AT HOME WITH THE
French
CLASSICS

For Millie and Fred —

With best wishes,

Richard Grausman

AT HOME WITH THE
French
CLASSICS

Richard Grausman

Illustrated by Donna Ruff

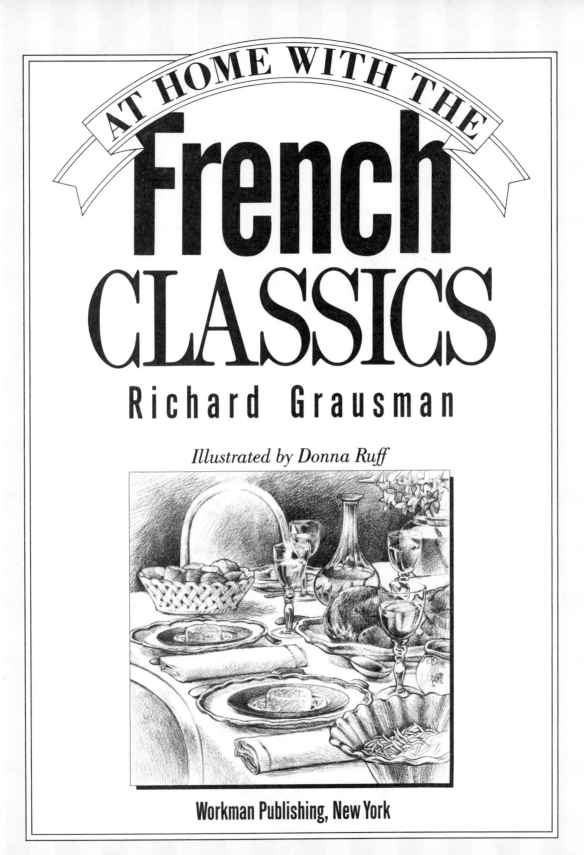

Workman Publishing, New York

Library of Congress Cataloging-in-Publication Data
Grausman, Richard.
At home with the French classics.

Includes index.
1. Cookery, French.   I. Title.
TX719.G756   1988   641.5944   88-40224
ISBN 0-89480-627-0
ISBN 0-89480-633-5 (pbk.)

Cover and book design: Kathleen Herlihy-Paoli
Book illustration: Donna Ruff
Front cover fabric: handwoven tablecloth by Gegia Bronzini, Italy;
courtesy of Lino Lana Seta, Inc., New York

Workman Publishing Company, Inc.
708 Broadway
New York, New York 10003

Manufactured in the United States of America
First printing November 1988

10 9 8 7 6 5 4 3 2 1

To Susan, Jennifer, and Deborah,
the three loves of my life;
and to my brother, Philip, and his
vast creative talent.

Acknowledgments

There are many people to thank for the creation of this book. My first thoughts and thanks go to my parents, Roland and Elizabeth Grausman, for their early nurturing and for their constant urging that I seek an enjoyable profession. Thanks must also go to Charles Merrels, for insisting that I take his place in a series of cooking classes that he was unable to attend in 1961; to the teacher of those classes, James Beard, whose praise and encouragement started me thinking in new directions; to Charles Narcess my chef-professor at Le Cordon Bleu in Paris, from whom I learned many of my teaching skills; to Elizabeth Brassart, owner and directress of Le Cordon Bleu for some forty years, for the confidence she showered upon me in making me her first representative outside France (1969–1984), and for her many years of support and close friendship; to my many students who have patiently awaited this book and whose enthusiasm and appreciation of my classes have helped me to become a better teacher.

I am indebted to my loving wife, Susan, without whose constant encouraging, reminding, assisting, and inspiring this book might never have been written; to my agent, Jane Dystel, whose persistent efforts brought me to the attention of my publisher; to Peter Workman, for his enthusiastic support and guidance in this project; to Sara Hertz and Debby Weiner, my very able assistants over the past two years, for the many hours they spent acquainting my friendly Macintosh with all I know about French cooking, as well as for their time-consuming recipe testing; and to my other testers around the country; Jill Prescott in Milwaukee, Valerie Steinau in Cincinnati, and Susan Damur and Barbara Robinson in Denver, for their work and helpful comments.

I would also like to express my gratitude to Kate Slate whose editorial and incredible organizational abilities helped me to find the beginning and end of this book; to my multi-talented friend Dorothy Monet, for her critical eye, help, and encouragement; to Kathy Herlihy-Paoli, for giving the book its graphic verve and individuality; to Bob Gilbert, for his close, tireless attention to detail; and to all those at Workman Publishing responsible for the production of the book; but especially to my editor, Sally Kovalchick, for her overall supervision. Last, but certainly not least, to Donna Ruff, for her illuminating drawings which add so greatly to the book.

Contents

Introduction

For close to two decades I have traveled from coast to coast, teaching and giving demonstrations for Americans on classic French cooking. Although many books have been written on the subject, I have come to realize that just as classical music can be transformed by the individual style and interpretation of the performing artist, so can recipes be "played" differently and thus made to reflect the personality and sensibilities of the individual cook.

The recipes in this book are my interpretations and updates of French classics, based on my years of teaching. No recipe has ever been added to my classes without my first asking: Is it really delicious? Does it deserve to be re-created? If the answer is yes, I then ask: Is it too rich? Too sweet? Too heavy? Too costly? Does it take too long to prepare? If the answer is yes again, which often is the case, I then go about changing it.

The most rewarding part of updating classic recipes is making them more compatible with today's health and calorie concerns. The results are the meals I've enjoyed day by day with my family, and friends, both informally and on the most festive occasions. Over the years I have found that the amounts of salt, sugar, butter, egg yolks, and cream called for in most classic French recipes far exceed the dishes' needs. I have, therefore, reduced such ingredients without altering the essential nature of the dishes. Salt, for example, is traditionally called for in all pastry recipes to enhance flavor; I find, however, that if sugar is present, salt is dispensable, and I have adjusted such recipes accordingly.

Most of the techniques used in preparing French classics are handed down from one generation of French chefs to the next by means of a strict apprentice system. Under this system you do as you're told and never ask why. In doing so you learn the "one right way." This system of learning may be one of the reasons that French cooking has remained distinctive through the ages and that many of the original techniques are still in use today. Although I was taught by chefs who trained under this system, I have learned through my own teaching that there is always more than one way to achieve a desired result.

In updating French recipes, my goal has been to provide clear, easy instructions, free of some of the restraints of the classic French kitchen and more appropriate to the time restraints of today's busy home cook. Where a step is not imperative, I have eliminated it. If a shortcut works, I have used it. When something can be done in advance, I do it.

It has also been a concern of mine that Americans are intimidated not only by the lengthy, detailed preparation they feel to be inherent in French cooking, but by the ingredients as well. Since my desire is for the American cook to feel comfortable and at home with the French classics, I have used ingredients in this book that for the most part can readily be found at local supermarkets. Those items that may not always be available, I have made optional or have given other, more accessible ingredients as substitutes.

Above all, my primary objective has been foolproof recipes that remain unmistakably French even though their proportions and preparation may have changed. It is my hope that this book will bring understanding and enjoyment of fine French cooking to all who read it, and give pleasure to all who feast from it.

Coming to Terms

One of the most important things I try to give my students, and that I hope my recipes succeed in doing, is the knowledge and therefore the confidence, to be creative. If you understand what it is that you want to accomplish, you most likely will find several ways of doing it. The techniques used in this book are those that work best for me. You may already know techniques that may be more efficient for you than mine. Give my methods a try, but if you find some of yours work better, continue to use them.

I also believe that there should be considerable flexibility in cooking, with your own palate and senses being the ultimate guides in seasoning a dish or in determining whether or not it is properly cooked. Unfortunately, I cannot watch *you* cook, as I do my students, or answer your questions. Therefore, what follows is some information that should help you understand a little better how I cook and why the recipes are written as they are.

Ingredients

As mentioned earlier, these recipes were developed using ingredients largely available in supermarkets. If I have called for an exotic ingredient, it is either presented as optional or given a substitute.

Unless otherwise specified, all fruits and vegetables are medium size.

Apples: In France I often use an apple called the Reinette du Canada, which has a firm flesh that is not too juicy, holds its shape when cooked, and can be browned like potatoes when sautéed. If you can find Russets (which are similar), you should try cooking with them, but in all the recipes in this book the widely available Golden Delicious has been used.

Bacon: I use slab, or unsliced, bacon in my recipes, preferably the smoked variety. Although smoked slab bacon is sometimes hard to find, most butchers will order it for you. When not available, use thick-sliced smoked bacon to achieve similar flavor results.

Butter: Although I use unsalted butter in almost all of my cooking, I realize that in some parts of the country it is hard to find fresh unsalted butter. For this reason, if you normally use lightly salted butter, continue to do so. However, I do specifically call for unsalted butter in some recipes, mostly pastry, and recommend that, in those instances, if possible, you try to get a good-quality unsalted butter.

Carrots: While carrots with the tops on are the freshest, and the bagged variety are the most common, I find that the large, loose ones are the best. In addition to finding them tastier, I also discover that I have fewer to peel. However, the carrots called for in the recipes are the average-size plastic bag variety.

Cheese: The cheese most commonly used in French cooking is Gruyère, but any Swiss-style cheese is fine. Try any of the following: Gruyère, Emmenthaler (called Emmental in France), Comté, Beaufort, or other cheeses sold in supermarket delis as "Swiss."

Eggs: All eggs used in this book, unless specifically mentioned, are USDA Grade A Large, weighing 60 to 65 grams or approximately 2 ounces each.

Flour: I use unbleached all-purpose flour because it has a better flavor than the bleached, but if you have bleached flour, use it.

Herbs: Fresh herbs will almost always be more satisfying than dried. However, dried herbs are more readily available. If a fresh herb is specifically called for in a recipe, it is usually because the herb is added at the end of the preparation, not cooked with it and dried herbs should not be substituted, for they will not impart the fresh taste and color desired.

There is no easy formula for substituting dried herbs for fresh, because the strength of an herb varies from plant to plant, season to season, and variety to variety. As a general rule, start by using whichever you have—fresh or dried—in the amount given in the recipe. You can always add more.

When buying dried herbs, try to get them in as whole a form as possible. For example, use thyme that is in leaf form, not powdered. A preground herb has a much greater chance of being flavorless when you buy it and will certainly lose any flavor it has fairly quickly.

Milk: I use whole milk. However, if you only use 2%, 1%, or skim milk, use what you have on hand. If you find that the results are too thin or not rich enough, use whole milk the next time you make the recipe.

Many classic French recipes call for milk to be scalded. This practice dates back to the days before pasteurization and was important for health reasons. Today, if I heat milk in a recipe, it is to shorten the overall cooking time.

Mushrooms: The mushrooms I use are button mushrooms, which get their name from their size, that of a suit button. They are always left whole in recipes. Some supermarkets package button mushrooms, but many don't. When button mushrooms are not available, larger mushrooms can be cut in half or quartered to approximate their size.

Oil: I use olive oil or such vegetable oils as soy, sunflower, peanut, and safflower. Many blended oils also work well. Find one that has a good, delicate taste. Generally speaking, and for most recipes, I use a light olive oil as opposed to the heavier, fruitier extra-virgin oils. However, in recipes originating in the south of France (Provence), or in dishes containing olives, a strong, fruity extra-virgin oil is desirable.

Onions: Our normal yellow cooking onion is similar to the strong yellow variety commonly used in France and is the one I have used for general cooking in this book.

For those recipes that call for pearl onions, if you can't get them, you can substitute small white onions. If they are too large, simply peel off one or two layers.

Salt: Although salt was, and in some cases still is, used as a preservative, it is mainly used as a taste enhancer. I tend to use it sparingly, and you may wish to increase the quantities I specify. You will note that in most recipes, especially where a sauce is used, you will be instructed to taste and adjust the seasoning, if necessary. A French chef will usually taste a dish just before serving it, and if he does not detect a hint of salt, he will add a little. The constant use of salt numbs our taste buds, and over a period of years you may find yourself increasing the amount of salt used. I have often eaten in French restaurants where I found the food too salty. More often than not, the chef had been cooking for many years.

I became aware of the effect that salt has on taste buds while teaching. When I started teaching, a good 30 percent of the people attending my classes found the food I prepared too salty, while about 10 percent thought it needed more salt. Over a three-year period, I found this remained constant no matter where I taught. Shortly after the birth of our first daughter, however, I was shocked to find that 90 percent of my classes suggested that I should use more salt. On reflection, I quickly realized what had happened during the six months I'd stopped teaching. For the last three months of my wife's pregnancy and the first three months of my child's life, the doctor had placed my wife on a low-salt diet, and since I was doing most of the cooking, I, too, was on the same diet. This was enough time to rejuvenate my taste buds, and so when I started teaching again, the food I cooked, which tasted fine to me, was undersalted for my audience.

Over the subsequent 14 years I have increased my use of salt slightly, and now find only about 30 percent of my students tell me I'm undersalting. Very few find I oversalt.

Sugar: Sugar, like salt, can be a very personal taste. What is too sweet for one is not sweet enough for another. I find many classic French desserts too sweet, and have adapted them over the years, removing sugar to suit my taste. In most cases sugar can be added or subtracted, but in some recipes the addition or removal of too much will alter the final product. Sugar, for example, is what gives a cookie its crunch. If the amount is cut down too much, the cookie's texture will be too cakelike.

Once you have made a recipe, feel free to adjust the sugar, a teaspoon or two at a time, until it is perfect for you.

Thickening Agents: In my recipes I usually give a choice of thickeners: arrowroot, potato starch, or cornstarch. I realize that cornstarch is the one most available in the American home, and in fact the one used in certain pastry preparations in France. But for cooking, and especially sauce making, I, along with most French chefs, prefer the use of arrowroot or potato starch. Both produce sauces that are brighter and of better consistency than those made with cornstarch. Arrowroot is found in the spice section of the supermarket, and potato starch is normally found in the kosher or foreign specialty section.

Truffles: French black truffles are most definitely not a supermarket item, and I have therefore made their use optional. Fresh truffles are fungi that grow underground and are prized for their unique flavor. They can range in size from ½ inch in diameter to as large as 2 inches and in their fresh form are rarely available in this country. I call for medium-size truffles, which measure about ¾ inch in diameter and come packed in cans or jars.

Vinegar: When vinegar is called for in a French kitchen, plain white distilled vinegar is used. For salad dressings, wine vinegars are used. The quality of commercial wine vinegars varies widely, and I find in general that white wine vinegars are milder than red ones. I also use sherry, balsamic, and a number of fruit vinegars from time to time.

Wines for Cooking: When a white wine is called for, I use light, dry inexpensive white wines from France, California, Spain, and Italy. Look for a light, delicate, and dry wine that is not too acidic, and similar in quality to a Mâcon Blanc. A few dishes are made with red wine. In these cases, I use a full-bodied red, such as Mâcon Rouge or Côtes-du-Rhône.

Ingredient Preparation

I assume that all vegetables and fruits are washed and trimmed. I only emphasize washing when the vegetable requires extra attention, as for leeks (see "Washing Leeks," page 211) or when my method is perhaps unexpected (see "Washing Mushrooms," page 214).

I assume that all vegetables that are ordinarily peeled you will peel, and I only indicate it when it's important (see "Peeling and Seeding Tomatoes," page 220).

I always rinse poultry and shellfish and have made it a point to include this reminder in the recipes, as I feel that many cooks skip this step. After rinsing, if what you are cooking is to be roasted or sautéed, it is important to dry it well so it will brown.

In cutting up ingredients, I use the following terms:

Finely Chopped: I use this term when I want something to be minced, but not so finely minced that it verges on a purée, as can sometimes happen if you use a processor.

Chopped: Cut into pieces about ¼ inch or less.

Diced: Small square pieces, usually between ¼ to ½ inch. When food is diced finer than ¼ inch it is considered chopped.

Julienne: Julienned ingredients are cut into thin strips about 2 inches long. They can be as fine as a hair or as thick as matchsticks and are often used as garnish.

Sliced on the Diagonal: Mostly used with carrots for greater surface area, better browning, and appearance.

Adjusting Seasoning

A good chef will always taste soups and sauces after making them to determine if additional seasoning is necessary. For this reason, I will remind you to taste and adjust seasoning. Many students have asked, "How do I know what to adjust?" Although the knowledge usually comes with experience, here are a few hints for the beginner.

Adjusting the seasoning usually refers to salt and pepper. If you like the way the sauce tastes as it is, then nothing needs to be added. If you think it is missing something, look at the ingredients in the recipe and see if you might need to add a small amount of one of them. For example, the sauce may have called for a small amount of either vinegar, lemon juice, port, Madeira, or Cognac. Perhaps a drop or two more is all that is needed to make the sauce perfect. Sometimes a specific herb is used to accent a sauce; if its flavor is not discernible on tasting, an additional pinch is probably necessary.

Everyone has a different sense of taste, so what seems like a perfect blend of flavors to one person may be bland to someone else. All these recipes have been tested for seasoning and I hope you will like them as they are, but please feel free to adjust any seasoning according to your own taste.

Measurements

Instead of giving precise cup measurements for many cooking ingredients—such as ½ cup chopped onion or 1 cup diced carrots—I list them as "1 onion, chopped" and "2 carrots, diced." There are two reasons for doing this. One is so that you can more easily visualize the recipe while shopping. Carrots and onions are found whole in the markets, not diced and measured in cups. The second, and perhaps more important, reason is that there should be flexibility in cooking, and no need for many ingredients to be measured precisely. It makes little difference to the end results if one reader uses a medium-small onion while another uses a medium-large one.

The pastry recipes, on the other hand, are more precise than most American recipes, and a quick reading of "The Metric System in Cooking and Baking" (page 404) will give you an understanding of some of the inaccuracies possible in measuring solids, and the importance for accurate measurement in pastry recipes.

Although I encourage the use of an ounce/gram scale for pastry making, following my precise cup measurements should give you the same results time after time. When I measure dry ingredients such as flour and sugar, I use the dip-and-level method: If, for example, a recipe calls for ⅔ cup flour, I **dip** the cup marked "⅓" (there are no ⅔-cup measures for dry ingredients) into the flour and scoop up more than the cup can hold. With the back of a knife I **level** it off, and then repeat the process to make ⅔ cup. If you usually spoon the flour into your cup before leveling, you will be using less flour than I do.

Oven Temperature

Oven temperature is very important, especially for baking. The oven temperatures in this book have been checked using a Taylor mercury thermometer. If your recipe takes more or less time than I have indicated it should, the calibration of your oven is probably incorrect. I have used ovens that have been off by 50 to 75 degrees. Sometimes these ovens are accurate at 475° but too hot at 350°. When I bake, I always use a thermometer to ensure an accurate temperature.

Placement in the Oven

Understanding how your oven works and where its "hot spots" are will allow you to use it more efficiently. The heat in most American ovens comes from the bottom and reflects off the top, making those two areas the hottest. Most ovens vent from either the front or back, causing one area to be slightly cooler than the other. When placing something in the oven, think of how you want it to cook. For even cooking and browning, the center is the optimal location. To prevent the browning of a baked custard or rice pudding, place it on the bottom rack of the oven. Most tarts should be baked on the bottom rack to ensure a dry crust, and moved to the top if their surface needs browning. Bake only one sheet of pastry or cookies at a time, or else the bottom of one sheet and the top of the other will be unevenly baked.

Convection Ovens: Theoretically convection ovens have no hot spots since they use fans to circulate the heat. This allows you to bake as many trays of pastry as the oven will hold without the uneven results of a conventional oven.

Tests for Doneness

"Cook until tender" or "cook until done" are terms often used in recipes that confuse many amateur cooks. "What is tender?" "How do you test for it?" and "What is meant by 'done?'" are questions often asked by students.

Vegetables: Vegetables are tender when the point of a knife penetrates them without resistance. This technique yields tender, not crunchy, vegetables. In most cases you should support the vegetable with a fork or spoon while inserting your knife. Potatoes tested this way will cling to the blade until fully cooked, at which point they will slide off. For those who prefer undercooked, crunchy vegetables, biting into one is the best way to check for doneness. Lift a string bean or broccoli stem from the pot, run it under cold water, and taste it. The difference between perfectly cooked and overcooked vegetables may be just a matter of seconds, so pay close attention while cooking them. Whatever your preference, test for doneness and don't rely solely on the times shown in recipes. Both altitude and freshness can affect timing considerably.

Meat: The single prong of a roasting fork or skewer is often used for testing the doneness of meat. Tough or raw meat will resist or cling to the prong, but when the meat is tender the prong will easily penetrate and release it. This is precisely the way to test meat in a stew or ragoût. Chicken, veal, and pork are pierced to release their inner juices for testing. Clear juices indicate that the meat is done; if the juices run pink, additional cooking is necessary.

Red meat to be served rare or medium-rare is pressed with a finger, not pierced, to ascertain doneness. The more meat is cooked, the firmer it becomes. Rare meat is soft, while medium-rare is springy to the touch.

To ensure that your meat will cook properly, see that it is dry and at room temperature before starting. When sautéing or grilling meat, wait for the first drops of blood or juice to appear on the uncooked surface before turning it. The meat is medium-rare when the interior juices begin to appear again on the surface after the meat has been turned.

Pastry: In the case of pastry, a variety of indicators are used to determine doneness. Among them are color, aroma, shrinkage, and texture. In the book, I have provided signs to assist you in determining proper cooking time.

Making Recipes Ahead of Time

The two main considerations of making food ahead of time are how to store it and how to ready it for serving. Most of the information necessary for preparing dishes ahead are contained in the recipes themselves, but I think it worth calling attention to two important aspects here as well.

Covering: Many foods, like soups and sauces, form crusts or skins if exposed to air. To prevent this I use plastic wrap *placed directly on the surface* of the mixture in question. A surface covered this way will not dry out, and the air that is ordinarily trapped and can promote bacterial growth is eliminated.

Reheating: Reheating does not mean recooking. In French cooking, reheating is an art. Food must be brought back to the temperature at which it will start to cook again without allowing any additional cooking. For some foods this can be done quickly, while for others it must be done slowly. You can reheat a soup or sauce over high heat, and serve it as soon as it comes to a boil. A large pot of stew, on the other hand, must reheat slowly, so that by the time the sauce is simmering, everything is just hot, not overcooked. In the same fashion, a rare roast beef must be reheated slowly so it will be warm when served but not cooked any more.

For warming or reheating sauces that are extremely sensitive to heat, such as *béarnaise* or *crème anglaise*, it is essential to use a water bath (*bain-marie*, see page 375).

Cooking Times

The timing given in recipes should be viewed merely as a guide, not an absolute. Keep an eye on what is happening in your pan, not just on the clock. If a recipe instructs you to "sauté onions over medium heat until browned, about 5 minutes," the important words are "until browned." If after 5 minutes your onions are still white, you'll know that my stove was hotter than yours, and that you can use higher heat. If, however, your onions start to burn after 2 minutes, you'll know to reduce your heat the next time.

It has often been said that a good cook needs to use all five senses while cooking, but little is said about our use of common sense. If a cake should be light brown after 30 minutes but is still white, don't remove it from the oven. If you are frying but it sounds like boiling, turn your heat up. If your nose tells you that something is burning, it probably is, so remove it from the heat.

Cooking Equipment

The variety and quality of cooking equipment on the American market today have vastly improved since I first started teaching nearly 20 years ago. Then I traveled from city to city with a duffle bag full of equipment for I never knew what would be waiting for me to use when I arrived. Today, when I travel, I take only my knives.

With the increased variety of kitchen equipment now available comes the dilemma of knowing what will best suit your needs. You may need a good saucepan, or a new knife, but which one is for you? The range of materials is baffling, and the price of some may astound you. You probably wonder if it really can make a difference to your cooking and if you shouldn't just make do with what you already have. Although a good cook can always figure out a way to make the best of what is available, good equipment can make the work much easier. A sharp knife, no matter what material it is made from, is a cook's most valuable tool. When shopping for a knife, pick it up and see how it feels in your hand. Some knives will be well-balanced, while others will be blade- or handle-heavy. Look for a knife with a thin, sharp blade. It is easier to maintain a sharp edge on a thin blade than on a thicker one. No matter what kind of knife you have, never allow it to get dull. Keep it sharp by frequently using a steel or other sharpening tool.

Several knives I use regularly are: A small, inexpensive, 2½-inch razor-sharp paring knife; a well-balanced, 8-inch hand-forged "Chef's" knife for general work and chopping; a 10- or 12-inch carving knife; a 6-inch slicing knife; and a 6- or 8-inch serrated knife for slicing bread, tomatoes, cakes, and other pastry.

Pans that conduct heat well heat up and transfer heat quickly, and cool down quickly. A pan made from a material that conducts poorly will heat up and transfer heat slowly, but will retain the heat for a long time.

Although it makes no difference what pan you choose when you boil water, it does make a difference when you boil milk. A good conductor can be used with any degree of heat, while a poor conductor should be used on low to medium heat, and only with care on higher heat. In a pan made from material that conducts well, milk will boil on high heat without burning or scorching, but not in a pan made from a lesser conductor. If you do use a poor conductor, pay closer attention to what you cook. Stir the contents of the pan more often, and adjust your heat carefully.

To find out if your pan conducts heat well, try this simple test. Off the heat, place

½ tablespoon of butter in the bottom of the pan. On the inside upper rim of the pan attach an even smaller amount of butter. Now place the pan on high heat. If your pan conducts heat well, you will notice that the butter on the bottom starts to melt immediately, and when it has, the butter on the rim will start sliding down to the bottom. With a poor conductor, you may find that by the time the butter on the rim starts to melt, the butter in the bottom has burned.

Pans are available in copper, aluminum, coated aluminum, cast iron, enamelled cast iron, stainless steel, heat resistant porcelain and glass, and a variety of combined materials. Listed below are some of the pros and cons of utensils made from these materials. Knowing these will help you when you are going to be using a pan for a specific purpose.

Pots and Pans

Copper: Excellent conductivity allows you to cook rapidly over high heat without worrying about sticking and burning. It also allows even cooking over low heat. It is lined with tin, nickel, stainless, or silver for general cooking, and unlined, for cooking sugar and jam. If you like shiny copper pans, be prepared to polish them frequently.

Aluminum: Also an excellent conductor of heat. Can be used with high or low heat. It is not recommended for boiling water because certain minerals cause a dark gray oxide to form making it difficult to clean. This does not happen when making soups and sauces. However, when cooking with tomatoes, vinegar, and other acidic ingredients which pit aluminum, use a utensil that is lined with stainless steel, a non-stick coating, or electro-plated with aluminum oxide. The latter creates a virtually indestructible dark gray coating with excellent cooking properties.

Cast Iron and Enamelled Cast Iron: Iron is a fairly poor conductor of heat, which means that it takes a long time to get hot, and once hot, it takes a long time to cool down. This property makes it an excellent material for casseroles or dutch ovens used in the oven for long slow cooking, for oven to table preparations, and for grill pans and griddles. However, when using cast iron for cooking sauces, care should be taken to stir often to prevent sticking and burning. You should, however, avoid using plain cast iron for cooking sauces containing wine, because a metallic taste often results.

Stainless Steel: By itself, a poor conductor of heat. Utensils made from thin sheets of the metal are usually strong and light and are excellent for boiling vegetables and for making stocks and soups. Aluminum- or copper-clad stainless steel makes excellent all-purpose pans.

Ovenproof Porcelain and Glass: Are very poor heat conductors but are excellent for low temperature oven cooking, and for oven to table serving.

Suggested Checklist of Some Basic Cooking Equipment:

A selection of sharp knives, a sharpening steel, and cutting boards

A set of copper- or aluminum-clad stainless-steel saucepans and stock pots for general use, including 1-, 2-, 3-, and 4-quart saucepans, a 7- or 8-quart soup pot, and a 12- or 16-quart stock pot

Several good conducting heavy saucepans, 1-, 2-, and 3-quart

10- and 12-inch straight-sided, cast-aluminum or cast-iron sauté pans or skillets, with lids

Nonstick omelet and crêpe pans

Cast-iron grill pan with raised ridges

Dutch ovens, 5- and 8-quart, at least one good for oven to table use

Gratin or baking dishes, and roasting pans

2 nonstick and 1 aluminum non-coated pastry sheets

Pastry cooling racks, and an oven thermometer

Gram/ounce scale, measuring cups and spoons

French rolling pin, tart pans, cake pans, bread pans, pastry brushes, pastry bags and tubes

Mixing bowls of different sizes; some metal and some glass

Colanders and strainers, with at least one fine-mesh sieve for sauces

8-inch sauce whisks; rubber, wooden, and long metal spatulas

Ladles and skimmer

Kitchen scissors, and fine grater

Food processor, and hand-held mixer

First

In France, a first course is called (confusingly) the *entrée*, which means "entry." And to properly begin a French meal, there must be one. This is true for the simplest family supper or the most elegant restaurant meal. At home the first course might be a soup or a crudité or perhaps something from the charcuterie, such as a slice of pâté. At a restaurant, the possibilities are expanded.

In this country, first courses are rare except in restaurants or for entertaining. Americans have a tradition of putting the main part of a meal on the table all at once. The French break the meal into courses, serve smaller portions, and spend more time at the table.

The first-course recipes in this chapter were designed to be part of a multicourse meal—just as the main courses in this book are designed to be preceded by a starter course. However, because this is not the way we eat on a daily basis, these first-course dishes are also perfectly suited as the main course for a lunch or light supper, and I have given a range of servings to indicate their dual nature.

Courses

Soups

Formal dining, in years past, always included a soup. It came *before* the first course, and in general it was a cream soup for luncheon and consommé for dinner. This style of dining has all but disappeared (although you can still experience it in some of the fine resort hotels of Europe). I generally use soup as a first course or, when served with bread, salad, and a dessert, as a main course—especially hearty soups such as Soupe de Poisson (page 24) or Potage de Pois Cassés (page 27).

Although the generic term for soups in French cooking is *potages*, the classic breakdown of types and terms is far more complex. Simply speaking, soups can be divided into two groups: clear soups (or consommés) and thickened soups. Thickened soups are classically further divided into *purées*, *veloutés*, and *crèmes*, and each follows certain rules. *Purées* are thickened with a purée of a starchy vegetable (such as potato or rice) or legumes (such as

lima, lentil, or pea). *Veloutés* are thickened with a light *velouté* sauce, while *crèmes* are thickened with a light béchamel. *Veloutés* are enriched, just before serving, with a liaison of egg yolks and butter, and *crèmes* are finished with heavy cream.

Over the years, these classic distinctions have been blurred. And in the case of my soups, they have been deliberately altered, to make them lighter than the classics that inspired them. I eliminate the egg yolk and butter enrichment and a good deal of the starch, and use heavy cream sparingly.

Consommé de Volaille
Chicken Consommé

One of the true tests of a good chef is his ability to make an excellent consommé. It should be crystal clear, full of flavor, yet not too salty, and it should have a lovely color ranging from light gold to deep amber. The process for making consommés is long and tedious, and it is rare to find them on restaurant menus today. If you do find one, you can be sure the chef is proud of it.

A classic consommé is made with a double-strength veal, beef, or chicken stock. This stock is further strengthened and then clarified (a process necessary for a perfectly clear soup). From beginning to end, making a consommé can take up to two days.

Since today people rarely are able or willing to devote so much time to making a soup, this version takes some shortcuts without shortchanging the taste. By starting with canned stock (see "Using Canned Stocks," page 348), the consommé takes less than an hour.

It can be served cold (it will be lightly jelled) or hot. If you are making a hot consommé and want to serve it in the French fashion, accompany it with a cooked garnish such as diced or julienned vegetables, shredded chicken, rice, or vermicelli.

Serves 6 to 8

2 quarts double-strength chicken stock, homemade*, or
    canned (see chart, page 349)
2 egg whites
4 envelopes unflavored gelatin, softened in ¾ cup cold water
1 pound ground skinless, boneless chicken breast
1 carrot, finely chopped
1 onion, chopped
1 leek (white part only), washed and chopped
2 stalks celery, chopped
1 large tomato, chopped
10 sprigs parsley, chopped
3 sprigs fresh tarragon or 2 teaspoons dried
20 sprigs fresh chervil or 2 teaspoons dried (optional)
1 teaspoon salt (omit if using canned stock)
⅛ teaspoon freshly ground pepper
2 tablespoons Glace de Viande (optional; page 352)

1. **Clarify the stock:** Place the stock in a 4- to 5-quart saucepan. Beat in the egg whites so they liquefy and blend with the stock. Add the softened gelatin and all the remaining ingredients.

2. Stir the mixture slowly and continually with a whisk over high heat until the first sign of boiling, about 12 min-

Consommés can be made from beef, veal, chicken, fish, or game. The name of the consommé changes depending on the garnish served with it. In the classic repertoire there are hundreds of different garnish combinations and, therefore, soup names. For example: *Consommé Bretonne* is garnished with julienne of leek, celery, onion, and mushroom and shredded chervil. *Consommé Solange* is garnished with pearl barley, squares of lettuce, and chicken julienne. *Consommé Rossini* is thickened with tapioca, flavored with truffle essence, and garnished with profiteroles stuffed with foie gras and chopped truffles.

utes. Immediately stop stirring; reduce the heat and simmer gently for 20 minutes. As the stock gets hot, it will become cloudy or milky.

3. Using a skimmer, gently remove most of the vegetables, chicken, and egg white from the surface of the stock. Line a strainer with a dampened kitchen towel or several thicknesses of dampened cheesecloth and pour the stock through it. The strained stock or consommé should be perfectly clear. If not, it may require a second straining.

4. **Degrease the consommé:** If, after straining, there are any remaining droplets of fat on the surface of the consommé, cut a paper towel into quarters. Place one square at a time on the surface of the soup and immediately draw it across and away. Continue this with as many squares as you need (cutting more paper towels, if necessary) until there is no more visible fat.

5. Serve hot or cold.

* If you are interested in making your own strong chicken stock, you might consider making the Poule au Pot on page 127. The chicken for this simple and delicious dish is cooked in chicken stock, thus creating a double-strength stock that could be used to make the consommé.

Variation

Consommé de Boeuf *(Beef Consommé):* A beef consommé is made in principally the same way. Replace the chicken stock with 2 quarts double-strength beef stock, homemade or canned (see chart, page 348). Use 1 pound ground beef instead of ground chicken breast. Before serving, stir in ¼ cup Madeira (optional).

The seasoned ground chicken and vegetables used to clarify the consommé do not have to be discarded once their job is done. After skimming them from the soup in step 3, set them aside, let cool, and refrigerate, covered. A quick béchamel flavored to taste with tomato paste or curry powder can be mixed with the ground chicken and served with rice—it goes very nicely with basmati or Texmati (available in Indian food markets or gourmet shops)—for an easy lunch or dinner. The chicken and sauce can also be used as a filling for crêpes.

Soupe à l'Oignon
Onion Soup

Although I normally make this soup with stock, a more delicate version can be made with water. The caramelized onions will provide the necessary flavor.

With the addition of bread and cheese, this simple soup becomes *soupe à l'oignon gratinée*, perhaps the most famous of all French soups. Without them, it makes a nice, very light first course.

Serves 6 to 8

3 tablespoons butter
1½ pounds onions (5 to 6 medium), halved and thinly sliced
½ teaspoon salt
¼ teaspoon freshly ground pepper
2 tablespoons all-purpose flour
9 cups beef stock, homemade or canned (see chart,
     page 348), or water
1 tablespoon Cognac
½ pound Swiss-style cheese, such as Gruyère or
     Emmenthaler, grated (about 2 cups)

1. In a large saucepan or 5-quart Dutch oven, heat the butter. Add the onions and cook over medium-high to high heat, stirring occasionally, until well browned. They will start to brown in 10 to 12 minutes. After another 20 to 25 minutes the onions should be dark drown, but not black. Season with the salt and pepper.

2. Reduce the heat to medium and stir in the flour. Brown lightly, about 3 minutes, stirring.

3. Add the stock, increase the heat to high, and bring to a boil, about 15 minutes. Reduce the heat to medium and simmer for 30 minutes. Skim off any foam or butter that comes to the surface. *(The recipe can be prepared ahead to this point. Let cool to room temperature, cover, and refrigerate. Bring to a simmer before proceeding.)*

4. Just before serving, add the Cognac. Pass the cheese separately.

Soupe à l'Oignon Gratinée
French Onion Soup

*S*oupe à l'oignon gratinée, listed on American menus as French onion soup and on French menus often simply as a *gratinée*, is served in restaurants throughout the world. Although there is no classic recipe for this classically French soup, most contain onions, stock, bread, and Swiss-style cheese, making it virtually a meal in itself. For this reason I usually serve it for lunch or supper with a mixed green salad, and some fruit or pastry for dessert.

The bread should be stale or toasted so it will float and support the cheese on the surface of the soup, where it can easily be browned or *gratinéed*.

Serves 6

Soupe à l'Oignon (at left)
Slices of stale or toasted French bread*, cut ½-inch thick
1 pound Swiss-style cheese, such as Gruyère or Emmenthaler, grated

1. Preheat the broiler.
2. Heat the soup to a simmer.
3. Place enough bread in each of 6 ovenproof bowls so the slices will cover the surface once the bowls are filled with the soup. Ladle the soup into the bowls.
4. Sprinkle the soup with the cheese and place the bowls on a cookie sheet and place under the broiler until the cheese has browned, 5 to 7 minutes.

* The number of bread slices you need will depend on the size of your soup bowls and the diameter of the loaf of bread. The object is to cover the surface of the soup with the bread, which floats to support the cheese. One or two slices per person is usually adequate.

An especially appealing feature of this recipe is that the basic onion soup can be made well in advance, then reheated and placed under the broiler for a superb last-minute meal. Special onion soup bowls, which can withstand the high temperature of a broiler, are used in this preparation. If you don't have onion soup bowls, use any ovenproof bowls with a 1-cup capacity.

Soupe de Poisson
Mediterranean Fish Soup

This soup, served with a green salad, rosé wine, and a fruit tart for dessert, makes a wonderful lunch or light supper. It is also the base for the Bouillabaisse Américaine on page 114. Most traditional recipes for this soup call for fish fillets to be cooked as part of the soup base and discarded. With today's fish prices, I find this wasteful and extravagant. In my *soupe de poisson*, I poach the diced fillets in the soup at the last minute and serve them with the soup. For an even heartier version I add scallops and/or shrimp, poaching them at the same time as the fish.

Serves 6

5 pounds fish heads and bones (see Note)
¾ cup olive oil, extra-virgin if available
2 onions, halved and sliced
2 leeks, washed and diced
½ fennel bulb, diced
About 15 sprigs parsley
3 pounds tomatoes, diced, or 6 pounds canned tomatoes,
    drained and chopped
5 garlic cloves, smashed
1 bay leaf
¼ teaspoon thyme
¼ teaspoon savory
2 to 3 large pinches saffron threads, to taste
Peeled zest of 1 orange
2 cups dry white wine
6 cups water
½ teaspoon salt
¼ teaspoon freshly ground pepper
1 pound skinless fish fillets (see Note), diced

Serving Suggestion: Accompany the soup with toasted slices of French bread, Aïoli (page 379), and grated Swiss-style cheese.

Note: This can be just about any fish you like. Just be sure that if you are using a strong-flavored fish, such as mackerel or bluefish, that it is very fresh.

1. In a large bowl or saucepan, soak the fish heads and bones in ice water for at least 20 minutes or until ready to use them.

2. In a large stockpot, heat the oil over medium heat. Add the onions, leeks, fennel, and parsley and sauté until the vegetables have softened without coloring, 4 to 5 minutes.

3. Add the tomatoes, garlic, bay leaf, thyme, savory, saffron, and orange zest. Stir well with a wooden spoon.

4. Drain the fish bones and heads and add to the pot along with the wine and water. Season with the salt and pepper. Bring to a boil over medium-high heat and cook for 30 minutes.

5. Strain the soup through a sieve, pressing as much liquid from the solid ingredients as possible. Discard the solids. *(The soup can be prepared ahead to this point. Let cool to room temperature, cover, and refrigerate for up to 3 days or freeze for up to 1 month. Bring the soup back to a simmer before proceeding.)*

6. Add the fish fillets and bring the soup back to a boil just before serving.

Potage au Cresson
Watercress Soup

This low-calorie variation of the classic watercress soup uses zucchini in place of potatoes. The small amount of cream used to enrich the soup can be omitted, reducing the calories even further.

I once made this soup for a well-known restaurant critic, who apologized for eating only half a serving, saying that it was a little too rich for someone on a diet. When I explained that the soup only had 70 calories per serving, I received a request for seconds.

This soup can be served hot or cold. If you are using a homemade chicken stock, the soup may jell when cold, making it too thick. If this happens, thin with water and adjust the seasoning. Try using yogurt instead of cream when serving the soup cold.

Serves 6

1 tablespoon butter
3 leeks (white part only), washed and diced
1½ pounds zucchini, peeled (see Note) and diced
4 cups chicken stock, homemade or canned (see chart, page 349)
1 bunch watercress, stems removed
¼ teaspoon salt
⅛ teaspoon freshly ground pepper
⅓ cup heavy cream

Note: I peel the zucchini so the color of the soup will be pale green like the classic version.

1. In a 4-quart pot, heat the butter. Add the leeks and gently sauté over medium-low heat until softened, about 3 minutes.

2. Add the zucchini and sauté for 2 minutes without browning. Add the stock and simmer until the zucchini is just tender, 3 to 4 minutes.

3. Bring the soup to a boil and add the watercress. Reduce the heat and simmer for 1 minute.

4. In a food processor or blender, blend the soup until smooth. Season with the salt and pepper. *(The soup can be prepared ahead to this point. Let cool to room temperature, cover, and refrigerate. If serving the soup hot, bring back to a simmer before proceeding.)*

5. Just before serving, stir in the cream.

Variation

Potage au Cresson et au Curry *(Curried Watercress Soup):* Reduce the amount of watercress to ½ bunch and add 1 tablespoon curry powder along with the stock in step 2.

Potage de Pois Cassés
Split-Pea Soup

Green split-pea soup is a hearty winter soup that, together with some warm bread, a piece of cheese, and fruit provides a very satisfying meal. In France, it is most often served with croutons (small cubes of fried bread), but because of their high calorie count, I rarely use them.

The traditional version of this soup was somewhat more time-consuming and arduous, the cook having to use a *tamis* (drum-shaped sieve) to achieve the proper consistency. The blender and food processor make this an easier operation for the modern-day cook.

I also use this recipe for lentil, bean, and other legume-based soups, and it can easily be cut in half for fewer servings.

Serves 8 to 10

2 pounds green split peas, washed and picked over
2 leeks, washed and diced
2 onions, each studded with 1 clove
2 large carrots, cut in half
2 stalks celery
Bouquet Garni (page 346)
1 ham bone, or ½ pound slab bacon, rind removed, or
*   ½ pound smoked sausage*
1 handful lettuce leaves (optional)
½ teaspoon salt
¼ teaspoon freshly ground pepper
3 quarts water
¼ cup dry sherry (optional)

1. Put all of the ingredients, except the sherry, into a stockpot. Bring the soup to a boil and simmer, partially

covered, until the peas are tender, about 1 hour.

2. Remove the meat and set it aside*. Discard the onions, bouquet garni, one of the carrots, and the celery.

3. In a blender or food processor, purée the ingredients remaining in the pot until they are smooth. If the soup is too thick, thin it with a little water or milk.

4. Dice the ham or sausage and add it to the soup. *(The soup can be prepared ahead to this point. Let cool to room temperature, cover, and refrigerate. Bring to a simmer before proceeding.)*

5. Just before serving, add the sherry.

* If you are using bacon, after removing it, rinse and dice it. Then sauté it before returning it to the soup in step 4.

Variation

Potage Paysan de Pois Cassés *(Country Split-Pea Soup):* As with most puréed soups, a coarser, more rustic version can be made. To do this, dice all the vegetables except for one of the onions, which you stud with the cloves. When the peas are soft, discard only the whole onion and the bouquet garni. Remove the ham or sausage after cooking, dice, and return to the soup. If using bacon, dice, sauté, and return to the soup.

Crème d'Asperges
Cream of Asparagus Soup

*C*rème d'asperges is also known as *crème Argenteuil* in honor of the region (in north central France) where the best asparagus are grown. (In fact, any dish that includes the name Argenteuil contains asparagus.) What made this a "cream" soup in the classic kitchen was that it was made with a light béchamel, though the

IMMERSIBLE BLENDER

The smoothness of a soup will vary with the machine you use to purée it. A blender will make the finest purée (although you will have to do most soups in batches). There are also a number of hand blenders (a gadget that has been available for years in France and has just recently made its way here) that will purée the soup directly in the pot. The result will be somewhat coarser, but cleanup will be easier. The food processor (which has supplanted the blender in most kitchens) will also make a slightly coarser purée, and must often be done in batches. The secret to getting a smooth soup in a food processor is to first purée the solids as fine as possible and then thin this purée with the liquid.

rules were often bent to make it with a thickened stock (*velouté*) or a combination of the two. I find the flavor better when made with stock alone (and even better if made with veal stock). This recipe produces a very light and delicately creamy soup, but for those who prefer theirs thicker or more creamy, it is an easy matter to add up to another tablespoon of arrowroot or double the cream.

Serves 8

2 tablespoons butter
3 pounds asparagus, well washed, tough ends removed,
    and cut into 1-inch lengths
¼ teaspoon salt
⅛ teaspoon freshly ground pepper
6 cups chicken stock, homemade or canned (see chart,
    page 349)
2½ tablespoons arrowroot, potato starch, or cornstarch,
    dissolved in 2½ tablespoons cold water
¼ cup heavy cream

1. In a large saucepan, heat the butter over medium-high heat. Add the asparagus and gently sauté until bright green, about 5 minutes. Season with the salt and pepper.

2. Add the stock and bring to a boil over high heat, skimming off any foam and impurities that rise to the surface. Boil gently for 4 to 5 minutes, or until the asparagus are tender. If desired, remove 16 to 24 asparagus tips and reserve for garnish.

3. Place the asparagus and stock in a blender, discarding any sand or grit that may remain at the bottom of the saucepan. Blend until smooth. Return the soup to the saucepan.

4. Bring the soup to a simmer, and whisk in the dissolved arrowroot to thicken. Stir in the cream. *(The soup can be prepared ahead. Let cool to room temperature, cover, and refrigerate. Bring to a simmer before serving.)* Place 2 to 3 of the reserved asparagus tips, if using, in each of 8 soup bowls and ladle in the soup.

Variation

Crème de Brocoli *(Cream of Broccoli Soup):* Use 3 pounds of peeled broccoli in place of the asparagus. Cut the stalks and florets into 1-inch pieces and cook as for the asparagus.

Crème de Maïs
Cream of Corn Soup

A classic cream of corn soup is made by puréeing cooked corn with a light béchamel sauce, and serving it with a few kernels of corn in each bowl. My version, with its added aromatic vegetables, is closer in appearance to an American corn chowder. I use half milk and half water to create a light yet creamy tasting soup. It is important to the appearance of the soup to dice the vegetables no larger than the corn kernels, and should you prefer a completely smooth soup, simply blend to a purée and strain. This soup can be made several days in advance and served hot or cold.

In the summer I use leftover cooked fresh corn, and switch to canned or frozen corn in the winter. When cutting the cooked corn from the cob, be sure to scrape the cobs with your knife, for there is often a lot of flavorful corn left after the kernels have been cut off.

Serves 6 to 8

5 tablespoons butter
1 onion, diced
2 carrots, diced
1 stalk celery, diced
⅓ cup all-purpose flour
4 cups water
4 cups milk
About 4 cups cooked fresh corn (from 5 to 6 ears), or
*   about 2 pounds canned or frozen corn*
½ teaspoon salt (omit if using canned corn)
⅛ teaspoon freshly ground pepper

1. In a large saucepan, heat the butter over medium heat. Add the diced vegetables and gently sauté for 2 to 3 minutes. Add the flour and cook, stirring occasionally, for 4 minutes. Make sure that neither the flour nor the vegetables begin to brown during this time.

2. Add the water, milk, and corn and bring to a boil over high heat, stirring occasionally, about 10 minutes.

3. Season with the salt and pepper. Simmer gently over medium-low heat for about 40 minutes. Skim the soup several times to remove the foam and butter that rise to the surface. Stir the soup each time after skimming. When finished, the soup should have a light, creamy texture. If too thick, add water. If too thin, boil to thicken. Taste and adjust the seasoning, if necessary. *(The soup can be prepared ahead. Let cool to room temperature, cover, and refrigerate. Bring to a simmer before serving.)*

4. Serve the soup hot or cold.

Salads

In France, a salad can be composed of many things — vegetables, meat, poultry, seafood, eggs, cheese, herbs, greens, or combinations thereof — just as long as it's dressed with a vinaigrette or a mayonnaise-based dressing. Salads can range in complexity from the simple raw vegetable salads called *crudités* to cooked vegetables dressed with vinaigrette or even cooked in a sort of vinaigrette — as are dishes prepared *à la grecque* (see Champignons à la Grecque, page 215).

A combination of ingredients artfully arranged in a salad bowl or on a plate is known as a *salade composée* — the most well-known example of which is probably *salade niçoise*. By tradition, the components of a *salade composée* are kept separate, not tossed together.

While most salads are served as a first course, and in some cases eaten as a main course, a *salade verte* (green salad) is served after the main course.

Salade d'Endives et de Pamplemousse Rose
Endive and Pink Grapefruit Salad

B elgian endive is often used in place of lettuce in a variety of simple French side salads. There are a number of special combinations (see Variations), but one of my favorites is the combination of endive and grapefruit, which will surprise you if you have never experienced it. Somehow, magically, each seems to cancel out the bitterness of the other.

Serves 6

2 tablespoons white wine vinegar
2 pinches salt
2 pinches freshly ground pepper
½ cup light vegetable oil
3 Belgian endives
3 pink grapefruit

1. In a small bowl (or jar), mix the vinegar, salt, and pepper together. Add the oil and mix until well blended.

2. Take off 12 of the larger outside leaves from each of the endives and set aside (reserve the smaller inside leaves for another use). Peel and section the grapefruit (see "How to Section an Orange," page 325). *(The salad can be prepared ahead to this point. Store the endive in a plastic bag in the refrigerator. Refrigerate the grapefruit in a colander so it does not sit in its own juices.)*

3. To serve, on each plate, place 6 endive leaves, rounded side down, in a flower pattern. Fill each leaf with a grapefruit section.

4. Whisk the vinaigrette to reblend and spoon it lightly over the grapefruit sections.

Variations

Salade d'Endives et de Cresson *(Endive and Watercress Salad):*
Belgian endive and watercress are both available in the
winter when other greens may not be at their best, and their
flavors combine very well. Use 3 Belgian endives, separated
into leaves, and 1 bunch of watercress, stems removed.
Add 1 teaspoon Dijon mustard to the vinaigrette. Arrange
the salad with the watercress in the center and the endive
leaves radiating out in a flower pattern and drizzle with the
vinaigrette. Or, alternatively, cut the endive leaves into
1-inch pieces and toss with the watercress and vinaigrette.

Salade d'Endives aux Noix *(Endive and Walnut Salad):* Walnuts
and Belgian endive make another traditional winter salad
that is often served with game. The flavor created by this
unusual combination is exceptional. Use 3 Belgian endives,
leaves separated and cut into 1-inch pieces, and 30 walnut
halves. Toss with the vinaigrette. In place of the vinaigrette
above you might try a walnut oil vinaigrette: Replace 2 tablespoons of the vegetable oil with 2 tablespoons of walnut oil.

Salade d'Endives et de Betteraves *(Endive and Beet Salad):* Bake
beets according to instructions in Betteraves au Four (page
200). Dice the beets, then toss lightly with 4 to 6 tablespoons (to taste) of Sauce Vinaigrette (page 383). Mound
the beets in the center of 6 individual salad plates or a large
salad bowl. Arrange the leaves of 3 Belgian endives so they
radiate out from the beets in a floral design. Chop a hard-
boiled egg and sprinkle it over the center of the beets. The
beets can be tossed with the vinaigrette in advance, but the
salad should not be assembled until just before serving (to
avoid discoloration).

**Washing Salad Greens: It is
important to wash the lettuce well, but most people
don't know this easy and
efficient method of doing
it. Wash each variety
separately in a large quantity of cold water. The
operative word here is
"large," the object being to
have enough water so the
lettuce can float. Swirl the
leaves around, turning
them over and over again
in the water, and in the
process, the dirt and sand
will drop to the bottom,
while any insects will float
to the surface along with
the leaves. Remove the
leaves, discard the dirty
water, and repeat this
process until you no longer
find dirt or sand at the bottom of your washing water.
Two to three washings are
generally sufficient.**

Storing Salad Greens: Spin dry
the leaves twice, using a
lettuce or salad spinner,
and place each variety of
salad green in a plastic bag
of its own. Washed, dried,
and packaged in this way,
the greens will stay fresh in
the refrigerator for several
days. When it is time to
make a salad, you can
choose from the variety
of prepared greens to
compose a salad to suit
your taste.

SALADE VERTE
Green Salad

In France, a simple green salad (*salade verte*) is made
with a lettuce similar to our Boston lettuce and tossed
with a vinaigrette. The salad can be modified by adding
and mixing greens. Most supermarkets today offer a variety
of salad greens for us to choose from: Boston, Bibb, curly
endive (chicory), romaine, watercress, and Belgian endive
(see Salade d'Endives et de Pamplemousse Rose, page 33)
are among the most frequently seen. There has also been a
recent surge in the popularity of European greens such as
arugula, radicchio, mâche, and frisée (baby chicory).

Salad dressings are generally variations of the vinaigrette (see Sauce Vinaigrette, page 383). The vinaigrette
can be modified by substituting small amounts of nut oil
(such as walnut, almond, or hazelnut) for an equal portion
of the oil called for; different types of vinegar, or lemon
juice can be used in place of the tarragon vinegar called for.

Beyond Simple Salade Verte: There are a large number of ingredients that can be added to your salads to change both
appearance and flavor. Some of these are: *Fresh Herbs:*
Chives, chervil, basil, and tarragon. Either chop the herbs
and sprinkle over the salad, or use a few small leaves mixed
in with the other greens. *Tomatoes:* When ripe, tomatoes
add wonderful flavor and color to a salad. Use tomatoes that
are not too large and cut them into wedges, or use cherry
tomatoes cut in half. When available, use the yellow or
golden varieties of tomatoes, as well as the red. *Avocado:*
Diced ripe avocado adds a subtle richness that is often
appreciated. *Green, Yellow, and Red Peppers:* Diced or julienned, sweet peppers add color, crunch, and flavor. *Cucumbers and/or Radishes:* Sliced cucumbers add a cool freshness to a salad, and sliced radishes add spicy freshness.
Cheese: When serving a salad as a first course, I often add
a little cheese: freshly grated Parmesan, diced hard cheese
(Swiss, Beaumont, St.-Nectaire), or a *chèvre* (goat cheese).

Salade de Crevettes et de Coquilles St.-Jacques
Shrimp and Scallop Salad

The repertoire of classic French recipes abounds in cold lobster presentations, most often made with a mayonnaise-based sauce. This recipe substitutes the much more available shrimp and sea scallops for the lobster and sauces them with a delicately seasoned vinaigrette. Both the seafood and the vinaigrette can be prepared well ahead of time and then tossed together at the last minute for easy entertaining. Serve this with warm French bread and a dry white wine such as Muscadet.

Serves 6

¾ pound large shrimp, shelled and deveined
¾ pound sea scallops, rinsed, tendon removed
3 tablespoons lemon juice or white wine vinegar
2 teaspoons Dijon mustard
½ cup vegetable oil
3 tablespoons light olive oil
Pinch each salt and freshly ground pepper, or more to taste
2 tablespoons chopped fresh herbs: dill, chives, or basil*
1 large head Bibb lettuce, separated into leaves

1. Place the shrimp and scallops in 3 quarts of boiling water. When the water returns to a boil, drain the seafood and refresh under cold running water.

2. Slice the shrimp in half lengthwise, and slice the scallops horizontally into 2 or 3 rounds. *(The seafood can be prepared up to 1 day ahead. Cover and refrigerate.)*

3. In a bowl large enough to hold the seafood, make the vinaigrette. First mix together the lemon juice and mus-

HOW TO CLEAN A SEA SCALLOP

Although many people do not bother with this, the tough tendon on the side of a sea scallop really ought to be removed, as it gets even tougher when it's cooked. After rinsing the scallops, grab the tendon, as shown above, and gently pull to remove.

Salade de Tomates
(Tomato Salad)

When tomatoes are in season, I like nothing better than to start an informal meal with a *salade de tomates.* Finding an American tomato with as much flavor as a French one is rare, but when I do, I like to take advantage of it and serve it in this simple French fashion. Slice the tomatoes (one medium-large tomato per person) and place them, in overlapping slices, on individual salad plates. Make a vinaigrette of three parts light olive oil, one part lemon juice, and 1 or 2 tablespoons chopped chives. Spoon 1 to 2 tablespoons of well-whisked vinaigrette over each portion of tomatoes and serve with warm French bread.

tard. Add the oils and whisk well. Season with the salt and pepper and stir in the chopped herbs. Refrigerate. *(This can be done ahead and taken out of the refrigerator when ready to assemble the salad.)*

4. To serve, arrange the Bibb lettuce on the serving plates. Whisk the vinaigrette until it is smooth, and toss the seafood in it. Either simply mound the seafood in the center of each plate, or arrange each plate by overlapping the shrimp and scallops to form a circular design.

* If more than one herb is available, use 1 tablespoon of each.

Salade de Volaille aux Pêches
Chicken Salad with Peaches

This dish is based on the memory of a salad I once had at the then three-star restaurant Lapérouse in Paris. Their salad was made with fragrant white peaches, which are more widely available in France than they are here, and it was served the way such salads are in France, with the various elements arranged separately on the plate. Instead of this classic presentation of a composed salad, I prefer to toss the salad. By combining the ingredients this way, all the flavors can enter your mouth at the same time, which to me is more enjoyable. Of course, this type of presentation is also less time-consuming.

This salad serves eight as a first course, but with larger portions (serving six), it makes a good main course for lunch, along with warm French bread and a chilled white or rosé wine.

Serves 6 or 8

*8 skinless, boneless chicken half breasts (about 3
    pounds), poached, chilled, and diced*
1 avocado, diced
2 white or yellow peaches, peeled and diced
Juice of 1 lime
2 stalks celery, chopped
3 scallions, chopped
2 hard-boiled eggs, chopped
¾ to 1 cup mayonnaise, to taste
¼ teaspoon salt
⅛ teaspoon freshly ground pepper
Pinch curry powder
1 head lettuce, separated into leaves
Tomato wedges or cherry tomatoes, for garnish

1. In a large bowl, toss the chicken, avocado, and peaches with half of the lime juice. Add the celery, scallions, and hard-boiled eggs.

2. Flavor the mayonnaise with the salt, pepper, curry powder, and remaining lime juice. Gently toss all ingredients with the flavored mayonnaise and refrigerate. *(The recipe can be prepared up to this point 1 day ahead.)*

3. Serve the salad on a bed of lettuce leaves and garnish with tomato wedges or cherry tomatoes.

Variations

Salade de Volaille aux Mangues *(Chicken Salad with Mangoes):* Substitute 1 mango for the peaches.

Salade de Fruits de Mer aux Pêches ou aux Mangues *(Seafood Salad with Peaches or Mangoes):* Substitute 2 pounds cooked lobster meat or shrimp for the chicken.

Salade de Volaille aux Mangues et au Gingembre *(Chicken Salad with Mangoes and Ginger):* Increase the curry powder to 1 to 2 teaspoons (to taste) and add 1 teaspoon chopped fresh ginger.

Eggs & Omelets

Although the egg has come under heavy attack for the cholesterol in its yolk, and although I no longer eat them as I once did, I have not given up the pleasure this most versatile of foods provides. Besides being an excellent source of protein, eggs are responsible for many of the masterpieces of French cooking.

As recently as 10 years ago, a French meal—usually lunch—often included an egg dish. Eggs—poached, soft- or hard-boiled, baked, fried, scrambled, or in an omelet—were offered as first courses, or as a completely separate course.

These days—although something like Oeufs Brouillés en Surprise au Caviar (page 41) might be the beginning of an elegant meal—people are more likely to serve these egg dishes with bread, salad, and dessert for a quick, nourishing light meal.

Oeufs Brouillés aux Truffes
Scrambled Eggs with Truffles

When properly made, *oeufs brouillés aux truffes* ranks in my mind as one of the top 20 dishes ever created. Most French recipes call for the eggs to be cooked in a water bath (*bain-marie*) or double boiler, but I have found that a nonstick pan over low heat works just as well, and if you are careful there will be no need for the extra butter or cream, thus saving a few calories.

The use of truffles here not only makes the dish, but, unfortunately, makes it a luxury as well. I now find that I serve this dish only occasionally for a brunch, or for a special, light Champagne supper. Serve the eggs with or on thinly sliced white toast.

The term "scrambled eggs" does not do justice to the French *oeufs brouillés*, a soft, moist, and creamy dish served as a first course and not for breakfast. Unlike the firm and often dry American scrambled eggs, *oeufs brouillés* are cooked, with butter, very slowly in a double boiler to achieve their silky consistency and are then finished with additional butter or cream.

Serves 4

8 eggs
2 black truffles, chopped
2 tablespoons butter
Pinch each salt and freshly ground pepper

1. In a bowl, beat the eggs well with a fork or whisk. Stir in the chopped truffles and allow the mixture to stand for 15 to 30 minutes.

2. In a 10-inch nonstick skillet, heat the butter over medium-low heat. Add the eggs and cook, stirring gently with a wooden spoon. As the eggs begin to set, keep them moving in the pan so they do not get too stiff. Remove the pan from the heat if necessary to keep them from drying out. The eggs should be creamy, soft, and shiny when finished, 3 to 5 minutes.

3. Sprinkle the eggs with the salt and pepper and serve immediately.

Variations

Oeufs Brouillés à la Ciboulette *(Scrambled Eggs with Chives):* Replace the truffles with 3 tablespoons chopped chives and eliminate the standing period in step 1.

Oeufs Brouillés en Surprise au Caviar *(Scrambled Eggs with Caviar):* Because the portions for this variation are smaller, it will serve 8 instead of 4. Replace the truffle with 2 teaspoons chopped chives and eliminate the standing period in step 1. To serve this dish as restaurants do, you must cut the tops off the egg shells and wash them so you can use them as serving containers. If you can manage this delicate operation (there are soft-boiled egg cutters on the market that work), fill the shells three-quarters full of eggs and top each one with 1 teaspoon of sturgeon, whitefish, or salmon caviar. A simpler presentation is to serve the eggs in small ramekins.

Oeufs Magda *(Scrambled Eggs with Dijon Mustard and Cheese):* Replace the truffle with 1 tablespoon chopped parsley, 1 teaspoon Dijon mustard, and 2½ to 3 ounces (¾ to 1 cup) grated cheese, to taste. Classically, Gruyère is used, but I like to use any one of a number of other cheeses, such as St.-Nectaire, Beaumont, or Brie. The softer cheeses cannot be grated, but should be simply diced or cut into small pieces and added to the eggs. Omit the standing period in step 1.

Omelette aux Fines Herbes
Herb Omelet

Many people shy away from making omelets, feeling that to make a good one requires the mastery of difficult techniques and the ownership of a specially treated pan. It is true that until the advent of nonstick surfaces, it was essential to have a well-seasoned omelet pan. Often the mere description of the seasoning process was enough to discourage a prospective omelet maker. But with nonstick pans and the simple technique used here, omelet making should not be intimidating.

There are numerous approaches to omelet making, but I find that the technique that produces the best texture in the eggs is something I call the "stir-and-shake" method. The object is to keep the eggs moving (if the egg is allowed to sit too long over heat, it becomes hard and tough). When the eggs first hit the hot pan, I rapidly stir them off the bottom of the pan (as you would making American scrambled eggs), at the same time shaking the pan gently. Then when the eggs are nearly set, I stop stirring and let the bottom of the omelet set, shaking the pan once or twice to keep it from sticking.

Everyone seems to have his own "secret" for making a light omelet. Some chefs add water or milk. (I know one who adds Tabasco sauce and swears by it.) I find that the water or milk makes the eggs thinner, which might seem to some to be lighter, but to me, the only "secret" is working rapidly so the eggs do not toughen.

An *omelette aux fines herbes* is one of the most popular omelets in France and one of the finest omelets I have ever eaten, but only when fresh herbs are used. It serves one as a main course or two as a first course.

Serves 1 or 2

3 eggs
1 teaspoon chopped fresh tarragon
1 teaspoon chopped fresh chives
1 teaspoon chopped fresh chervil or parsley

HOW TO FOLD AN OMELET

1. Stir the eggs until they are nearly set. Stop stirring and let the bottom of the omelet firm slightly.

2. Place the filling across the center of the omelet.

3. Push the omelet forward so the opposite side rises up.

4. Fold the risen portion to overlap the first fold.

5. Turn the omelet out folded side down onto a serving platter.

Pinch each salt and freshly ground pepper
½ tablespoon butter

1. In a bowl, beat the eggs with the chopped herbs, salt, and pepper until just blended.

2. Heat a 7- to 8-inch nonstick omelet pan and heat the butter over medium-high heat.

3. Add the egg mixture to the pan and rapidly and constantly stir it with a wooden spoon. If you can, gently shake the pan at the same time. When the eggs are nearly set but with a little liquid still remaining, stop stirring and shake the pan for a couple of seconds, making sure that the bottom of the pan is completely covered by the egg. At this point the eggs should be set, yet still moist. Stop shaking the pan and allow the bottom of the omelet to firm slightly, 4 to 5 seconds. (After making several omelets, you will be able to stir and shake the pan simultaneously.)

4. Fold the omelet into thirds by lifting the handle and tilting the pan at a 30-degree angle. With the back of the spoon, fold the portion of the omelet nearest the handle toward the center of the pan. Gently push the omelet forward in the pan so the unfolded portion rises up the side of the pan. Using the spoon, fold this portion back into the pan, overlapping the first fold. Turn the omelet out onto a serving plate so it ends up folded side down (see "How to Fold an Omelet," at left). Serve immediately.

Omelette Turque
Omelet with Sautéed Chicken Livers

This is a delicious way to use chicken livers and a good example of a filled omelet, in which the flavorings are not mixed with the eggs but folded inside the cooked omelet. If you are lucky enough to have duck, squab, or pheasant livers, use them in place of the chicken livers. It serves one as a main course or two as a first course.

Serves 1 or 2

1½ tablespoons butter
1 shallot, chopped
3 chicken livers, rinsed and cut into chunks
Pinch thyme
Salt and freshly ground pepper
2 tablespoons Madeira
2 teaspoons Glace de Viande (optional; page 352)
3 eggs

1. **Make the filling:** In a 7- to 8-inch nonstick omelet pan, heat 1 tablespoon of the butter over medium-high heat. Add the shallot and sauté until softened but not browned. Add the livers and sauté them just until all sides are colored. Season with the thyme and 1 or 2 pinches of salt and pepper, to taste.

2. Add the Madeira (flame, if desired; see instructions in Bananes Flambées au Rhum, page 322) and reduce the liquid by half. Add the *glace de viande*, toss the livers just to coat with the sauce (the livers should still be pink in the center), and remove from the heat. Using a slotted spoon, separate the livers from the sauce and keep both warm while you make the omelet.

3. In a small bowl, beat the eggs with a pinch of salt and pepper until just blended.

4. Wipe out the omelet pan and reheat over medium-high heat and heat the remaining ½ tablespoon butter.

5. Add the egg mixture to the pan and rapidly and constantly stir with a wooden spoon. When the eggs are nearly set but with a little liquid still remaining, stop stirring and shake the pan for a couple of seconds, making sure that the bottom of the pan is completely covered by the egg. At this point, the eggs should be set, yet still moist. Stop shaking the pan and allow the bottom of the omelet to firm

OMELET PANS

An omelet pan has sloping sides, and the most popular size is 7 or 8 inches, which will make a 2- to 3-egg omelet. Even better for a 2-egg omelet is a 6-inch omelet pan. You can use larger pans to serve more people, but if you are a beginner, the smaller pan will be easier to work with. If I'm serving more than two people, I almost always use a smaller pan and make several omelets.

slightly, 4 to 5 seconds. (After making several omelets, you will be able to stir and shake the pan simultaneously.)

6. Before folding the omelet, place the livers across the center of the omelet. Fold the portion of the omelet nearest to you so it partially covers the livers. Gently push the omelet forward in the pan so the unfilled portion rises up the side of the pan. Using a wooden spoon, fold this portion over to enclose the filling.

7. Turn the omelet, folded side down, out onto a plate (see "How to Fold an Omelet," page 42) and pour the reserved sauce around it. Serve immediately.

Variations

Omelette à la Ratatouille *(Ratatouille Omelet):* Substitute 2 to 3 rounded tablespoons of Ratatouille Niçoise (page 218) for the chicken liver filling.

Omelette au Fromage *(Cheese Omelet):* The cheese for this omelet is always Gruyère or Emmenthaler. If you use another cheese it is no longer *omelette au fromage* but, for example, *omelette au Camembert.* In place of the chicken liver filling, place 2 to 3 rounded tablespoons (about 1 ounce) of grated Swiss-style cheese, such as Gruyère or Emmenthaler, across the center of the omelet before folding.

Ingredients used to flavor an omelet are sometimes mixed with the eggs before cooking (as in Omelette aux Fines Herbes), while others are folded inside the omelet (as in Omelette Turque) after it is cooked. Although the choice of where to place the ingredients is often a personal one, I like to avoid mixing anything with the eggs that would cause them to discolor, such as tomatoes or sautéed mushrooms.

Soufflés

The soufflé is perhaps the most famous creation ever to come out of the French kitchen. Light, airy, and delicately flavored, it is most often described in celestial terms. Restaurants rarely offer soufflés on their menus, but many will prepare one if ordered in advance. I was taught that a soufflé must be made and baked at the last possible moment, and that it can never wait for your guests but rather your guests must wait for it.

Over the years I have learned and refined techniques that will allow you to prepare most soufflés in advance (see "Preparing Soufflés for the Oven Ahead of Time," page 302), and to bake them without collars in 10 minutes or less. I cook soufflés in a very hot oven (475°) so that the surface sets immediately in the high heat, as do the sides as they rise from the mold. The resulting light crust holds the soufflé together as it rises and eliminates the need for the paper collar often used to

The variety of soufflés that can be made is almost endless. Just keep in mind that all the ingredients added to the soufflé base should be fully cooked or ready to eat, because the soufflé cooks so rapidly that there is not enough time for raw ingredients to cook. Nor should the added ingredients contain excess moisture, since they will alter the soufflé's consistency.

give extra height and support. (A note of caution, however: This high-temperature method only works with molds no larger than 4 to 5 cups.)

Traditionally, a soufflé is made of a base, a purée or flavoring, and stiffly beaten egg whites. For most classic first-course soufflés, the base is essentially a thick béchamel sauce (made with butter, flour, and milk) to which a flavoring (cheese, spinach, ham) and egg yolks are added, before being lightened with stiffly beaten egg whites. Although this base is called for in most soufflé recipes, in my experience even fairly proficient cooks have problems with it. If the base is undercooked, it will be too thin and the soufflé will break off as it rises out of the mold. If overcooked, it will be too thick to easily incorporate with the beaten egg whites, and the results are often heavy or lumpy.

A dessert soufflé, on the other hand, doesn't seem to suffer these problems and it uses a base made without butter. I have therefore adapted this idea for savory soufflés, using what is effectively a sugarless pastry cream (*crème pâtissière salée* or *sans sucre*) as a base.

Should you encounter problems while learning to make soufflés, see the "Soufflé Problem-Solving Chart" on page 54.

Soufflé au Jambon
Ham Soufflé

A ham soufflé makes a wonderful lunch or light supper when served with a green salad and dessert. The ham used can be your own leftover baked ham, boiled ham from the supermarket, or smoked or Black Forest ham from a gourmet shop. The soufflé serves two for lunch or four as a first course.

Serves 2 or 4

Butter and all-purpose flour for soufflé mold
1 cup milk
3 egg yolks
1 tablespoon water
3 tablespoons all-purpose flour
⅛ teaspoon freshly ground pepper
1 tablespoon Madeira
1 teaspoon Dijon mustard
¼ pound ham (boiled, baked, or smoked), finely chopped
4 egg whites
⅛ teaspoon cream of tartar

1. Preheat the oven to 475°. Liberally butter a 4-cup soufflé mold and lightly dust with flour, tapping out any excess.

2. In a small saucepan, bring the milk to a boil over medium heat. While the milk is heating, whisk the egg yolks and water together in a small bowl. Add the 3 tablespoons flour to the yolks and blend until smooth and free of lumps.

3. Before the milk boils, pour about ¼ cup of it into the egg yolk mixture to thin it. When the remaining milk boils, add it to the egg yolk mixture and stir well.

BEATING EGG WHITES:
The Magic of the
Copper Bowl

A firmly beaten egg white is the "secret" of the success of all soufflés and many desserts; and there is no firmer egg white than the one that has been beaten by hand with a balloon whisk in an unlined copper bowl.

When egg whites are beaten in a copper bowl, the copper combines with the protein to form a polymer. Simply put, this means that the protein molecules and the copper combine to form a strong chemical chain. This allows you to beat the egg whites until they are very stiff without their breaking down.

When egg whites are not beaten in a copper bowl, a little cream of tartar should be added to the egg whites. Cream of tartar is a potassium salt. The potassium reacts with the egg whites as the copper does, although the chemical chain formed is not as strong. Nevertheless, with cream of tartar you can beat egg whites until they are stiff.

There's no reason for you to go out and buy a copper bowl unless you have poor results with the present procedure. If you are planning to buy one, however, I recommend a 10-inch-diameter bowl. With this size bowl you can beat 3 to 9 egg whites. A balloon whisk is used for beating egg whites. Most egg white whisks are made with wooden handles to differentiate them from sauce whisks, whose handles are metal. For bowls ranging in size from 10 to 14 inches I use a 14- to 16-inch balloon whisk. Many people use large sauce or smaller balloon whisks with their large copper bowls, making their task much more difficult.

Before each use, the bowl should be cleaned with a little vinegar and salt, and then rinsed out with cold water and dried.

4. Return the egg–milk mixture to the saucepan and whisk rapidly over medium-high heat, whisking the bottom and sides of the pan until the mixture thickens and boils, about 30 seconds. (Turning the pan as you whisk helps you easily reach all areas of the pan.) Continue to whisk vigorously for 1 minute while the soufflé base gently boils. It will become shiny and easier to stir.

5. Reduce the heat to medium and allow the soufflé base to simmer while you season it with the pepper, Madeira, mustard, and ham. Remove the pan from the heat and cover.

6. In a large bowl, beat the egg whites with the cream of tartar until stiff peaks form, about 3 minutes.

7. Pour the warm soufflé base into a large bowl, and with a whisk fold in one-third of the beaten egg whites to lighten it. Some egg white will still be visible. With a rubber spatula, fold in the remaining egg whites. Stop folding as soon as the mixture is blended; a little egg white may still be visible.

8. Pour the soufflé mixture into the prepared mold, leveling the surface with your spatula. If any of the batter touches the rim of the mold, run your thumb around the rim to clean it off. *(You can prepare the soufflé ahead to this point; see "Preparing Soufflés for the Oven Ahead of Time," page 302.)*

9. Bake on the lowest rack in the oven for 5 minutes. Lower the temperature to 425° and bake for another 5 to 7 minutes. The soufflé should rise 1½ to 2 inches above the mold and brown lightly on the top. The top of this soufflé has a tendency to crack slightly. Serve immediately.

Variation

Soufflé au Saumon Fumé *(Smoked Salmon Soufflé):* Substitute ¼ pound finely chopped smoked salmon (or any other smoked fish) for the ham. Omit the Madeira and mustard. Add 2 tablespoons chopped chives or dill with the fish in step 5.

Soufflé aux Epinards
Spinach Soufflé

This is a very light version of a spinach soufflé, and because it is made with frozen spinach, it is also quick and easy. Just be sure to squeeze the spinach as dry as possible. The measurement for nutmeg here is for 2 or 3 pinches, which is difficult to measure accurately, so if in doubt, skimp: although a little nutmeg enhances the flavor of spinach, too much will overpower it. The soufflé serves two for lunch or four as a first course.

Serves 2 or 4

Butter and all-purpose flour for soufflé mold
5 ounces frozen spinach or the washed leaves from
    1 pound fresh
1 cup milk
3 egg yolks
1 tablespoon water
3 tablespoons all-purpose flour
½ teaspoon salt
⅛ teaspoon freshly ground pepper
2 to 3 pinches freshly grated nutmeg
4 egg whites
⅛ teaspoon cream of tartar

1. Preheat the oven to 475°. Liberally butter a 4-cup soufflé mold and lightly dust with flour, tapping out any excess.

2. If using frozen spinach, cook according to package directions, then drain and refresh under cold running water. If using fresh spinach, drop the leaves into boiling water and cook 3 minutes. Drain and refresh under cold running water. Squeeze the spinach to extract as much

A finished soufflé will be firm and dry around the outside edge and soft and creamy in the center. Since most Americans are used to soufflés that are considerably drier, they often feel they have made a mistake when they find the creamy center. If you prefer a drier center, allow the soufflé to remain in the oven for 3 to 4 minutes longer.

You can vary the flavor of this soufflé by adding 1 ounce grated Swiss-style cheese, such as Gruyère or Emmenthaler. You might also want to add some crumbled bacon, or a few mushrooms that have been chopped and sautéed. Just remember that the more you add, the heavier the soufflé becomes. If you decide to use all of the above-mentioned ingredients in the soufflé, add one more egg white to provide a little extra lift.

moisture as possible, and finely chop. Set aside.

3. In a small saucepan, bring the milk to a boil over medium heat. While the milk is heating, whisk the egg yolks and water together in a small bowl. Add the 3 tablespoons flour to the yolks and blend until smooth and free of lumps.

4. Before the milk boils, stir about ¼ cup of it into the egg yolk mixture to thin it. When the remaining milk boils, add it to the egg yolk mixture and stir well.

5. Return the egg–milk mixture to the saucepan and whisk rapidly over medium-high heat, whisking the bottom and sides of the pan until the mixture thickens and boils, about 30 seconds. (Turning the pan as you whisk helps you easily reach all areas of the pan.) Continue to whisk vigorously for 1 minute while the soufflé base gently boils. It will become shiny and easier to stir.

6. Reduce the heat to medium and allow the soufflé base to simmer while you season it with the salt, pepper, and nutmeg, and add the reserved spinach. Remove the pan from the heat and cover.

7. In a large bowl, beat the egg whites with the cream of tartar until stiff peaks form, about 3 minutes.

8. Pour the warm soufflé base into a large bowl, and with a whisk fold in one-third of the beaten egg whites to lighten it. Some egg white will still be visible. With a rubber spatula, fold in the remaining egg whites. Stop folding as soon as the mixture is blended; a little egg white may still be visible.

9. Pour the soufflé mixture into the prepared mold, leveling the surface with your spatula. If any of the batter touches the rim of the mold, run your thumb around the rim to clean it off. *(The soufflé can be prepared ahead to this point; see "Preparing Soufflés for the Oven Ahead of Time," page 302.)*

10. Bake on the lowest rack in the oven for 5 minutes. Lower the temperature to 425° and bake for another 5 to 7 minutes. The soufflé should rise 1½ to 2 inches above the mold and brown lightly on the top. The top may be slightly cracked, but this is not a problem. Serve immediately.

Soufflé au Roquefort
Roquefort Cheese Soufflé

Since the ingredients for a cheese soufflé are generally at hand, it's easy to prepare an elegant lunch or light supper for unexpected guests. This particular version was inspired by a soufflé I had years ago at the restaurant Taillevent in Paris, but the cheese soufflé most commonly served in France is a *soufflé au fromage* (see Variation) made with Gruyère or Emmenthaler. If Roquefort is too difficult to find, substitute another blue cheese.

Serves 2 or 4

Butter and all-purpose flour for soufflé mold
1 cup milk
3 egg yolks
1 tablespoon water
3 tablespoons all-purpose flour
1 teaspoon Dijon mustard
⅛ teaspoon freshly ground pepper
Pinch freshly grated nutmeg
2 ounces Roquefort cheese, crumbled (about ⅔ cup)
4 egg whites
⅛ teaspoon cream of tartar

1. Preheat the oven to 475°. Liberally butter a 4-cup soufflé mold and lightly dust with flour, tapping out any excess.

2. In a small saucepan, bring the milk to a boil over medium heat. While the milk is heating, whisk the egg yolks and water together in a small bowl. Add the 3 tablespoons flour to the yolks and blend until smooth.

3. Before the milk boils, stir about ¼ cup of it into the egg yolk mixture to thin it. When the remaining milk boils,

add it to the egg yolk mixture and stir well.

4. Return the egg–milk mixture to the saucepan and whisk rapidly over medium-high heat, whisking the bottom and sides of the pan until the mixture thickens and boils, about 30 seconds. (Turning the pan as you whisk helps you easily reach all areas of the pan.) Continue to whisk vigorously for 1 minute while the soufflé base gently boils. It will become shiny and easier to stir.

5. Reduce the heat to medium and allow the soufflé base to simmer while you season it with the mustard, pepper, and nutmeg. Stir in the cheese and mix well until it melts completely and the mixture comes to a boil. Remove the pan from the heat and cover.

6. In a large bowl, beat the egg whites with the cream of tartar until stiff peaks form, about 3 minutes.

7. Pour the warm soufflé base into a large bowl, and with a whisk fold in one-third of the beaten egg whites to lighten it. Some egg white will still be visible. With a rubber spatula, fold in the remaining egg whites. Stop folding as soon as the mixture is blended; a little egg white may still be visible.

8. Pour the soufflé mixture into the prepared mold, leveling the surface with your spatula. If any of the batter touches the rim of the mold, run your thumb around the rim to clean it off. *(You can prepare the soufflé ahead to this point; see "Preparing Soufflés for the Oven Ahead of Time," page 302.)*

9. Bake on the lowest rack in the oven for 5 minutes. Lower the temperature to 425° and bake for another 5 to 7 minutes. The soufflé should rise 1½ to 2 inches above the mold and brown lightly on the top. Serve immediately.

Variation

Soufflé au Fromage *(Cheese Soufflé):* Substitute 2 ounces grated (rounded ⅔ cup) Swiss-style cheese, such as Gruyère or Emmenthaler for the Roquefort. *In step 5, when you add the cheese, be sure to return the soufflé base to a boil so the cheese loses its stringiness.*

SOUFFLE PROBLEM-SOLVING CHART

PROBLEM	CAUSE	SOLUTION
Heavy uncooked bottom.	Unstable egg whites that break down. Soufflé made too far in advance.	Make sure you use cream of tartar. Make next soufflé just before baking.
Burnt top.	Rack is too high in the oven.	Bake on lowest rack in oven.
Top domed instead of flat.	Sides stuck to the mold as it rose. Mold was insufficiently buttered or insufficiently filled.	Very carefully loosen edge of soufflé with point of a knife and return to oven.
Top is concave, not flat after the prescribed cooking time.	The center needs more cooking.	Reduce oven heat by 50° and continue cooking for 2 to 5 minutes.
Soufflé rises abnormally high on one side.	A trapped air pocket expands to push portion of soufflé too high.	When making your next soufflé, take care not to trap air when filling the mold.
Pieces of soufflé break off as it rises.	Soufflé base is too thin or liquidy.	When making same soufflé again, add more flour or less liquid to base.

Fish Mousses

There are two types of classic fish mousse. One fish mousse is made with cooked fish and served cold. If you have ever made a salmon mousse with mayonnaise, heavy cream, and gelatin, you are familiar with this style. But hot fish mousses, *mousselines de poisson*, are made differently.

Classically a *mousseline de poisson* was made by pounding uncooked fish in a large mortar with a pestle until the strands of muscle fiber were stretched and broken down to form a gummy, springy paste. Egg whites were then pounded into the fish paste. Once smooth, this paste was forced through a fine sieve, leaving any bones, tendons, or fibrous tissue behind. This refined fish paste was then chilled, and cream would be added until it became the consistency of creamy mashed potatoes.

Over the years, machines have been used to speed this lengthy process. The food processor's metal blade is usually so efficient that it cuts fish, bones, tendons, and all so small that it is not necessary to put it through a sieve, making the whole process quick and easy.

Although much faster than the original method, the texture of the mousseline is not as smooth. To improve the mousseline's texture, I use half fish and half shrimp. The shrimp pulverizes into a paste that, when poached, is very smooth. Blended with the fish, it produces a wonderful flavor and texture.

The fish mousseline is technically designed as a hot dish—as in the recipes that follow—but it is also good served cold, although you would then serve it with a cold rather than a hot sauce.

Mousseline de Poisson
Basic Fish Mousseline

One of the most sublime preparations to come out of the French kitchen is a well-made fish mousseline. Essentially a fish purée bound by egg whites and enriched by heavy cream, it can be poached, steamed, or baked. It can be used as a stuffing, as in Saumon Farci aux Deux Sauces (page 61); or baked in a mold and served with a sauce, as for Coquilles St.-Jacques en Surprise (page 60) or Turban de Fruits de Mer (page 58); or it can be spoon-molded to make quenelles or small dumplings (see "Spoon-Molding Dumplings," page 82) and served with the Sauce Aurore (page 361) or Sauce au Safran à la Tomate Fraîche (page 362). You can use the mousseline plain or

Unless you have tasted a hand-pounded mousseline, you would not notice that one made with a processor is a little grainy instead of being silky smooth. To improve the texture of the processor-made mousseline, I occasionally use the plastic blade instead of the metal one. In effect, the duller plastic blade pounds the fish instead of cutting it. However, a mousseline made this way must then be forced through a food mill to eliminate any bones or tendons. To me, the end results are noticeably smoother; however, I go to this extra effort only for very special occasions.

change its flavor and appearance by adding chopped truffles and chopped fresh herbs.

Before molding or using the mousseline, you should test its consistency by poaching a teaspoonful in a saucepan of simmering water. It should hold its shape, yet not be too firm or springy when eaten.

Serves 8 to 10

When choosing a fish to use for a mousseline, look for the freshest possible. The fresher the fish, the better the mousseline will be. When inland, look for thick fillets from large fish, which hold their freshness longer than thin ones.

1 pound skinless, boneless firm, fresh fish, cut into
    2-inch chunks
1 pound shrimp, shelled and deveined*
4 egg whites
1 teaspoon salt
¼ teaspoon freshly ground pepper
⅛ teaspoon freshly grated nutmeg
2½ cups heavy cream

1. Place the fish and shrimp in a food processor fitted with the metal blade. Process the fish until it becomes a gummy paste.

2. Add the egg whites one by one and process until the mixture is very smooth. Blend in the salt, pepper, and nutmeg. Add 2 cups of cream quickly in a steady stream. Turn off the processor as soon as the cream is incorporated. Too much processing at this point can cause the cream to turn to butter.

3. Place the fish mixture in a bowl and place the bowl in a larger bowl containing ice and a little water. When the mixture is cold, it will stiffen and hold more cream. Stir in the remaining cream a little at a time. Poach a spoonful of the mixture to determine if it needs more seasoning, egg white, or cream. If it's too firm and springy, it needs more cream; if it's soft, a little more egg white. *(The mousseline can be made up to 1 day in advance. Cover, and refrigerate until ready to use.)*

* You can omit the shrimp if you want and use 2 pounds of fish. The mousseline will have a somewhat grainier texture.

Variation

Terrine de Poisson *(Fish Terrine):* Follow the instructions for constructing the Terrine Maison aux Pruneaux (page 64), using the uncooked fish mousseline in place of the ground meats. Use lightly poached salmon, lobster, or sea scallops in place of the strips of ham and chicken. Bake like the terrine in a 400° oven until springy to the touch, about 1 hour.

Turban de Fruits de Mer
Fish Mousseline Ring with Seafood

A spectacular presentation can be created by molding a fish mousseline in a ring mold. When baked and unmolded, the ring, or "turban," is filled with seafood and topped with one of several highly refined sauces. A classic turban is made by first lining the mold with fillets of sole. I find that this adds neither contrast of texture and color nor a smoother surface to the dish. And because it is time consuming and expensive, I have eliminated that aspect of the dish.

Although I have specified the use of small shrimp and bay scallops, if sea scallops are fresher, use them along with medium-size shrimp. Oysters can be used in place of or in addition to the mussels, and poached mushrooms (Champignons Pochés, page 110) can be added if desired.

If saffron is not available or not appreciated, serve the turban with a tomato-flavored sauce (Sauce Aurore, page 361). The mousseline and the sauce can be prepared a day before serving.

Serves 8 to 10

HOW TO CLEAN MUSSELS

Pull the beard off mussel with paring knife and thumb as above. Rub the mussels vigorously against each other in large bowl of water. Remove the mussels and pour off dirt and water. Repeat until water is clean.

Butter for ring mold
Mousseline de Poisson (page 56)
2 pounds mussels, scrubbed and debearded
2 shallots, minced
½ cup dry white wine
½ pound small shrimp, shelled and deveined
½ pound bay scallops, rinsed
Sauce au Safran à la Tomate Fraîche (page 362)

1. Preheat the oven to 350°. Butter a 1½-quart ring mold.

2. Fill the mold with the *mousseline de poisson* and smooth the surface. Place the mold in a baking pan. Pour in enough boiling water to reach halfway up the mold and bake until the top is springy to the touch and a cake tester inserted into the center comes out clean, 30 to 40 minutes.

3. Meanwhile, place the mussels, shallots, and wine in a large saucepan. Cover and steam over high heat, shaking the pan several times to toss the mussels. The mussels will open and be cooked after about 5 minutes of steaming. Remove the mussels from their shells and set aside. Discard any that have not opened.

4. Strain the mussel liquid through a fine-mesh sieve into a small saucepan, discarding any sand or grit that may remain at the bottom of the pan. Boil over high heat until reduced to ¼ cup, about 5 minutes. Set aside.

5. Bring a large saucepan of water to a boil over high heat and drop in the shrimp and scallops. When the water returns to the boil, drain the shrimp and scallops immediately and refresh under cold running water. Set aside.

6. In a large saucepan, reheat the *sauce au safran à la tomate fraîche* over medium heat. Add the shrimp, scallops, mussels, and reduced mussel cooking liquid to the sauce. Heat, stirring occasionally, until the sauce begins to simmer; do not boil.

7. To assemble, unmold the mousseline onto a large warmed serving platter and use paper towels to absorb any excess moisture. With a slotted spoon, transfer the shellfish to the center of the ring. Spoon the sauce over the shellfish and around the sides of the mousseline ring.

Coquilles St.-Jacques en Surprise
Fish Mousseline with a
Hidden Scallop

The "surprise" element of these ramekin-molded mousselines is the scallop that is hidden inside each one.

The fish mousseline can be made and molded in the ramekins up to one day in advance of serving. The ramekins cook rapidly on top of the stove in a covered skillet partially filled with simmering water.

Serves 10

10 sea scallops, rinsed, tendon removed
Butter for ramekins
Mousseline de Poisson (page 56)
Sauce Beurre Blanc (page 376), Sauce Hollandaise
    (page 373), Sauce Aurore (page 361), or Sauce au
    Safran à la Tomate Fraîche (page 362)

If 2 chopped truffles or ¼ cup freshly chopped chives are added to the mousseline, the color contrast with the hidden scallop is even more dramatic.

1. In a medium saucepan of simmering water, poach the scallops for 15 seconds. Drain immediately and set aside.

2. Butter ten ¾-cup ramekins and divide the mousseline equally among them. Bury a scallop in the center of each portion. *(The recipe can be prepared a day ahead to this point. Cover and refrigerate.)*

3. Place the ramekins in a large skillet with a cover. Add water to come ½ inch up the sides of the ramekins. Cover and steam the mousseline over medium-high heat until it puffs and is springy to the touch at the center of each ramekin, about 10 minutes.

4. **To serve:** Unmold the mousselines onto paper towels to drain off the excess moisture, and place them on individual serving plates. Serve with your choice of sauce.

1. Score the fish along its back, from head to tail.

2. Peel the skin down to the belly and remove. Leave the skin on the head intact.

Saumon Farci aux Deux Sauces
Mousseline-Filled Salmon with Two Sauces

A fish mousseline can be used to stuff any size fish. I once sailed on the *S.S. France* and was served one of their specialties, a turbot stuffed with a lobster mousseline. Because there were 12 of us at table, they served an 18-pound turbot.

A more manageable-size fish is the baby Coho salmon or salmon trout that has recently come onto the market. These small salmon are a perfect size for this recipe. Often sold boned, the fish can be easily stuffed and poached. Wrap the fish in plastic wrap to hold it and stuffing together while poaching.

Serves 4

2 small (about 1 pound each) whole salmon, boned, with head and tail on
½ recipe Mousseline de Poisson (page 56)
½ recipe Sauce Beurre Blanc (page 376)
½ recipe Beurre Blanc au Cresson (page 377)

1. Fill the cavity of each fish with the mousseline, smoothing with a spatula.

2. Wrap each fish in plastic wrap or aluminum foil and place in a single layer in a large skillet, fish poacher, or shallow roasting pan. Pour in enough boiling water to reach halfway up the fish. Cover and simmer over moderate heat until the mousseline is firm, about 20 minutes.

3. Unwrap and drain the fish on paper towels. Place the fish on a warmed platter. Carefully peel the skin from the exposed side of the body. For presentation, spoon the *sauce beurre blanc* around the fish on half of the platter. Spoon the *beurre blanc au cresson* around the other half.

Pâtés & Terrines

I remember eating pâté often as a child. It was served on crackers or small rounds of toast as an hors d'oeuvre. It was always smooth and livery tasting. Years later, after my interest in French cooking had taken hold and I was living in France, I learned that the majority of pâtés were more of a coarse, chunky variety—sort of like meat loaf—and only those made from liver (goose, duck, chicken, and pork) were smooth.

Now that the full range of pâtés has been discovered on this side of the Atlantic, there is still a tendency to lump them all under the heading of pâté, whereas there are distinct differences. Literally speaking, something called pâté is baked in a crust designed to be a strong, edible, decorative container. A terrine, on the other hand, is baked in a ceramic mold (called a terrine). In fact, the mold is often

designed to look like a pâté's crust. Then there are the galantines and ballotines—the aristocrats of the pâté world. Instead of a crust or a mold, the pâté mixture is usually poached or baked wrapped inside the skin of a chicken or duck and coated in aspic.

Although the container changes, the components and techniques for making a pâté, terrine, galantine, or ballotine are pretty much the same. They all contain a seasoned ground meat called a forcemeat, or *farce*, and strips of meat or poultry to add both a contrasting texture and a pattern to the sliced pâté. Most are served cold, with or without an aspic.

For this book, I have omitted pâtés baked in a crust (*en croûte*), because I don't feel the crust is worth the effort and even properly made is so thick that it's close to inedible. And I've omitted galantines and ballotines, because they are really quite a time-consuming (though rewarding) production.

In the recipes for Mousse de Foie de Volaille (a simple, rich, smooth mousse that is vastly different from the pâté I knew as a child) and for Terrine Maison aux Pruneaux that follow, I have removed a great deal of the fat called for in their classic counterparts, using just enough to give the pâtés the proper texture and taste.

Terrine Maison aux Pruneaux
Home-Style Pâté with Prunes

This terrine is a good all-purpose recipe that can serve as a guide for numerous variations. You can use different meats or different flavoring and decorative ingredients (see Terrine Variée, page 66).

Although this is a typical terrine, it differs from most in its fat content. Most recipes call for the baking mold to be lined with thin sheets of pork fat, and the meat itself covered with the same fat. This method originated in the days before refrigeration, to protect the terrine from airborne bacteria by completely sealing it with fat. Since most people today have refrigerators, I have omitted it from the recipe. I have also omitted the strips of pork fat traditionally used merely to make a mosaic pattern in the sliced pâté.

Although the terrine is usually served cold, you will find it delicious served hot with a purée of potatoes. The seasoned ground meat can be shaped into patties, pan fried like sausage, and served with eggs for breakfast or with vegetables for dinner. Mixed with some cooked rice or bread crumbs, it can also be used to stuff cabbage or green peppers.

Serving Suggestion: Slices of the terrine can be served as a first course, or with a mixed green salad, warm French bread, and dessert for lunch or light supper. Serve the terrine with *cornichons*, small French pickles.

Wine: Both white and red wines are suitable for terrines.

Serves 8

4 shallots
5 large sprigs parsley, stems removed
¼-inch slice (about ¼ pound) ham (boiled, baked, or smoked), cut into ¼-inch-wide strips
½ pound skinless, boneless chicken breast, cut into ¼-inch strips

If you have any chicken and ham strips left over they are delicious quickly sautéed and eaten on their own or used to fill an omelet.

There are a number of attractive white porcelain terrines that can be used for pâté. Those with ducks or rabbits on their lids can also be used, although technically they should have the meat of those animals in them. Most people, however, will use a ceramic or glass loaf pan, and instead of bringing the terrine to the table, will present slices of the pâté on a platter or individual plates.

1 teaspoon salt
¾ teaspoon freshly ground pepper
½ teaspoon thyme
¼ cup plus 2 tablespoons dry white wine
2 tablespoons Cognac
3 tablespoons Madeira
5 ounces fresh pork fat, cut into chunks
8 to 14 pitted prunes, marinated in Madeira (page 341)
¾ pound lean pork, ground
¾ pound veal (shoulder), ground
⅛ teaspoon ground allspice
1 egg
1 tablespoon potato starch or cornstarch

1. In a food processor, finely chop the shallots and parsley.

2. Place the strips of ham and chicken in a shallow dish and sprinkle with half of the shallot mixture, ¼ teaspoon of the salt, ¼ teaspoon of the pepper, and ¼ teaspoon of the thyme. Moisten with the 2 tablespoons white wine, 1 tablespoon of the Cognac, and 1 tablespoon of the Madeira.

3. Add the pork fat and 4 of the prunes to the remaining shallot mixture in the processor and process to grind the fat, about 10 seconds.

4. Add the ground lean pork and veal and season with the allspice and the remaining salt, pepper, and thyme. Moisten with the remaining wine, Cognac, and Madeira. Add the egg and potato starch and process to combine, about 15 seconds.

5. Divide the seasoned ground meat into four even portions. Spread one portion evenly over the bottom of a terrine or 4- to 5-quart loaf pan, using your fingers to make sure the corners are filled in.

6. Completely cover the ground meat with alternating strips of chicken and ham, placing them lengthwise. You may have to cut the strips to fit the terrine. Cover the strips with another layer of ground meat, again using your fingers if necessary to spread the mixture evenly.

7. Press as many of the remaining prunes as needed halfway into the layer of ground meat to make a tight, compact row down the center. Cover with the third layer of ground meat.

8. Cover the ground meat again with the chicken and ham strips. Cover with the final portion of ground meat, pressing it down with your hands to fit the terrine. Cover with the terrine lid or aluminum foil. *(If time permits, let the terrine stand in the refrigerator overnight before baking to allow the flavors to fully develop.)*

9. Preheat the oven to 400°.

10. Place the terrine in a larger baking pan and place on the lowest rack in the oven. Add boiling water to come 1½ inches up the sides of the terrine. Bake for 1 hour.

11. Lower the oven temperature to 350° and bake an additional 30 minutes. When done, the melted fat and juices should be clear and not cloudy. The meat will have shrunk away from the sides of the terrine and a cake tester inserted into the center of the terrine will come out hot to the touch. If tested with a meat thermometer, the internal temperature should be about 160°.

12. Remove the terrine from the oven, but keep it covered in the pan of water. Evenly weight the surface of the terrine with a 4- to 5-pound weight (e.g., 2 large cans of tomatoes), and allow to cool. If your terrine has a lid, remove it and replace it with aluminum foil before weighting.

13. When cool, about 1½ hours, remove the weight, cover the surface with plastic wrap, and refrigerate. The terrine is best eaten several days after it has been cooked, or it can be frozen for later use.

Variation

Pâté de Campagne *(Country-Style Pâté):* For a country-style pâté, simply omit the ham and chicken strips and the prunes and grind up ½ pound of pork liver with the meat and pork fat.

Terrine Variée:
• Use duck, pheasant, rabbit, or hare in place of the chicken, and the name changes to Terrine de Canard, Faisan, Lapin, etc., Lièvre aux Pruneaux.
• Use chicken livers (soaked in Armagnac or Cognac) in place of the prunes. Use about the same number of livers as prunes. Substitute strips of beef tongue for the ham.
• Add about 2 tablespoons green peppercorns or 1 medium truffle, chopped, to the ground meat to change both flavor and appearance.
• Instead of cutting them into strips, cut the chicken and ham into dice and stir into the seasoned ground meats. This will save time and produce a more typical, though less sophisticated, looking terrine.

Mousse de Foie de Volaille
Chicken Liver Mousse

Serving Suggestion: Serve the
mousse on thin toast points
as an hors d'oeuvre, or
mold and decorate with
aspic to serve as a first
course (see "How to Deco-
rate a Mousse," page 68).

This is a quick and easy recipe for chicken liver
mousse. Traditionally, an equal amount of butter is
mixed with the livers to make the mousse. I have used
what I consider to be the minimum amount for a successful mousse. When available, use duck, goose,
pheasant, or pigeon livers.

Serves 12

2 sticks (8 ounces) plus 3 tablespoons butter
3 shallots, chopped
1 pound chicken livers, rinsed and dried
½ teaspoon thyme
½ teaspoon salt (omit if using salted butter)
⅛ to ¼ teaspoon freshly ground pepper, to taste
¼ cup Madeira
2 teaspoons Glace de Viande (optional; page 352)
2 teaspoons Cognac

1. In a 10-inch skillet, heat 3 tablespoons of the butter
over medium heat. Sauté the shallots quickly until they are
softened but not browned, 2 to 3 minutes.

2. Add the livers, increase the heat, and sauté just until
all sides have been colored lightly, 2 to 3 minutes. Season
with the thyme, salt, and pepper. Transfer the livers to a
food processor or blender.

3. Add the Madeira and *glace de viande*, if using, to the
skillet and reduce by half over high heat, about 45 seconds. Set aside.

4. Purée the livers and the remaining 2 sticks butter
until smooth. Mix in the reduced pan liquid and Cognac.
Taste and adjust the seasoning, if necessary.

5. Pour the mousse into a porcelain mold or individual molds for serving and cover the surface with plastic wrap. Refrigerate for a minimum of 2 hours. Serve with toast or crackers.

HOW TO DECORATE A MOUSSE

For an impressive finishing touch that's worth the effort, you can layer the top of your molded *mousse de foie de volaille* with aspic. To make an aspic, add 4 packages of unflavored gelatin to either the Consommé de Volaille (page 19) or Consommé de Boeuf (page 21). Cool the aspic to room temperature and pour a thin layer over the mousse. Place the mousse in the refrigerator to set the aspic. The unused portion of the aspic can either be reheated and served as a hot consommé or poured into a shallow baking dish or roasting pan, chilled until set, and then chopped and served with the mousse. If you would like to decorate the mousse further (see below), save some of the aspic for the final decorations.

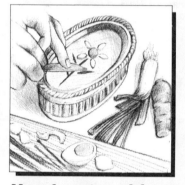

Move the moistened deco-ration to the chilled mousse with the point of a knife.

To make simple decorations, use tomato skin, hard-boiled egg white, and leek, scallion, parsley, or tarragon leaves. (The leaves should be blanched in boiling water for 5 to 10 seconds and refreshed under cold running water to set their color.) Plan the design and cut everything into the desired shapes before placing on the mousse.

When you are ready to decorate, moisten the decoration by spooning some liquid aspic over it. With the point of a knife, move the decoration to the chilled mousse (the decorations can also be placed directly on top of a mousse that hasn't been coated with aspic). Refrigerate the mousse until the aspic on the decorations has set, about 15 minutes. Cover with another thin layer of liquid aspic and chill for at least 1 hour.

A decorated mousse.

Crêpes

Crêpes are one of those specialties that go in and out of fashion. Although at one time in this country there were restaurants that served nothing but crêpes, recently they have waned in popularity.

Now with America's revived interest in pasta, it may be time to reevaluate the crêpe. The French use first-course crêpes much the same way Italians use cannelloni. Instead of a square of pasta, the French use this thin, delicate pancake to fold around a filling, which is coated with a sauce and baked.

Crêpes freeze exceptionally well, and if you prepare some to have on hand, making stuffed crêpes can be easy. When I make crêpes to freeze for future use, I do not put waxed paper between each crêpe as most cookbooks instruct. I generally freeze the crêpes in a stack, in the quantity that I am most likely to need (assuming two to three crêpes per person). When I'm ready to use them, I put the whole stack to warm in an oven or defrost in a microwave, making them pliable and easy to use.

HOW TO SEASON A CREPE PAN

If you buy a French steel crêpe pan, wash and dry it well before its first use. This should be the only time you wash the pan. Give the pan its first seasoning by placing it on the stove and filling it three-quarters of the way up with vegetable oil. Turn the heat to medium-high and heat until the oil begins to smoke, then turn off the heat and allow the pan to cool. Pour off the oil and wipe out the pan with a paper towel. Each time you use the pan, heat about ¼ inch of vegetable oil in it until the oil smokes. Pour off the oil immediately, and add ⅛ teaspoon salt. Using a paper towel, scrub the pan with the salt. The scrubbing will clean the pan and it will be ready for your batter. When you finish with the pan, wipe it with a paper towel and store it in a plastic bag to prevent dust from collecting on it.

Crêpes Salées
First-Course Crêpes

The batter for these basic crêpes can be used for all first-course crêpes. In addition to the salt and pepper, you can add seasoning to the batter based on what the filling will be. A touch of freshly grated nutmeg for a spinach filling, or a little curry powder for creamed chicken or seafood are just two examples of spices that can be added. I often add chopped chives or a few thinly sliced scallions, which add both color and flavor to the crêpe.

The number of crêpes that you can make from this recipe will depend on how thin the batter is and how thin you make the crêpes. If you let the batter rest after making it, the flour swells, making the batter smoother and thicker. If you find your first crêpe too thick, add a little more milk to the batter. When cooking the crêpes, once the pan is coated with the batter, any excess should be poured out to keep the crêpes thin.

I use a nonstick crêpe pan and recommend it, but if you prefer to use a traditional metal crêpe pan, you will have to season it first (see "How to Season a Crêpe Pan," page 69). Even if your pan is nonstick, you should lubricate it with a touch of oil or butter for the first few crêpes if you want to be able to flip the crêpes (which is especially fun for children) as instructed in step 4. Otherwise, the crêpe batter will stick to the pan as it cooks, and you won't be able to shake the crêpe loose to flip it. It is, however, an easy matter to loosen and turn the crêpe with a coated spatula (so as not to scratch the pan).

Once made, the stacked crêpes should be tightly wrapped in plastic wrap and stored in the refrigerator for up to 2 days, or frozen for several months. To use them, simply reheat in a 250° oven until warm, about 15 to 20 minutes. When warm, the crêpes will be pliable and will separate easily.

Makes 16 to 24 six-inch crêpes

1 cup plus 1 tablespoon (150 g) all-purpose flour
3 eggs
1½ cups milk
¼ teaspoon salt
⅛ teaspoon freshly ground pepper
3 tablespoons melted butter or vegetable oil

1. In a bowl, stir the flour, eggs, ½ cup of the milk, the salt, and pepper with a whisk until you have a smooth batter. Add the remaining 1 cup milk and stir well. If time permits, allow the batter to rest 30 minutes. (As the batter rests, the granules of flour absorb the milk and swell, creating a smoother batter and a slightly stronger crêpe than if used right away.)

2. Whisk in the melted butter just before using.

3. Heat a 6-inch crêpe pan, either well seasoned or with a nonstick surface, over medium-high heat. The pan is ready when a drop of water dances on the hot surface of the pan. Hold the pan in one hand, tilting it slightly. Using a small ladle or coffee measurer, pour about 2 tablespoons of batter into the pan where the sides and bottom meet. Now turn the pan in a circular motion to spread the batter evenly. The amount of batter used should just coat the bottom of the pan. Any excess should be poured back.

4. Cook the crêpe until the edge begins to brown. Turn the crêpe, carefully lifting it with a spatula, or flip it. To flip, first make sure that the crêpe is sliding in the pan by shaking it vigorously if necessary. Flip with a forward and upward motion of your hand, keeping your eye on the crêpe. Although your first few crêpes may land on the floor, you will soon be catching them as they turn over. Cook the second side for only 10 to 15 seconds and slide the crêpe onto a plate. If overcooked, crêpes become dry and brittle.

The batter can also be made in a blender. Place all ingredients in the container of the blender and turn the blender on and then off again. Scrape down the flour that has stuck to the sides of the blender and blend again until smooth.

5. Repeat until all the crêpes are made, stacking them one on top of the other and allowing them to cool. The top surface of the crêpe should be medium brown in color, and the underneath pale yellow. If after making two crêpes you find the color either too dark or too light, adjust your heat accordingly. At the same point, if you find the crêpe is too thick, add a little more milk to thin the batter.

Crêpes au Jambon Sauce Mornay
Ham and Mushroom Crêpes with Cheese Sauce

I find it difficult to actually give recipes for stuffed crêpes, because to me they are perfectly designed for using leftovers and are an inspiration of the moment, not something for which you should go shopping. They are easy to make and elegant to serve and can be made when you're in the mood to use the leftover lamb, turkey, or ham in your refrigerator and then reheated and served later. They can be eaten on the spot, of course, but you can also stuff, sauce, and store them for up to 2 days in the refrigerator or a month well wrapped and frozen.

This is one of my favorite crêpe recipes. It can be made totally in advance and reheated just before serving. Using a processor to chop all the ingredients makes this very easy.

Serves 8

16 Crêpes Salées (page 70)
Butter for serving dish

Crêpes Farcies
(Stuffed Crêpes)

A *crêpe farcie* (stuffed crêpe) can be a wonderfully elegant creation, with the crêpe batter, filling, and sauce all designed to go with one another and seasoned accordingly. Or they can dress up leftovers for a simple family meal. The possible combinations of ingredients for stuffing crêpes is limited only by your imagination, but there are some guidelines for a stuffing mixture that to me has the proper consistency and will hold together, and there are some combinations of stuffings and sauces that are also typically French.

Basic Stuffing Formula: For each 6-inch crêpe, use 3 tablespoons of diced or chopped cooked ingredients (such as meat, fish, shellfish, poultry, vegetables, cheese, or combinations) bound together with 1 tablespoon or so of the sauce you will be using to cover the crêpes.

Suggested Combinations:
• Diced chicken and mushrooms with a *velouté* flavored with tarragon.
• Shrimp, crab, lobster, or scallops with a curry-flavored béchamel.

• Fill with the four-cheese mixture from Ravioli aux Quatre Fromages (page 96) and serve with a tomato sauce sprinkled with grated Parmesan.

Crêpes Soufflés
(Soufflé-Filled Crêpes)

You can also stuff a crêpe with soufflé batter and then bake it to cook and puff the soufflé. Use any of the first-course soufflés in the book, and follow the instructions for the dessert version of this soufflé-filled crêpe in "Dessert Crêpe Variations," page 321.

¼ pound ham (boiled, baked, or smoked), finely chopped
5 sprigs parsley, chopped
Duxelles (page 212)
Sauce Mornay (page 358)
1 or 2 tablespoons milk
1 ounce Swiss-style cheese, such as Gruyère or Emmenthaler, grated (about ⅓ cup)

1. Preheat the broiler.
2. Place a stack of crêpes, light side facing up, on a plate. Butter 8 individual oval gratin dishes or 1 large baking dish.
3. Stir the chopped ham and parsley into the *duxelles*. In a saucepan, bring the *sauce mornay* to a simmer. Add enough sauce to the ham and parsley to bind it, about ¼ cup. Taste and adjust the seasoning if necessary.
4. Place about 3 tablespoons of filling down the center of the first crêpe. Lift up one edge of the crêpe to cover the filling. Do the same with the other edge, totally enclosing the filling. Place your palms over the crêpe, and with your fingertips facing each other, roll the crêpe onto your hands and transfer it to the baking dish. The fold of the crêpe should be on the bottom. Repeat with the remaining crêpes. If you are using the individual gratin dishes, place 2 crêpes in each.
5. Reheat the remaining sauce. Thin with the milk and bring to a boil, whisking well. Spoon the sauce over the crêpes to completely cover. Sprinkle the grated cheese over all the crêpes. *(The crêpes can be prepared in advance up to this point. Cover and refrigerate for up to 1 day or wrap tightly and freeze for up to 1 week. Return to room temperature before using.)*
6. Place the crêpes under the broiler for about 5 minutes, or until the sauce browns lightly. Warn your guests that the dishes are *très chaud* (very hot). (If the crêpes have been made ahead and refrigerated or frozen, reheat in the upper third of a 475° oven until the sauce is bubbling and the surface has browned lightly, 10 to 15 minutes. This will take a few extra minutes if the crêpes have been frozen.)

Quiches

Originally a quiche was a rich cheese custard tart from Alsace and Lorraine. Sometimes it would be made with the addition of ham or bacon. To this day in France, if you order quiche, you will probably be served a classic quiche Lorraine.

However, the spirit of nouvelle cuisine and the generally eclectic approach Americans have toward cooking has made this simple classic a blueprint for a multitude of added ingredients. Perhaps the most surprising and delicious quiche I've tasted in this country was made with jalapeño peppers and Monterey Jack cheese. Another of my favorites is one made with crab and a curry-flavored custard in a puff pastry shell (see Quiche au Crabe à l'Orientale, page 78).

The classic custard used for a quiche combines eggs and heavy cream to make a very rich filling. I prefer a lighter custard, using milk instead of cream and fewer eggs to bind it. By using a shallow tart pan with a removable bottom instead of a deep quiche mold or pie dish, the resulting crust will not be soggy and the thinner portions more suitable for a first course.

To come up with your own combinations of ingredients for a quiche, use enough diced ingredients to cover the bottom of the tart shell (about 2 cups).

HOW TO LINE A TART PAN

1. Lightly butter your tart pan. You need only a very small amount of butter for this purpose. The butter is just to hold the pastry in the pan.

2. Dust the pastry and work surface lightly. Roll out the pastry (keeping it round), lifting and rotating it one quarter turn after each roll. Dust between each roll. Continue rolling in this fashion until the pastry is about ¼ inch thick.

3. Roll the pastry onto the rolling pin, turn it

Tarte à l'Oignon
Onion Tart

This simple onion tart, a member of the quiche family, reminds me of many wonderful meals I have had at inexpensive restaurants in rural France.

In the traditional recipe, the onions are cooked slowly until soft and then mixed with a thick béchamel sauce into which several eggs have been beaten. The finished tart makes a hearty first course.

My recipe is made with the light custard mixture I use for most of my quiches, to make it less filling and easier to fit into a contemporary dinner menu.

Serves 6 to 8

Pâte Brisée (tart pastry, page 241)
1 tablespoon butter
3 onions, halved and thinly sliced
2 eggs plus 1 egg yolk
1½ cups milk
¼ teaspoon salt
⅛ teaspoon freshly ground pepper
2 pinches freshly ground nutmeg

1. Preheat the oven to 475°.

2. Line a 9½- or 10-inch tart pan with removable bottom with the pastry (see "How to Line a Tart Pan," page 75).

3. Line the pastry with aluminum foil and weight with 1 pound dried beans or rice. Bake on the middle rack of the oven for 20 minutes, until the edges of the pastry begin to color. Remove the foil and beans from the pan.

4. Meanwhile, in a large, heavy-bottomed saucepan, heat the butter over medium heat. Add the onions and cover with a tight fitting lid. Gently steam the onions in their

own moisture until soft, uncovering to stir occasionally, about 20 minutes. Lower the heat, if necessary, to keep the onions from browning.

5. In a bowl, beat the eggs and yolk lightly. Blend in the milk, salt, pepper, and nutmeg.

6. Spread the cooked onions evenly over the bottom of the tart shell. Pour the custard into the pan to within ⅛ inch of the top of the crust; you may not use all of it (see Note, page 77). Holding the tart pan by the outer rim (so you do not dislodge the bottom), place the pan on the middle rack of the oven.

7. Bake about 20 minutes, or until the custard puffs.

8. Unmold as soon as possible (see "Unmolding a Tart or Quiche," page 246). Allow to cool for at least 10 minutes before serving. The tart is delicious served at any temperature. *(The onion tart can be made in advance. It will keep well in the refrigerator for several days. Reheat in a 350° oven for 10 to 15 minutes before serving.)*

Quiche Lorraine
Quiche with Ham

Quiche Lorraine is the best known of all quiches. Traditionally made in a deep crust, one slice can often serve as a light meal. I prefer it made in a shallower tart shell and served as a first course. Recipes for this classic quiche vary in a number of ways. Often, half an onion will be chopped, sautéed, and added to the filling, crumbled bacon used instead of ham, and the custard made with more eggs and heavy cream.

I prefer making my quiche with a light and delicate custard, making it easy to eat as a part of an entire meal.

Serves 6 to 8

90 degrees, and unroll it onto your lightly floured work surface. Continue this rolling, lifting, and turning process until the pastry is about ⅛ inch thick. Your pastry should be about 14 × 14 inches.

4. Roll the pastry onto the pin, and unroll it into the tart pan. The pastry will overlap the pan an inch or more.

5. Lifting the edge of the pastry with one hand, gently press the pastry into the sides of the pan with the back of your bent index finger.

6. Cut off the excess pastry by rolling the pin across the top of the pan. Remove the cut off pastry from the outer edge of the pan (see also "Making a Decorative Rim," page 242). To help prevent the pastry from bubbling up during baking, prick the bottom all over with the sharp point of a paring knife. Do not use a fork for this purpose, for the holes created may be too large and allow liquids to leak out. (At this point the pastry can be covered with plastic wrap and refrigerated or frozen along with any unused pastry.)

Note: If you make a border for the top of the tart, you will have a deeper shell, capable of holding most of the custard filling. If the pastry is simply cut off at the top of the pan, it will form a shallower tart shell, requiring less custard.

Pâte Brisée (tart pastry, page 241)
1 tablespoon Dijon mustard
2 eggs plus 1 egg yolk
1½ cups milk
¼ teaspoon salt
⅛ teaspoon freshly ground pepper
Pinch freshly grated nutmeg
¼ pound ham (boiled, baked, or smoked), diced, or
    8 strips of cooked bacon, crumbled
¼ pound Swiss-style cheese, such as Gruyère or
    Emmenthaler, diced, sliced, or grated (about 1⅓ cups)

1. Preheat the oven to 475°.
2. Line a 9½- or 10-inch tart pan with removable bottom with the pastry (see "How to Line a Tart Pan," page 75).
3. Line the pastry with aluminum foil and weight with 1 pound dried beans or rice. Bake on the middle rack of the oven for 20 minutes, until the edges of the pastry begin to color. Remove the foil and beans from the pan and spread the mustard over the bottom of the pastry. Lower the oven temperature to 425°.
4. In a bowl, beat the eggs and yolk lightly. Blend in the milk, salt, pepper, and nutmeg.
5. Spread the ham and cheese evenly over the bottom of the tart shell. Pour the custard into the tart shell to within ⅛ inch of the top of the crust; you may not use all of it (see Note). Holding the tart pan by the outer rim (so as not to dislodge the bottom), place the pan on the middle rack of the oven.
6. Bake 25 to 30 minutes, or until the custard puffs.
7. Unmold as soon as possible (see "Unmolding a Tart or Quiche," page 246). Allow to cool for at least 10 minutes before serving. The quiche is delicious served at any temperature. *(The quiche can be made in advance. It will keep well in the refrigerator for several days. Reheat in a 350° oven for 10 to 15 minutes before serving.)*

Quiche au Crabe à l'Orientale
Curried Crab Quiche

While planning a series of classes on the French island of Martinique in the Caribbean, I was inspired to take the classic quiche of the island's motherland and combine it with the wonderful local seafood. Although I originally made this with *langouste* (rock lobster), which is plentiful in the Caribbean, I ultimately substituted crab, which is far more available elsewhere. Shrimp, scallops, lobster, or mussels can also be used with excellent results (see Note).

The custard for the quiche is delicately flavored with curry powder, Cognac, and Madeira and is made with milk instead of cream. The tart shell is made with puff pastry, which bakes quickly and doesn't need prebaking. Feel free, however, to use *pâte brisée*.

Serves 6 to 8

½ recipe Pâte Demi-Feuilletée (page 277), or 1 pound
    store-bought puff pastry, or Pâte Brisée (page 241)
2 eggs plus 1 egg yolk
1½ cups milk
2 tablespoons Madeira
2 tablespoons Cognac
½ teaspoon curry powder
¼ teaspoon salt
⅛ teaspoon freshly ground pepper
¾ pound crabmeat, fresh or frozen, picked over to remove
    any shell or cartilage

  1. Preheat the oven to 475°.
  2. Roll out the pastry about 1/16 inch thick. Line a 9½- or 10-inch tart pan with removable bottom with the pastry and prick the pastry well all over with the point of a sharp

Serving Suggestion: If you serve the quiche as a first course, you might follow it with grilled lamb chops and vegetables, or a sautéed chicken or veal dish. Since such a meal starts with pastry, fruit or sorbet makes a good dessert.

Note: If you do substitute another kind of shellfish for the crab, be sure to cook it first. Crabmeat is already cooked when purchased.) Also, be sure to cut the seafood into bite-size pieces.

knife. Freeze the lined tart pan until you are ready to bake your quiche. (If you are using *pâte brisée*, line the tart pan as per "How to Line a Tart Pan," page 75, and blind-bake the shell as in step 3 of Quiche Lorraine, page 77.)

3. In a bowl, combine the eggs, egg yolk, milk, Madeira, Cognac, curry powder, salt, and pepper and mix well with a whisk without vigorously beating.

4. Cover the bottom of the tart shell with the crab meat and fill three-quarters full with the custard mixture (there may be some custard left over; see Note, page 77).

5. Holding the tart pan by the outer rim (so as not to dislodge the bottom), place it on the bottom rack of the oven. After 5 minutes, reduce the temperature to 425° and bake an additional 25 to 30 minutes, or until the pastry is golden brown and the custard begins to puff and brown lightly.

6. Unmold as soon as possible (see "Unmolding a Tart or Quiche," page 246). Allow to cool for at least 10 minutes before serving. The quiche is delicious served at any temperature. *(The quiche can be made up to a day in advance. Keep well refrigerated. Reheat in a 350° oven for 10 to 15 minutes before serving.)*

Cream-Puff Pastry

Most people know *pâte à choux* or cream-puff pastry in its dessert form—such as cream puffs or éclairs—but the dough is also used for first courses.

First-course cream-puff pastries can be filled with numerous savory mixtures. For a hot presentation, the fillings can be similar to those used in the puff-pastry cases (see Bouchées de Fruits de Mer, page 86). Or served cold, the pastry can be filled with salads.

The recipes that follow are for two uses of cream-puff pastry that are a little more unusual. For Gnocchi à la Parisienne (page 80), the pastry is poached in small dumpling form and served with a sauce. For the Gougère Soufflé (page 82), a cheese-flavored cream-puff pastry is baked in the form of a ring and then filled with a cheese soufflé.

Gnocchi à la Parisienne
Parisian-Style Cream-Puff Dumplings

Gnocchi are Italian dumplings made from potatoes. If you've ever had them, you probably remembered them long after the meal was over as they tend to be heavy and often, in the hands of an inexperienced cook, leaden.

Although these Parisian-style dumplings are called gnocchi and have the same shape, the similarity to the Italian dish ends there. French gnocchi are made from cream-puff pastry piped from a pastry bag into simmering water and poached. The resulting dumplings are light and delicately flavored.

FORMING *GNOCCHI*

Traditionally, these dumplings are served with a Mornay sauce, which I find much too heavy. Instead I serve them with a sauce of cream and fresh tomatoes, which makes this a much lighter fresher dish.

Serves 4 to 6

2 ounces Swiss-style cheese, such as Gruyère or
    Emmenthaler, grated (about ⅔ cup)
Double recipe Pâte à Choux Salée (page 269)

Sauce Crème à la Tomate Fraîche
(Cream Sauce with Fresh Tomato)
1 cup heavy cream
⅛ teaspoon salt
⅛ teaspoon freshly ground pepper
2 tomatoes, peeled, seeded, chopped, and well drained
1 ounce Parmesan cheese, grated (about ¼ cup)
2 tablespoons chopped fresh chives or 1 tablespoon
    chopped fresh basil, tarragon, or parsley

1. Stir the grated Gruyère cheese into the *pâte à choux*. Fill a pastry bag fitted with a ½-inch (#6) plain tube with the mixture*.

2. Fill a large Dutch oven or flameproof casserole three-quarters full of water and bring to a simmer. Resting the tube on the edge of the pan, gently squeeze the pastry to approximately 1 inch in length and cut off the gnocchi with the point of a knife. (If the pastry clings to your knife, dip the knife into the hot water.)

3. As the gnocchi simmer, they will rise to the surface of the water and become springy to the touch when fully cooked, approximately 10 minutes.

4. Drain the gnocchi on paper towels. *(The gnocchi can be made 1 day in advance. Cover and refrigerate until you are ready to serve them.)*

5. **Make the *Sauce Crème à la Tomate Fraîche*:** In a large saucepan, bring the cream to a boil and season with the salt and pepper. Add the gnocchi to the cream to reheat.

6. When the cream has thickened slightly, gently stir

in the tomatoes and half the cheese. Taste and adjust the seasoning if necessary.

7. Pour into a warm serving dish; sprinkle with the chopped herbs and serve immediately. Pass the remaining Parmesan cheese separately.

* The gnocchi can also be formed into small spoon-shaped dumplings; see "Spoon-Molding Dumplings."

Variations

Gnocchi Verts *(Green Gnocchi):* I often make green gnocchi by coloring the dough with a dried purée of watercress or spinach as I do when making green noodles (see Pâtes Fraîches Vertes, page 92). Try coloring half the recipe green and serving a combination of green and white Gnocchis à la Parisienne.

Gnocchi aux Herbes *(Gnocchi with Herbs):* In step 1, stir 2 tablespoons minced fresh herbs, such as chives or tarragon, into the dough.

Gougère Soufflée
Cheese Soufflé in a Cream-Puff Ring

A *gougère* is simply baked cream-puff pastry to which Gruyère (Swiss) cheese has been added. It is a traditional dish from the Burgundy region of France. The pastry, with chunks of cheese stirred in, is spooned out onto a pastry sheet in a ring or baked as small cream puffs and served with cocktails.

I have taken the somewhat rustic *gougère* and transformed it into an elegant first course. Based on a cream-puff pastry dessert called Paris-Brest (page 275), the

SPOON-MOLDING DUMPLINGS

The spoon-molding method of making gnocchi can also be used with the Mousseline de Poisson (page 56) to make quenelles.

1. Dip two spoons into hot water and scoop the pastry with one spoon.

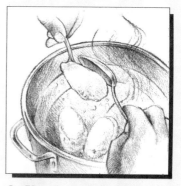

2. Use the second spoon to scoop and mold the pastry as it drops into simmering water.

gougère is baked in its traditional ring form, but filled with an airy cheese soufflé and placed in a hot oven just before serving to warm the soufflé.

Serves 6 to 8

Butter and all-purpose flour for baking sheet (optional)
2 ounces Gruyère, or other Swiss-style cheese, grated
    (about ⅔ cup)
Pâte à Choux Salée (page 269)
1 egg, beaten
Soufflé au Fromage (page 53)

1. Preheat the oven to 475°. Use a nonstick baking sheet, or butter and flour a baking sheet or line it with nonstick parchment paper.

2. Stir three-fourths of the grated cheese into the *pâte à choux*. Fill a pastry bag fitted with an ¹¹⁄₁₆-inch (#9) plain tube with the mixture. Squeeze a ring of pastry about 7 inches in diameter and 1 inch wide onto the baking sheet. (Use a pot lid to draw the outline of the circle.) You can also use a spoon to make the ring, although it will have a rougher look. Brush the ring lightly with the beaten egg and sprinkle with the remaining cheese.

3. Place in the oven for 5 minutes. Lower the temperature to 400° and bake another 25 to 30 minutes, or until light brown all over.

4. While the pastry is still warm, cut off the top one-third with a serrated knife and reserve. Allow both portions of the pastry to cool on a pastry rack. *(The pastry shell can be made 1 day in advance and stored in a plastic bag, unrefrigerated.)*

5. When you are ready to serve, preheat the oven to 475°. Place the bottom of the pastry ring on a baking sheet and fill with the cheese soufflé so that it is rounded on top. Gently replace the top of the ring and bake on the lowest rack of the oven for 3 to 4 minutes, or until the soufflé just begins to rise.

6. Using two metal spatulas, gently transfer the filled pastry ring to a serving platter lined with a doily. Use a serrated knife to cut into individual portions and serve warm.

Puff Pastry

The secret to puff pastry's wonderful flakiness and glorious flavor is in the butter. Because it is so rich, I find that I reserve it for special occasions and only make it once or twice a year.

Although making puff pastry is certainly not quick and easy, using what's called rough puff pastry instead of the classic puff pastry, as I do, greatly simplifies the procedure, shortening it by about 2½ hours. I would suggest to anyone approaching puff pastry for the first time that you try the following recipes with store-bought puff pastry first, to get a feel for the dough and its rich and buttery results. Then I recommend that you try it with homemade rough puff pastry (Pâte Demi-Feuilletée, page 277). I think you will be surprised not only by the difference in taste, but also by the relative ease with which you can make a truly impressive pastry.

_____

Feuilletés d'Anchois
Puff Pastry with Anchovy Butter

T his delicious puff-pastry hors d'oeuvre is excellent with cocktails. Those who do not like the taste of anchovies will find the warm strips of flaky pastry filled with the delicately flavored anchovy butter a pleasant surprise.

As with most puff-pastry items, the pastry can be formed on the pastry sheets and frozen, ready to bake when needed. The pastry can be baked several hours in advance and reheated shortly before serving. The anchovy butter can also be made in advance.

Serves 10 to 12

Butter for baking sheet
½ recipe Pâte Demi-Feuilletée (page 277) or 1 pound
    store-bought puff pastry
1 egg, beaten

Beurre d'Anchois
(Anchovy-Flavored Butter)
1 stick plus 2 tablespoons butter, softened to room
    temperature
10 anchovy fillets, finely chopped
Juice of ½ lemon
1 teaspoon Dijon mustard
⅛ teaspoon freshly ground pepper

1. Preheat the oven to 400°. Lightly butter a 17- × 14-inch baking sheet.

2. Roll the pastry into a rectangle large enough to cover the baking sheet and ⅛ inch or less thick. Sprinkle the baking sheets with water. Lift the pastry onto a rolling pin and unroll it onto the baking sheet, pressing down gently.

Trim away excess pastry. Brush the pastry with the beaten egg and place in the refrigerator for 15 minutes.

3. Cut the chilled pastry into strips 3½ inches long and 1 inch wide. (There should be a total of 64 strips.) *(The pastry can be made ahead up to this point. Refrigerate or freeze. The strips can be baked without defrosting, although the cooking time will be longer by about 1 minute.)*

4. Bake the pastry strips in the lower third of the oven for 20 to 25 minutes, or until the pastry has risen and browned evenly. Transfer to a rack to cool. While still warm, split the strips in half horizontally. *(The strips can be baked in advance and reheated in a 350° oven for 3 minutes before serving.)*

5. **Make the Beurre d'Anchois:** Cream the butter with a whisk. Add the minced anchovy fillets, lemon juice, mustard, and pepper and blend well.

6. Spread the bottoms of the pastry strips evenly with the anchovy butter, replace the tops, and serve lukewarm.

Variation

Feuilletés au Fromage *(Puff Pastry with Gruyère):* Omit the Beurre d'Anchois. In step 3, after brushing with the egg, sprinkle the top of the pastry with an even layer of grated Gruyère cheese (about ½ cup). Cut into strips, bake as directed, and serve warm.

Bouchées de Fruits de Mer
Shrimp and Scallops in Puff-Pastry Shells

*B*ouchées are puff-pastry shells that can be filled with seafood, chicken, or sweetbreads along with a sauce and served as a first or main course. The shells

To save time, you can make the *bouchées* in advance, up to the point of baking. Cover them with plastic wrap and refrigerate for a day or freeze them for up to a month (bake them without thawing). Or, you can bake them ahead of time and reheat them (3 minutes in a 350° oven) and then fill them just before serving. (In France, every pastry shop sells fully baked shells that only need reheating.) Of course to save even more time, you can use the ready-to-bake frozen pastry shells available in supermarkets here.

can also be filled with fruit and served as dessert: For example, use the *bouchées* in place of the square-cut puff-pastry case in Feuilleté aux Fraises (page 279).

Seafood tossed in a rich white wine sauce and served in warm, flaky puff-pastry shells makes a delicious and elegant first course, especially if served with Champagne. Once the *bouchées* are made, this dish is also quick and relatively easy to make.

If you are making your own pastry shells, you will need two round pastry cutters: one 3½ or 4 inches in diameter, fluted if possible; the other 2 to 2½ inches in diameter and plain. The smaller cutter can also be used to make *petites bouchées* (small pastry shells), which can be filled and used for hors d'oeuvres.

Although I heartily recommend making this as a first course, with puff-pastry shells, I often serve the seafood and sauce with rice as a main course to serve four.

Serves 8

Butter for baking sheet and skillet
½ recipe Pâte Demi-Feuilletée (page 277), or 1 pound
*   store-bought puff pastry, or 8 puff-pastry shells*
1 egg, beaten
3 medium shallots, finely chopped
½ pound mushrooms, sliced
1 pound sea scallops, rinsed, tendons removed
1 pound medium shrimp, shelled and deveined
About 1 cup dry white wine

Sauce Vin Blanc
(White Wine Sauce)
3 egg yolks
1 stick (4 ounces) butter, softened to room temperature
¼ teaspoon salt
⅛ teaspoon freshly ground pepper

1. Preheat the oven to 400°. Lightly butter a large baking sheet.

2. Roll out the pastry into a large sheet approximately ⅛ inch thick. Using a 3½- to 4-inch round or fluted cutter, cut out 16 rounds. Using a plain 2- to 2½-inch cutter, cut out the centers of eight of the rounds, creating rings of pastry. (Use the centers for another purpose.)

3. Sprinkle the baking sheet with water. Place the solid rounds on the baking sheet, pressing down lightly. Brush the tops lightly with the beaten egg. Place a pastry ring on the top of each round to form a border. Press the two pieces of pastry together gently. Brush the surface lightly with the beaten egg. Prick the center several times with the point of a knife. *(The* bouchées *can be made ahead up to this point. Refrigerate or freeze them. They can be baked without defrosting, although the baking time will be longer by about 1 minute.)*

4. Place the pastry in the middle of the oven and bake for 20 to 25 minutes, or until the pastry has risen and colored evenly to a golden brown. Allow to cool on a pastry rack and cut out the center, leaving a well to be filled. *(These pastry shells can be baked in advance and reheated in a 350° oven for 3 minutes before serving.)*

5. Lightly butter a 12-inch skillet and sprinkle with the chopped shallots. Add the mushrooms, scallops, and shrimp to the pan in that order. Pour in enough white wine to come halfway up the seafood. Cut a piece of wax paper to fit over the surface of the seafood, and cover the pan with a lid.

6. Place the pan over low heat and bring slowly to a simmer, 10 to 15 minutes. When the seafood begins to simmer, it should be done. Check to make sure the seafood has turned opaque. If not, simmer an additional minute, but do not overcook.

7. Transfer the seafood and mushrooms to a bowl and keep warm. Reduce the liquid over high heat until about ½ cup remains, and pour it into a small saucepan.

8. **Make the Sauce Vin Blanc:** To the reduced poaching liquid in the saucepan add the egg yolks, and whisk over medium-high heat until thick and fluffy, 2 to 3 minutes. Reduce the heat to low and immediately beat in

MAKING *BOUCHEES*

Langues de Boeuf
(Puff-Pastry Cookies)

You will have small, round scraps left over from cutting out the *bouchées*. You can either save them for another purpose, or use them to make a cookie called a *langue de boeuf* (ox tongue). Roll the rounds out in sugar until they are very thin and about 4 inches long (sort of tongue shaped). Bake on a lightly buttered sheet in a 475° oven until puffed and brown, about 4 minutes.

the butter, 1 tablespoon at a time, adding the last tablespoon of butter off the heat. Season with the salt and pepper.

9. Pour off and discard any liquid the seafood may have accumulated. Toss the seafood with the sauce and fill the warm pastry shells, allowing some of the seafood and sauce to overflow onto the plates.

Variation

Bouchées à la Normande *(Shrimp, Mussels, and Oysters in Puff-Pastry Shells):* Omit the scallops. Steam 16 scrubbed oysters and 16 scrubbed and debearded mussels in the cup of dry white wine over high heat until the shells open, about 5 minutes. Strain the cooking liquid and use in step 5 to poach the mushrooms and shrimp. Remove the cooked mussels and oysters from their shells (discarding any that have not opened) and toss with the white wine sauce, shrimp, and mushrooms in step 9.

FRENCH ROLLING PINS

A French rolling pin, made from a single piece of wood, is about 19 to 20 inches long and 1½ to 2 inches in diameter. A French pin has greater surface area and is especially helpful when rolling large pieces of dough (as for pasta) or when transferring dough from work surface to pastry sheet or tart pan. A French pin is rolled with an open hand. As the fingertips and palm run over the top of the pin, a downward pressure is exerted to flatten the dough.

Pasta

Making pasta and bread is very much alike. Each uses flour and water to make an inexpensive product that is enjoyed by all. In developing a recipe to teach, I wanted to create one that would be easy to roll out by hand (since many people do not have pasta machines) and delicious enough for my students to want to make on special occasions.

A good noodle exhibits a slightly chewy or springy texture when eaten. The elastic texture is developed by kneading and rolling the dough. This same elasticity makes noodles difficult to roll out. Over the years, chefs have added butter, cream, oil, or extra egg yolks to help relax the dough, making it easier to roll.

I add about three times as much oil as others do, making the dough relatively easy to roll and stretch. You can vary the type of oil used to change the flavor of the dough.

Pâtes Fraîches
Fresh Pasta

The difficult part of making pasta for me is the kneading process. Although there are those who will insist on kneading by hand and rolling by machine, I find the opposite easier. What normally takes many minutes of strenuous hand labor requires only seconds to accomplish with a food processor.

In addition to the sauces on these pages, I also like to serve homemade noodles with butter, Sauce Crème à la Tomate Fraîche (page 81), or Sauce Tomate (page 372).

Makes about 1 pound / Serves 4 or 6

2 cups (300 g) all-purpose
3 eggs
3 tablespoons vegetable oil
1 tablespoon water
1½ teaspoons salt

If you have a pasta rolling machine, you may think it easier to use; however, the majority of my students who have tried the recipe both by hand and by machine report that the machine method took longer and was more involved.

1. Place the ingredients in a food processor and process until a smooth, soft dough forms, about 1 minute. If the dough is too sticky, add more flour, 1 teaspoon at a time. If the dough is too firm, add more water, ½ teaspoon at a time.

2. Remove the dough from the machine and divide in half. Shape each half into a rough square or rectangle. Wrap in plastic wrap and refrigerate for 30 minutes or more. *(If the dough is not to be used within 24 hours, freeze it and bring back to room temperature before proceeding.)*

3. Dust the work surface and the dough lightly with flour and roll one of the squares of dough into a sheet as thin as possible, between ¹⁄₁₆ and ¹⁄₃₂ of an inch and about 16 × 18 inches, dusting and turning the dough so it does not stick to the work surface. If the dough becomes too elastic to flatten or roll out, allow it to rest, covered with plastic wrap to prevent drying, for 3 to 5 minutes before continuing. (If you have the space, roll out both pieces of dough at the same time, alternating from one to the other as they build up tension.)

4. **Cut into noodles:** Lightly dust the surface of the dough to prevent sticking and fold the fully rolled out dough in half, then in half again, always folding in the same direction. Using a large chef's knife, cut crosswise to form noodles of a desired width (for extremely thin, delicate noodles, see "Stretching Noodles," page 94). The noodles can be cooked at this point if desired. *(You can make the noodles ahead to this point. Allow the noodles to dry on a flat surface or draped over a drying rack for 15 to 30 minutes. They will still be flexible, but may begin to crack when folded. Place the noodles in plastic bags and freeze if not using within 24 hours. Frozen pasta does not have to be thawed before cooking.)*

5. To cook the noodles, drop them into a large amount of boiling water and cook until tender yet chewy, 3 to 5 minutes. The drier the noodles are, the longer they will take to cook.

6. To serve, drain the noodles and toss them with butter or one of your favorite sauces.

Pâtes Fraîches Vertes
Fresh Green Pasta

I use watercress to make green pasta because it produces a lovely color and a fresh taste, but you can use spinach or basil, or combinations such as watercress, tarragon, chives, and a touch of parsley and basil.

In addition to adding color and flavor, the purée makes the dough less elastic and easier to roll out.

Serve this with Sauce Tomate (page 372), or substitute it for the gnocchi in the recipe for Gnocchi à la Parisienne (page 80), or for the plain pasta in Pâtes Fraîches aux Petits Pois (page 93).

Makes about 1 pound / Serves 4 or 6

2 bunches watercress, stems removed
2 cups (300 g) all-purpose flour
3 eggs
3 tablespoons vegetable oil
2 teaspoons water
1½ teaspoons salt

1. Plunge the watercress into a saucepan of boiling water and blanch for about 45 seconds. Drain and refresh under cold running water. Place in a food processor and process until puréed, 1 to 2 minutes. Transfer the purée to a sieve lined with a double thickness of paper towel and set over a bowl. Gently press out as much moisture as possible; set aside the watercress liquid. Press the watercress purée dry between two thicknesses of paper towel, changing the towel frequently. The purée should be as dry as possible.

2. Place the purée, 2 teaspoons of the reserved watercress liquid, and the remaining ingredients in a food processor and process until a smooth, soft dough forms, about 1 minute. If the dough is too sticky, add more flour, 1 tea-

As with any pasta, if I'm not cooking it right away, I dry or partially dry the finished pasta before placing it in plastic bags. (If the pasta is not partially dried first, it may stick together.) It can be refrigerated for a few days, but I prefer freezing it. Like all fresh pasta, it can be frozen for several months. In certain areas of the country where humidity may be extremely high, stickiness may cause drying to be a problem. In such cases, dusting the noodles with cornmeal will prevent this.

spoon at a time. If the dough is too firm, add more water, ½ teaspoon at a time.

3. Proceed as for Pâtes Fraîches (page 90) from step 2 through step 4.

4. To cook the noodles, drop them into a large amount of boiling water and cook until tender yet chewy, 4 to 5 minutes. The drier the noodles are, the longer they will take to cook.

5. To serve, drain the noodles and toss them in butter or one of your favorite sauces.

Pâtes Fraîches aux Petits Pois
Noodles with Cream, Peas, and Parmesan

Although spectacular when made with fresh noodles and fresh, sweet peas, this recipe is so good that I often make it with packaged pasta and frozen baby peas. The peas can be taken from the freezer and heated in the cream while it thickens in step 2. (Increase your cooking time by 1 to 2 minutes.)

Pasta of all shapes and sizes can be cooked, according to the manufacturer's instructions, and mixed with the cream, peas, ham, and cheese.

Serves 4 or 6

Pâtes Fraîches (page 90) or 1 pound packaged pasta
1 cup heavy cream
⅛ teaspoon salt
⅛ teaspoon freshly ground pepper
1 cup fresh or frozen baby peas, cooked
1 ¼-inch-thick slice ham (boiled, baked, or smoked), diced
2 ounces Parmesan cheese, grated (about ½ cup)

1. If making your own pasta, follow the Pâtes Fraîches recipe (page 90) through step 3. In step 4, cut the noodles into ¼-inch widths. Continue with the recipe through step 5.

2. While the noodles are cooking, in a small saucepan bring the cream to a boil over medium-high heat. Season with the salt and pepper and allow to boil gently until the cream thickens enough to coat a spoon, about 30 seconds. Gently stir in the peas, ham, and half the cheese. Heat for several seconds.

3. When the noodles have finished cooking, drain them in a colander and rinse under hot water. Transfer them to a warm serving bowl and pour the cream and hot pea sauce over.

4. Serve with the remaining cheese on the side.

Nouilles aux Morilles
Noodles with Morels

In France, although *nouilles* (egg pasta noodles) are traditionally served as a garnish or accompaniment rather than as a first course, the Italian use of pasta for a first course is gaining popularity in this country. Thus I have adapted a typical French pasta side dish and made it an elegant first course with the addition of morels. While both dark brown and white morels are available, I recommend using only the more robust-flavored brown ones for this recipe. Try preparing this recipe with dried Shiitake or dried chanterelle mushrooms as well. In France, this cream sauce with mushrooms is often served with sautéed chicken and veal. The noodles serve four as a main course or six as a first course.

Serves 4 or 6

STRETCHING NOODLES

Instead of rolling the dough paper thin before cutting it into noodles, I find it easier and more fun to stop rolling when the dough is about $1/16$ inch thick, and after cutting into noodles, to stretch them the rest of the way to increase their length and thinness.

It is extremely important to allow the noodles to rest, covered with plastic wrap, before stretching them. A 2-foot cut noodle that has not rested will snap or break before being stretched to 4 feet, but after resting for 1½ hours it can easily be stretched up to 8 feet.

Once stretched, finding a place to hang the noodles to dry can become a problem. Cut in half, they usually hang nicely over the backs of kitchen chairs, over a clothes drying rack, or simply on your countertop. I recall seeing, while driving through Naples years ago, women hanging their pasta up to dry on their outdoor clotheslines. For those who wish to try this method, be warned that I also recall seeing the neighbors' dogs nibbling on the ends.

FRESH MORELS

Pâtes Fraîches (page 90) or 1 pound packaged fettuccine
1 ounce dried morel mushrooms
1½ cups heavy cream
½ teaspoon salt
⅛ teaspoon freshly ground pepper
2 ounces Parmesan cheese, grated (about ½ cup)

1. If making your own pasta, follow the Pâtes Fraîches recipe (page 90) through step 3. In step 4, cut the noodles into ¼-inch widths. Continue with the recipe through step 4.

2. Meanwhile, in a small bowl of cold water, soak the dried mushrooms. Stir the mushrooms in the water as they soak, making sure that there is sufficient water in the bowl for them to float, and allow any dirt or sand to fall to the bottom of the bowl. As the mushrooms swell in size and soften, the water will become brown and it will acquire the strong flavor of the mushroom. This will take 10 to 15 minutes.

3. When the mushrooms are soft, gently squeeze them over the bowl and then place them in a small saucepan. When the dirt has fallen to the bottom of the bowl and the water in the bowl is clear, very carefully pour it into the saucepan with the mushrooms, and discard the dirt at the bottom.

4. Bring the mushrooms and liquid to a boil and gently boil until only 1 teaspoon of liquid remains, about 4 minutes. Add the cream, season with the salt and pepper, and set aside.

5. In a stockpot, bring 4 quarts of water to a boil. Add the noodles and boil until tender yet chewy, 3 to 5 minutes (about 5 minutes longer for packaged pasta). Stir the noodles several times to prevent them from sticking together.

6. While the noodles are cooking, bring the cream and mushrooms to a boil. When the noodles have finished cooking, drain them in a colander and rinse under hot water. Transfer them to a warm serving bowl and cover with the sauce. Toss with half of the grated Parmesan cheese.

7. Serve the noodles with the remaining cheese and additional pepper on the side.

Ravioli aux Quatre Fromages
Ravioli with Four Cheeses

Ravioli, although Italian in origin, have been used quite imaginatively by French chefs for hundreds of years. If you enjoy making pasta, you will find making ravioli a very creative experience. You can make miniature ravioli to serve in soups and ragoûts, or extra-large ones that can serve as individual portions for a first course. The ravioli for this recipe will serve six as a main course and 12 as a first course.

If you are not up to making your own pasta, try making ravioli with wonton skins, which can be found in most supermarkets. Two wonton skins will make four standard-size ravioli or one giant one.

The options for making ravioli ahead of time are many. You can freeze the ravioli before cooking them and cook them later without defrosting (they'll take a little longer to cook). Or you can cook the ravioli, refrigerate them, and reheat in the sauce later. Or you can combine the cooked ravioli and sauce before refrigerating or freezing and then reheat the whole dish later.

Serves 6 or 12

Pâtes Fraîches (page 90)
2 ounces Swiss-style cheese, such as Gruyère or
    Emmenthaler
1 ounce Parmesan cheese
½ pound cream cheese
¼ pound ricotta cheese
12 fresh basil leaves
1 egg, beaten with a pinch of salt
Sauce Tomate (page 372)

RAVIOLI GUIDELINES

The types of ravioli fillings are endless, and I leave them to your imagination, with just a few guidelines. Fillings used should not require additional cooking. Fillings should be relatively dry. If necessary, use bread crumbs to absorb excess liquid. Try fillings of cooked meat, poultry, seafood, brains, sweetbreads, tongue, mushrooms, spinach, vegetable purées, cheese, or combinations thereof. If you *do* use cheese, just keep in mind that dry cheeses (such as Parmesan) and low-fat cheeses do not generally soften when boiled and the resulting filling will be dry or coarse.

Although traditional sauces are based on cheese, cream, or tomato, any sauce that complements your filling can be used.

1. Make the Pâtes Fraîches through step 3 of the recipe, rolling each rectangle of dough as thin as possible into a sheet approximately 16 × 19 inches, dusting and turning the dough so it does not stick to the work surface. If the dough becomes too elastic to roll, cover it with plastic wrap to prevent drying, and allow it to rest for 2 or 3 minutes before continuing. If you have the space, roll out both pieces of dough at the same time, alternating from one to the other as they build up tension. Cover the pasta with plastic wrap while you make the cheese filling.

2. In a food processor, finely chop the Swiss-style and Parmesan cheeses. Add the cream cheese, ricotta, and basil leaves and process well.

3. Brush a light coat of beaten egg on one of the sheets of pasta. With a pastry bag fitted with a ½-inch (#6) plain tube, or with a spoon, drop the cheese filling onto the sheets of pasta in ½-teaspoon mounds spaced about ¾ inch apart.

4. Roll up the second sheet of pasta onto your rolling pin and unroll to cover the filling. Press the dough together firmly around the filling to seal. Using a knife or ravioli cutting wheel, cut between the rows of filling to form little square ravioli. At this point, let the ravioli rest at least 15 to 20 minutes: If the egg sealant is not allowed to dry, the filling will escape during cooking. *(If the ravioli will not be used within a few hours, freeze them in layers separated by sheets of plastic wrap. Do not defrost before cooking.)*

5. To cook the ravioli, cook them in a large quantity of boiling water until tender, 8 to 10 minutes (1 minute or so longer for frozen). Drain in a colander or on paper towels. *(The ravioli can be cooked in advance, cooled, covered, and refrigerated until ready to use. For reheating information, see Note.)*

6. Serve with the tomato sauce.

If you are not interested in ravioli at all, make the cheese filling to spread on crackers or to fill cherry tomatoes to serve as an hors d'oeuvre.

Note: To reheat the ravioli, place them in an ovenproof serving dish and cover with the sauce. Place the dish in a 400° oven until the sauce bubbles, 10 to 15 minutes (slightly longer for frozen). You can also combine the ravioli and sauce in the serving dish and refrigerate or freeze.

The main course provides the focal point of a French meal and is the course around which the balance of the menu is planned. It can be as simple as a grilled steak or a roast duck, as hearty as a robust ragoût, or as elegant as a rack of lamb or a poached fish served with a rich sauce. Once chosen, it should be complemented by an appropriate first course and dessert.

The repertoire of French main courses is so large it could easily take up a book on its own. I have therefore omitted those recipes that require an excess amount of time and attention, as well as those which call for ingredients too hard to locate in this country, and for which no good substitutes exist. The recipes that follow are my timeless favorites.

Courses

Seafood

In France, fish dishes are the aristocrats of the culinary repertoire. Fish are accorded a respect and admiration that is born of several things. First, fish has always been expensive, making it a rarity and a delicacy. Second, because of the delicate taste of most fish, it has always been served with highly refined sauces. If you go to a restaurant that is known for its fish dishes in France, be assured the sauces will be well prepared.

In this country, on the other hand, fish has not enjoyed such esteem. While it has always been inexpensive (relative to France), good, fresh fish has been available to only a small percentage of the country. Many American cooks never see anything but pre-packaged fillets in their supermarkets.

Over the past few years, however, interest in eating fresh fish has grown tremendously. What may have initially started as a concern for healthful eating has turned into an appreciation of the

Fish does not freeze well. The texture of the muscle changes and there is considerable loss of flavor and moisture when it is defrosted. When frozen fish is my only choice, I choose thick over thin fish, for its texture will be better.

Unlike fish, shellfish such as shrimp and scallops do freeze well. Once defrosted, however, they deteriorate rapidly. Ask for freshly defrosted shrimp. They should have a pleasant smell and be firm, not soft, to the touch. If they are soft or old, they will be mealy when cooked. Scallops should be smooth and shiny, not dull or dry looking, and exhibit a sweet sea smell.

flavors and textures unique to seafood. With this increased interest has come greater availability, larger variety, better handling methods, fish farming—and higher prices.

When shopping for fish, there are some things to know in order to judge its freshness. Whole fish fresh from the sea have a smell of the ocean water. They have shiny, slippery skins, and a flesh that is firm to the touch. Their eyes are clear and their gills are crimson in color. Fish that is past its prime will have an unpleasant odor, dull, dry skin, and flesh that yields to the press of a finger, retaining its imprint. The eyes will be cloudy and the gills will be gray. Fresh fillets of fish will be firm to the touch and glistening in appearance. Fillets not worth purchasing will be soft, dull, and dry looking.

If you have bought fish and won't be home for several hours, ask the market to surround your package of fish in a bag of crushed ice. This is especially important in the summer.

With the expanding number of fish varieties now appearing in our markets, you shouldn't be limited by the few types of fish mentioned in this chapter. If the fish looks fresh, try it. Some of the following recipes are quick and easy, others are a little more complex. If you try them all, you will learn a great deal about cooking seafood.

Lotte à l'Américaine
Monkfish in a Spicy Tomato Sauce

America has just begun to appreciate the monkfish, or angler fish. Of course the French have known about it all along, and chances are, if you've traveled at all in France, you've encountered it on restaurant menus as *lotte*.

In this country, until recently, the monkfish was inexpensive and largely ignored, perhaps because of the way it has been marketed: for example, it has been called, among other names, "ugly fish," which indeed it is. It has a giant head with bulging eyes and looks almost prehistoric. Since the price of monkfish here has risen from about one dollar a pound to over six dollars a pound in only two years, I take this as an indication that, for many, this fish is becoming more beautiful.

In spite of its looks, monkfish is a delicious and extremely firm-fleshed fish (it is often called the poor man's lobster, although the resemblance is in its texture and not in its taste). It has tough and leathery skin with no scales and a large backbone, leaving the flesh free of any smaller bones. There is a strong membrane covering the flesh, which must be removed before cooking since it becomes rubbery and unpleasant (this membrane is often not removed by the fish market).

You will notice in this recipe that the fish cooks a long time. Any other fish would fall apart under such conditions, but monkfish becomes deliciously tender. The only substitute for monkfish would be cut-up lobster.

Serves 6

Serving Suggestion: Start with artichokes vinaigrette. Serve the fish with rice (Riz Pilaf, page 234). For dessert, strawberries with zabaglione (Fraises au Sabayon, page 323).

Wine: Chilled white or rosé.

In France, where fish are always sold with the heads on, I found it curious that *lotte* are always displayed headless. When I finally asked a fisherman why, he said it was bad luck to look into the eyes of a *lotte* and therefore their heads were cut off at sea.

There are a number of ways to prepare monkfish. You can grill it whole over a hot fire, then slice it and serve with Sauce Béarnaise (page 374). Or you can braise it with a little rosemary, white wine, and shallot, and make a simple cream sauce with the reduced cooking liquid.

3 tablespoons olive oil, extra-virgin if available
3 pounds monkfish fillet, membranes removed, cut into
    2-inch pieces
1 onion, chopped
3 shallots, chopped
5 garlic cloves, chopped
¼ cup Cognac
½ cup dry white wine
3 pounds tomatoes, peeled, seeded, and diced, or 6 pounds
    canned tomatoes, drained and diced
2 teaspoons tarragon
¼ teaspoon salt
⅛ teaspoon freshly ground pepper
2 to 4 pinches cayenne pepper, to taste*
1 tablespoon tomato paste
2 tablespoons butter
Chopped parsley, for garnish

1. In a 10- to 12-inch skillet, heat 2 tablespoons of the olive oil over high heat until it is very hot (smoking). Add the fish and quickly cook until the fish is firm, about 2 minutes. Remove and drain the fish, reserving the pan juices.

2. Reduce the heat, add the remaining 1 tablespoon olive oil and the onion, and sauté until softened but not browned, about 3 minutes. Add the shallots and garlic and cook, stirring, for 15 seconds. Return the fish to the pan, remove from the heat, add the Cognac, and flame. (See flaming instructions in Bananes Flambées au Rhum, page 322.)

3. Add the wine, reserved pan juices, tomatoes, tarragon, salt, pepper, and cayenne pepper. Boil gently, uncovered, until the fish is tender, 15 to 20 minutes.

4. With a slotted spoon, remove the fish to a warm serving dish. Add the tomato paste to the sauce and boil rapidly to thicken, about 5 minutes. Taste and adjust the seasoning, if necessary. Stir in the butter. Pour the sauce over the fish and sprinkle with parsley.

* If you want to make this sauce spicier, add more cayenne, but wait until the fish has cooked and adjust the seasoning at the end.

Filets de Saumon Grillés
Grilled Salmon Fillets

Most French recipes call for grilling salmon steaks (*darnes de saumon*), but I prefer to use fillets, and ideally the tail section*. A 6-ounce tail fillet is a perfect individual serving, easy to cook and easy to serve.

It was actually by accident that I came upon my technique of cooking the fish fillets. For years I tried to find a way to grill fillets on both sides without having them either stick to the grill or fall apart in the turning process. One day when in a hurry, I just threw them onto a hot, unoiled grill. Unable to turn them, I covered them with a lid. When cooked, I found that because the skin was firmly stuck to the grill, I was able to easily slide a metal spatula between the skin and the fish, and lift the fish to a waiting plate. In doing so, all I had left behind was a piece of (often strong tasting) skin. The end results were succulent and delicious, and I have grilled fish fillets this way ever since.

Serves 6

6 salmon fillets, unskinned (about 6 ounces each)
2 to 3 tablespoons soy sauce, or lemon or lime juice
    (optional)
1 stick (4 ounces) butter, melted
2 tablespoons chopped fresh chives, tarragon, or basil

1. Rinse the fillets under cold water and pat dry with paper towels. If not extremely fresh, or if desired, sprinkle them with soy sauce or lemon or lime juice. *(This can be done several hours in advance of cooking. The fish should be kept refrigerated until shortly before grilling.)*

GRILLING FISH

If you find yourself fortunate enough to be near a source of fresh fish, you will want to grill it often, for it is healthy, quick, and delicious.

Cooking a whole fish or steaks on a grill can be difficult. The flesh of most fish is delicate, and tends to stick. Coat the metal grates with a vegetable oil spray to help prevent major sticking.

For large whole fish that are hard to turn, use aluminum foil strips to form a sling. This makes it easier to support the fish when lifting it. Should you have one of the special hinged fish grills that encloses the fish and allows you to easily turn it, so much the better.

Boneless steaks, such as swordfish and tuna, which have firm flesh, are ideal for grilling. Have the fish cut into 1¼- to 1½-inch steaks, and remove all the skin and fat. Steaks like salmon and halibut that do have a bone are grilled and served with the skin on. Make sure these fish are very fresh. If they are not, skin and bone them before cooking and serve them as medallions.

Grill fish steaks as you would a grilled rib steak (Côte de Boeuf Grillée, page 161), but cook the swordfish until medium-well to well done. Cook tuna rare to medium. Serve with melted butter and chopped fresh herbs, or with a Sauce Beurre Blanc (page 376).

Fillets and sides of fish should be prepared as for Filets de Saumon Grillés (page 104), except for monkfish, which should be grilled as whole fillets, skinless and membrane-free, and then sliced after cooking.

2. Preheat your grill so it is very hot. If you do not have a lid, make one by loosely covering the grill with heavy-duty aluminum foil or use a large domed pot lid to cover the fish while it is cooking.

3. Combine the melted butter and the herbs.

4. Grill the fillets until the fish is fairly firm yet springy to the touch, 5 to 10 minutes. Moisture or juices from the fish will pool on the surface of the fish and become opaque in appearance.

5. Slide a metal spatula between the skin and the fish. Lift the fish onto a plate, leaving the skin on the grill to be scraped off later. Pour a little of the herb butter over the fish and serve immediately.

* If you are planning to serve salmon tails, make sure you order them in advance. There are only two tail fillets per fish, so it is very possible the market will not have enough for you. If your fish market is obliging, they will fillet a whole fish and sell you what you need. I try to get 5- to 6-ounce pieces cut so they are of even thickness.

Rouget à la Suzanne
Baked Red Snapper in a Mediterranean Tomato Sauce

This low-calorie version of a Mediterranean-style fish dish (named for my wife, Susan) is actually a combination of two classic snapper presentations. *Rouget à l'algéroise* is made with a tomato sauce containing fennel and saffron; and *rouget à la portugaise* uses a fresh tomato sauce made with shallots, garlic, and parsley. Both use considerably more olive oil than I have used here.

When snapper is not available, try another similar-size fish, such as bluefish or black sea bass.

Serves 6

½ tablespoon olive oil, extra-virgin if available
4 pounds tomatoes, peeled, seeded, and diced or 6 pounds
    canned tomatoes, drained and diced
3 shallots, finely chopped
2 garlic cloves, finely chopped
1 small bulb fennel, finely diced*
1 pinch saffron
½ teaspoon salt
¼ teaspoon freshly ground pepper
10 sprigs parsley, chopped, plus 8 whole sprigs, for garnish
1 whole red snapper (4 to 5 pounds)

1. Preheat the oven to 350°.

2. In a large skillet, heat the oil over high heat. Add
the tomatoes, shallots, garlic, and fennel and cook, stirring
occasionally, until the tomatoes soften but still have some
shape, about 5 minutes. The tomatoes' excess moisture
should have evaporated, but if not, strain and reserve the
tomatoes and return the excess liquid to the pan. Cook the
liquid over high heat until it is reduced to a syrup. Return
the tomatoes to the pan, and season with the saffron, salt,
and pepper. Stir in the chopped parsley. *(The sauce can be
made ahead of time. Let cool to room temperature, cover,
and refrigerate.)*

3. Place a layer of the sauce on a large, deep ovenproof
serving platter. Place the fish on the platter and cover all
but the head and tail with the remaining sauce. Bake 50 to
60 minutes, until a knife penetrates easily to the bone.

4. Decorate the platter with parsley sprigs and serve.

   * If fennel is not available, either leave it out or use
¼ teaspoon anise seed or fennel seed for a similar flavor.

Serving Suggestion: Start with
Quiche Lorraine (page 76).
Riz Pilaf (page 234), made
with a touch of saffron and
1 teaspoon of tarragon,
makes an excellent accom-
paniment for the fish.
Follow with a mixed green
salad made with an olive
oil and lemon juice vinaigrette. For dessert, serve
fruit sorbet and cookies.

Wine: Chilled rosé or red.

In French cooking, a *point*
is the amount of powdered
spice that can be lifted on
the tip (point) of a paring
knife and is basically equal
to a pinch. The technique
is used with strong spices,
such as cayenne, which
you might not want to get
on your fingers.

Filet de Saumon Poché Sauce Beurre Blanc
Poached Salmon Fillets with Butter Sauce

Serving Suggestion: Unless a vegetable is poached along with the fish, the fish is usually served only with rice or steamed potatoes. The delicate flavor of the fish and sauce go well with the relatively bland flavor of the starches, while a more assertive vegetable would upset the balance of flavors.

Wine: Muscadet, Pouilly-Fuissé or Chardonnay.

Poaching small fish or fish fillets is a quick technique used in French restaurants. Although classically such a dish would be made by poaching the fish in a court bouillon (light vegetable stock), I find the use of court bouillon advantageous only when poaching fish to be served cold (see Saumon Poché Sauce Verte, page 108). So I just poach fish fillets (salmon as here, or another thick fish such as sea bass or striped bass) in water, sometimes adding an acid such as vinegar, wine, or lemon juice if the fish is not extremely fresh.

The traditional sauce for poached fish is Sauce Hollandaise (page 373), but I prefer to serve it with the *sauce beurre blanc.* You should have everything you want to serve ready before starting to poach the fish since it cooks in just a few minutes.

Serves 6

3 pounds salmon fillet, skinned, cut into individual serving pieces, and rinsed well in cold water
⅓ cup distilled vinegar, juice of 1 lemon, or 1 cup dry white wine (optional*)
Sauce Beurre Blanc (page 376)

1. Place enough water in a large nonaluminum skillet or Dutch oven to cover the fillets by an inch or more and bring to a boil. If the fish is not extremely fresh, add the vinegar, lemon juice, or white wine.
2. Place the fish into the boiling water and adjust the heat so that the water barely simmers; do not let it boil.

Cooking time is approximately 10 minutes per inch of thickness of the fish. When done, the fish will be firm yet springy to the touch.

3. Remove the fish from the water using a skimmer or slotted spoon and drain on paper towels.

4. **To serve:** Place the fish on warm plates or a platter and cover with *sauce beurre blanc.*

* If the fish is not absolutely fresh, add one of these three acidic ingredients to rejuvenate the fish's flavor. I most often use vinegar.

Saumon Poché Sauce Verte
Cold Poached Salmon with
Green Mayonnaise

H ere is a classic summer buffet dish in France. Poaching a whole salmon is an elegant way to serve this majestic fish, provided you have a fish poacher the size of your salmon. The fish is cooked in a light vegetable stock (court bouillon) in which it is then allowed to partially cool, thus keeping the fish moist and flavorful.

**PRESENTATION OF
THE SALMON**

This is a wonderful dish for entertaining, since it is done well ahead of time and is as simple as it is impressive. For a slightly more decorative presentation than the one given here, you can coat the salmon with the green mayonnaise and use cucumber slices to create a scale pattern on top of the fish.

Serves 6 to 8

2 quarts water
2 carrots, sliced
1 onion, sliced

When poaching large pieces or whole fish, it is important to start with a cool or cold stock (with small fish or fillets you start with boiling stock). Fish does not need much heat to cook and is therefore poached at a simmer, with the heat slowly penetrating and evenly cooking the fish. If you place the fish in hot stock, or if you bring the cold stock to a simmer too rapidly, it will usually overcook the outside while undercooking the center of the fish.

1 shallot, sliced
Bouquet Garni (page 346)
½ cup white (distilled) vinegar
3- to 4-pound center cut of fresh salmon or 5-pound whole salmon
3 lemons, sliced
1 bunch parsley
Sauce Verte (page 381)

1. **Make the court bouillon:** In a 4-quart saucepan, combine the water, carrots, onion, shallot, bouquet garni, and vinegar and simmer for 20 minutes. Strain, discarding the solids, and let cool to room temperature.

2. Place the salmon in a fish poacher, or in a pan large enough to hold it, and cover it with the court bouillon. Slowly bring to a simmer over medium to medium-high heat, about 20 minutes.

3. Allow the fish to simmer, but not boil, for 10 minutes. Remove from the heat and let stand 15 to 20 minutes.

4. Remove the fish from the bouillon and transfer it to a serving platter lined with a white cloth napkin or paper towel to absorb the excess moisture and keep the fish from sliding on the platter. Cover with plastic wrap and refrigerate (up to 24 hours ahead).

5. **To serve:** Remove the skin (see "How to Skin a Cooked Fish for Presentation," page 61) from the top side of the fish and decorate both the fish and platter with lemon slices and sprigs of parsley. Serve the *sauce verte* on the side, or coat the fish with the sauce.

Variation

The salmon can also be served hot. If the salmon is extremely fresh, you can simply poach it in lightly salted water, otherwise use the same court bouillon as for the cold salmon. After poaching, let the salmon stand in the hot poaching liquid for 5 minutes. Prepare for serving as you would for the cold salmon, but serve with Sauce Hollandaise (page 373).

Filet de Sole Granville
Fillet of Sole with Shrimp, Mushrooms, and Truffles

This is an example of just how good a classic recipe can be. Sole Granville was originally made with a whole fish that was surrounded by shrimp and mushrooms and decorated with truffles. I use sole fillet in place of the whole fish, and often leave out the truffle. I have also cut back considerably on the egg yolks, cream, and butter normally used in the recipe.

In France this would be made with Dover sole—a firm and delicious fish, which you *can* get in this country both fresh and frozen. If your market has Dover sole, I recommend trying it here, but failing that, you can use any of the many varieties of flat fish native to American waters: the most common are gray, lemon, Rex, and petrale sole; flounder; fluke; and dab. The two varieties I find closest in texture to Dover sole are gray sole and petrale sole.

Serves 6

Champignons Pochés
(Poached Mushrooms)
¾ pound button mushrooms, washed
Juice of ½ lemon
Pinch salt and freshly ground pepper

Sauce Parisienne
4 tablespoons butter
3 tablespoons plus 1 teaspoon all-purpose flour
2 cups fish stock (page 349)
¼ teaspoon salt
⅛ teaspoon freshly ground pepper

Two things that can help not perfectly fresh fish taste fresher are skinning and soaking the fish before cooking. Cooking the skin heightens any bad flavors that exist in the fish itself. If you simply remove the skin and soak the fish in ice water for 10 to 15 minutes, you can prevent bad odors and give it a fresher taste and better smell.

When working with fish, keep a bowl of water containing several tablespoons of vinegar nearby, and use this acidulated water to rinse your hands and to wipe knives and countertops to help prevent fish odors from developing.

SKINNING FISH FILLETS

1. Place the fillet on a cutting board, skin side down. Start at the tail and cut a little of the fish away from the skin so you can grab the skin with your fingers.

2. With your knife held at about a 30-degree angle to the table or cutting board, slice back and forth between skin and fish while at the same time pulling the skin in the opposite direction.

Oysters, mussels, or clams can be steamed in white wine and the resulting cooking liquid used with, or in place of, the fish stock called for here. Add the cooked shellfish to the sauce; if you wish to change the color and flavor of the sauce, you can add saffron, curry, or tomatoes.

2 egg yolks
⅓ cup heavy cream
¾ pound shrimp, shelled, deveined, and cooked
1 black truffle, diced (optional)

Fish and Finishing

2 to 3 tablespoons butter
3 shallots, chopped
2 pounds gray sole fillets, folded in half (see "Folding a
    Fillet," page 113)
½ cup fish stock (page 349)
½ cup dry white wine
1 black truffle, sliced (optional)

1. **Poach the mushrooms:** In a saucepan, combine the mushrooms with enough water to come halfway up their sides. Add the lemon juice, salt, and pepper. Cover the pan and bring to a boil over high heat. Reduce the heat and simmer gently for 2 to 3 minutes. *(The mushrooms can be poached ahead of time. Store them in their poaching liquid.)*

2. Drain the mushrooms, reserving the poaching liquid. Place the poaching liquid in a small saucepan and reduce over high heat to ¼ cup, about 3 minutes.

3. **Make the sauce:** In a medium saucepan, heat 3 tablespoons of the butter over medium-high heat. Stir in the flour and cook until pale yellow and frothy, 30 to 45 seconds.

4. Add the fish stock and the reserved reduced mushroom liquid. Bring to a boil while whisking. Reduce the heat and simmer for 5 to 10 minutes, skimming off the butter and impurities as they rise to the surface. Season with the salt and pepper and whisk well.

5. In a small bowl, blend the egg yolks and cream together. Remove the sauce from the heat and add the egg yolk–cream mixture. Return to medium heat and whisk the sauce until it returns to a simmer. Remove from the heat and gently stir in the mushrooms, shrimp, and diced truffle. Cover the surface of the sauce with plastic wrap. *(The sauce can be made 1 day ahead to this point and refrigerated.)*

6. **Prepare the fish:** Butter a 12-inch skillet with 1 tablespoon of the butter and sprinkle with the chopped shallots. Place the folded fillets in the pan and add the fish stock and wine. Cut a piece of wax paper to fit over the surface of the fish. Place it on the fish and cover with the pan lid. *(The fish can be prepared up to 1 hour in advance and kept at room temperature.)* Reheat the sauce in a water bath (*bain-marie*).

7. Bring the fish to a simmer over medium heat. It should be white and opaque throughout, about 10 minutes.

8. With a skimmer or slotted spoon, transfer the fish to a hot platter, overlapping the fillets around the outside of the platter. Cover loosely with foil to keep warm. Blot up any excess liquid from the platter with paper towels. Reduce the fish poaching liquid over high heat until only 2 tablespoons remain, 4 to 5 minutes.

9. With a slotted spoon or skimmer, remove the shrimp, mushrooms, and diced truffle from the sauce and place in the center of the platter.

10. Strain the reduced fish poaching liquid into the sauce. Taste and adjust the seasoning, if necessary, and whisk well over high heat until the sauce just begins to boil. Remove the sauce from the heat, beat in the remaining tablespoon of butter, to taste, and spoon or pour the sauce over the sole. Use the sliced truffle to decorate the fish and serve immediately.

Serving Suggestion: Start with a chicken consommé (Consommé de Volaille, page 19) or a cream of asparagus soup (Crème d'Asperges, page 28). Serve the fish with steamed rice. For dessert, serve puff pastry with strawberries (Feuilleté aux Fraises, page 279).

Wine: Top-quality white Burgundy or Champagne.

Goujonnettes de Sole
Strips of Fried Sole, Fried Parsley, and Onion Rings

A *goujon* is a small, 2- to 3-inch minnowlike fish that is caught in the rivers of France. *Goujons* are usually deep fried and served as an hors d'oeuvre with

Wine: Serve the fish with a dry white wine, such as Muscadet or Pouilly-Fuissé.

FOLDING A FILLET

In France, sole fillets are
cut in half, down the middle, into two long, thin
fillets (each fish thus yields
four fillets). An American
sole is larger than a French
Dover sole, so I often halve
the individual fillets as well.

To make a fillet of sole
easier to remove from the
poaching liquid, and to
create an attractive package
for presentation, it is cus-
tomarily folded in half (or
sometimes rolled up to
form something called a
paupiette) before being
placed in the liquid. When
folding a fillet, the smooth
outside of the fillet (where
the skin was) should be on
the inside, and the inside
(where the bones were)
should be on the outside. If
you don't want to remember
any of this, just try folding
in both directions; the one
in which the fish folds flatter
is the correct one.

lemon and fried parsley. These crunchy, tender fish
are eaten head and all, for their bones are hardly
noticeable. A number of restaurants in towns border-
ing rivers will serve them while you sip an apéritif and
contemplate the menu. This is a wonderful way to start
a meal.

Goujonnettes de sole, or *filets de sole en goujon*,
is fillet of sole that is cut to resemble *goujons* and
then served in the same way. This classic is beginning
to reappear on restaurant menus using a variety of
the newly available fish, such as mahi-mahi or orange
roughy.

In addition to the fried parsley (if you've never
tasted it, you will be pleasantly surprised), I have
included some fried onion rings for all those who like
them as much as I do.

The key to this dish is to work quickly so the food
will still be hot when it gets to the table. In a restaurant
the fish and vegetables would be fried simultaneously
in separate deep-fryers. Since this is impractical for
the home kitchen, I recommend frying the onions first
and keeping them warm in a 250° oven, and then frying the fish and parsley.

Serves 6

1½ pounds fillet of sole
2 cups milk
½ teaspoon salt
¼ teaspoon freshly ground pepper
About 1 cup all-purpose flour, for dredging
3 onions, cut into rings
2 to 2½ quarts vegetable oil, for deep-frying
1 bunch parsley, stems removed
3 lemons, cut in half
Sauce Rémoulade (page 382)

1. Preheat the oven to 250°.
2. Cut the fillets in half lengthwise (follow the "seam"

down the middle of the fillet). Cut the fillet halves on the diagonal to form strips about 2½ to 3 inches long and ½ inch wide.

3. To 1 cup of the milk add the salt and pepper. Soak the fish in the seasoned milk for 10 minutes.

4. Drain the fish and toss the fish in the flour to coat each piece just before frying.

5. Place the onion rings in the remaining 1 cup milk to moisten. Drain and toss in the flour to coat.

6. In a deep-fryer, heat the oil to very hot (just smoking). Add the onion rings and cook until golden brown, 1 to 2 minutes. Drain on paper towels and keep warm in the oven.

7. Let the oil get very hot again and fry the fish, in 3 batches, until golden brown and crunchy, 2 to 3 minutes per batch. Drain on paper towels, and keep warm.

8. Fry the parsley for about 5 seconds. Drain on paper towels. Serve the fish with the parsley, fried onion rings, lemon halves, and *sauce rémoulade* on the side.

Bouillabaisse Américaine
Mediterranean Fish Stew

The name *bouillabaisse* probably causes most cooks to bolt in the other direction because of what seems to be a complicated and time-consuming dish that calls for fish that they can't even pronounce, let alone even find in the market. My version uses only seafood easily available and is really just an elaboration of my Soupe de Poisson (page 24), which you can make well ahead of time (and even have stored in the freezer).

The only ingredients the least bit difficult to find are fresh fennel, saffron, and savory. For the fennel,

Serving Suggestion: Serve this hearty soup with a green salad and a fruit tart for dessert and you will have a wonderful meal.

Wine: Accompany the meal with a chilled rosé de Provence and the flavors will make you feel as though you were on the Côte d'Azur.

you can substitute 1 teaspoon of anise or fennel seed or 1 tablespoon of an anise-flavored apéritif such as Pernod or Ricard. Unfortunately, there is no substitute for saffron if you want this to be a *bouillabaisse* instead of just a fish stew, although it will still be very good. If you do not have savory, omit it.

To serve the *bouillabaisse*, toasted slices of French bread are placed on the table with dishes of *aïoli* and *rouille*. Each diner spreads one of the two flavorful mayonnaises on the toast rounds before adding them to the bowl with the soup and fish.

Serves 6 to 8

2 tablespoons olive oil, extra-virgin if available
1 onion, halved and sliced
1 leek, washed and diced
½ fennel bulb, diced, or 1 teaspoon anise or fennel seed,
    or 1 tablespoon Pernod or Ricard
2 garlic cloves, smashed
5 sprigs parsley, chopped
1 tomato, peeled, seeded, and diced
½ bay leaf
1 pinch savory (optional)
1 pinch thyme
1 pinch saffron
½ teaspoon salt
⅛ teaspoon freshly ground pepper
2 pounds live lobster, cut into serving pieces
2 pounds mussels (optional), scrubbed and debearded
2 pounds fish fillets (see Note), cut into chunks
Soupe de Poisson (page 24), prepared through step 5;
    omit the fish fillet
2 pounds shrimp, shelled and deveined
1 pound sea scallops, rinsed, tendon removed
1 loaf French bread, sliced and toasted
½ recipe Aïoli (page 379)
½ recipe Rouille (page 380)

Note: Use any fish that appeals to you, the freshest possible and preferably thick over thin pieces. Try for 1 pound each of two types. And avoid strongly flavored fish such as mackerel and bluefish unless they are extremely fresh.

1. In a large stockpot, heat the oil over medium heat. Add the onion, leek, and fennel and cook until tender, about 5 minutes. Stir in the garlic, parsley, tomato, bay leaf, savory, thyme, saffron, salt, and pepper and cook for 1 minute.

2. Place the lobster, mussels, and fish fillets in the pot and cover with the cold *soupe de poisson*. Bring to a boil over medium heat, about 20 minutes, and boil gently for 1 minute.

3. Add the shrimp and scallops. When the soup returns to a boil, the shellfish and fish should all be done. If not, simmer an additional minute.

4. Remove the fish and shellfish and place on a large serving platter.

5. Bring the soup back to a boil, taste, and adjust the seasonings, if necessary. Strain, if desired, into a large soup tureen and bring to the table.

6. Place some of the fish and seafood in a large individual soup bowl and ladle the hot soup over it. Serve with the toasted French bread and bowls of the *aïoli* and *rouille*.

Crevettes à la Provençale
Shrimp in a Garlic-Tomato Sauce

This flavorful recipe is fast and easy. Shrimp are sautéed and then added to a *sauce provençale* made with ingredients typical of the south of France: tomatoes, garlic, and olive oil. Traditionally this sauce is covered and cooked slowly. I use high heat instead to cook it rapidly, and have also reduced the quantity of olive oil used to about half. The recipe serves four as a main course with rice pilaf or six as a first course.

Serving Suggestion: Serve with a salad and rice pilaf (Riz Pilaf, page 234). For dessert, serve a fruit tart.

Wine: Côtes-du-Rhône or chilled rosé de Provence.

Serves 4 or 6

The *sauce provençale for crevettes à la provençale* is extremely simple and, therefore, quite versatile. It can also be used with fish, chicken, veal, pasta, and omelets. Using the proportions here you can make larger quantities, although unless you have a professional stove, do not try to make any more than a double recipe. You need a great amount of heat to evaporate the liquid from the tomatoes rapidly without cooking them to a purée. The sauce as I have designed it should, if possible, retain the texture of the diced tomatoes. You can also vary the sauce by adding ¼ pound of sautéed sliced mushrooms.

4 tablespoons olive oil, extra-virgin if available
2 pounds tomatoes, peeled, seeded, and diced or 4 pounds canned tomatoes, drained and diced
3 garlic cloves, finely chopped
¼ teaspoon salt
⅛ teaspoon freshly ground pepper
6 sprigs parsley, chopped
1½ pounds shrimp, shelled and deveined

1. **Make the *sauce provençale*:** In a skillet, heat 2 tablespoons of the oil over high heat until it is smoking. Add the tomatoes. (Be careful; the hot oil may spatter.) Toss or stir quickly. Add the garlic and cook until most of the liquid has evaporated, 3 to 5 minutes. Season with the salt and pepper, remove from the heat and stir in three-fourths of the chopped parsley. Pour the sauce into a bowl and set aside. *(The sauce can be made 1 day in advance. Cover and refrigerate.)*

2. In a skillet, heat the remaining 2 tablespoons oil over medium-high heat. Add the shrimp and sauté until they change color and begin to curl, 2 to 3 minutes.

3. Add the *sauce provençale* to the cooked shrimp and bring to a boil. Transfer the shrimp and sauce to a hot serving platter and sprinkle with the remaining chopped parsley.

Crevettes à l'Orientale
Shrimp with Curry, Ginger, and Tomato

If a classic French dish has the word *orientale* or *indienne* in its name, it generally signifies that a curried sauce is a part of the presentation. In most cases, curry powder is used to flavor a flour-based sauce,

such as béchamel or *velouté*. In this lightened version
of a French curry dish, I use cream and fresh tomatoes
for the sauce and add two Oriental or Indian ingredients that have become easy to find in our supermarkets: fresh coriander (cilantro) and fresh ginger.
However, if you can't find fresh coriander, use parsley;
if you can't find fresh ginger, leave it out.

Serves 6

1 tablespoon vegetable oil
1 onion, chopped
3 garlic cloves, chopped
1 piece (1 to 1½ inches) fresh ginger, peeled and chopped
2 to 3 teaspoons curry powder, to taste
2 to 3 pinches cayenne pepper, to taste
¼ cup dry white wine
1 cup heavy cream
¼ teaspoon salt
⅛ teaspoon freshly ground pepper
2 pounds large shrimp, shelled and deveined
2 pounds tomatoes, peeled, seeded, chopped, and drained
   or 4 pounds canned tomatoes, chopped and drained
12 sprigs fresh coriander (cilantro), chopped

Serving Suggestion: Watercress soup (Potage au
Cresson, page 25) or
another light vegetable
soup makes a good first
course. Serve the curry
with plain rice (Riz au
Blanc, page 233) or rice
pilaf (Riz Pilaf, page 234)
and your favorite chutney.
Follow with a mixed green
salad and a soufflé or a
fruit sorbet for dessert.

Wine: Dry white or rosé.

1. In a 12-inch skillet, heat the oil over medium-low
heat. Add the onion and gently cook until softened, about
5 minutes. Add the garlic, ginger, curry powder, and cayenne pepper and stir with a wooden spoon. Add the wine
and boil over high heat until reduced by half, 10 to 15 seconds. Stir in the cream and season with the salt and pepper.
*(This sauce can be made up to 2 hours in advance and held
at room temperature.)*

2. About 5 minutes before serving, bring the sauce to a
boil, add the shrimp, and cook rapidly, turning the shrimp
occasionally, until they change color and begin to curl, 2 to
3 minutes. Stir in the tomatoes and two-thirds of the coriander. (Do not boil the sauce after the tomatoes have been
added or it will become watery.) Transfer to a warm serving platter and sprinkle with the remaining coriander.

1. Place the blade of a small kitchen scissors into the intestinal tract.

2. Cut through the shell down the back of the shrimp to the tail.

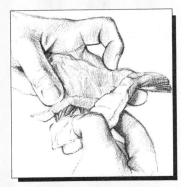

3. Peel off the shell, remove the vein, and rinse.

SHELLING AND DEVEINING SHRIMP

There are two schools of thought on the subject of shelling and deveining shrimp. Those who believe it is either unhealthy or undesirable to eat the intestinal tract of the shrimp remove the shell and "vein" before cooking. Those who feel it is important to cook shrimp in their shells, for the added flavor, eat the cooked shrimp, intestine and all.

I like the increased flavor offered by the shells, and do not object to the occasional grittiness of the vein. However, since I find that the ease of eating unshelled shrimp generally outweighs the added flavor, I usually remove the shell and veins before cooking.

The system I use for shelling and deveining shrimp was taught to me many years ago by the wife of a fisherman in East Hampton, Long Island.

Shrimp shells can be used to make a flavorful liquid that can be used in a sauce, or to make a rice pilaf. This way, you can take advantage of the shells' flavor. Once the shells are removed, rinse them well and place them in a saucepan. Cover them with cold water, bring to a boil, and simmer them for 15 minutes to extract their flavor.

Homard Grillé
Grilled and Steamed Lobster

The first time I ever had grilled lobster was in France in a small town on the Brittany coast. The region is renowned for its lobsters. The small half-lobster that was served was very delicious and very expensive, but the flavor was superior to any steamed lobster I had ever eaten, although its claws and legs were dry.

Over the years I have re-created the delicious flavors of a grilled lobster and solved the problem of dry
claws and legs. I cook the body of the lobster on the
grill, to develop its flavor, and steam the claws and legs
separately, to keep them moist and sweet.

Serves 6

3 lobsters (3 to 4 pounds each*), split
2 tablespoons chopped fresh herbs, such as tarragon,
   chives, dill, or basil
1 stick (4 ounces) butter, melted
2 lemons, cut into wedges (optional)
2 sticks (8 ounces) melted butter, for dipping (optional)

1. Place the lobsters on a large tray or baking sheet.
Cut off the antennae, and if the two halves have not been
completely separated, use a pair of scissors to do so. Have
the claws and legs ready to go into a large pot containing
1 to 2 inches of boiling water when you put the bodies on
the grill.

2. Add the chopped herbs to the 1 stick of melted butter and use a pastry brush to coat all the interior parts of
the lobster.

3. Place the lobsters, shell side down, on a very hot
grill and cover. If your grill does not have a cover, make
one with aluminum foil. Put the legs and claws into the pot
of boiling water, cover, and steam until the bodies on the
grill are done, 10 to 15 minutes. When done, the juices in
the shell will be sizzling, the meat will be opaque and firm
to the touch, and (if female) the roe, which is dark green
when raw, will be red.

4. **To serve:** Lift or slide the bodies onto individual
serving plates. Bring the legs and claws to the table in a
large bowl, and serve with lemon wedges and melted butter, if desired.

* These large-size lobsters can be hard to find, so you
will most likely have to order them in advance.

PREPARING A LOBSTER FOR GRILLING

Lobsters are generally split
in half lengthwise for grilling to avoid boiling inside
their shells, and to gain
flavor from the grill.

After you split the lob-
ster, remove the stomach
(which is found in the head
area) and the intestine (a
small clear or black tube
running the length of the
lobster), if you find it.
Twist the claws and legs
from the body and keep
separate for steaming. The
claw shell, which is softer
before being cooked,
should be cracked now.

Because lobster meat
breaks down or spoils rapidly once the lobster is
dead, they are most often
split just before grilling. If
you are unable to kill and
split the lobsters yourself,
have the market do it for
you no more than four
hours in advance and keep
the lobsters well iced until
you are ready to cook them.

Poultry

In France, it is not at all uncommon for a home cook to prepare recipes for guinea hen, goose, pheasant, squab, quail, and partridge in addition to chicken, duck, and turkey. For most American families, duck is an adventure.

In either country, however, chicken is the clear favorite. There are more French recipes for chicken than any other bird—in fact, more than for any other food. Its delicate flavor lends itself to a host of sauces as well as numerous cooking methods. Chicken can be grilled, sautéed, oven-roasted, spit-roasted, fried, poached, and braised.

Duck, whose popularity in this country has recently gained momentum, is a less versatile, dark-meat bird that needs more assertively flavored sauces. In America, where the predominant breed of duck available (the White Pekin) is fairly fatty, roasting is really the best method of cooking.

When roasting duck, or indeed any

poultry (under 7 pounds), I use the high-temperature method that is used in France to produce wonderful flavors in a short time. I also roast all birds on their sides instead of breast up. This places the joints, which take longer to cook, in the path of the most direct heat, and prevents overcooking the breast.

The recipes in this chapter include light-meat fowl (chicken and pheasant) and dark-meat fowl (duck and squab). Among the white-meat poultry recipes is a recipe for rabbit, which is treated in much the same way as chicken and for which chicken can easily be substituted.

Poularde Truffée et Farcie
Roast Stuffed Chicken with Truffles

*D*indonneau truffé, or truffled turkey, is a specialty in France for Christmas and New Year's. When I was living in Paris in the late '60s, I would see stacks of truffled turkeys in the windows of charcuterie shops a week to ten days before the holidays. (The shops, which were never heated, were as good as refrigerators in the winter.) Each turkey had slices of truffles placed under the skin, where they developed flavor while the turkeys gently aged. The flavor that the truffle adds to the roast bird is heady and earthy, and incomparable. Trying to describe a truffle to someone who hasn't had one is impossible, like trying to describe the taste of a mushroom.

Sliced truffles are a superb flavoring for any and all roast poultry, but there is something particularly satisfying in using them to flavor chicken—it changes the ordinary into something extraordinary.

I roast chicken in a manner that most Americans will find unusual. First, I roast at 475°. A bird of the

Serving Suggestion: Roast potatoes or rice, carrots (Carottes à l'Etuvée, page 202), and broccoli (Purée de Brocoli, page 205) go beautifully with the chicken.

Wine: A fine red Bordeaux from Médoc or Graves is equal to the elegance of this dish.

MAIGRE-GRAS AND FAT SEPARATOR

A **maigre-gras** is a sauce-boat used in France that has two sides. One side pours off the fat, the other the sauce. One version of a fat separator typically found on the American market looks like a small watering can. The spout keeps the fat separate.

same size cooked at the more usual, lower temperature of 350° to 375° could take up to 2 hours; my 4-pound chicken is done in 1 hour. I also lay the chicken on its side instead of breast up. This exposes the thickest parts of the bird, the joints, to the hottest part of the oven so they will cook in the same time the breast does—instead of cooking the chicken breast side up, which results in breast meat that is overcooked while the joints are not fully done.

The stuffing used in this recipe is my favorite. It is a good basic stuffing recipe (which can have other ingredients, such as dried fruit or chopped cooked chestnuts, added to it) and, like all the stuffings I use in roasted fowl, is fully cooked. Using a cooked stuffing eliminates the need for extra time in the oven. If you can't get truffles, eliminate them. You will still have a delicious, stuffed roast chicken. If you like the stuffing, triple the recipe for your next turkey.

Serves 6

1 chicken (4 to 5 pounds), rinsed and patted dry; neck, gizzard, and wing tips reserved

1 medium black truffle, about 1 inch in diameter, cut into 10 thin slices

½ pound slab smoked bacon, rind removed and diced, or ½ pound thick-sliced smoked bacon, diced

2 onions*

3 chicken livers, coarsely chopped

1 cup unseasoned bread crumbs

½ teaspoon salt

¼ teaspoon freshly ground pepper

1 teaspoon thyme or 4 sage leaves, chopped

½ cup Madeira

1 carrot, sliced ½-inch thick*

3 tablespoons butter, softened to room temperature

1 cup water

1. Starting at the neck, separate the skin from the body of the chicken by inserting your fingers underneath the skin and loosening any membranes you encounter (see "Truffling a Chicken"). Place 3 truffle slices on each side of the breast and 2 on each leg. *(This can be done 1 to 2 days in advance, and the chicken should be covered with plastic wrap and refrigerated. Bring back to room temperature before proceeding.)*

2. Preheat the oven to 475°.

3. In a large skillet, sauté the bacon over medium-high heat until it is half cooked. Finely chop 1 onion, add it to the pan, and cook, with the bacon, over medium-high heat until the onion is softened, but not browned, 2 to 3 minutes.

4. Add the livers and brown them quickly over high heat, about 30 seconds. Remove the mixture from the heat and add the bread crumbs, which will absorb the fat. Season with the salt, pepper, and thyme. If the stuffing is too dry, moisten it with 1 tablespoon of the Madeira. Taste and adjust the seasoning with salt and pepper. *(The stuffing can be made several hours in advance of roasting, but should not be refrigerated.)*

5. Stuff and truss the chicken just before roasting (see "How to Truss a Bird," page 150).

6. Place the chicken on its side in a nonstick roasting pan or on a rack in a roasting pan. Quarter the remaining onion and arrange it, the carrot, and reserved wing tips, neck, and gizzard around the chicken. Spread the butter over the chicken and sprinkle with salt and pepper.

7. Roast the chicken for 30 minutes. Turn it onto its other side and roast another 30 minutes. Baste every 15 minutes. Turn the chicken breast up for the last 5 or 10 minutes, if necessary, for even browning. The chicken is done when, if poked at the leg joint with a fork, the juices run clear. Allow the chicken to stand 10 to 15 minutes before carving.

8. To make a simple pan juice, deglaze the pan by adding the remaining Madeira and the water to the pan and stirring to loosen the caramelized bits from the bottom and sides of the pan. Over high heat, reduce by about half.

TRUFFLING A CHICKEN

In preparing the chicken for truffling, it is necessary to separate the skin from the meat. This is done quite easily once the thin membrane connecting the two is broken. Pull the neck skin back over the breast and you will find the membrane. Holding the skin up, puncture the membrane with your fingernail and spread it apart with your fingers. Once under the skin, you will find that you can easily slide your hand along the surface of the meat. As you reach down toward the leg and second joint, you will find your way impeded by another membrane. Break this one and your hand slides over the leg.

The truffles, which are very thinly sliced, are fragile and need to be protected as you move them to their resting place under the skin. I use my first two fingers like chopsticks to hold the truffle between the nail of one and the flesh of the other. Once I reach the spot where I want to deposit the truffle, I simply slide it off my nail and onto the meat with the upper finger.

Although the chicken will not develop the same flavor, other ingredients can be placed under the skin of the bird in a similar way. Some suggestions include wild mushrooms, prosciutto, or smoked ham.

Taste and adjust the seasoning, if necessary. Strain, remove the fat, and serve with the carved chicken.

* The quartered onion and carrot slices are added to the roasting pan to add flavor and color to the pan and ultimately to the sauce. But they are also there to keep the chicken fat that is rendered out during the roasting from burning. To do this, they must cover a good part of the pan bottom (without being so close together that they won't cook). Therefore, if you have a very large roasting pan, and the quantity of onion and carrot called for here does not seem like enough, add more.

Poularde Pochée à l'Estragon
Poached Chicken with Creamy Tarragon Sauce

A *poularde pochée à l'estragon* is a sumptuous and elegant dish. A whole chicken is poached in a veal or chicken stock with a few aromatic vegetables. The resulting fortified stock is turned into a creamy white tarragon sauce. In restaurants, the dish would only be offered if two or more people were sharing it. Although at the three-star restaurant Oustaù de Baumanière in Les-Baux-de-Provence (in the south of France), I was allowed to order *poularde à l'estragon* just for myself. The entire chicken was brought to the table in a huge white tureen, my piece carved off and the rest returned to the kitchen. (The staff ate well that day.)

In updating this recipe, I use chicken parts or boneless breasts in place of the whole chicken. This shortens the cooking time and allows me to easily pre-

Serving Suggestion: Start with a first course of asparagus. Serve the chicken with plain rice (Riz au Blanc, page 233) or rice pilaf (Riz Pilaf, page 234). For dessert, serve a sorbet and cookies (Tuiles aux Amandes, page 282) or Oranges au Champagne (page 325).

Wine: Champagne or chilled Chardonnay.

pare this dish for a large dinner party. To make things simple, I prepare the chicken and sauce in advance. The chicken is then reheated in barely simmering stock and served with the reheated sauce.

Serves 6

3½ pounds chicken parts or 6 boneless, skinless half breasts (about 2 pounds)
1 carrot, sliced
1 onion, quartered
Bouquet Garni (page 346)
1 tablespoon tarragon
2 quarts chicken stock, homemade or canned (see chart, page 349)
½ teaspoon salt (¼ teaspoon if using canned stock)
⅛ teaspoon freshly ground pepper

Sauce Velouté
2½ tablespoons butter
3 tablespoons all-purpose flour
½ cup heavy cream
2 teaspoons tarragon

1. In a 4-quart Dutch oven or saucepan, combine the chicken, vegetables, bouquet garni, tarragon, and stock (it is not necessary for the stock to cover the chicken completely). Bring to a boil over high heat and season with the salt and pepper. Reduce the heat, cover, and simmer for 25 minutes for chicken parts, 15 minutes for breasts, or until the juices run clear when the chicken is pierced with a fork.

2. Remove the poached chicken pieces and skin them. Strain the stock. Measure out 3 cups of the stock, skim to remove any fat, and set aside. Return the remaining stock and the chicken to the Dutch oven and keep warm. *(If you are preparing the chicken in advance—up to 2 days— refrigerate it in the poaching liquid. Before proceeding, bring the stock and chicken to a bare simmer. When ready to serve, remove the chicken to a heated platter and keep warm. Reserve the remaining poaching liquid for another use.)*

FRENCH CHICKEN TERMS

Americans are often confused by all the different names used in French chicken recipes: *poussin*, *poulet*, *poularde*, *poule*, and *coq* being only some of them. These terms correspond to the terms we use to indicate size (and often age) of a chicken. A *poussin* is a baby chicken. A *poulet* is a broiler or a fryer, depending on its size. A *poularde* is a roaster. A *poule* is a stewing hen. And a *coq* is a rooster.

3. **Make the *velouté* sauce:** Place 1 cup of the skimmed stock in a small saucepan. Reduce over high heat until only 2 or 3 tablespoons remain, about 7 minutes.

4. In another small saucepan, heat the butter over medium heat. Add the flour and whisk until the mixture becomes pale yellow and frothy, 30 to 45 seconds. Add the remaining 2 cups skimmed stock and stir with a whisk until the sauce comes to a boil, 2 to 3 minutes. When it comes to the boil, whisk vigorously for about 10 seconds, then reduce the heat and simmer gently, whisking the sauce well from time to time until the sauce is the consistency of heavy cream, 2 to 3 minutes. Skim the surface of butter and impurities several times during the cooking, and follow by whisking the sauce well each time.

5. Add the reduced stock, cream, and tarragon. Bring the sauce back to a boil, reduce the heat, and simmer until the sauce is the consistency of heavy cream, about 10 minutes. Taste and adjust the seasoning, if necessary. *(The sauce can be prepared up to 2 days in advance. Cover the surface with plastic wrap, let cool, and refrigerate. Before serving, bring to a boil and whisk well.)*

6. **To serve:** If you have not already done so, remove the chicken from the poaching liquid (reserve for another use) and drain on paper towels. Place the chicken in a deep serving dish and pour the sauce over it. You can strain the hot *velouté* sauce over the chicken, removing the tarragon as it is done in the classic style, or omit the straining, if you prefer.

What *poule au pot* does, in essence, in addition to producing a lovely and tender chicken dish, is make a double-strength chicken stock. The same basic ingredients that go into regular-strength chicken stock are here cooked in stock instead of water. In France, the resulting soup would be served as a separate course (followed by the chicken and vegetables). But you can also save it and use it as the basis for Consommé de Volaille (page 19), and serve the chicken and vegetables simply, with mustard and *cornichons* (small French pickles).

Poule au Pot
Chicken in a Pot

When you're not feeling your best or you are in the mood for a light meal, this dish of tender chicken and vegetables simmered in stock is just right.

Ordinarily, the soup and the chicken would be served as separate courses, but I prefer to skin the chicken and take the meat off the bone, making the dish both easier to eat and easier to make ahead of time. You can also simplify things by using canned chicken stock if you don't have homemade.

Serves 4 to 6

1 chicken (about 4 pounds) cut into 8 serving pieces, or
    equivalent parts, rinsed
3 quarts chicken stock, homemade or canned (see chart,
    page 349)
1 leek (white part only), washed and cut into 2-inch pieces
2 onions, quartered*
2 small white turnips, peeled and quartered (optional)
3 carrots, cut into 2-inch pieces
2 stalks celery, cut into 2-inch pieces
Bouquet Garni (page 346)
½ teaspoon salt (¼ teaspoon if using canned stock)
⅛ teaspoon freshly ground pepper
½ cup rice, cooked; or ¼ pound cooked thin egg noodles;
    or 6 new potatoes, diced and cooked

1. In a large stockpot or flameproof casserole, combine the chicken and stock. Bring to a boil, uncovered, over high heat, about 20 minutes. Skim the foam, fat, and impurities that rise to the surface.

2. Add all the remaining ingredients except the cooked rice, noodles, or potatoes. Bring back to a boil, reduce the heat, and simmer, partially covered, for 30 minutes. The chicken should be cooked and vegetables should be tender. If not, cook an additional 5 to 10 minutes. Skim occasionally to remove fat, foam, and impurities that rise to the surface.

3. Remove the pot from the heat and uncover. Transfer the chicken and vegetables to a large bowl. Discard the bouquet garni. Skim the surface of the soup to remove all fat. Strain, if necessary.

4. When the chicken is cool enough to handle, skin it

TO CUT A COOKED BIRD INTO SERVING PIECES

1. Turn the bird on its side. Slice down the body to remove the leg and second joint.

2. Pull the leg away.

3. Separate the leg at the second joint.

4. Slice along the breast to remove the wings and a small piece of breast.

5. Run your knife down between the breast and the carcass and lift the breast away.

6. Diagonally slice the breast into pieces.

and pull the meat off the bones. Return the chicken to the pot along with the vegetables.

5. **To serve:** Bring the soup to a simmer. Place the rice, noodles, or potatoes in a strainer or colander and dip into the top of the soup to heat them. Place some of the vegetables, chicken, and rice (or noodles or potatoes) in each of four deep soup bowls. Ladle some of the soup over all and serve.

* Do not trim off the root ends of the onions before quartering in order to keep the onion layers together.

Variation

Poule au Pot Sauce Suprême (*Chicken in a Pot with Velouté Sauce*): Prepare a Sauce Velouté (page 360) with the stock. Add ½ cup heavy cream to the sauce and simmer until the sauce thickens enough to coat a spoon, 10 to 15 minutes. Serve the chicken (skinned, but not pulled from the bones) and vegetables on a platter accompanied by plain rice (Riz au Blanc, page 233) and the sauce.

CUTTING POULTRY INTO SERVING PIECES

To halve (for 1-pound bird): Cut out the back and remove the breastbone.

To quarter (for 2-pound bird): Above steps, plus separate the breasts from the legs.

To cut into 8 serving pieces (for 3- to 4-pound bird): Remove leg and second joint. Remove the back and then the remaining backbone. Cut through the white cartilage covering the sternum from the inside—do not cut through the breastbone. Pry the breasts back to reveal the breastbone and remove it with your fingers. Halve the breast and cut each half in two with poultry shears or a cleaver. Turn the leg and second joint skin side down; you will see a line of fat on the inside of the second joint. Where that line ends is the proper place to separate the leg and joint.

Coq au Vin
Chicken in Red Wine

*C*oq au vin was originally designed to make a tough rooster (*coq*) tender enough to eat. The earliest versions came from the Loire Valley, where the French kings lived, and the wines used in the dish were Bourgueil and Chinon, which come from the same area. These same wines are available to us today, and using a plump, tender chicken in place of the firmer-fleshed rooster produces a succulent masterpiece.

When this dish was made with a rooster, its blood was saved, diluted with a little vinegar to prevent coagulation, and used to thicken the sauce. For everyone's convenience, I, along with most cooks, use flour to thicken the sauce in this more contemporary version.

Classic *coq au vin* recipes call for the chicken to be flamed with Cognac. I have omitted this step from the recipe, finding it adds little to the final flavor of this dish.

Chicken, veal, and fish are normally cooked in white wine, if wine is called for, but *coq au vin* requires a full-bodied red wine to produce its rich sauce. Sometimes a red wine of unusual quality and character is used; in these cases the dish takes on the name of the wine. *Coq au Chambertin* is an example of this. Some California Zinfandels work extremely well with this recipe, as do many of the wines of Spain, and a French Mâcon Rouge is always a good choice.

This dish can be fully prepared one to two days in advance and reheated on top of the stove or in a 350° oven for about 45 minutes before serving.

Serves 4 to 6

Serving Suggestion: As a first course I often serve artichokes, asparagus, or a vegetable soup. I usually serve warm French bread with the meal and a mixed green salad before serving dessert, my favorite being Tarte Tatin (page 245).

Wine: When choosing a wine to drink with a *coq au vin*, look for a full-bodied red. My preference has always been a mature Burgundy or, when available, a Chinon or Bourgeuil from the Loire Valley. If none of these are available, try one of the many fine reds from Spain or Portugal.

3 tablespoons vegetable oil

1 chicken (3½ to 4 pounds), cut into 8 serving pieces, rinsed, and patted dry

1 onion, diced

3 tablespoons all-purpose flour

3 shallots, sliced

4 garlic cloves, sliced

2 cups full-bodied dry red wine, such as Pinot Noir, Côtes-du-Rhône, or Zinfandel

1½ cups beef stock, homemade or canned (see chart, page 348)

1 teaspoon tomato paste

1 teaspoon Glace de Viande (optional; page 352)

Bouquet Garni (page 346)

½ teaspoon salt (¼ teaspoon if using canned stock)

¼ teaspoon freshly ground pepper

20 pearl onions, peeled, root ends trimmed but left intact to hold the onions together

½ pound smoked slab bacon, cut into ½-inch rectangles

½ pound mushrooms, washed, dried, and halved or quartered, to match size of the onions

5 sprigs parsley, chopped for garnish

1. In a large flameproof casserole, heat the oil over high heat. Add the chicken and brown well on one side, about 3 to 4 minutes; turn and partially brown the other side, about 1 minute.

2. Add the diced onion and reduce the heat slightly. Sauté the onion until it begins to brown, 2 to 3 minutes.

3. Sprinkle the chicken with the flour. Shake the casserole and turn the chicken so the flour mixes with the hot oil. Reduce the heat to medium and cook, stirring occasionally, until the flour browns, about 3 minutes.

4. Add the shallots, garlic, wine, stock, tomato paste, *glace de viande*, and the bouquet garni. Stir well and season with the salt and pepper. Reduce the heat to medium-low, cover, and simmer for 30 minutes. *(The recipe can be prepared to this point several days in advance. Let cool to room temperature, cover, and refrigerate or freeze. Bring back to a simmer before continuing in step 9.)*

5. Drop the pearl onions into a large saucepan of boiling water and cook until tender, 10 to 15 minutes. Drain.

6. Place the bacon in a medium-size saucepan, cover with cold water, and, over medium-high heat, bring to a boil. Drain, rinse with cold water, and repeat this blanching process to extract the bacon's excess saltiness.

7. In a 10- to 12-inch skillet, sauté the bacon chunks over medium-high heat until crisp on the outside, yet still soft on the inside. Drain on paper towels.

8. Remove all but 2 tablespoons of the bacon fat from the pan, add the mushrooms, and sauté over high heat until browned, 2 to 3 minutes. Season to taste with salt and pepper and remove the mushrooms to a bowl. Add the pearl onions to the pan and brown, stirring, 2 to 3 minutes, then add to the mushrooms.

9. When the chicken is tender, remove it to an oven-proof serving dish or clean casserole. Discard the bouquet garni. Strain the sauce through a double-mesh sieve and remove any fat remaining on the surface. The sauce should be the consistency of heavy cream. If it is too thick, add a little water; if too thin, boil it to thicken.

10. Add the bacon, mushrooms, and onions to the chicken, and pour the sauce over all evenly. Before serving, heat to a simmer and simmer for 5 minutes. This can be done on top of the stove or in the oven, depending on the serving dish used. Sprinkle with the parsley and serve.

Poulet Sauté à la Portugaise
Chicken with Mushrooms, Tomatoes, and Olives

The classic recipe for *poulet sauté à la portugaise* presents the chicken in a tomato sauce garnished with tomatoes and sliced mushrooms. The rendition that I have been teaching for the past 16 years adds both black and green olives to the garnish. Also, the mushrooms are quartered so they are approximately the same size as the olives. If button mushrooms are available in your area, you can use them whole.

Although I usually serve this colorful dish during the summer when tomatoes are best, I prepare it in the winter using good-quality canned tomatoes.

To make things easier, I often cook the chicken in the sauce one or two days before I am going to serve it. I cook the mushroom, tomato, and olive accompaniment on the day of serving, add it to the chicken, and reheat everything together in a 300° to 350° oven for about 45 minutes. The thick sauce will thin to its proper consistency after the tomatoes are added.

Serves 4 to 6

Serving Suggestion: Serve rice pilaf (Riz Pilaf, page 234) with the chicken. Salad and dessert—fruit sorbet and cookies—are all you need to accompany this dish.

Wine: I would serve either a Portuguese red or a chilled Beaujolais with this summer ragoût.

4 tablespoons butter
1 chicken (3½ to 4 pounds), cut into 8 serving pieces, rinsed, and patted dry
2 onions, diced
⅓ cup all-purpose flour
2 garlic cloves, finely chopped
2 shallots, finely chopped
2 cups beef stock, homemade or canned (see chart, page 348)
1 cup dry white wine
Bouquet Garni (page 346)
1 tablespoon tomato paste
½ teaspoon salt (¼ teaspoon if using canned stock)
¼ teaspoon freshly ground pepper
3 ounces (about ¾ cup) green olives*
1½ tablespoons vegetable oil
¾ pound mushrooms, washed, dried, and quartered
2 pounds tomatoes, peeled, seeded, and quartered, or 4 pounds canned tomatoes, drained and quartered
3 ounces (about ¾ cup) black olives*
3 sprigs parsley, chopped, for garnish

1. In a flameproof casserole, heat the butter over high heat. Add the chicken and brown well on one side, about 3 to 4 minutes; turn and brown the other side, about 3 minutes. Add the onions, reduce the heat to medium-high, and cook until golden, about 3 minutes.

2. Stir the flour into the butter. Reduce the heat to medium and cook, stirring or shaking the casserole occasionally, until the flour is light brown, 3 to 5 minutes.

3. Add the garlic, shallots, stock, wine, bouquet garni, tomato paste, salt, and pepper. Stir gently with a wooden spoon.

4. Cover, reduce the heat to medium-low, and simmer until the chicken is tender and offers no resistance when pierced with a roasting fork, 25 to 35 minutes. Skim the fat from the surface of the sauce several times during the cooking period. Discard the bouquet garni. *(The dish can be made to this point 1 or 2 days in advance. Let cool to room temperature, cover, and refrigerate. To reheat, continue with the recipe through step 7 and reheat the entire dish in a 300° to 350° oven for about 45 minutes.)*

5. Place the green olives in a saucepan and cover with cold water. Bring to a boil, drain, and rinse with cold water. Taste the olives. If they are still salty, repeat the procedure until they are just slightly salty to the taste.

6. In a 12-inch skillet, heat the oil over high heat. Add the mushrooms and sauté, tossing, shaking, or stirring them occasionally, until they are browned, about 3 minutes. Season to taste with salt and pepper.

7. Add the green olives, mushrooms, tomatoes, and black olives to the chicken. Simmer for 5 minutes.

8. **To serve:** If not already in an attractive casserole, transfer to a hot serving dish and sprinkle the chicken with chopped parsley.

* There are many varieties of both pitted and non-pitted olives available, so choose those whose flavor you prefer. Although pitting olives takes time, the effort will be appreciated by your guests when entertaining.

GRADATIONS OF GARLIC

The strength of garlic flavor varies with the way it is prepared and when it is added to a dish. The subtlest way of using it is to add it to a liquid, without sautéing it first, so that it blends with the other flavors and does not stand out, as in *coq au vin* or for glazed garlic (Ail Glacé, page 206).

For a more distinct garlic flavor, the garlic should be sautéed first before adding it to a liquid, as in Ratatouille Niçoise (page 218). For the strongest flavor, garlic is added either raw (as in Aïoli, page 379) or close to the end of the cooking (as in Sauce Provençale, page 117).

Poulet au Riesling
Chicken with Riesling

Serving Suggestion: This recipe, as with a number of others, was designed to have a subtle blend of beige and cream colors. No touch of green is necessary on the plate, but you can start your meal with a vegetable or a mixed green salad. Serve the chicken with buttered noodles. For dessert, serve an Alsatian fruit tart (Tarte Alsacienne aux Fruits, page 248).

Wine: Chilled Riesling.

This Alsatian specialty is quick and easy to prepare. Classically, *poulet au Riesling* was made by simmering the chicken in a combination of wine and water. The resulting stock was thickened to make a *velouté* sauce, which was further enriched with egg yolks and cream. Mushrooms were poached separately and their liquid reduced and added to the sauce.

In this recipe, the mushrooms are cooked with the chicken, eliminating two steps, and only the cream is used in the sauce. Omitting the butter, flour, and egg yolks from the sauce yields a smaller quantity of sauce with a greater intensity of flavor.

Serves 4

3 tablespoons butter
1 chicken (2 to 2½ pounds), quartered, or 4 skinless,
  boneless half breasts (about 1½ pounds), rinsed and
  patted dry
¼ teaspoon salt
⅛ teaspoon freshly ground pepper
1 onion, halved
2 shallots, finely chopped
¼ pound mushrooms, washed, dried, and sliced
¾ cup plus 1 teaspoon Riesling wine
¾ cup heavy cream

1. In a large skillet, heat the butter over medium heat. Add the chicken and brown it lightly, about 3 minutes on each side.

2. Pour off any excess cooking fat. Season the chicken with the salt and pepper. Add the onion to the pan, cover,

and sauté gently over low heat for 15 minutes (10 minutes if using breasts).

3. Add the shallots, mushrooms, and the ¾ cup wine to the chicken. Cover and simmer until the chicken is tender and juices run clear when the chicken is pierced with a roasting fork, about 10 minutes.

4. Transfer the chicken and mushrooms to a serving platter and keep warm. Discard the onion and reduce the liquid over high heat to about ⅓ cup, about 2 minutes.

5. Add the cream and boil to thicken, stirring gently, about 1 minute. Taste and adjust the seasoning, if necessary, and stir in the 1 teaspoon wine.

6. Spoon or pour the sauce over the chicken.

Variations

Poulet ou Côte de Veau à la Crème *(Chicken or Veal Chops with White Wine and Cream):* In place of the ¾ cup Riesling use any dry white wine. In step 5, add 1 teaspoon Cognac to the sauce in place of the Riesling. For the veal version, use four 1¼-inch-thick veal chops in place of the chicken. Serve with rice instead of noodles.

Poulet au Champagne *(Chicken with Champagne):* Use Champagne in place of the ¾ cup Riesling and 1 teaspoon Cognac in place of the Riesling in step 5. Serve with rice instead of noodles.

Poulet Vallée d'Auge *(Chicken with Apples and Cider):* This dish is named for the valley of the Auge River, which passes through Normandy, where most of France's apples grow. Use apple cider (French apple cider, if you can find it) in place of the ¾ cup Riesling and 1 teaspoon Calvados (or applejack) in place of the Riesling in step 5. Serve with sautéed apples instead of noodles.

Sauce Crème
(Cream Sauce)

A classic cream sauce is Sauce Béchamel (page 357) with the addition of 1 cup of heavy cream. Once the cream is added, the sauce is boiled to reduce it to the desired consistency. Contemporary cream sauces are made just with heavy cream and reduced cooking liquids, or Glace de Viande (page 352) or other glazes.

Examples of contemporary cream sauces can be seen in the Steak au Poivre (page 159) and in the Poulet au Riesling (page 135).

Poulet au Vinaigre de Xérès
Chicken with Sherry Vinegar

Serving Suggestion: **Start with
a mixed salad. Serve the
chicken with carrots
(Carottes Glacées au
Madère, page 203) and
mashed potatoes (Purée de
Pommes de Terre à l'Ail,
page 232). For dessert,
serve poached pears
(Poires au Porto, page
324) and macaroons
(Macarons, page 288).**

Wine: **A moderately priced
Spanish red.**

This is a variation of legendary chef Fernand Point's
famous recipe, *poulet au vinaigre*. When I first
tasted this dish, I was surprised to find that it did not
exhibit the sharpness of the vinegar. Later, when I
made the dish I realized that reducing the vinegar
until only a small amount remained cut the sharpness.

In this recipe, the unique flavor created by the
sherry vinegar will be a pleasing surprise. Sherry
vinegar, having a rich sherry taste, is available in many
gourmet stores, but if you have difficulty finding it, try
the recipe with a good balsamic or red wine vinegar.

Serves 4

4 tablespoons butter
*1 chicken (2 to 2½ pounds), quartered, or 4 boneless,
    skinless half breasts (about 1½ pounds), rinsed and
    patted dry*
¼ teaspoon salt
⅛ teaspoon freshly ground pepper
1 onion, cut in half
¼ cup sherry vinegar
2 shallots, finely chopped
3 garlic cloves, finely chopped
1 cup dry white wine
1 tablespoon tomato paste
2 teaspoons Glace de Viande (optional; page 352)
4 sprigs parsley, chopped

1. In a 12-inch skillet, heat 2 tablespoons of the butter
over medium-high heat. Add the chicken and brown well
on both sides, about 3 to 4 minutes per side. Season with
the salt and pepper.

2. Pour off any excess cooking fat. Add the onion to the pan, cover, and sauté gently over low heat for 15 minutes (10 minutes if using breasts).

3. Remove the chicken, but leave the onion, and pour off and reserve any pan juices. Add the vinegar and reduce until almost all of the liquid is evaporated, about 1 minute. Add the shallots, garlic, wine, and reserved pan juices. Return the chicken to the pan, cover, and simmer until the chicken is tender and juices run clear when the chicken is pierced with a roasting fork, about 10 minutes.

4. Remove the chicken and keep it warm on a serving platter. Discard the onion.

5. Stir in the tomato paste and *glace de viande*. Taste and adjust the seasoning with salt and pepper, if necessary. The sauce should be the consistency of light cream; if it is not, boil to thicken. Remove the pan from the heat and stir in the remaining 2 tablespoons of butter and the parsley. Pour the sauce over the chicken.

FERNAND POINT

A master chef, responsible for many of France's modern classic recipes, Fernand Point was the acknowledged king of French cooking and the teacher of many of today's most highly acclaimed chefs, including Paul Bocuse and the Troisgros brothers. Until his death in 1955, Point was the chef/owner of the famous restaurant called La Pyramide in Vienne, south of Lyons in the Rhône Valley.

Poussins aux Herbes et à la Moutarde
Broiled Baby Chickens or Cornish Hens with Herbs and Mustard

A *poulet grillé à la diable* is a grilled chicken coated with mustard and bread crumbs. I have always found the result too dry, and, in fact, classically this dish is served with a sauce (called *sauce diable*), which compensates for the dryness.

Instead of coating the chicken with bread crumbs, I use only mustard and a number of herbs normally found in a *sauce diable*, retaining much of the dish's original character. The resulting moist and tender chicken needs no sauce other than the simple pan juices.

A *poussin* is a tender and juicy baby chicken weighing about one pound. Although they have been popular in Europe for many years, *poussins* have only recently begun to appear in the selective American supermarket. If they are not yet available in your area, use one of the suggested substitutions below.

Changing the herbs used or adding a touch of curry powder will lead to many variations, as will the use of Madeira or sherry in place of the white wine.

Serves 4 to 6

Serving Suggestion: I normally serve the chicken with buttered noodles, rice, or baked potatoes, and accompany it with peas, green beans, or another green vegetable. Sometimes I serve the vegetable as a first course such as buttered broccoli or artichoke vinaigrette.

Wine: Dry red.

3 poussins or Cornish hens (about 1 pound each),
    split in half, rinsed, and patted dry*
3 tablespoons Dijon mustard
1 tablespoon tarragon
2 teaspoons basil
2 teaspoons thyme
⅛ teaspoon salt
⅛ teaspoon freshly ground pepper
¾ cup dry white wine

1. Place the chicken pieces skin side up in a roasting pan and spread half of the mustard over them. Sprinkle with half of the herbs and season with half the salt and pepper. Turn the pieces skin side down and repeat the seasoning process. *(This can be done up to 12 hours in advance of cooking. Cover well and refrigerate.)*

2. Preheat the broiler.

3. Place the hens 3 to 4 inches below the broiler, skin side down. When they have browned well on one side, 8 to 10 minutes, turn and broil on the other side, until well browned, about 7 minutes.

4. Deglaze the pan by adding the wine, tilting the pan, and stirring to loosen the caramelized bits on the bottom of the pan. Baste the pieces with the liquid and broil for an additional 1 to 2 minutes; the juices of the chicken should

run clear when it is pierced with a fork. The alcohol in the wine will evaporate and may ignite, but the flames will cease in seconds.

5. Serve the chicken with some of the pan juices.

✳ If you cannot find *poussins* or Cornish hens, use a 2- to 2½-pound broiler cut into quarters or 4 chicken half breasts (1½ to 2 pounds).

Variation

Poussins Grillés ou Rôtis (*Grilled or Roasted Baby Chickens or Cornish Game Hens*): If you have a grill or grill pan, you might want to grill the *poussins*. Or roast them as for squab (page 146). Simply grilled or roasted, they are good served with either Champignons à l'Ail (page 214), made with wild mushrooms, or rice with wild mushrooms (Riz Sauvage Forestière, page 236).

Suprêmes de Volaille Basquaise
Sautéed Breast of Chicken with Ham, Peppers, and Tomatoes

The robust flavors of ham, peppers, and tomatoes are typical of the Basque region in the Pyrénées Mountains of southwestern France. Anything served with this combination is labeled *basquaise*. The area is renowned for its pork, and especially the cured hams produced in and around the city of Bayonne. Bayonne ham is either sliced thin and eaten with fruit, like Italian prosciutto, or diced and used to add flavor to a variety of dishes. Bayonne ham is very difficult to find in America, but prosciutto is a good substitute.

Instead of making a flour-thickened sauce for this

Serving Suggestion: Start with **Terrine Maison aux Pruneaux (page 64). Serve the chicken with rice (Riz Pilaf, page 234). For dessert, serve peach Melba and cookies (Biarritz, page 286).**

Wine: Dry red.

A *suprême* of chicken is technically a boned breast of chicken with the skin and the wing's first joint attached. When sautéed and presented on a plate or platter, it has a more attractive shape and has better color than the boned and skinless breasts or cutlets we find in our markets.

dish, as is the custom, I deglaze the pan in which the chicken is cooked with the juices from the tomato, pepper, and ham mixture and reduce them to form a sauce.

Serves 4 to 6

2 tablespoons vegetable oil or rendered pork fat*
2 onions, halved and sliced
3 garlic cloves, chopped
2 green bell peppers, cut into julienne
2 red bell peppers, cut into julienne
¼-inch slice Bayonne ham or prosciutto (about
    ¼ pound), diced
¼ teaspoon salt
⅛ teaspoon freshly ground pepper
1½ pounds tomatoes, peeled, seeded, and diced or
    3 pounds canned tomatoes, drained and diced
3 tablespoons butter or rendered pork fat*
6 skinless, boneless chicken half breasts (about 2 pounds),
    rinsed and patted dry

1. In a medium saucepan, heat the vegetable oil over medium-low heat. Add the onions, cover, and cook gently until they are softened but not browned, 4 to 5 minutes.

2. Stir in the garlic, green and red peppers, and the ham. Season with the salt and pepper. Cover and cook gently until the vegetables are almost tender, about 5 minutes.

3. Add the tomatoes and cook an additional 3 to 4 minutes. The tomatoes should be soft but still hold their shape. Drain the vegetables, reserving the liquid, and set aside. *(The recipe can be prepared in advance to this point. Cover, let cool, and refrigerate. Reheat the ham and vegetables in a small amount of the reserved liquid before proceeding.)*

4. In a large skillet, heat the butter over medium-high heat. Add the chicken breasts and cook for 4 to 5 minutes per side, or until the juices run clear when the chicken is pierced with a fork and it is just slightly springy to the touch. Season to taste with salt and pepper. Remove to a serving platter and keep warm.

5. Pour off any remaining fat and deglaze the pan by adding the reserved vegetable liquid and stirring to loosen the caramelized bits on the bottom and sides of the pan. Reduce the liquid until it has the consistency of light cream. To serve, arrange the vegetables and chicken on a warm platter and pour the sauce over the chicken.

* Pork fat is the fat typical of *basquaise* dishes. To render pork fat, dice about ¼ pound fresh pork fat and melt over medium heat. Measure out the quantity called for and save the remainder for another use or discard.

Variation

Poulet Rôti Basquaise *(Roast Chicken with Ham and Vegetables):* You can also roast a chicken and serve it surrounded by the ham and vegetable mixture (steps 1 through 3).

Suprêmes de Faisan au Genièvre
Boned Breast of Pheasant with Juniper

The combination of juniper berries and game birds is classic. The birds are usually roasted, and the juniper berries are used to flavor an accompanying sauce or stuffing.

The following recipe finds its inspiration in the traditional use of juniper with game birds, but gets its innovation from serendipity. A number of years ago, a student presented me with several pheasants. Unfortunately, they had already been skinned, making them unsuitable for roasting. So I improvised. I took a handful of juniper berries (which by good fortune were

Serving Suggestion: To start, I would serve a pâté or a consommé made with the rest of the pheasant. Serve the pheasant breasts on a bed of buttered noodles or with wild rice.

Wine: Both white and red Burgundies will go well with this deliciously different pheasant dish.

FRESH JUNIPER BERRIES

I have made pheasant with juniper using dried store-bought berries instead of fresh ones, and although my guests always enjoy it, I am always disappointed. For this reason I recommend that you use fresh berries whenever possible. Juniper berries can be found on juniper trees, bushes, and ground covers. They may be large or small. Normally green on the tree, they turn dark blue or black a week or so after picking (this is how you find them in the store). They can be used green from the tree, and will have a stronger taste of resin and be more bitter than the riper dark berries. As with any unfamiliar fruit or plant, if you have questions about what you are picking, consult a local nursery.

fresh, because there were juniper bushes nearby), crushed them, and coated the pheasant breasts as I would for a *steak au poivre*. I then sautéed them and flamed them with gin (which is flavored with juniper). I then added *glace de viande* and finished the sauce with some cream.

The results so pleased me that I wanted to re-create the recipe the next time I had fresh juniper. Unfortunately I didn't have the pheasants, so I decided to try chicken breasts. Although chicken is more delicate in taste, it is similar in size, cooking properties, and texture. The dish was delicious. Try it with chicken, but if you can get pheasant—commercially raised pheasant is available—try the recipe in its original form.

Serves 4 to 6

*6 individual skinless, boneless pheasant or chicken half
    breasts (about 2 pounds)*
½ cup juniper berries, preferably fresh, crushed
1 tablespoon butter
¼ teaspoon salt
⅛ teaspoon freshly ground pepper
¼ cup plus 1 teaspoon gin
1 tablespoon Glace de Volaille (optional; page 353)
1 cup heavy cream

1. Lightly coat the pheasant breasts with the juniper berries and wrap in plastic wrap. Let stand at room temperature for 2 hours. *(If you are preparing this more than 2 hours in advance, wrap well and refrigerate.)*

2. In a 10- to 12-inch skillet, heat the butter over medium-high heat. Add the pheasant breasts and sauté until lightly browned, about 3 minutes. Turn the breasts, season with the salt and pepper, cover, reduce the heat to medium-low, and continue cooking until done, 5 to 7 minutes. The breasts should be slightly springy to the touch. If soft or very springy, they need longer cooking; if firm to the touch, they are overcooked.

3. Remove the pan from the heat, add the ¼ cup of gin, and flame (see flaming instructions in Bananes Flambées au Rhum, page 322). When the flames die, transfer the breasts to a warm platter or serving plates. Most of the juniper berries will have fallen from the breasts during cooking and should be left in the pan. Add the *glace de volaille* and stir until dissolved. Add the cream, increase the heat to high, and bring to a boil. Taste and adjust the seasoning, if necessary. At this point the sauce should be thick enough to lightly coat a spoon. Add the teaspoon of gin to the sauce.

4. **To serve:** Pour the sauce over the breasts. Serve only a few berries with the sauce, to indicate where the flavor comes from, and tell your guests that they need not eat them, for most will find them too bitter.

Lapin Sauté à la Moutarde et au Romarin
Sautéed Rabbit with Mustard and Rosemary Sauce

In case you think I've taken leave of my senses, in France rabbit is treated much like chicken. Small young rabbits are tender like chicken, but have a more robust flavor. It is an inexpensive and widely used meat in France, only recently becoming popular in the United States.

I have had many students who refuse to eat rabbit for a variety of reasons, most of which stem from childhood memories of their Easter bunnies. The following recipe, which combines the flavors of mustard, rosemary, and Cognac, has convinced many skeptics that rabbit is worthy of serious consideration. For those

Serving Suggestion: Start with melon. Steamed rice or buttered noodles and sautéed mushrooms (Champignons à l'Ail, page 214) are the ideal accompaniments for this cream-sauced dish. Follow with a mixed green salad and a fruit tart for dessert.

Wine: Dry white.

already convinced, who would like more rabbit rec-
ipes, substitute rabbit for chicken in recipes such as
Poulet au Vinaigre de Xérès (page 137) and Poulet ou
Côte de Veau à la Crème (page 136).

Serves 6

3 tablespoons vegetable oil
2 rabbits (2½ pounds each), cut into serving pieces
    (ask the butcher to do this)
½ teaspoon salt (¼ teaspoon, if using canned stock)
¼ teaspoon freshly ground pepper
1 onion, finely chopped
2 garlic cloves, finely chopped
3 shallots, finely chopped
¼ cup plus 1 teaspoon Cognac
1 cup dry white wine
1 cup chicken stock, homemade or canned (see chart,
    page 349)
3 teaspoons rosemary, fresh if available
1 tablespoon Dijon mustard
1 teaspoon Glace de Viande (optional; page 352)
1 cup heavy cream
6 sprigs parsley, chopped

1. In a large skillet, heat the oil over high heat. Add
the rabbit pieces and brown lightly, 3 to 4 minutes on each
side. Season with the salt and pepper.

2. Pour off the excess oil and add the onion, garlic, and
shallots to the pan. Reduce the heat to medium and cook
for 2 minutes without browning.

3. Remove the pan from the heat, add the ¼ cup
Cognac, and flame (see instructions for flaming in Bananes
Flambées au Rhum, page 322). When the flames die, add
the wine, stock, and 2 teaspoons of the rosemary. Cover
and simmer until the rabbit is tender, 30 to 40 minutes,
turning the pieces halfway through the cooking.

4. Remove the rabbit pieces to a serving platter and
keep warm. Reduce the liquid in the skillet over high heat
to about ¾ cup, about 10 minutes.

5. Whisk in the mustard and the *glace de viande*. Add the cream and the remaining 1 teaspoon rosemary, and boil the sauce until it thickens enough to lightly coat a spoon. *(The dish can be prepared ahead to this point. Return the rabbit to the sauce, cover, and refrigerate. Before serving, slowly return to a simmer, then remove the meat to a serving platter and proceed.)*

6. **To serve:** Stir the 1 teaspoon Cognac and three-fourths of the chopped parsley into the sauce and pour it over the rabbit. Sprinkle with the remaining parsley.

Variation

Poulet Sauté à la Moutarde et au Romarin *(Sautéed Chicken with Mustard and Rosemary Sauce):* Substitute a 3½-pound chicken cut into serving pieces. Reduce the mustard and rosemary to 2 teaspoons each.

Pigeonneaux aux Olives
Squabs with Olive Sauce

Green olives and dark-meat birds such as squab (and duck) are traditional companions in France. The olives are used not only to flavor the sauce but are treated as an accompaniment to the squab. Blanching them several times to extract salt makes the olives a lovely and delicately flavored vegetable.

Whereas classic recipes for squab with olives cook the birds in the sauce, I have designed this recipe so the sauce can be prepared several days in advance, if desired, and simply reheated for serving.

Making the sauce ahead of time also gives the birds time to age, something I do to improve their

Serving Suggestion: Begin with a shrimp or lobster salad, or Salade d'Endives et Pamplemousse Rose (page 33). Steamed potatoes or rice go well with the sauce. For dessert, serve Gâteau Moka (page 256).

Wine: Both Châteauneuf-du-Pape and Hermitage wines will complement the olive sauce.

BLANCHING

Food is blanched either by adding it to already boiling water, or starting it off in cold water and bringing it to a boil. The latter, cold-water blanching, is used to extract, as in blanching olives or bacon, excess salt. Blanching in boiling water is used to retain flavor, color, and nutrients for such things as herbs or green vegetables. Blanching is also used to loosen the skin of tomatoes, peaches, and almonds, making them easier to peel.

taste. Many people complain that squab has a gamey or livery taste. I have noticed this taste whenever the birds are very fresh, but by allowing them to age for a few days, the strong taste disappears and is replaced by a uniquely delicious flavor. If the birds you have are frozen, defrost them in the refrigerator and let them age 2 to 3 days before roasting. If they are freshly killed, allow them to age 4 days in the refrigerator.

Serves 6

6 squabs (about 1 pound each), rinsed and patted dry
¼ cup olive oil, extra-virgin if available
1 onion, diced
1 small carrot, diced
⅓ cup all-purpose flour
2 cups dry white wine
4 cups beef stock, homemade or canned (see chart, page 348)
3 shallots, sliced
3 garlic cloves, sliced
1 tablespoon tomato paste
Bouquet Garni (page 346)
1 tablespoon Glace de Viande (optional; page 352)
¼ teaspoon freshly ground pepper
¾ pound pitted green olives
6 tablespoons butter
¼ teaspoon salt

1. Remove the squabs' hearts, necks, wing tips, and gizzards and set aside. Truss the birds (see "How to Truss a Bird," page 150).

2. In a medium saucepan, heat the oil over medium-high heat. Add the hearts, necks, wings, and gizzards and brown, 5 to 7 minutes. Add the onion and carrot and brown them lightly, 3 to 4 minutes.

3. Reduce the heat to medium, sprinkle the flour into the pan, and brown well, stirring occasionally, about 4 minutes. By the time the flour is browned, the carrot and onion will be dark brown.

4. Add the wine, stock, shallots, garlic, tomato paste, bouquet garni, *glace de viande*, and the pepper. Simmer the sauce for 1 to 1½ hours, stirring from time to time and skimming off any fat or foam that comes to the surface.

5. Meanwhile, blanch the olives by placing them in a saucepan and covering with cold water. Bring to a boil, drain, and rinse with cold water. Taste the olives. If they are still salty, repeat the procedure until the olives are just slightly salty to the taste.

6. When the sauce is done, it will have a rich brown color and be the consistency of light cream. Strain the sauce through a fine-mesh sieve. Add the olives and simmer, covered, for 10 to 15 minutes. Taste and adjust the seasoning, if necessary. *(The sauce can be made several days in advance. Let cool to room temperature, cover, and refrigerate. Just before serving, bring to a boil.)*

7. Preheat the oven to 475°.

8. Place the birds on their sides in a roasting pan, dot with the butter, and season with the salt and additional pepper to taste. Roast until tender and the juices run clear when the birds are pricked with a roasting fork, about 15 minutes on each side, basting two or three times. Turn the squabs breast side up for an additional 5 to 10 minutes. (I generally roast squabs until thoroughly cooked, yet still moist and tender. Many people enjoy these birds medium-rare, and if this is your preference, reduce the cooking time by 10 minutes.)

9. Using a large fork, lift the squabs to allow the interior juices to drain. Then partially carve them to let juices out further. Place the squabs on individual serving plates, and surround with olives and sauce.

Variations

Pigeonneaux Grillés aux Olives *(Grilled Squabs with Olive Sauce):* Make the olive sauce (steps 2 through 6). Cut the squabs in half and grill them for 5 to 7 minutes on each side. Serve each half on a plate covered with the olives and sauce. Serve the other half as a second serving.

SERVING SMALL BIRDS

When serving a whole small bird with a sauce, it is necessary to carve it part way to let out the excess juices. If this is not done, the plate will fill with these juices and dilute your sauce. If you serve the birds without a sauce, then these juices are desirable. To partially carve the squabs, pass your knife along the body and under the legs and second joints until it reaches the hip joints. Then make one or two slices into each breast. Although I prefer serving small birds whole in this fashion, I realize that some guests will have difficulty in cutting them. The birds can be cut in half for easier serving.

Pigeonneaux Sautés aux Olives *(Sautéed Squabs with Olive Sauce):* Make the olive sauce (steps 2 through 6). Cut the squabs in half and brown in butter or oil, 3 to 4 minutes on each side. When browned, reduce the heat to low and cook, covered, for 15 minutes longer. Serve as above.

Canard aux Olives *(Duck with Olive Sauce):* Make the olive sauce (steps 2 through 6) using the duck hearts, necks, wings, and gizzards. Roast a 5-pound duck at 425° for 30 minutes on each side and 10 minutes breast up. Omit the butter and the basting. When serving duck with olive sauce, a quarter of the duck is served per person and covered with the sauce.

Canard à l'Orange
Duck with Orange Sauce

PRESENTATION OF THE DUCK

A classically prepared *canard à l'orange* is one of the most satisfying and delicious dishes in the French culinary repertoire, yet no one—including most restaurants—seems to have the patience for it anymore.

Admittedly still a fairly time-consuming affair, my version does manage to make things easier. To begin with, I make the sauce a day or more in advance (which has the beneficial side effect of allowing the ducks to age and improve in flavor), and I prepare the sectioned oranges for the accompaniment the night before. I have also shortened the time in the oven by using a high-temperature roasting method, a technique that works well to remove excess fat yet leaves the meat succulent and tender. Finally, to avoid any last-minute scramble, I carve the duck before the guests arrive, and then reheat it briefly in a hot oven just before serving.

Serves 6

2 ducks (about 5 pounds each), rinsed and patted dry
2 tablespoons duck fat (see step 1) or vegetable oil
1 onion, diced
1 small carrot, diced (optional)
3 tablespoons all-purpose flour
¾ cup dry white wine
2 cups beef stock, homemade or canned (see chart,
    page 348)
2 shallots, sliced
2 garlic cloves, sliced
Peeled zest of 1 orange
Bouquet Garni (page 346)
2 teaspoons tomato paste
1 teaspoon Glace de Viande (optional; page 352)
¼ teaspoon salt
⅛ teaspoon freshly ground pepper
2 tablespoons sugar
1 tablespoon water
¼ cup white (distilled) vinegar
2 tablespoons Madeira
1 tablespoon plus a dash Cognac
6 large oranges

1. **Prepare the ducks for roasting:** Cut off the wing tips and set aside with the necks, hearts, and gizzards. Chop the liver and set aside if you would like to use it in the sauce (see step 6). Remove the fat from the tail section and set aside. Truss the ducks (see "How to Truss a Bird," right). *(If you are making the sauce ahead of roasting the ducks, wrap the ducks in plastic wrap and refrigerate.)*

2. Cut the necks, wings, hearts, and gizzards into small pieces. If you do not have a nonstick roasting pan, save the wing tips to use as a makeshift roasting rack (see step 11).

3. In a medium saucepan, heat some of the duck fat over medium heat. Pour out all but about 2 tablespoons of the rendered fat. Add the cut up parts and giblets and cook over medium-high heat until browned, about 5 minutes.

HOW TO TRUSS A BIRD

1. Cut off the wing tips.

2. Push the tail of the bird into the body cavity.

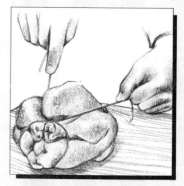

3. Wrap a length of string around the legs and cross over as shown. Bring the string between the legs and breast to the front of the bird.

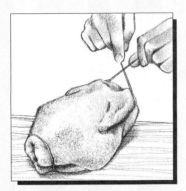

4. Turn the bird breast side down, tie securely across the back in front of the wings.

5. A fully trussed bird.

Add the onion and carrot and cook until lightly browned, about 3 minutes. Reduce the heat to medium, add the flour, and brown well, being careful not to burn the onion, about 3 minutes.

4. Add the wine and stock and bring to a boil, stirring. Reduce the heat to medium-low and add the shallots, garlic, orange zest, bouquet garni, tomato paste, *glace de viande*, salt, and pepper. Simmer until the sauce is thick enough to coat a spoon, 45 minutes to 1 hour, skimming frequently to remove all fat and impurities.

5. **Meanwhile, make the sweet-and-sour caramel flavoring:** In a small heavy saucepan, moisten the sugar with the water. Bring to a boil over high heat and cook, without stirring, until a deep amber color—dark, but not burned. Quickly pour in the vinegar—it will spatter violently for a second—and allow the mixture to boil for a moment. Remove from the heat.

6. When the orange sauce has finished simmering, remove from the heat and stir in the chopped liver, if using. Strain the sauce through a fine-mesh sieve. Taste and adjust the seasoning, if necessary.

7. Add about half of the caramel flavoring to the orange sauce. Taste and add more, if necessary, to offset the bitterness of the orange zest. Stir in the Madeira and the 1 tablespoon Cognac. *(The sauce can be made up to 3 days ahead. Cover with plastic wrap to prevent a skin from forming, and refrigerate. If the sauce was made with the liver, reheat in a water bath* [bain-marie]. *If not, simply bring to a simmer before serving.)*

8. With a vegetable peeler, remove the zest from 2 of the oranges and cut into very fine julienne. In a small saucepan, bring the julienne zest and water to cover to a boil. Drain and reserve the julienne.

9. Peel and section all of the oranges, making sure they are completely free of all membranes (see "How to Section an Orange," page 325). Pour off any juice that collects. *(The oranges can be prepared ahead of time. Cover and refrigerate.)*

10. Preheat the oven to 475°.

11. Prick the ducks all over with a fork to allow the fat to drain during cooking. Place the ducks on their sides in a large roasting pan, preferably nonstick, or rest the duck on the reserved wing tips (see "If You Don't Have a Nonstick Roasting Pan," opposite). Season lightly with salt and pepper. Place the roasting pan in the middle of the oven and roast for 15 minutes.

12. Reduce the heat to 425° and roast for another 15 minutes, then turn the ducks onto their other sides and with a bulb baster remove as much fat from the pan as possible.

13. Continue roasting for another 30 minutes or so (roasting time is about 15 minutes per pound). For the last 5 to 10 minutes of cooking, turn the ducks breast side up for even color. The ducks are done when their cavity juices run clear. Let the ducks sit 10 minutes before carving.

14. Carve the ducks into individual serving pieces and place them on an ovenproof serving platter and let them sit until about 5 minutes before serving time.

15. Preheat the oven to 500°.

16. Add the reserved julienned zest to the sauce and reheat in a water bath (*bain-marie*).

17. When ready to serve, place the duck in the upper third of the oven for 3 to 5 minutes to reheat. Meanwhile, sprinkle the orange sections with a dash of Cognac and warm them in a covered skillet over low heat, 3 to 4 minutes (save any juices that collect to thin the sauce, if necessary).

18. **To serve:** Surround the duck with the orange sections and pass the sauce separately.

Canard Rôti
Roast Duck

Although *canard à l'orange* is probably the best known treatment of duck, its rich, full flavor combines well with the tart-sweetness of many fruits. This is a basic recipe for a simple roast duck—delicious in its own right—to which you can add one of three fruit sauces in the recipes that follow. As with my Canard à l'Orange (page 149), the duck is roasted quickly at high temperature, carved ahead of time, and then reheated before serving.

Serves 6

2 ducks (about 5 pounds each), rinsed and patted dry
2 onions, quartered
1 carrot, thickly sliced
1 stalk celery, cut into 4 pieces
2 shallots, halved
4 sprigs parsley
1 bay leaf
¼ teaspoon thyme
½ teaspoon salt
¼ teaspoon freshly ground pepper
2 cups water or chicken stock (optional; see step 7)

1. Preheat the oven to 475°.

2. **Prepare the ducks for roasting:** Cut off the wing tips and set aside with the necks, hearts, and gizzards. Truss the ducks (see "How to Truss a Bird," page 150). Prick the ducks all over with a fork to allow the fat to drain during cooking. Place the ducks on their sides in a large nonstick roasting pan, or rest them on the reserved wing tips (see "If You Don't Have a Nonstick Roasting Pan," left).

3. Place the necks, giblets, wing tips (if not already under the duck), vegetables, and herbs around the duck. Sprinkle all with the salt and pepper. Place the roasting pan in the middle of the oven and roast for 15 minutes.

4. Reduce the heat to 425° and roast for another 15 minutes, then turn the ducks onto their other sides and with a bulb baster remove as much fat from the pan as possible.

5. Continue cooking for another 30 minutes or so (roasting time is about 15 minutes per pound), and for the last 5 to 10 minutes of cooking, turn the ducks breast side

Serving Suggestion: To start, serve a mixed green salad. With the duck, serve a potato and a green vegetable. For dessert, serve chocolate mousse (Mousse au Chocolat, page 315).

Wine: Dry red.

IF YOU DON'T HAVE A NONSTICK ROASTING PAN

If you don't have a nonstick roasting pan, cut each wing at the first joint from the body. Cut the resulting portions at the joint, yielding 4 three-inch pieces. Place the pieces down the middle of the roasting pan, about 2 inches apart, to form a rack for the duck to rest on.

up, for even color. The ducks are done when their cavity juices run clear.

6. At this point, if you are preparing one of the ducks with fruit, follow the instructions in the appropriate recipe.

7. If, however, you are serving a plain roast duck, let it sit for 10 to 20 minutes before carving while you make a simple pan juice. Pour the fat from the roasting pan, retaining the vegetables and duck parts in the pan. Place the pan over high heat, add 2 cups of water or stock, and bring to a boil, then reduce the heat and simmer for 10 minutes, stirring the vegetables from time to time.

8. Strain the liquid into a small saucepan, discarding the solids. Over high heat, cook until reduced to 1 cup, about 10 minutes. Skim off any remaining fat.

Canard au Cidre
Duck with Apples and Cider

Inspired by a wonderful dish I had years ago at the restaurant Taillevent in Paris, this duck is accented by apples in numerous forms, from a garniture of apples flamed with Calvados (apple brandy) to the French apple cider used in the sauce. Unlike American cider, French apple cider—which along with Calvados comes from Normandy—is sparkling and mildly alcoholic and comes both sweet and dry (for cooking, use the dry variety). Although it is imported to this country, it is not always easy to find, so substitute a good apple juice or cider. If you *can* get French apple cider, buy some to serve with the duck; failing that, serve either Champagne or a fine red Bordeaux.

Serves 6

Serving Suggestion: As with most duck presentations, I serve wild rice or a combination of wild rice and mushrooms (Riz Sauvage Forestière, page 236) followed by a green salad. For dessert, serve Gâteau Chocolat au Grand Marnier (page 254).

Wine: If in Normandy, I might order an excellent dry cider to drink, but at home I serve either Champagne or a fine red Bordeaux.

PROFESSIONAL TEST FOR DONENESS

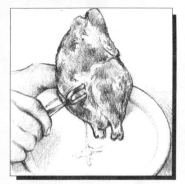

The professional way of judging the doneness of poultry is to collect the last couple of drops of cavity juices on a white plate to see if they are running clear. To pour the cavity juices out, pick up the duck by inserting a roasting fork—a French roasting fork works best—between the leg and breast and into the backbone.

Canard Rôti (page 152)
6 large Golden Delicious apples
1 cup dry white wine
2 cups dry French or American apple cider
1 teaspoon Glace de Viande (optional; page 352)
¾ cup heavy cream
4 to 5 drops white (distilled) vinegar (optional)
2 tablespoons butter
1 tablespoon sugar
¼ cup Calvados, applejack, or Cognac

1. Roast the ducks as per the Canard Rôti recipe.
2. While the ducks are roasting, peel, core, and slice the apples ¼ inch thick. As you work, place the apples in a large skillet and moisten them with the wine to prevent discoloration. Add any remaining wine to the apples in the skillet.
3. Cover the pan and poach the apples over medium heat until tender but not soft, 5 to 7 minutes. Drain the apples, reserving the poaching liquid. Set both aside.
4. When the ducks are done, place them on a carving board. *(If the ducks are cooked several hours in advance of serving, allow them to cool completely before carving.)* Pour the fat from the roasting pan, retaining the vegetables and duck parts in the pan. Place the pan over high heat, add the cider, the reserved apple poaching liquid, and the *glace de viande*. Bring to a boil, reduce the heat, and simmer for 10 minutes, stirring the vegetables from time to time.
5. Strain the liquid through a fine-mesh sieve into a small saucepan, discarding the solids. Over high heat, cook until reduced to 1 cup, about 10 minutes. Skim off any remaining fat. Add the cream and boil to thicken the sauce enough to lightly coat a spoon. Taste the sauce; if it is too sweet, add the vinegar, a drop at a time, to taste. *(The sauce can be made several hours ahead. Cover with plastic wrap to prevent a skin from forming. Remove the wrap and gently reheat before proceeding.)*
6. Preheat the oven to 500°.
7. Carve the ducks into individual serving pieces and

place in a roasting pan or on an ovenproof platter. Place
the platter in the upper third of the oven for 3 to 5 minutes
to reheat the duck.

8. **To serve:** In a skillet, reheat the apples with the
butter and sugar. Remove the pan from the heat, add the
Calvados, and flame (see flaming instructions in Bananes
Flambées au Rhum, page 322).

9. Place the apples on the platter with the duck. Serve
the sauce separately.

Canard aux Pêches
Roast Duck with Peaches

Fresh fruit in season is really the only choice here.
If you're inspired to roast a duck in early summer,
make it with cherries (see Variation, below). If it's mid
to late summer, make the duck with peaches—white
peaches, if you can get them.

Serves 6

Canard Rôti (page 152)
12 peaches
1 cup dry white wine
2 cups beef stock, homemade or canned (see chart, page 348)
2 teaspoons Glace de Viande (optional; page 352)
*2 teaspoons arrowroot, potato starch, or cornstarch, dissolved
    in 2 teaspoons cold water*
2 tablespoons butter
1 to 2 tablespoons sugar, to taste
¼ cup Cognac

1. Roast the ducks as per the Canard Rôti recipe.
2. While the ducks are roasting, peel, pit, and slice
the peaches and place them in a skillet. Moisten them with

Serving Suggestion: Start with
seafood salad. Accompany
the duck with wild rice or
fried potatoes. Finish with
sorbet and cookies (Tuiles
aux Amandes, page 282).

Wine: Either red Burgundy
or Bordeaux.

DOUBLE-MESH SIEVE

Whenever a sauce requires straining, a very fine strainer is used to obtain as smooth a sauce as possible. Classically, and in professional kitchens, a conical strainer, known as a *chinois* or China cap, is used. Recently, a double-mesh sieve, actually a larger version of a tea strainer, has appeared on the market. If a double-mesh strainer is not available, I use as fine a strainer as I have at hand and line it with cheesecloth if some is convenient.

the wine to prevent discoloration. Add any remaining wine to the peaches in the skillet.

3. Cover and poach the peaches over medium heat until tender, 3 to 5 minutes. Immediately drain the peaches, reserving the poaching liquid. Set both aside.

4. When the ducks are done, place them on a carving board. *(If the ducks are cooked several hours in advance of serving, allow them to cool completely before carving.)* Pour the fat from the roasting pan, retaining the vegetables and duck parts in the pan. Place the pan over high heat and add the reserved poaching liquid, the stock, and *glace de viande*. Bring to a boil and reduce the heat. Simmer 10 minutes, stirring the vegetables from time to time.

5. Strain the liquid through a fine-mesh sieve into a small saucepan, discarding the solids. Over high heat, cook until reduced to 1½ cups, 8 to 10 minutes. Skim off any fat that comes to the surface. Thicken with the dissolved arrowroot. The sauce should lightly coat a spoon. If too thick, add 1 to 2 tablespoons water to thin.

6. Preheat the oven to 500°.

7. Carve the ducks into individual serving pieces and place in a roasting pan or on an ovenproof platter. Place the platter in the upper third of the oven for 3 to 5 minutes to reheat the duck.

8. **To serve:** In a skillet, reheat the peaches with the butter and sugar. Remove the pan from the heat, add the Cognac and flame (see flaming instructions in Bananes Flambées au Rhum, page 322). Place the peaches on the platter with the duck. Serve the sauce separately.

Variation

Canard aux Cerises *(Roast Duck with Cherries):* Substitute 1½ pounds cherries, pitted, for the peaches. Omit the sugar. Use ¼ cup kirsch in place of the Cognac. Do not poach the cherries, but add the white wine to the roasting pan in step 4. In step 5, add the cherries and kirsch to the sauce. To serve, spoon the cherries and the sauce over the duck.

Meat

Traditionally, meat prepared for roasting and braising in France is wrapped in a thin sheet of pork fat that is intended to keep it moist while cooking. Lean roasts are often larded (strips of pork fat are woven into the roast) to add interior fat for moisture and flavor. Although the exterior fat is often removed before serving, the interior fat remains to be eaten. In America, the fat is left on the meat for the same reasons.

The fat, although flavorful in itself, adds little to the flavor of the meat. I find that a combination of the animal's diet, proper aging, and the interior fat, in combination with the final cooking is what determines its flavor.

Therefore, for most cuts of meat, I remove as much exterior fat as possible before cooking. If I want to take advantage of any flavor the fat might have, I will use some of it together with, or in place of, butter or oil to baste or sauté the meat.

Steak au Poivre
Pepper-Coated Steak with Cognac and Cream

A *steak au poivre* is a thick slice of beef coated with cracked pepper, pan fried, and flamed with Cognac. It is served rare to medium-rare with a cream sauce, potato, and watercress. Although there are many variations on this classic preparation, most of which include the use of a brown sauce and various other ingredients, none equal the flavor created by the combination of steak, pepper, Cognac, and cream.

The only updating necessary for this French bistro classic is the careful removal of all exterior fat. If the butcher has not already done so, make sure that, when you trim the fat, your knife passes under the fat as well as the membrane lying next to the muscle, so that only red meat is visible when finished. By doing this, you avoid eating unnecessary fat.

Any good individual beef steak can be used for this recipe, but I prefer boneless shell or strip steak, and my second choice is a boneless sirloin. Both cuts have excellent flavor and texture. Allow the meat to come to room temperature, 1 to 2 hours, before sautéing.

When cooking the steaks, it is important to have enough oil in your pan to fry the pepper as well as the meat. If not fried, the amount of pepper used will be too hot to eat. Start with just enough oil to coat the bottom of your pan (this is sufficient for sautéing the steak) and then add another tablespoon of oil (this is for frying the pepper).

Serves 4

¼ cup black peppercorns*

4 boneless shell, strip, or sirloin steaks, 1¼ inches thick,
    completely trimmed

2 to 3 tablespoons vegetable oil

¼ teaspoon salt

¼ cup plus 1 teaspoon Cognac

¾ cup heavy cream

1 bunch watercress, stems removed

1. Crush the peppercorns, a few at a time, using the bottom of a heavy saucepan (see "Cracking Pepper," below).

2. Place the steaks on the crushed pepper to coat both sides.

3. Cover the bottom of a skillet with a thin layer of oil and heat over medium-high heat. Add the steaks and sauté them until rare or medium-rare, 4 to 5 minutes on each side. Season the steaks with the salt and remove them from the pan. Discard the oil.

4. Return the steaks to the pan and remove the pan from the heat. Add the ¼ cup Cognac, and flame (see flaming instructions in Bananes Flambées au Rhum, page 322). When the flames die, remove the steaks to a serving platter or individual plates and keep warm.

5. Add the cream to the pan and bring to a boil over high heat, stirring until the cream has thickened enough to coat a spoon. Stir in the teaspoon of Cognac and salt to taste. Spoon the sauce over the steaks and serve with watercress.

* If it is your first time eating a pepper steak, you may want to use commercially cracked pepper, or scrape some of the pepper off before serving it. Once you become a *steak au poivre* lover, you will find yourself seeking pepper in spice stores in search of the ultimate aroma.

CRACKING PEPPER

Cracking pepper is easy if you use a heavy-bottomed saucepan as a lever. Crush 8 to 10 peppercorns at a time, placing them under the portion of the pan nearest the handle. Holding the pan down at the opposite end, use the handle to press down on the peppercorns to crush them. A coffee grinder also works well, but if you are not careful you will have a very "hot" cup of coffee in the morning. Most other machines (such as food processors and blenders) create partially crushed and partially powdered pepper.

Côte de Boeuf Grillée
Grilled Rib Steak

**Serving Suggestion: With
grilled beef, I generally
serve Ratatouille Niçoise
(page 218) and new pota-
toes steamed in their skins
and tossed in a little chive
butter. I often accompany
the meat with a Sauce
Béarnaise (page 374).**

**Wine: A full-bodied red is
always enjoyable with this
meal.**

The American or English rib roast does not exist
in France. Instead of roasting three or more ribs
together, the French cut them into individual ribs and
sauté or grill them to serve two people.

There is no better way to cook a steak than on a
grill. I can remember 20 years ago that a steak charred
black on the outside and pink on the inside was considered perfection. I also remember pouring water
onto a fire to douse the flames that were engulfing the
steak. To prevent this from happening, I now remove
all the fat before cooking. By eliminating the exterior
fat, you prevent flare-ups and avoid the consumption of
unnecessary fat.

There is a considerable amount of fat on the rib,
and it is always a challenge to remove as much as possible without losing the shape of the steak. It is equally
important that the bone be trimmed of fat.

Serves 6

*3 rib steaks with bone, each 1½ inches thick
Salt and freshly ground pepper, to taste
1 bunch watercress, stems removed, for garnish*

1. Trim as much of the fat from the steaks as possible
and let them come to room temperature, 1 to 2 hours,
before cooking.

2. Place the steaks on a very hot grill close to the coals.
Cook the steaks 4 to 5 minutes per side with the lid down.
Halfway through the cooking on each side, lift and rotate
the meat 90 degrees, to enhance both the flavor and appearance. Once the meat has been turned, salt and pepper the
first side. Check the firmness of the meat from time to time,

noticing the changes that occur. Medium-rare is springy to the touch and well done is firm. If after the meat has been turned you see juices beginning to pool or come to the surface, you have reached medium-rare and are approaching medium. Remove from the heat immediately.

3. Bring the steaks to the table on a large carving board surrounded by the watercress. At the table, bone the steak and slice it thinly across its width on the diagonal to form broad slices.

GRILLING BEEF

Although most cuts of well-aged beef are good on the grill, my favorites are strip or shell steaks, whole fillets of beef, and rib steaks. I watch for sales of these cuts. When I find a good price on a shell or strip roast, I have the "tail" ground for hamburger and the rest completely trimmed of fat and cut into steaks. When buying fillet I have the long wide tendon or "silverskin" removed as well as all the fat. It should then be tied to form an evenly cylindrical roast, which will cook in 15 to 20 minutes on a very hot grill. A standing two- or three-rib roast of beef can be cut into two or three individual steaks, each one enough to serve two or three people.

A good piece of beef should be cooked rare or medium-rare for you to enjoy its flavor and tenderness. The most difficult part of grilling a steak is to cook the meat evenly. Often the meat is well done on the outside, and raw at the center. To avoid this, always have the meat at room temperature, and grill steaks that are not too thick. Thickness is more important than weight. Ideal thickness, I have found, is 1¼ to 1½ inches.

CAST-IRON GRILL PAN

If you do not have access to a grill, do not despair. Most foods (including grilled steak) can be just as easily prepared on the stovetop using a cast-iron grill pan. These pans are either round or square and can be flat like a griddle or have sides like a skillet. What they all have in common are the ridges on the bottom that resemble a grill top.

Tournedos Charlemagne
Fillet Steaks with Mushrooms and Béarnaise Sauce

The combination of beef, mushrooms, and *sauce béarnaise* is a treat for any steak lover. This is my adaptation of the classic *filet de boeuf Charlemagne*, in which the fillet of beef is roasted, then sliced and reconstructed with a layer of cooked shallots and mushrooms (*duxelles*) between the slices. Just before serving, the roast is reheated and coated with the *sauce béarnaise*. This classic presentation is only for experienced cooks, while the following recipe is for everyone. It can easily serve six with the addition of two more steaks. All accompaniments should be ready to serve before cooking the fillet steaks.

Serves 4

2 tablespoons butter
4 large shallots or 1 onion, finely chopped
¾ pound mushrooms, washed, dried, and finely chopped
Salt and freshly ground pepper, to taste
1 teaspoon tomato paste
Sauce Béarnaise (page 374)
1 tablespoon vegetable oil
4 fillet steaks, cut 1 to 1¼ inches thick
1 bunch watercress, stems removed, for garnish

1. In a skillet, heat the butter over medium heat. Add the shallots and sauté until softened, 3 to 4 minutes. Add the mushrooms and sauté over high heat, stirring occasionally, until most of the moisture has evaporated, about 5 minutes. Season with salt and pepper. Remove from the heat and stir in the tomato paste.

2. Make the *sauce béarnaise* and keep warm in a water

Serving Suggestion: Sautéed or roasted potatoes are excellent with the steaks and can be reheated when the mushroom mixture is reheated. Follow with a mixed green salad.

Wine: A good red Bordeaux will complement these steaks well.

bath (*bain-marie*) while you sauté the steaks.

3. In a 10-inch skillet, heat the oil over medium-high heat. Add the fillet steaks and sauté until rare or medium-rare, 2 to 3 minutes each side. Season with salt and pepper. Place the steaks on a serving platter or plates.

4. **To serve:** Cover each fillet with a layer of the warm mushroom mixture and coat with *sauce béarnaise*. Garnish with the watercress.

Filet de Boeuf Rôti
Roasted Fillet of Beef

This very elegant cut of meat is perfect for entertaining: it cooks quickly, slices easily, goes well with a variety of sauces, but is also excellent by itself. However, because it is relatively thin and cooks quickly, it can be difficult to brown (unless cooked on a grill). In my method I put the roasting pan in the oven for 10 minutes before putting the roast in. This way, the roast enters a hot pan and starts to cook immediately.

In France, a *filet de boeuf* would be wrapped in a sheet of pork fat (called a bard), but I omit it. I also trim off all the fat from the fillet.

Fillets are tender and are served rare or medium-rare to retain their juices. Although a sauce is not necessary, the Béarnaise (page 374), Bordelaise (page 366), and Madeira (page 365) sauces all complement the beef and create an elegant presentation.

Serves 8 to 10

1 beef fillet (7 to 8 pounds untrimmed, 4 to 5 pounds well trimmed), tied every 2 inches for roasting (ask the butcher to do this)

Serving Suggestion: Start with a seafood salad. With the fillet, serve carrots (Carottes à l'Etuvée, page 202), cauliflower (Purée de Chou-Fleur, page 204) and buttered peas. For dessert, serve Gâteau Chocolat au Grand Marnier (page 254). A *filet de boeuf rôti* is also delicious served cold with a Sauce Raifort (page 383).

Wine: Red Bordeaux.

2 tablespoons vegetable oil or melted butter
1 carrot, cut into ¼-inch slices
1 onion, halved and cut into ¼-inch slices
2 cups beef stock, homemade or canned (see chart, page 348)
⅛ teaspoon salt
⅛ teaspoon freshly ground pepper
Sauce of choice (see above; optional)

1. Preheat the oven to 475°.

2. Lightly coat the meat and a roasting pan with the oil. Place the sliced vegetables in the pan and heat in the preheated oven for 10 minutes, or until the vegetables start to sauté.

3. Add the fillet to the pan and roast for a total of 25 to 30 minutes for medium-rare. Turn the roast every 6 to 7 minutes to brown it evenly. The roast should be springy to the touch when done.

4. Transfer the roast to a carving board, and deglaze the pan and vegetables by adding the stock and stirring to loosen the caramelized bits on the bottom and sides of the pan. Boil to reduce by half and strain; discard the vegetables. Season the roast with salt and pepper.

5. **To serve:** Cut the fillet into slices about ¼ inch thick and serve with a little of the pan juices, or your favorite sauce.

Poitrine de Boeuf Braisée au Gingembre et Coriandre
Braised Brisket with Ginger and Coriander

This recipe is a wonderful example of how ingredients not normally associated with classic French cooking can be used to bring new life to a traditional dish.

I really should call this recipe Boeuf Braisé Deborah, for it was created on the evening my wife gave birth to our second daughter, Deborah. One of the nurses who attended my wife was from the British West Indies, and a food enthusiast. When she found out my profession, she asked me for my chocolate mousse recipe. In return she gave me her favorite recipe, chicken cooked with fresh ginger, garlic, tomatoes, fresh coriander, and hot pepper.

When I returned home, I took out the brisket of beef I had in the refrigerator and started to prepare a classic braised beef. Finding a piece of ginger in the vegetable drawer, I thought of the nurse's chicken recipe. Although I did not have fresh coriander, I did have coriander powder and dried hot peppers. My older daughter, Jennifer, and my gourmet mother-in-law were both so pleased with the results that I have been teaching this recipe ever since.

Serves 6 to 8

3 tablespoons vegetable oil
3 to 4 pounds breast of beef (first-cut brisket)
2 onions, halved and thickly sliced
4 large carrots, thickly sliced on the diagonal
3 tablespoons all-purpose flour
2 garlic cloves, chopped
2 shallots, chopped
1 inch fresh ginger, sliced, or more to taste
2 cups dry red wine
1½ cups beef stock, homemade or canned (see chart, page 348)
2 teaspoons ground coriander
2 teaspoons tomato paste
1 to 2 dried red chili peppers (optional), to taste
Bouquet Garni (page 346)
⅛ teaspoon salt
⅛ teaspoon freshly ground pepper
12 to 16 small new potatoes, peeled

Serving Suggestion: Start with a salad of endives and pink grapefruit (Salade d'Endives et Pamplemousse Rose, page 33). For dessert, serve a Crème Renversée au Caramel (page 307).

Wine: Dry red.

1. In a flameproof casserole or large Dutch oven, heat the oil over high heat. Add the meat when the oil is hot and brown it, about 3 minutes on each side. Remove the meat.

2. Add the onions and carrots and cook over high heat until they are lightly browned, about 10 minutes.

3. Add the flour and cook, stirring occasionally, over medium heat until browned, 3 to 5 minutes.

4. Add the garlic, shallots, and ginger, and stir for 10 seconds before adding all of the remaining ingredients except for the potatoes.

5. Return the meat to the casserole, cover, and simmer over medium-low heat until tender, 2½ to 3 hours. This can be done on top of the stove or in a 300° to 350° oven.

6. Add the potatoes during the last hour of cooking. If your casserole is too small to hold them, boil or steam them separately.

7. When the meat is tender, discard the bouquet garni. Reserving all of the cooked vegetables, strain the cooking liquid, which has thickened to form a sauce, through a fine-mesh sieve. Skim to remove all fat. *(This recipe can be prepared up to this point in advance. Reheat the meat and vegetables before serving.)*

8. Slice the brisket and serve it with the potatoes and vegetables. Spoon some of the sauce over all and serve the remaining sauce separately.

Variations

Boeuf Braisé *(Braised Beef):* Omit the ginger, coriander, and chili peppers and you have my basic braised beef recipe.

Boeuf Braisé à l'Hongroise *(Braised Beef with Onions and Paprika):* Use the basic Boeuf Braisé (above) and omit the carrot, add another onion and 1 tablespoon of paprika.

Boeuf Braisé à l'Alsacienne *(Braised Beef with Cabbage and Juniper):* Omit the coriander and chili pepper. In place of the ginger, use 15 juniper berries. Add a whole head of cabbage cut into wedges at the same time as the potatoes in step 6.

Boeuf Bourguignon
Burgundy-Style Beef Stew

On a winter night, or after a full day of skiing, nothing is quite as satisfying as a hearty *boeuf bourguignon*. In France this ragoût is made with fresh unsmoked bacon, which is hard to find in most American markets. I use smoked bacon and remove the excess salt and smoky flavor by blanching it twice. The delicate smoky taste that is left creates additional character not found in the original recipe, giving this version a sauce that is fuller and more robust.

Traditionally, *boeuf bourguignon* is made with a local, full-bodied Burgundy made from the Pinot Noir grape. Use any similar imported or domestic wine.

Serving Suggestion: Start with artichokes vinaigrette and serve lime mousse (Mousse au Citron Vert, page 317) for dessert.

Wine: Pinot Noir or red Burgundy.

Serves 6

¼ cup vegetable oil
3 pounds beef chuck (see Note), trimmed, cut into 1½- to
    2-inch cubes, and patted dry on paper towels
1 onion, diced
1 small carrot, diced
⅓ cup all-purpose flour
¼ cup Cognac (optional)
3 cups dry red wine
1½ cups beef stock, homemade or canned (see chart,
    page 348)
2 shallots, sliced
4 garlic cloves, sliced
1 tablespoon tomato paste
1 teaspoon Glace de Viande (optional; page 352)
Bouquet Garni (page 346)
½ teaspoon salt
¼ teaspoon freshly ground pepper

Note: Although in most of my cooking, and in nearly every meat dish, I seek ways of reducing or omitting unnecessary fat, this is a place where the fat in the meat is absolutely necessary. Chuck, which is the meat called for here, is layered with fat, which essentially bastes the meat from the inside as it cooks. Many people make the mistake of substituting beef round for the chuck because it contains less fat. I advise against doing so.

24 pearl onions, peeled, root end trimmed but left intact to
    hold the onions together
12 to 18 new potatoes, peeled
1 pound smoked slab bacon, rind removed, cut into
    ½-inch rectangles
¾ pound mushrooms, washed, dried, and halved or
    quartered to match the size of the onions
6 sprigs parsley, chopped, for garnish

1. In a large flameproof casserole, heat the oil over high heat. When the oil begins to smoke, add the beef cubes and brown well on all sides, turning the pieces only after they have browned, about 7 minutes. This can be done in two batches if your casserole cannot hold the meat in one layer. Add the onion and carrot to the casserole, reduce the heat to medium-high, and brown the vegetables lightly, about 3 minutes.

2. Sprinkle the flour over the meat and vegetables and cook over medium heat, stirring occasionally, until evenly browned, about 5 minutes.

3. Remove the casserole from the heat, add the Cognac, and flame (see flaming instructions in Bananes Flambées au Rhum, page 322). When the flames die, add the wine, stock, shallots, garlic, tomato paste, *glace de viande*, bouquet garni, salt, and pepper. Cover, reduce the heat to medium-low, and simmer, occasionally skimming off the fat or foam that rises to the top, until the beef is tender, about 1½ hours. The cooking time will vary depending on the cut and aging of the meat. It might take as long as 2½ to 3 hours. To test for doneness, stick one prong of a roasting fork into a piece of the meat and lift it from the casserole. If the meat clings to the fork, it needs more cooking. If it drops from the fork, it is tender and ready to serve. *(The recipe can be prepared to this point in advance. Let cool to room temperature, cover, and refrigerate or freeze.)*

4. Meanwhile, drop the pearl onions into a large saucepan of boiling water and cook until tender, about 10 minutes; drain well.

5. Boil or steam the potatoes until tender, about 20 minutes. Drain.

6. Place the bacon in a small saucepan and cover with cold water. Bring to a boil, drain, and rinse under cold running water. Repeat this process one more time and drain well.

7. In a 12-inch skillet, sauté the bacon until it is crisp on the outside, yet soft on the inside, about 5 minutes. Drain on paper towels.

8. Remove all but about 2 tablespoons of fat from the skillet, add the mushrooms, and sauté over high heat until browned, 3 to 5 minutes. Season with salt and pepper to taste and remove the mushrooms to a bowl.

9. Add the boiled onions to the pan and sauté until browned, about 5 minutes.

10. When the beef is tender, remove it with a skimmer or slotted spoon and place it in an attractive oven-to-table casserole. Add the onions, mushrooms, and bacon.

11. Remove any fat from the surface of the cooking liquid. If the sauce is too thick, add a little water; if too thin, boil it to reduce and thicken. The sauce should be the consistency of heavy cream. Adjust the seasoning of the sauce and strain it over the meat and vegetables. *(The stew can be prepared up to 2 days in advance. As with all ragoûts, the flavor actually improves if made at least 1 day in advance. Let cool, cover, and refrigerate. Before serving, reheat the ragoût and simmer for 5 minutes.)* Sprinkle with chopped parsley and serve.

COMPLETELY TRIMMED RACK OF LAMB

A rack of lamb contains 6 to 8 chops, and when found in a supermarket, will have bones ranging

Carré d'Agneau Vert Pré
Rack of Lamb with Watercress

The name of this superb French dish comes from its presentation. The lamb is surrounded by watercress as if it were in a green *(vert)* prairie *(pré)*.

Rack of lamb is not only one of the most delect-

from 3 to 4 inches in length. It is usually covered by a thick layer of fat. Although the backbone or chine bone of the chops will have been cut through with a band saw to facilitate carving, they will still be attached. When roasted as is, the rack will leave large unattractive bones and quantities of fat on the diners' plates.

To make the cooking easy and to improve the presentation, I ask the butcher to cut the rib bones 2 inches from the eye, and to remove the chine and feather bones. I also have all visible fat removed, leaving only the eye of the chop. If there is still fat on the rack when you get it home (butchers are often reluctant to trim *all* the fat off, because it makes it look like you're not getting enough for your money), you can remove the rest yourself by peeling away the fat covering the meat. Once you have uncovered the eye of the rack, use a knife to slice the fat away from the bones. You will find that you have removed a small piece of meat that is embedded in the fat, and you can trim this and reserve it for later use in a lamb stew.

able cuts of lamb, it is also an expensive and, to some, intimidating one. Even though they have probably cooked lamb rib chops (which before they are cut apart comprise a rack), most people will rarely make a rack of lamb at home, thinking of it as a restaurant specialty. However, not only is it not hard to make, it is a good deal less expensive at home.

Since the racks cook quickly, have your vegetable dishes ready to reheat, and roast the racks while eating your first course.

Serves 4 to 6

2 racks of lamb (8 chops each), completely trimmed (see "Completely Trimmed Rack of Lamb," page 170)
1 teaspoon thyme
½ teaspoon rosemary
¼ teaspoon salt
⅛ teaspoon freshly ground pepper
1 bunch watercress, stems removed

1. Preheat the oven to 475°.

2. Season both sides of the racks with the herbs, salt, and pepper, and place in a roasting pan bone side down. (If seasoning in advance, do not salt until just before roasting.)

3. Place in the oven and lower the temperature to 400°. Depending on their size, the racks will take 20 to 30 minutes to cook to medium-rare. When done, they will be springy to the touch.

4. **To serve:** Transfer the lamb to a serving platter or carving board and surround with watercress. Slice into individual chops by cutting between the bones, and serve 2 to 3 chops per person.

Variation

Carré d'Agneau Vert Pré Sauce Béarnaise ou Choron (*Rack of Lamb with Béarnaise or Choron Sauce*): Omit the herbs and serve with Sauce Béarnaise (page 374) or Sauce Choron (page 376).

Navarin d'Agneau
French Lamb Stew

An Irish stew is perhaps the best-known lamb ragoût in the world, but a *navarin d'agneau* is the best-tasting one.

I have taught this recipe in many cities throughout the country, and often have had students tell me that at least one member of their family doesn't eat lamb. They check the recipe further and find the turnips. Now matters are much worse, for no one in their family eats turnips! Can the turnips be left out? Not if the stew is to be a *navarin*.

Luckily, my students go home, follow the recipe, and re-create what they had in class. The reports I get back are not only that the *navarin* was a success, but that "they even wanted more turnips." If you are among those who do not like lamb or turnips, be encouraged that you are in for a tasty surprise.

As with any stew, this not only can be made ahead of time, but it improves with age.

Serving Suggestion: When serving *navarin d'agneau*, I often start with a seafood salad and finish with a pastry like Choux Soufflés au Chocolat (page 272).

Wine: Red Bordeaux.

Serves 6

4 tablespoons vegetable oil
2½ pounds boned shoulder of lamb (see Note), trimmed
    and cut into 1½-inch cubes
¼ cup all-purpose flour
3 cups beef stock, homemade or canned (see chart, page 348)
1 cup dry white wine
1 tablespoon tomato paste
3 garlic cloves, finely chopped
Bouquet Garni (page 346)
½ teaspoon salt
¼ teaspoon freshly ground pepper

Note: As in *boeuf bourguignon*, this is one place where using a leaner cut of meat will detract from the recipe. The lamb shoulder's fat content will produce moist and tender meat. Your butcher may suggest boned leg of lamb instead, but you should insist on the shoulder.

TURNING VEGETABLES

In much of French cooking, vegetables are "turned" (pared into uniform foot-ball or olive shapes) to add to the attractiveness of a dish. In France the vege-tables in a *navarin d'agneau* or other ragoûts would be turned, but it's not worth doing unless you think your guests will appreciate it. To turn large root vegetables (potatoes, turnips, carrots) first cut them into chunks, then trim them to an olive shape with a paring knife.

4 large carrots, cut into 1-inch pieces
18 pearl onions, peeled, root end trimmed but left intact to hold the onions together
3 small to medium white turnips, peeled and quartered
18 small new potatoes, peeled
Chopped parsley, for garnish

1. In a large flameproof casserole, heat 3 tablespoons of the oil over high heat until it begins to smoke. Add the cubes of lamb and brown well on all sides, turning the pieces only after they have browned. If your casserole is not large enough to hold the lamb in one layer, this can be done in two batches.

2. Sprinkle the flour over the meat and brown over medium heat, 3 to 5 minutes.

3. Add the stock, wine, tomato paste, garlic, and bou-quet garni. Stir with a wooden spoon. Season with the salt and pepper. Bring to a boil, then reduce the heat to medium-low, cover, and simmer.

4. Meanwhile, in a 10- to 12-inch skillet, heat the remaining 1 tablespoon oil over high heat. Add the carrots and brown, shaking the skillet frequently. Remove the car-rots and set aside. Next, brown the pearl onions and tur-nips in the same skillet.

5. After the lamb has been simmering for 30 minutes, add the browned carrots. After another 15 minutes, add the onions and turnips. Check both meat and vegetables for tenderness from time to time, and if one of the vege-tables is fully cooked before the rest, remove it to prevent overcooking. While everything is gently cooking, skim off all the fat and impurities that come to the surface. Total cooking time will be about 1½ hours. *(The stew can be made several days ahead to this point. Remove the bouquet garni. Let cool to room temperature, cover, and refrigerate or freeze. Bring slowly back to a simmer while you cook the potatoes; see next step.)*

6. Boil or steam the potatoes until they are tender, about 20 minutes. (If boiled, drain them.) Add them to the casserole when all ingredients are tender, and cook 5 min-utes longer.

7. Skim any fat remaining on the sauce, and remove the bouquet garni. Transfer the stew to a hot serving dish and sprinkle with chopped parsley just before serving.

Variation

Navarin Printanier *(French Lamb Stew with Spring Vegetables):* This version of a *navarin* takes its name from the spring-time (*printanier*) vegetables that are added to it. In step 6, along with the cooked potatoes, add about ½ pound cooked peas and ¼ pound cooked green beans.

Gigot d'Agneau Rôti
Roast Leg of Lamb

A leg of lamb is a luxury in France, and most families reserve it for special gatherings and Sunday lunches. Simply roasted with garlic and herbs, it is most often served with fresh green beans in spring and summer, and one of a variety of dried beans, such as *flageolets* (pale green kidney beans), in the winter. Potatoes are often roasted in the pan with the lamb.

If you have ever roasted a leg of lamb, you will discover that I do a number of things differently. First, I have the butcher cut out the "H" (also known as the "aitch") or hip bone (see "French-Style Leg of Lamb," page 175), which makes the leg easier to carve. Second, as with most meat, I remove as much fat as possible. (Normally, and especially in France, a leg of lamb is roasted with a layer of fat covering it.)

In this recipe, as in many leg of lamb recipes, garlic is imbedded in the meat before roasting. Most cooks will make random slits in the meat and insert the gar-

Serving Suggestion: Serve with glazed garlic (Ail Glacé, page 206) and green beans (Haricots Verts, page 207) or white beans with garlic and tomato (Haricots à la Bretonne, page 209).

Wine: Good dry red.

FRENCH-STYLE LEG OF LAMB

A leg of lamb is cut differently in France than in America. A French leg ends at the hip, whereas the American leg contains a part of the hip or sirloin. The shank bone on a French leg is left intact and serves as a handle, which you use to turn the leg while cooking and to hold while carving. Some American butchers crack or break this shank bone and fold it back against the leg, or cut it off.

To get a French-style leg, ask your butcher to leave the shank bone intact and uncut. Have him remove the "H" or hip bone. Once removed, you will see the ball joint of the leg. The meat will now extend beyond the ball joint, and should be cut off to form a well-shaped leg. Freeze this meat for future use.

lic slices. When eating the lamb, a diner often gets a bite that is more garlic than lamb. To avoid this, I place the slices of garlic near the bone along its length and at both ends of the leg. In this way the leg is lightly scented with garlic without being objectionably strong.

Serves 6

1 leg of lamb (see "French-Style Leg of Lamb," left)
(6 to 7½ pounds untrimmed or 4 to 5 pounds trimmed)
2 garlic cloves, sliced
1 tablespoon light olive oil
2 teaspoons thyme
1 teaspoon rosemary
⅛ teaspoon salt
⅛ teaspoon freshly ground pepper

1. Preheat the oven to 475°.
2. Make several small deep incisions into the leg of lamb along the length of the bone. Insert the garlic slices, placing them as close to the bone as possible. Rub the leg with the oil and sprinkle all over with the herbs. Season with the salt and pepper.
3. Place the lamb in a roasting pan and roast for 15 minutes. Lower the oven temperature to 400° and roast for another 15 minutes.
4. Turn the leg and roast for another 20 minutes, or until springy to the touch.
5. Remove the roast when done and allow the leg to stand, covered, for 10 to 15 minutes before carving.

Variations

Gigot d'Agneau Sauce Choron (*Roast Leg of Lamb with Choron Sauce*): Omit the garlic and rosemary and serve with Sauce Choron (page 376), a tomato-flavored béarnaise sauce.

Gigot d'Agneau à la Moutarde (*Roast Leg of Lamb with Mustard*): Substitute 2 to 3 tablespoons of Dijon mustard for the olive oil.

Gigot en Chevreuil
Leg of Lamb Prepared as Venison

Marinating lamb in the same marinade used for venison is the basis for this classic recipe. If you have never prepared game, making this recipe and its suggested sauces will give you the experience necessary to do so when you have the opportunity.

I have slightly altered the classic wild game marinade (*marinade pour gibier*) by using half the normal amount of vinegar, and by using red wine instead of white because I find the sauces made from the marinade fuller in both flavor and color.

By using a simple brown sauce (Jus Lié, page 364) as a base instead of the classic brown game sauce, the sauces are all easy to make, and any one of them turns this leg of lamb into a unique taste experience.

Serves 8

Marinade Pour Gibier (page 368)
1 leg of lamb (see "French-Style Leg of Lamb," page 175)
     (6 to 7½ pounds untrimmed or 4 to 5 pounds trimmed)
1 tablespoon light olive oil
2 teaspoons thyme
1 teaspoon rosemary
⅛ teaspoon salt
⅛ teaspoon freshly ground pepper
Sauces Poivrade, Grand Veneur, et Chevreuil (page 366)

1. Two to four days before you want to serve the lamb, start to marinate it (see instructions in the marinade recipe).
2. Preheat the oven to 475°. Remove the lamb from the marinade and dry it well. Strain the marinade and reserve it and the vegetables for the sauces.

GRILLING LAMB

To prepare a leg for grilling, I have the leg butterflied (boned and cut to lie flat). However, some parts are thicker than others, making even cooking a little difficult, and when carving you find yourself cutting several different muscles, some with and some against the grain. To avoid this, after the leg is butterflied, I trim it of all its fat, and am left with individual muscles, which I then grill like steaks.

At least 1 hour before grilling, I sprinkle or rub the leg with seasonings. Unlike other cuts of lamb whose flavors are relatively delicate, the leg is stronger in flavor and can support fairly robust seasonings, such as mustard or rosemary, garlic, ginger, or even crushed juniper berries.

When grilling a rack of lamb, the cooking time on a hot covered grill is generally 13 to 14 minutes. I often season the lamb several hours in advance of cooking, though I am careful not to salt the meat until just before grilling so as not to extract the natural moisture. In general, I do not season any grilled meat with salt until after it has been browned.

3. Rub the lamb with the oil and sprinkle all over with the thyme and rosemary. Season with the salt and pepper.

4. Place the lamb in a roasting pan and roast for 15 minutes. Lower the temperature to 400° and roast for another 15 minutes and turn the leg.

5. Meanwhile, begin making the sauces.

6. Roast the lamb for another 20 minutes or until it is springy to the touch.

7. Remove the roast when done and allow the leg to stand, covered, for 10 to 15 minutes before carving. Serve the sauces on the side.

Médaillons de Porc Sauce Robert
Pork Medallions with a Mustard Brown Sauce

*S*auce Robert with pork is a traditional French combination. Although a classic *sauce Robert* is a bit of an undertaking, I make mine with a Jus Lié (page 364) instead of a demi-glace, which cuts out 2 hours of preparation. In another slight twist on the original sauce, I deglaze the sauté pan with Cognac and add the flavorful juices to the sauce.

Since the *sauce Robert* is made in advance, preparation of this dish on the day you serve it is very easy.

Serving Suggestion: I like to serve the medallions on a large round platter with a mound of cooked carrots (Carottes à l'Etuvée, page 202) in the center. Not only is this an attractive presentation, but it is a delicious combination as well.

Wine: Dry red.

Serves 6

1½ tablespoons butter
6 medallions of pork, cut from 6 center rib chops,
    1 to 1¼ inches thick
Pinch salt
Pinch freshly ground pepper
¼ cup Cognac
Sauce Robert (page 367)
3 sprigs parsley, chopped

1. In a 12-inch skillet, heat the butter over high heat. Add the medallions and brown quickly on one side, about 1 minute. Turn and season with the salt and pepper.

2. Cover the pan, reduce the heat to medium-low, and cook gently until the meat is well done, firm or just slightly springy to the touch, 10 to 12 minutes.

3. Transfer the meat to a warm platter and keep warm. Over high heat, reduce the pan juices to a glaze, until no liquid remains. Discard any butter remaining in the pan.

4. Remove the pan from the heat, add the Cognac, and flame (see flaming instructions in Bananes Flambées au Rhum, page 322). When the flames die, return the pan to the heat and stir to loosen the glaze in the pan. Add the *sauce Robert*, bring to a simmer, and stir in the parsley. Pour the sauce over the medallions and serve.

Variation

Côtes de Porc Sauce Robert *(Pork Chops with a Mustard Brown Sauce):* Although the medallions make a very elegant presentation, there is no reason why you can't serve Sauce Robert (page 367) with pork chops. If you do so, increase the cooking time by about 3 minutes.

Rôti de Porc aux Pruneaux
Roast Pork with Prunes

In the Loire Valley, the flavorful combination of pork and prunes is often seen in local restaurants, especially in and around the town of Tours. Usually served as a ragoût, chunks of pork are cooked with the prunes in a sauce made with white wine and finished with a little heavy cream.

I have taken the components and flavor combina-

When you order the roast for Rôti de Porc aux Pruneaux, make sure that the butcher gives you the rib bones with the backbone removed so they can be cut up and scattered in the roasting pan. These will be delicious to nibble on before your guests arrive.

tion of a simple pork ragoût and rearranged them in an elegant main course for a dinner party. Instead of chunks of pork, prunes, and a sauce all cooked together, I serve a pork roast accompanied with prunes and white raisins poached in a full-bodied red wine. The poaching liquid is then used to make a light but intensely flavored sauce.

Serves 6 to 8

Serving Suggestion: **Begin with a soup, cream of asparagus (Crème d'Asperges, page 28) or cream of broccoli (Crème de Brocoli, page 30). With the pork roast, serve mashed potatoes (Purée de Pommes de Terre à l'Ail, page 232). For dessert, serve Paris-Brest (page 275).**

Wine: **Full-bodied red, such as Châteauneuf-du-Pape.**

2½ pounds boned* pork roast (center cut rib section, 8 ribs)
¼ teaspoon salt
⅛ teaspoon freshly ground pepper
½ teaspoon thyme
1 bay leaf, crumbled
2 onions, quartered
3 large carrots, thickly sliced
6 tablespoons butter
1½ pounds pitted prunes
½ cup white raisins
1 bottle dry red wine, such as a Côtes-du-Rhône
1 cup beef stock, homemade or canned (see chart, page 348)
1½ teaspoons arrowroot, potato starch, or cornstarch, dissolved in 1½ teaspoons cold water
2 tablespoons port

1. Preheat the oven to 475°.

2. Season the roast with the salt, pepper, thyme, and bay leaf. Place in a roasting pan with the vegetables. In a small saucepan, heat 4 tablespoons of the butter and pour over the roast. Place in the oven and reduce the temperature to 425°. Roast until the juices run clear, about 1 hour and 10 minutes.

3. While the pork is roasting, combine the prunes, raisins, wine, and stock in a medium saucepan. Cover and simmer over medium heat until the prunes are tender, about 30 minutes. Drain the fruit, reserving the poaching liquid. Return about ¼ cup of the poaching liquid to the fruit. Set the fruit and any remaining poaching liquid aside.

4. When the roast is done, allow it to stand 10 to 15 minutes before carving. Remove the fat from the roasting pan. Deglaze the pan by adding the reserved poaching liquid and stirring over high heat to loosen the caramelized bits on the bottom and sides of the pan. Strain through a fine-mesh sieve into a saucepan.

5. Bring the sauce to a boil and add the dissolved arrowroot to thicken it slightly. If the sauce is too thick, add a little water to thin it; if too thin, boil to reduce and thicken it. Season with salt and pepper to taste and stir in the port. Just before serving, beat in the remaining 2 tablespoons butter, 1 tablespoon at a time. Do not allow the sauce to boil once the butter has been added.

6. **To serve:** Slice the roast and arrange it on a platter. (When slicing the roast, I always leave a small piece—2 to 3 inches—unsliced. Placed at one end of the platter and followed by the overlapping slices, this makes an attractive presentation.) Surround it with the prunes and raisins. The carrots and onions from the roasting pan may be mixed with the fruit. Spoon some sauce over the meat and fruit and serve the remaining sauce separately.

＊ The roast should be tied like a fillet of beef in one long roast. I have seen butchers in some parts of the country who will cut the roast in half and tie the two pieces together to form a short, thick roast that takes twice as long to cook. If the roast is not boned, add 20 minutes to the roasting time.

To make entertaining easy, I generally have the roast, sauce, and prunes cooked in advance of my guests' arrival and only need to reheat, carve, and serve. Once roasted, I wrap the meat in aluminum foil. If the meat has cooled by the time I am ready to serve, I reheat it in a 350° oven for 10 to 15 minutes.

Variations

Rôti de Porc Grand-Mère *(Roast Pork with Carrots and Onions):* Omit the prunes, raisins, red wine, beef stock, arrowroot, and port. Serve the roast with the carrots and onions from the roasting pan and mashed potatoes.

Rôti de Porc Sauce Robert *(Roast Pork with a Mustard Brown Sauce):* Omit the prunes, raisins, red wine, beef stock, arrowroot, and port. Serve the roast with Sauce Robert (page 367).

Cassoulet Maigre
White Bean Casserole with Duck, Pork, Lamb, and Sausage

What baked beans are to Boston, *cassoulet* is to the southwest of France. Toulouse, Carcassonne, and Castelnaudary have competed for generations for the top honors as the city with the best *cassoulet*. Each town has its own special version of this legendary dish.

All versions of *cassoulet* contain beans as well as a combination of meats. Although made from scratch in restaurants, it is often seen as a way to use up leftovers in the home. I have made a number of changes that may be noticeable to those familiar with traditional *cassoulet* recipes. I have eliminated most of the fat by omitting the unsmoked bacon or salt pork normally used. I have also omitted the goose or duck fat that usually accompanies the traditional *confit* (preserved duck or goose). The fresh duck that I use in the recipe can be skinned to remove all fat, if desired. The pork rind also found in other recipes has been omitted because it is not readily available in our markets. Also omitted are the bread crumbs normally added during the last hour of cooking to absorb the excess fat and to form a crust. Because I have omitted so much fat from the recipe, I have dubbed it *maigre*, meaning "thin."

Although the purist may be skeptical of my omissions, I hope that you will consider the ease of preparation, the healthier, lowered fat content, and the wonderful flavors of the finished recipe when passing final judgment on my version.

The preparation of the *cassoulet* is divided into two procedures. The beans are actually the recipe for

Haricots à la Bretonne (page 209), and should be made a day or two in advance. And the *cassoulet* itself should be made one or two days ahead of time (an ideal dish for entertaining), because it tastes best when reheated.

Serves 8

1 duck (4½ to 5 pounds), rinsed and patted dry
2 tablespoons butter or vegetable oil
1½ pounds boned pork shoulder, cut into 1½- to
*   2-inch cubes*
1½ pounds boned lamb shoulder, cut into 1½- to
*   2-inch cubes*
2 pounds Hungarian, Polish, or any good sausage,
*   cut into 2-inch pieces*
½ teaspoon salt
¼ teaspoon freshly ground pepper
⅔ cup dry white wine
2 teaspoons Glace de Viande (optional; page 352)
Haricots à la Bretonne (page 209), prepared 1 day or
*   more in advance, at room temperature*

1. Remove the legs and second joints from the duck and cut into four pieces. Remove the breast meat by cutting next to the bone. Cut each breast in half and remove any excess fat.

2. In a large skillet, heat the butter over high heat. Add the duck pieces, pork, lamb, and sausage and sauté until browned, about 5 minutes. This can be done in as many batches as necessary. Season with the salt and pepper and remove the meat from the pan. Pour off the fat.

3. Deglaze the pan by adding the white wine and stirring to loosen the caramelized bits on the bottom and sides of the pan. Reduce the liquid over high heat by half, about 1 minute. Stir in the *glace de viande*. Add this liquid to the beans.

4. Preheat the oven to 350°.

5. In a large casserole, layer the meat and beans. Cover and cook until the meat is tender, about 2 hours. Adjust

the heat, if necessary, so that the beans simmer gently. *(The recipe can be, and is best if, made ahead of time. Let cool to room temperature, cover, and refrigerate. Reheat in a 350° oven until the beans and meat are hot and simmering, about 1 hour.)*

Potée Ma Façon
One-Pot Meal with Chicken, Pork, Sausage, and Vegetables

Serving Suggestion: When I want to make a slightly more formal presentation, I serve cantaloupe with port as a first course instead of the soup. (I save the soup to serve the next day with any leftover meat or vegetables.) The meats are sliced and served on one platter and the vegetables are attractively arranged on another. For dessert, serve a fruit tart (Tarte Alsacienne aux Fruits, page 248).

Wine: Chilled Beaujolais.

A *potée* is a wonderful and warming, peasant-style one-pot meal. Although there are almost as many variations of this regional classic as there are towns in France, a *potée* almost always contains pork, cabbage, potatoes, and, usually, sausage. Then, depending on the region, it might also contain beef, lamb, rabbit, goose, duck, pheasant, or partridge—plus any number of root vegetables and sometimes dried beans.

The main meat in my version of a *potée* is chicken, which in times past would rarely have been squandered on such a humble dish because it was much too expensive. These days, just the reverse is true. The meats that used to be cooked in a *potée* are now far more costly than chicken, so my modern-day *potée* is a departure from the authentic but is in keeping with its spirit.

This dish can easily be made in advance by shortening the cooking time in step 3 to 15 to 20 minutes. Allow to cool uncovered before refrigerating, and bring to a boil before serving.

Serves 10

1 smoked pork shoulder or beef tongue
1 large whole carrot plus 8 carrots cut into 2-inch lengths
1 whole onion plus 4 onions quartered*
3 cloves
1 head garlic
4 stalks celery
Double Bouquet Garni (page 346)
12 peppercorns
6 quarts water
1 chicken (3½ to 4 pounds), trussed (see "How to Truss a
  Bird," page 150)
4 white turnips, peeled and quartered
1 cabbage, cored and quartered
4 large potatoes, peeled and quartered, or 16 small new
  potatoes, peeled
1 Polish sausage, about 2 pounds

Potée is normally served in large soup plates. The soup or broth is served first, often poured over stale or toasted French bread. The meat and vegetables follow, usually piled high on a single platter, and are eaten on the same soup plates. This is a very informal way of serving, and ideal for friends and family. An assortment of strong, mild, and sweet mustards is served as a perfect accompaniment.

1. In a large stockpot, combine the pork shoulder (or beef tongue), 1 whole carrot, the whole onion, the cloves, the head of garlic, celery, bouquet garni, peppercorns, and water and bring to a boil. Simmer uncovered for 1 hour.

2. Remove the meat and strain the broth. Discard the other ingredients and return the broth to the stockpot. Add the chicken, pork (or tongue), the cut carrot lengths, quartered onions, turnips, and cabbage to the broth. Bring to a boil over high heat. Reduce the heat and simmer covered for 15 minutes.

3. Add the potatoes and sausage and simmer until the vegetables are tender, about 30 minutes. *(The recipe can be made ahead. Cool to room temperature, cover, and refrigerate. To avoid overcooking the vegetables when reheating, shorten the cooking time in this step by about 15 minutes. They finish cooking when you bring this to a boil before serving.)*

4. **To serve:** Serve the broth first, followed by platters of meat and vegetables accompanied by an assortment of strong and mild mustards.

* You can replace the 4 quartered onions with 32 pearl onions to be added in step 3. Peel the pearl onions, leaving their root ends trimmed but intact so they will not fall apart.

Médaillons de Veau à la Brunoise
Veal Medallions with Diced Vegetables

I n French cooking a *brunoise* is a combination of diced aromatic vegetables—usually carrots, onions, celery (both root and stalk), white turnips, and leeks—used to give flavor to soups and sauces. (It is similar to a *mirepoix*; see Artichauts Barigoule, page 198.) Ordinarily, a *brunoise* is treated as an additive and used in relatively small quantities. But the effort involved in preparing a *brunoise* has always seemed out of proportion to me, so in this dish I use the *brunoise* not only to enhance the flavor of the sauce, but as the accompanying vegetable as well.

Serves 6

2 tablespoons butter
3 large carrots, diced
3 onions, diced
3 stalks celery, diced
1 white turnip, peeled and diced (optional; see Note)
1 leek (white part only), washed and diced (optional;
*   see Note)*
⅛ teaspoon salt
⅛ teaspoon freshly ground pepper
Pinch of thyme
6 medallions of veal (boned rib chops), 1 to 1¼ inches thick
2 small black truffles (optional; see step 5), 1 diced and
*   1 sliced*
¼ teaspoon arrowroot, potato starch, or cornstarch dissolved
*   in 1 teaspoon cold water*
1 teaspoon Glace de Viande (optional; page 352)
2 tablespoons Madeira
1 tablespoon Cognac
3 sprigs parsley, chopped, for garnish (optional; see step 5)

Serving Suggestion: I normally present the vegetables mounded in the center of a large, round platter with the medallions set around them in a circle. If a round platter is not available, I place the medallions down the center of an oval platter, and spoon the vegetables on either side of them. Serve the veal with buttered noodles or sautéed potatoes. Begin the meal with asparagus or a green salad and end with Floating Island (Ile Flottante Cardinale, page 314).

Wine: Red Bordeaux.

Note: Although the turnip and leek are technically part of a *brunoise*, they can be left out with no ill effect. A *brunoise* also includes celery root (celeriac). If you can find it in your market, use a chunk of celery root about the size of a white turnip and dice as for the other vegetables.

1. In a large skillet, heat 1 tablespoon of the butter over medium heat. Add the diced vegetables and cook until just tender and lightly colored, 10 to 15 minutes. Season with the salt, pepper, and thyme. Remove the vegetables from the pan and set aside.

2. Heat the remaining 1 tablespoon butter in the pan. Add the veal and cook over medium-high heat until brown on both sides, 2 to 3 minutes. Season with salt and pepper to taste. Pour off any excess butter.

3. Spread the cooked vegetables and diced truffle over the veal, cover, and cook over low heat until the veal is firm to the touch, 12 to 15 minutes. Using a skimmer or slotted spoon, remove the veal and vegetables to a serving platter and keep warm.

4. Add the dissolved arrowroot to the pan to lightly thicken the pan juices. Stir in the *glace de viande*, Madeira, and Cognac. Taste and adjust the seasoning, if necessary.

5. **To serve:** Spoon the light sauce over the veal and top each medallion with a slice of truffle. If the truffle is not used, sprinkle chopped parsley over the vegetables and serve.

Variations

Côtes de Veau à la Brunoise *(Veal Chops with Diced Vegetables):* Substitute 1¼-inch-thick veal chops for the medallions and cook about 15 minutes in step 3.

Médaillons de Porc à la Brunoise *(Medallions of Pork with Diced Vegetables):* Substitute medallions of pork (cut from center rib chops) and omit the truffles.

Suprêmes de Volaille à la Brunoise *(Chicken Breasts with Diced Vegetables):* Substitute 6 boneless chicken breasts (about 2 pounds), and cook 10 to 20 minutes in step 3.

Médaillons de Veau Orloff
Veal Medallions with Duxelles and Sauce Mornay

Serving Suggestion: Start with a salad (Salade d'Endives et de Cresson, page 34) or a chicken consommé (Consommé de Volaille, page 19). In addition to the rice, I serve the veal with baby peas or asparagus tips, which go well with the dish, and their green accent makes this an attractive presentation. Oranges au Champagne (page 325) with Madeleines (page 284) make a fitting ending for this elegant meal.

Wine: White Burgundy or red Bordeaux.

Veal Orloff, formally known as *veau Prince Orlov*, is a classic dish I have not seen in many years. Traditionally it is made with either a saddle or a top round of veal, which makes this a very expensive dish, and when prepared in classic fashion, a difficult one as well.

I used to prepare this recipe by roasting the veal, then slicing and reconstructing it with a layer of *duxelles* (cooked shallots and mushrooms) between the slices. The roast was then coated with *duxelles*, placed in the center of an ovenproof platter, and coated with two layers of Mornay sauce. Just before serving, the roast was reheated and browned in a hot oven. The completed roast was then served surrounded by steamed white rice.

This presentation was actually an adaptation (by a chef at the Cordon Bleu in Paris) of the Escoffier classic in which the veal slices were layered with *soubise* (a bland onion and rice purée). In the adapted recipe, the *soubise* was replaced by *duxelles*, thus creating an elegant dish whose wonderful combination of flavors deserves to be rediscovered.

Today, to get the same flavors without the elaborate preparation, I use boned veal rib chops (medallions), sautéing them instead of roasting. The medallions can be completely cooked and assembled several hours before serving and then reheated.

Serves 8

2 tablespoons vegetable oil or butter
8 medallions of veal (boned rib chops), 1 to 1¼ inches thick
Pinch each salt and freshly ground pepper
Duxelles (page 212) made in advance and bound with
*   3 tablespoons of the Mornay sauce*
Sauce Mornay (page 358), made in advance
About ½ cup milk
1 ounce Swiss-style cheese, such as Gruyère or Emmenthaler,
*   grated (about ⅓ cup)*
1½ recipes Riz au Blanc (page 233)

1. Preheat the oven to 475°.

2. Coat a large skillet, two if necessary, with the oil or butter and sauté the medallions over medium-high heat until medium well done, about 4 minutes on each side. Cover the pan after turning the medallions. The veal will be firm, yet slightly springy to the touch, and you will see juice pooling on the surface of the meat. Remove the pan from the heat. Season with the salt and pepper.

3. Divide the *duxelles* into 8 equal portions. Place the veal on an ovenproof serving platter and spread each medallion with a thick layer of *duxelles*.

4. Heat the *sauce Mornay* to a boil, adjust the seasoning, and thin with 2 tablespoons of milk. Spoon an even coating of hot sauce over each medallion. Thin the remaining sauce with enough milk until it is the consistency of cream, about 5 tablespoons, and bring to a boil. Coat each medallion with a second, thinner coating of sauce.

5. Sprinkle a little of the cheese over each medallion and place in the upper third of the oven until the sauce bubbles and the cheese is golden brown, about 10 minutes.

6. Serve the veal surrounded by the *riz au blanc*.

Variation

Suprêmes de Volaille Orloff *(Chicken Breasts with Duxelles and Sauce Mornay):* Replace the veal with 8 boneless chicken breasts (about 2½ pounds). Cook for 5 minutes on each side in step 2.

Blanquette de Veau aux Morilles
Veal Stew with Wild Mushrooms

Serving Suggestion: Start with a salad. Serve the *blanquette* with rice (Riz au Blanc, page 233). For dessert, serve a sorbet and cookies (Tuiles aux Amandes, page 282).

Wine: Dry white.

A *blanquette* is a ragoût made in a white sauce enriched with heavy cream and egg yolks. (Although it is usually made with veal, recipes exist for *blanquettes* made with chicken, lamb, or fish.) A *blanquette de veau* normally contains button mushrooms, but I make mine with dried *morilles* (morels). These wild mushrooms, prized in France for their unique robust and earthy flavor, transform the *blanquette* of the bistro into one for the palace.

Serves 6

1 ounce dried morel mushrooms*
8 cups cold water
3 pounds veal shoulder, cut into 1½-inch cubes
1 onion, studded with 2 cloves
1 large carrot
2 leeks, washed
1 turnip
2 stalks celery
Bouquet Garni (page 346)
25 to 30 pearl onions, peeled, root ends trimmed but left
    intact to hold the onions together
2½ tablespoons butter
3 tablespoons all-purpose flour
½ teaspoon salt
¼ teaspoon freshly ground pepper
2 egg yolks
⅓ cup heavy cream

1. Place the dried morels in a small bowl, cover with 2 cups of the cold water, and let stand until softened, about 30 minutes. Remove the morels and squeeze gently to

remove as much liquid as possible. Strain the soaking liquid through a sieve lined with a double thickness of cheesecloth or paper towel; set aside.

2. Place the veal in a large casserole and cover with cold water, about 6 cups. Bring to a boil over high heat, skimming the foam from the surface frequently.

3. Add the reserved morel soaking liquid, the clove-studded onion, the carrot, leeks, turnip, celery, and bouquet garni. Reduce the heat to medium and simmer for 30 minutes.

4. Add the pearl onions and simmer for 35 minutes.

5. Add the morels; continue to cook until the veal is tender, 10 to 15 minutes longer.

6. Drain the meat and vegetables, reserving the stock. Put the veal, pearl onions, and morels in a large saucepan. Discard the other vegetables and bouquet garni.

7. Strain the reserved veal stock into a saucepan and boil over high heat until reduced to 3 cups, about 10 minutes.

8. In a small saucepan, heat the butter over medium-high heat. Add the flour and cook, stirring frequently, until the roux is pale yellow and frothy, 30 to 40 seconds. Add 2½ cups of the reduced veal stock and stir well with a whisk until the sauce thickens and comes to a boil, 2 to 3 minutes. Reduce the heat to maintain a gentle simmer and season the sauce with the salt and pepper. Whisk vigorously for about 10 seconds. Simmer gently, whisking the sauce from time to time, until the sauce is the consistency of heavy cream, about 5 minutes. Skim off any butter that comes to the surface.

9. Reduce the remaining ½ cup of reserved veal stock over high heat until only a few teaspoons remain and whisk into the sauce. Remove the sauce from the heat.

10. In a small bowl, mix the egg yolks and cream together and gradually whisk in ½ cup of the hot sauce. Whisk the warmed egg yolk mixture into the sauce. Return the sauce to the heat and bring just to a simmer, whisking constantly. Remove the sauce from the heat and pour it over the veal, onions, and morels. *(The recipe can be pre-*

With the recent interest in wild mushrooms in this country, both domestic and imported morels are available. Morels also come in both dark brown and white varieties, but I recommend using only the more robust-flavored brown ones for this recipe.

pared to this point several days in advance. Cover the surface with plastic wrap, let cool, and refrigerate.) .

11. Before serving, reheat the veal and vegetables in a boiling water bath (*bain-marie*), gently stirring occasionally, until the sauce and veal are hot, 15 to 20 minutes.

* If morels are unavailable, you can always make the more usual version of this dish by using ¾ pound regular mushrooms. Wash them and add in step 5.

Variation

Blanquette de Volaille aux Morilles *(Boneless Chicken Stew with Wild Mushrooms):* Substitute 2½ pounds skinless, boneless chicken breasts, cut in large chunks, for the veal. Omit steps 3 and 4. After step 2, add the reserved morel soaking liquid, the clove-studded onion, the carrot, leeks, turnip, celery, *bouquet garni*, and pearl onions and simmer for 35 minutes, or until the pearl onions are tender.

Escalopes de Veau Chasseur
Sautéed Veal Chops with Mushrooms and Tomato Sauce

Serving Suggestion: Begin your meal with a green vegetable or salad and accompany the veal with rice (Riz Pilaf, page 234) or buttered noodles. Serve fresh fruit for dessert.

Wine: Dry red.

When you see a dish called *chasseur* (which means "hunter") in France, you know right away that it will contain mushrooms. For this *chasseur*, I use wild mushrooms in place of the usual button mushrooms.

Normally, the veal would be floured before being sautéed in a preparation like this one. Unless browned quickly, however, the flour becomes pasty and unappetizing, and, for this reason, it has been omitted.

Serves 4

3 tablespoons butter
1 pound veal scallops
¼ teaspoon salt
⅛ teaspoon freshly ground pepper
½ pound fresh Shiitake or porcini mushrooms, washed,
    dried, and sliced
2 shallots, finely chopped
¼ cup dry white wine
½ cup beef stock, homemade or canned (see chart, page 348)*
1 teaspoon Glace de Viande (optional; page 352)
1 tablespoon tomato paste
1 teaspoon Cognac
3 sprigs parsley, chopped, for garnish

1. In a large skillet, heat the butter over medium-high to high heat. Add the veal and cook until lightly browned, about 2 minutes on each side. Season with the salt and pepper. Transfer the veal to a serving platter and keep warm.

2. Add the mushrooms to the pan and brown lightly, about 2 minutes. Add the shallots and cook for 20 to 30 seconds.

3. Add the white wine and cook until the liquid is reduced by half, about 1 minute. Stir in the stock, *glace de viande*, and tomato paste, and bring the mixture to a boil. Taste and adjust the seasoning, if necessary. Add the Cognac.

4. **To serve:** Pour the sauce over the veal. Sprinkle with chopped parsley.

* For a slightly thicker sauce, use Jus Lié (page 364) in place of stock.

GAS VS. ELECTRICITY AND A LITTLE HISTORY

The often-heard statement "Chefs prefer gas" originates from the fact that chefs like to have as much heat as possible. Most commercial gas stoves or ranges give off more heat than electric ones. However, when it comes to modern home equipment, the opposite is often true. The only advantage of a residential gas range over an electric one is the ability one has to adjust its temperature instantly. When working on an electric range, you must either anticipate temperature changes or use two burners set at different temperatures for rapid adjustments.

The trade-off is that although it is easier to adjust the heat on a gas burner, an electric one distributes low heat over a larger area, making slow or low-heat cooking easier. While living in France in the late '60s and early '70s, I often thought how smart the French were. The average home range came equipped with both gas and electric burners. I soon found that the combination was not due to a preference for both, but a need for at least one. It seemed that quite frequently the electric power workers went on strike, and although the power cuts usually lasted only a few hours, no Frenchman ever wanted to be without the means to prepare a meal. When planning a kitchen, you may want to consider both.

When it comes to making decisions on today's home appliances, a lot depends on the cost and availability of gas and electricity in your area. Since both work well, choose the one that is most economical. Compare the BTU output (the amount of heat per burner) of the various appliances available, and choose one with the highest output rating.

PROFESSIONAL RANGES

The use of professional ranges in homes has become popular in recent years, and I am often asked for my opinion on their use. If you are regularly cooking for 12 or more, a professional range will definitely make your task easier, and even though it takes more time to clean than a normal home range, you will be happy to do it. However, if you regularly cook for fewer than eight, you will find the burners of a professional range too large for your pots, the heat produced too much for your kitchen, and the added cleaning not worth the effort.

Vegetables

Other

Classic French cooking established a tradition—still alive today—in which the vegetables served with a main course were an integral part of it. In fact, the name of a dish indicated what those vegetables would be. For example, a dish with *Richelieu* in its title always contained a garnish of stuffed tomatoes and mushrooms, braised lettuces, and roast potatoes.

On the home cooking level this is not necessarily the case. The French do not share the American belief that a main course absolutely must be served with a vegetable. The recipes in this section are designed as accompaniments, although several are suggested as first courses.

Vegetables & Accompaniments

Compote de Pommes
Applesauce

Although some might wonder what applesauce is doing in a section on vegetables, I have included it here because I use it as an accompaniment to pork, veal, ham, goose, duck, and chicken. I serve the applesauce both warm, as the French do, and cold.

Applesauce is traditionally made by quartering unpeeled apples, cooking them with water to cover, and then pushing the cooked apples through a fine-mesh sieve or food mill, leaving the skins and seeds behind. Because of insect sprays and waxed skins, I prefer to peel and core the apples before cooking them, thus also eliminating the need for a food mill or sieve. Instead of cooking the apples in water, I cook them simply in their own moisture (*à l'étuvée*) until they are soft enough to whisk into a smooth sauce.

The quantities given here are merely to give you an idea as to how much applesauce you will get from 3 pounds of apples. Obviously, you can make as much or as little as you like. Be sure you have a saucepan with a heavy bottom and tight-fitting lid.

To "quarter" and core apples for the Alsatian Fruit Tart (page 248) and other recipes, stand the apple on end and cut off two thick slices from either side of the stem. Cut off the remaining two sections from the core. You will be left with a square-cut core and four pieces of apple.

Makes about 3½ cups

3 pounds apples, peeled, cored, and cut into chunks
Sugar, to taste

1. Place the apples in a saucepan and set, tightly covered, over very low heat. Within 5 to 10 minutes steam will appear when the lid is lifted. Cook, stirring occasionally, until the apples are soft enough to whisk into a smooth sauce, 15 to 20 minutes.
2. Taste and add a little sugar, if necessary.

Asparagus are best when freshly picked from the garden. They are sweet and tender and can be eaten raw. After a few days, however, they lose their natural sweetness, and their outer skin becomes bitter and tough. For this reason I peel all asparagus unless they are pencil thin, or come freshly picked from the garden. The cooking time, as for most green vegetables, will depend on their freshness. Taste a piece of the raw asparagus; if it is sweet it will take only a few minutes to cook. If it is bitter, it may take three times as long.

Serving Suggestion: At home I serve asparagus hot as a first course topped with melted butter and a little salt and pepper. On more formal occasions, I serve asparagus with Sauce Hollandaise (page 373), or *à la milanaise* with melted butter and freshly grated Parmesan cheese. Asparagus can also be served warm or chilled with a Sauce Vinaigrette (page 383), and are good with a mayonnaise or Sauce Verte (page 381) when accompanying a cold poached fish.

Asperges
Asparagus

The luscious white asparagus of France and Belgium are grown under mounds of earth to prevent them turning green (in much the same way Belgian endive is grown). I can remember in the late '60s tasting these delicately flavored vegetables for the first time and wondering why we didn't grow them in the United States. Ten years later Paris restaurants were proudly offering green asparagus on their menus in March. Heralded in the press as the first asparagus of the year, they were arriving from California by air.

Serves 8

3 pounds asparagus, washed

1. Cut or break off any dry ends from the asparagus. If the asparagus are larger than pencil thickness, peel the spears to ensure even cooking. Lay them flat on a cutting board to avoid breakage, and with a vegetable peeler, peel the entire spear from just below the point. Tie them in eight bundles (optional). If the asparagus are not to be cooked immediately, hold them in cold water.

2. Place the asparagus in a large saucepan with 5 to 6 quarts of water. Bring to a boil and cook until the point of a knife penetrates the spear without resistance, 3 to 7 minutes depending on their freshness. (If you are serving the asparagus cold, refresh them in cold water to stop their cooking and to set their color.)

3. Drain the asparagus on paper towels before placing them on individual plates or a serving platter. If tied, use the string to help lift the asparagus from the water to the towels, and then to the plates where the string should be cut and removed.

Artichauts Barigoule
Braised Artichokes with Ham and Vegetables

Classically, artichokes were most often presented as artichoke bottoms (*fonds d'artichaut*), cooked and then filled with many different ingredients, such as cooked peas, mushrooms, chicken livers, and even poached eggs. They were then topped with *sauce Mornay*, *hollandaise*, or *béarnaise*. The filled and sauced bottoms were usually used as a garnish on a platter accompanying a main-course presentation.

Because of the time involved, I rarely serve artichoke bottoms. Instead, my favorite way of serving artichokes is to braise them.

The following recipe is an adaptation of a traditional one from the south of France called *artichauts à la Barigoule* in which the artichokes are stuffed with ground and seasoned pork before braising.

I find eating the artichokes together with the diced braising vegetables and ham much more enjoyable than with the pork stuffing. Serve the artichokes in large, flat soup plates surrounded by the diced vegetables and braising liquid. Place a large bowl on the table for everyone to use to discard their leaves. The leaves are plucked then dipped into the braising liquid before being eaten. When all the leaves are gone, the delectable bottom is left to be eaten with the remaining broth, ham, and vegetable combination.

Serving Suggestion: To round out a light meal of braised artichokes, just serve some warm French bread, a piece of cheese, and fruit.

Serves 4

4 medium to large artichokes
½ lemon

3 tablespoons olive oil, extra-virgin if available
2 onions, diced
2 carrots, diced
2 stalks celery, diced
1 ¼-inch-thick slice of ham (about ¼ pound) (boiled, baked, or smoked), diced
2 garlic cloves, chopped
1 small bay leaf
½ teaspoon thyme
⅛ teaspoon salt
⅛ teaspoon freshly ground pepper
1 cup dry white wine
2 cups beef stock, homemade or canned (see chart, page 348)

For anyone who has never encountered an artichoke, it is helpful to know a bit about its construction. The edible portion of the artichoke is the fleshy bottom to which all the leaves are attached (each leaf, too, has a small tender and edible portion at its base). Also attached to the artichoke bottom, in its center, is a mass of hairlike fibers called the "choke," which must be removed (except in baby artichokes). If eaten, they can get caught in the throat. The choke of a cooked artichoke can be easily scooped out with a spoon, although for some more elegant presentations, the choke should be removed before serving so your guests won't have to worry about it.

1. Wash the artichokes in cold water. Cut off the stems and top third of the leaves. (A serrated knife works best.) Rub the cut areas with the lemon to prevent discoloration. With scissors, trim the thorns from the uncut leaves.

2. Place the artichokes in a large kettle of boiling water and blanch for 10 to 15 minutes to make the choke easy to remove. With a slotted spoon, lift the artichokes out and place them upside down on a plate to cool. Spread the leaves apart and, using a spoon, remove the small center leaves and choke.

3. In a large Dutch oven, heat the olive oil over medium heat. Add the diced vegetables and ham and sauté until lightly browned, about 6 minutes. Stir in the garlic, herbs, salt, pepper, wine, and stock.

4. Place the artichokes bottom side down on the mixture of vegetables and ham and bring the liquid to a boil. Cover, reduce the heat to low, and simmer until a knife enters the bottom of an artichoke without resistance and the leaves pull off easily, 40 to 50 minutes. *(The artichokes can be cooked ahead of time. Allow to cool uncovered, then cover and refrigerate. When ready to serve, heat to a simmer, covered, and serve.)*

5. **To serve:** Place each artichoke in a large soup plate with some of the vegetables and braising liquid surrounding it. Serve hot.

Betteraves au Four
Oven-Baked Beets

You can live in France and never know that beets grow in the ground, or have leafy tops, or require long cooking. French markets sell beets fully cooked, ready to peel and eat. In this country, however, this convenience is not afforded the home cook. Although most cooks boil beets, causing a good deal of the color and flavor of the vegetable to be lost, I prefer to bake them in the oven as you would a baked potato. Baking beets enhances both their color and flavor. Once cooked, they can be refrigerated for up to one week and kept for quick use — cold in salads or reheated and served as a hot side dish.

Serves 6

6 large beets

1. Preheat the oven to 400°.
2. Trim beets of all stems, leaves, and roots. (The leaves can be added to soups or cooked like spinach for a vegetable. However, I rarely eat them.) Wash and scrub the beets as you would a baking potato.
3. Wrap the beets in aluminum foil. (If they are not wrapped, the beet juice tends to seep and burn in the roasting pan.) Place the beets in a roasting pan and bake until a knife easily pierces the center of each beet, about 45 minutes. Remove from the oven and allow to cool.
4. When ready to use, peel away the outer skin and slice, dice, or julienne. The beets can be served either as a salad tossed with a vinaigrette or as a vegetable warmed with a little butter.

Serving Suggestion: The beets can be served sliced and tossed with a vinaigrette as a first-course salad accompanied by warm French bread. They can also be served diced with Belgian endive (see Salade d'Endives et de Betteraves, page 34). To serve the beets as a hot vegetable, reheat them in a covered saucepan over low heat with a small amount of butter for 5 to 10 minutes. Toss the beets to coat them with the butter and serve. I especially enjoy beets served with roasted or grilled chicken and veal.

In the past few years a new variety of golden beet has been developed and can be found in many farmers' markets. Its unique color makes it very appealing, and it has a slightly milder taste than the purple variety. It looks and tastes wonderful in a summer salad.

Brocoli
Broccoli

Serving Suggestion: **To dress up the presentation, replace the butter with a Sauce Hollandaise (page 373) that has been flavored very lightly with lemon. Broccoli also makes an excellent purée (see Purée de Brocoli, page 205).**

Broccoli is one of the most common American vegetables, but is rarely used in France—although Catherine de Médici brought it from Italy to France hundreds of years ago. Delicate and sweet in flavor when freshly picked, broccoli takes on a strong, disagreeable odor and flavor when it is stale. Freshly picked broccoli cooks in only 3 to 4 minutes. However, after a few days, the outer skin of the stalk toughens, increasing the cooking time dramatically. For best results, I always peel broccoli before cooking. It is not difficult, and allows the stalk and flower to cook in the same amount of time, avoiding the problem of undercooked stalks and overcooked flowers.

Although there are many ways to prepare broccoli, I enjoy it best when simply steamed or boiled and served with melted butter and a sprinkle of salt.

Serves 4

1 bunch broccoli
3 tablespoons butter, melted
⅛ teaspoon salt

1. Trim any dried ends from the stalks. Peel the stalks: Look at the cut end and you will see a pale green stalk with a dark green edge. Insert your knife just behind this edge and hold the peel firmly between your thumb and the blade of the knife. Pull the peel down toward the flower. If the broccoli is fresh, it will peel easily from "stem to stern." If the broccoli is not fresh, the peel will break off every inch or two, making the peeling process a little more time consuming, but all the more important.

2. In a large pot of boiling water, cook until a knife penetrates the stalk easily, 3 to 7 minutes. Since cooking time is directly related to freshness, when broccoli peels easily you know the cooking time will be short. Conversely, when the peeling is difficult, the broccoli will take longer to cook.

3. Drain the broccoli on paper towels. Serve with melted butter and a sprinkle of salt.

Carottes à l'Etuvée
Waterless Cooked Carrots

Of all the wonderful recipes I have taught over the years, this simple preparation of carrots has received more praise from my students than any other.

In America, carrots are typically cooked in water, drained, and then tossed in butter. Because their flavor is diluted by excess moisture, many think of carrots as a bland and uninteresting vegetable. The best French method for cooking the vegetable is embodied in the classic recipe *carottes Vichy*. Originally designed as part of a healthful regime for those who went to the spas in Vichy for their rejuvenating waters, the recipe calls for the carrots to be boiled in mineral water until it all evaporates. By adding a tablespoon or two of butter, the carrots become coated once the water is gone. My method of preparing carrots goes one step further, using the carrots' own moisture to gently cook them. When fully cooked the moisture is gone, leaving the carrots with a sweeter and more intense flavor, as well as with a deeper and more vibrant color.

Serves 6

STEAMING VEGETABLES

There is a certain fallacy in the wisdom of steaming green vegetables, a cooking method that is very much in favor these days. Steaming is really only best for green vegetables that are straight out of the garden, or at least no more than two or three days from being picked. Steaming heightens a fresh vegetable's natural sweet flavors.

However, the delicate sweetness of a fresh vegetable changes soon after it is picked, and within several days is replaced by a stronger, sometimes bitter taste. (This is particularly true of broccoli and spinach.) Steaming will only accentuate this off taste, and therefore I do not recommend its use for older vegetables.

Less fresh vegetables are far better when they are boiled or blanched in large quantities of water. This method yields a more delicately flavored vegetable and is my choice for most of the green vegetables I purchase in supermarkets.

2 pounds carrots, sliced, diced, or julienned
2 tablespoons butter
3 sprigs parsley, chopped

1. Place the carrots and butter in a saucepan over very low heat and cover with a tight-fitting lid. The carrots will slowly steam in their own moisture. Shake the pan from time to time. To check the correct amount of heat, lift the lid after 10 minutes. You should see steam and only barely hear the carrots cooking. If there is no steam, increase the heat. If you hear sizzling or boiling, reduce the heat. As the carrots cook you will notice a combination of water and butter at the bottom of the pan.

2. Cook until the carrots are tender. Depending on their size, they will take 15 to 40 minutes. Remove the lid and increase the heat to allow any remaining moisture to evaporate quickly. There should now be only a little clear butter at the bottom of the pan.

3. Gently toss the carrots to coat with the butter. If you are not ready to serve the carrots, or if you are preparing them in advance, remove the pan from the heat. Reheat before serving over medium-high heat. Sprinkle with chopped parsley and serve.

Over the past 10 to 12 years the style of preparing vegetables has gravitated toward the undercooked, with many cooks going to the extreme of serving them almost raw. I enjoy both raw and cooked vegetables, but rarely have I liked those caught somewhere in between, where they have the virtues of neither. For me a perfectly cooked vegetable is one that you feel on your teeth but do not hear while eating.

Variations

Carottes au Gingembre *(Carrots with Ginger):* Add 1 teaspoon (or more to taste) of chopped or julienned fresh ginger to the carrots while cooking and sprinkle with chopped fresh coriander (cilantro) instead of parsley.

Carottes Glacées au Madère *(Glazed Carrots with Madeira):* Add 2 tablespoons of Madeira when reheating the carrots in step 3. Wait until all the liquid has evaporated and the carrots become glazed with the Madeira.

Purée de Carottes *(Puréed Carrots):* Simply use a food mill or processor to purée any of the above. Add ¼ cup of milk or heavy cream to thin and smooth out the purée.

Purée de Chou-Fleur
Cauliflower Purée

There are a number of ways to make French vegetable purées. One classic method mixes a thick béchamel sauce with the puréed vegetable to enrich and smooth its texture (see Purée d'Epinards, page 205).

In the method I use most often, I purée the vegetable together with cooked potato or rice for body and smoothness. Most classic purées usually include large quantities of butter or heavy cream. In fact, the purées are stirred over heat to dry them out so they can be moistened with either milk or cream. I omit this step because I prefer the lighter, less rich purée that results.

Use this recipe as a guide for puréeing other vegetables. I use a ratio of potato to vegetable of 1 to 3 or, at most, 1 to 2.

Serves 6 to 8

1 head cauliflower (about 3 pounds), cored and separated
    into florets
1 to 1½ pounds potatoes, peeled (2 to 3 large potatoes)
¼ to ½ cup milk
3 tablespoons butter
¾ teaspoon salt
⅛ teaspoon freshly ground pepper

1. Boil the vegetables until tender, about 15 minutes for the cauliflower and 30 minutes for the potatoes.

2. Drain the vegetables and purée them together in the food processor. (Using a food processor to purée potatoes alone will make them pasty, but using it to purée them together with another vegetable works exceptionally well.)

I have always enjoyed cauliflower, in all the many ways it can be served. Hot, with a butter, cheese, or curry sauce; cold, with mayonnaise or vinaigrette; and raw, as a crudité. On the other hand, my family is, at most, indifferent to it. Over the years, whenever I have suggested cauliflower for dinner, I have always been outvoted; that is, until recently.

One night I made dinner and, without asking, served a purée of cauliflower with broiled chicken and string beans. The purée, which was enough for six, was devoured by four, and I now receive frequent requests for it.

When boiling vegetables for a purée, I find that very little additional liquid is necessary for the purée, and any left over cooking liquid makes a nice light soup.

The purée should be moist enough, but if it isn't, add some milk.

3. Stir in the butter and season with the salt and pepper. Blend well. *(The purée can be made a day or two in advance and covered with plastic wrap to prevent it from drying out. Reheat in a water bath [bain-marie] or microwave oven.)*

Variations

In step 1, when you cook the cauliflower, add one or all of the following: 1 onion, diced; 2 garlic cloves, or 2 carrots, thickly sliced.

Purée de Navets *(Turnip Purée):* To use turnips in place of cauliflower, boil equal amounts of potatoes and turnips, cut into chunks, until tender, about 15 minutes for turnips and 30 minutes for potatoes. Prepare as above.

Purée de Brocoli *(Broccoli Purée):* Substitute 3 pounds of broccoli for the cauliflower.

Purée d'Epinards
Creamed Spinach

In this type of vegetable purée, a béchamel sauce is added for rich and creamy results.

Serves 4

2 packages frozen spinach (about 19 ounces total)
Sauce Béchamel (page 357)
¼ teaspoon salt
⅛ teaspoon freshly ground pepper
⅛ teaspoon freshly grated nutmeg

1. Prepare the spinach according to the package directions. Squeeze dry to remove all excess moisture. There should be about 1 cup of spinach.

2. In a food processor, purée the spinach. Add the béchamel, ½ cup at a time, and process just to mix after each addition.

3. Season with the salt, pepper, and nutmeg. *(The purée can be prepared a day or two in advance, covered with plastic wrap to prevent it from drying out, and refrigerated. Reheat in a water bath* [bain-marie] *or microwave oven.)*

Ail Glacé
Glazed Garlic

These tender, glazed garlic cloves are gently boiled in beef or chicken stock. The flavor, though obviously garlic, is much milder than you might expect. They are ideal for serving with roast leg of lamb and are also good served with roast chicken or sautéed rabbit.

The glazed garlic can be prepared in advance and reheated in several additional tablespoons of stock. Make sure you boil the additional stock so that it, too, thickens to glaze the garlic.

Serves 6

3 medium to large heads garlic, split into cloves and peeled
1 cup beef stock or chicken stock, homemade or canned
(see chart, pages 348–349)

1. Trim the root ends from the peeled garlic cloves and place the cloves in a small heavy-bottomed saucepan. Pour in just enough stock to cover them.

2. Bring the stock to a boil. Reduce the heat to medium and boil gently until all the moisture from the stock evapo-

PEELING GARLIC

Each clove in a head of garlic is protected by a tight-fitting skin, which can be difficult to peel. It's easy, however, if the skin is loosened. Place a garlic clove on your work surface. Put gentle, but increasing downward pressure on the clove until you hear it snap, crack, or pop. The skin will have loosened itself from the garlic, and will come away easily. Too much pressure will smash or crack the garlic (or send it flying across the room) as well as loosening its skin, which in many cases is fine, but if you want the cloves to retain their shape (as in Ail Glacé, above) you must take care not to exert too much pressure.

Many chefs use the side of a knife blade or a cleaver to press garlic, but I find it safer to use either my fingers or a flat wooden spatula.

rates, about 20 minutes. Toss the garlic cloves to glaze them with the reduced stock.

Variation

Échalotes ou Petits Oignons Glacés *(Glazed Shallots and Pearl Onions):* Shallots and pearl onions can be glazed in the same way as garlic. Use just enough stock to cover them and boil as long as needed for the stock to reduce and form a glaze. Both are good when served with steaks, roast beef, grilled or roast chicken, and veal.

Haricots Verts
Green Beans

Green beans or string beans, as they are more commonly known, are the most frequently served green vegetable in France. Although most varieties of green beans today are stringless, this was not always the case. One of the purposes of snapping off the ends of the beans was to remove the tough fibrous strands that ran down the sides of the bean. Although with today's stringless beans a number of chefs have chosen to cut off only the end of the bean, I continue to cut or snap off both ends for aesthetic reasons.

Serving green beans is easy when they are cooked in advance. Reheating or sautéing them in a little butter will eliminate any excess water and heighten their flavor. Sprinkle with salt and pepper just before serving.

Serves 6 to 8

2 pounds green beans, trimmed
3 tablespoons butter
¼ teaspoon salt
⅛ teaspoon freshly ground pepper

1. Place the beans in a large pot containing 5 quarts of rapidly boiling water. Cook until tender, 5 to 7 minutes.

2. Drain the beans and refresh under cold running water to stop the cooking and set the color; drain well. *(This can be done several hours in advance.)*

3. **To serve:** Sauté (or reheat) the beans in butter over medium to medium-high heat, tossing frequently, until they are hot and lightly coated with butter, 2 to 3 minutes. Season with the salt and pepper and serve.

Variations

Haricots Verts à l'Ail *(Green Beans with Garlic):* For a delicate garlic flavor, heat 2 whole cloves of garlic in the butter before reheating the beans. Discard the garlic before serving. For a stronger garlic accent, chop 1 to 2 garlic cloves (to taste). Heat in the butter and toss with the beans before serving.

Haricots Verts aux Echalotes *(Green Beans with Shallots):* Gently sauté 2 finely chopped shallots (or ½ onion, finely chopped) in the butter before reheating the beans.

Haricots Verts Amandine *(Green Beans with Almonds):* Sauté and lightly brown ½ cup sliced or slivered almonds in the butter and toss with beans to reheat and serve.

Haricots Verts aux Herbes *(Green Beans with Herbs):* Sprinkle with 2 tablespoons chopped fresh parsley or 1 tablespoon chopped fresh tarragon, basil, or mint just before serving.

Haricots Verts à la Crème *(Green Beans with Cream):* Use ½ cup heavy cream in place of the butter to reheat the beans.

Haricots Verts en Salade *(Green Bean Salad):* Toss chilled cooked beans in a bowl with a chopped shallot and enough Sauce Vinaigrette (page 383) to coat. These beans are also excellent served with a tomato salad.

As with most vegetables, the cooking time for green beans depends on their freshness. A common belief is that the younger the vegetable, the faster it cooks, yet when picking large and small beans from the same plant, I find they are both tender after the same amount of cooking. I once took 5 pounds of freshly picked beans, and cooked them a pound at a time over a period of 10 days. Each time I cooked them, it took longer to achieve the same degree of tenderness. The first day they cooked in about 3 minutes, while on the tenth day it took 7 to 8 minutes. I have bought beans in the market that have taken more than 10 minutes of cooking to become tender. When cooked this long, the beans lose their color, and invariably have poor flavor.

Haricots à la Bretonne
White Beans with Garlic and Tomatoes

Brittany-style white beans are dried white beans that are cooked and mixed with a fresh tomato sauce. They are excellent when served with roast lamb, but more important, they serve as my base for a marvelous *cassoulet* (Cassoulet Maigre, page 181).

After cooking the beans, I reduce the cooking liquid, which is usually discarded, to form a sauce. This recipe can be used to cook other beans and legumes (such as pinto beans, limas, black-eyed peas, and lentils), which can be served with or without the reduced liquid and/or the tomato sauce.

Serves 10 to 12

2 pounds dried white beans, washed and drained
1 large carrot
1 onion, studded with 2 cloves, plus 3 onions, chopped
1 head garlic, unpeeled, plus 4 garlic cloves, chopped
2 Bouquet Garni (page 346)
*5 tablespoons butter**
2 pounds tomatoes, peeled, seeded, and chopped or
    4 pounds canned tomatoes, drained and chopped
½ teaspoon salt
¼ teaspoon freshly ground pepper
*3 sprigs parsley, chopped, for garnish**

1. Place the beans in a large casserole or saucepan, cover with cold water, and bring to boil over high heat. Remove from the heat and allow to stand covered for 20 to 30 minutes.

2. Rinse the beans in cold water, drain, and return them to the casserole with the carrot, cloved onion, head of garlic, and one bouquet garni. Add water to cover by 1 inch

(2 to 2½ quarts). Bring to a boil over high heat, then reduce the heat to medium-low and simmer, partially covered, until the beans are tender yet still firm, 1 to 1½ hours.

3. Drain the beans, reserving the cooking liquid, and discard the carrot, onion, head of garlic, and bouquet garni. Reduce the liquid over high heat until it thickens and only 1 cup remains. Pour this sauce over the beans and set aside.

4. In a skillet, heat 3 tablespoons of the butter over low heat. Add the chopped onions, cover, and cook slowly until soft, about 6 minutes.

5. Add the tomatoes, chopped garlic, and remaining bouquet garni. Season with the salt and pepper, cover, and simmer gently until the tomatoes soften and a sauce forms, about 30 minutes. Remove the bouquet garni.

6. Add the tomato sauce, which should not be watery, to the cooked beans. *(At this point the beans may be stored in the refrigerator for several days or frozen.)*

7. Before serving, bring the beans slowly to a boil. Stir in the remaining 2 tablespoons butter and sprinkle with chopped parsley. Serve hot.

* If you are making these beans for the Cassoulet Maigre (page 181), omit the final butter and parsley from step 7.

Poireaux
Leeks

Leeks, known in France as poor man's asparagus, are generally used in America only by those who can find them. Although they are commonplace in Europe, they can be difficult to find here, which is a shame because this member of the onion family has a wonderful and delicate flavor.

WASHING LEEKS

Leeks must be cleaned well, since dirt collects in their leaves as they grow up through the soil.

1. Cut off the roots and trim away any dried leaves. Then insert a paring knife through the white of the leek, just below the green, with its sharp edge facing up, toward the leaves. Pull the knife up through the leaves. Give the leek a quarter turn and make a second similar cut.

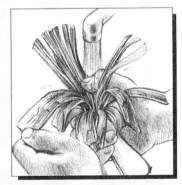

2. Spread the leaves of the leeks and wash thoroughly.

A leek looks sort of like an enormous scallion. It has long dark green leaves, a long white body, and white roots. A leek is usually filled with soil and needs careful washing (see "Washing Leeks," opposite). The green leaves are rarely eaten, but are used in some stocks and soups. They are also blanched, to brighten them, and then cut and used in decorating aspic-coated presentations. Many recipes call for the use of "the white part only," and in these cases the leaves can be discarded or saved for a soup.

Leeks are used as ingredients in stocks and soups, but they are also excellent on their own.

Serves 6

12 leeks, washed
Sauce Hollandaise (page 373) or Sauce Vinaigrette (page 383)

1. Lay the leeks flat in a skillet, add ½ inch of water, bring to a simmer, and cook covered, until tender, about 10 minutes.

2. **To serve:** Cut the leeks in half lengthwise and place two leeks (4 halves) on individual plates to be sauced. Serve warm with *sauce hollandaise* or at room temperature with *sauce vinaigrette*.

Poireaux à la Crème
Leeks in Cream

The classic version of this recipe first cooks the white parts of the leeks whole for 10 to 15 minutes in boiling water, and then boils them in heavy cream for an additional 20 to 30 minutes, producing a very delicate but very rich vegetable.

In the following recipe I dice, julienne, or chop the white parts of the leeks and cook them slowly in a little butter until they are tender. I then add just enough cream to bind them.

Serves 4

4 leeks (white parts only), washed and diced, chopped,
*   or julienned*
1 tablespoon butter
¼ cup heavy cream
Salt and freshly ground pepper

1. Place the leeks and butter in a medium saucepan over very low heat, cover with a tight-fitting lid, and slowly steam the leeks in their own moisture. Cook the leeks until tender, 8 to 10 minutes.

2. Remove the lid and increase the heat to allow any excess moisture to evaporate.

3. Add the cream and cook, uncovered, boiling if necessary, to thicken slightly. The cream should hold the leeks together. Season to taste with salt and pepper.

Serving Suggestion: I often use leeks prepared this way as a bed on which to place a grilled or sautéed pork or veal chop, or a breast of chicken. The combination is delicious. Serve the combination with buttered noodles or steamed potatoes and a chilled dry white wine.

Duxelles
Shallot and Mushroom Stuffing

A *duxelles* is one of the foundations of French cooking. It is used by itself, or mixed with chopped meats and herbs, to form stuffings. To chop the mushrooms by hand is time-consuming and tedious, but a food processor will do the work in seconds.

Makes 1½ cups

Serving Suggestion: Use the *duxelles* to stuff mushroom caps, or to flavor an omelet, béchamel sauce, or a simple broiled chicken.

**VEGETABLE
PREPARATION**

2 tablespoons butter
5 shallots or 1 onion, finely chopped
1 pound mushrooms, washed, dried, and finely chopped
¼ teaspoon salt
⅛ teaspoon freshly ground pepper

1. In a large skillet, heat the butter over medium-high heat. Add the shallots and cook until softened but not browned, about 2 minutes.

2. Add the mushrooms, increase the heat to high, and sauté until most of the water has evaporated and the mushrooms begin to brown, about 5 minutes. Season with the salt and pepper and remove from the heat.

Champignons à la Crème
Mushrooms in Cream Sauce

*C*hampignons à la crème is one of the most satisfying ways to serve mushrooms, and it makes an excellent first course served simply on a piece of toast, puff pastry, or more elaborately in a puff-pastry *bouchée* (see Bouchées de Fruits de Mer, page 86). You may also serve it as an accompaniment to sautéed veal or chicken.

Serves 6

1 tablespoon butter
1 shallot, finely chopped
1 pound mushrooms, washed, dried, and sliced
¼ teaspoon salt
⅛ teaspoon freshly ground pepper
1 cup heavy cream
1 to 2 teaspoons dry sherry or Madeira, to taste (optional)

1. In a medium saucepan, heat the butter over medium

heat. Add the shallot and sauté for about 2 minutes without browning.

2. Add the mushrooms, sprinkle with the salt and pepper, and cover tightly with a lid. Reduce the heat to medium-low and steam the mushrooms slowly in their own moisture for about 10 minutes.

3. Remove the mushrooms with a skimmer or slotted spoon and set aside. Reduce the cooking liquid over high heat until only 3 tablespoons remain, about 3 minutes.

4. Add the cream and boil, uncovered, until the sauce thickens slightly. Return the mushrooms to the sauce. *(The mushrooms can be made in advance up to this point. Cover the surface with plastic wrap and refrigerate.)*

5. **To serve:** First bring to a boil, then taste and adjust the seasoning, if necessary. Add the sherry or Madeira and spoon over warm toast or a piece of puff pastry.

Variation

Champignons Sauvages à la Crème *(Wild Mushrooms in Cream Sauce):* Use, in the same way, any of the many varieties of fresh wild mushrooms you find in the markets.

Champignons à l'Ail
Mushrooms and Garlic

S autéing mushrooms concentrates their flavor by extracting excess moisture while they are browning. Adding garlic to the browned mushrooms creates a flavor combination that goes especially well with grilled, sautéed, and roasted game birds and poultry. You will also enjoy this combination with grilled veal chops.

In France, both cultivated and wild mushrooms are used in this recipe. A number of different mushrooms have become available recently, so try this recipe with

WASHING MUSHROOMS

Washing mushrooms is an important and often debated technique. There are those who say that mushrooms should never be washed, but merely brushed with a mushroom brush, or simply wiped with a damp towel, for if washed they will become waterlogged. Anyone trying these techniques on large quantities of mushrooms will know that they can be extremely time-consuming, and not very efficient at removing all the dirt.

Mushrooms grow in dirt or sandy soil and can be quickly and easily washed to remove all traces of grit without fear of damage. It is most important, however, that the mushrooms be fresh and tightly closed. If the mushrooms are older, and their gills are showing, washing them *will* waterlog them.

To wash mushrooms, you'll need a large bowl and colander. First trim away any dried stems and place the mushrooms in a large bowl. Place the bowl under cold running water. As the bowl fills with water, use your hands to agitate the mushrooms. The light mushrooms will float on the surface, while the heavier dirt falls to the bottom. Once the bowl is full, immediately lift the mushrooms out of the water and into the colander. Pour the water out and, starting with a clean bowl, repeat the process. After each washing, feel the bottom of the bowl. When no trace of grit can be found at the bottom, the mushrooms are clean.

Two to three washings taking no more than a total of 2 minutes are all that is normally required. With this technique, you should be able to wash 1 to 3 pounds of mushrooms very quickly.

If you are sautéing the mushrooms, it is important that they be dry, so once washed, allow them to air dry, or if in a hurry, dry them with paper towels.

any of the varieties you find in your market.

The unsalted butter (or oil) specified in this recipe is important to the proper sautéing of the mushrooms. The object is to sauté them quickly over high heat to drive out the excess moisture so they will brown. The salt in salted butter extracts moisture from the mushrooms, making it more difficult to brown them. Too much liquid, or heat insufficient to evaporate the moisture, and the mushrooms will boil instead of sauté.

Serves 6 to 8

3 tablespoons unsalted butter or light olive oil
1½ pounds mushrooms, washed, dried, and quartered
4 to 5 garlic cloves, chopped, to taste
6 sprigs parsley, chopped
¼ teaspoon salt
⅛ teaspoon freshly ground pepper

1. In a large skillet, heat the butter over high heat. Working in batches if necessary, add only the number of mushrooms that will cover the bottom of the pan in one layer. Sauté until browned, about 4 minutes.

2. Add the garlic and parsley and toss or stir quickly. Season with the salt and pepper. Remove from the heat and arrange on a serving platter or in a vegetable dish. Serve hot.

Champignons à la Grecque
Marinated Mushrooms

Greek-style vegetables are served as a first course in France, but can easily be added to a summer buffet. Some chefs prepare the mushrooms with tomatoes; others do not include them. I enjoy them both ways, and use tomatoes in the summer or whenever I find them red, ripe, and full flavored.

Although mushrooms are my favorite, pearl onions are also excellent prepared in a similar fashion (see Variation).

Serves 4 to 6

½ cup dry white wine
¼ cup light olive oil
Juice of 1 lemon
3 shallots, finely chopped
1 garlic clove, finely chopped (optional)
2 tomatoes, peeled, seeded, and diced (optional)
Bouquet Garni (page 346)
10 peppercorns, crushed
1 teaspoon salt
Pinch ground coriander (optional)
1½ pounds button mushrooms, washed (if using larger
      mushrooms, quarter them)

1. Place all of the ingredients except the mushrooms in a large, non-aluminum saucepan. Bring to a boil, reduce the heat, and simmer for 5 minutes.

2. Add the mushrooms to the simmering liquid and simmer, covered, for 5 to 6 minutes. With a slotted spoon, transfer the mushrooms to a serving bowl. Discard the bouquet garni.

3. Reduce the liquid to approximately ¾ cup and pour over the mushrooms. Refrigerate and serve chilled.

Variation

Petits Oignons à la Grecque *(Marinated Pearl Onions):* Substitute 1½ pounds of pearl onions, peeled, for the mushrooms. Add ½ cup water to the marinade in step 1. In step 2, cook the onions until tender, about 30 minutes.

Tomates à la Provençale
Broiled Tomatoes with Garlic and Herbs

When tomatoes are ripe and in season, the preparation of this recipe will fill your kitchen with the aromas of southern France.

Serves 6

3 medium to large tomatoes
3 tablespoons olive oil, extra-virgin if available
2 garlic cloves, finely chopped
1 shallot, finely chopped
¼ teaspoon thyme
5 sprigs parsley, chopped
About ⅓ cup bread crumbs
Pinch each salt and freshly ground pepper

1. Cut the tomatoes in half crosswise and place cut side up in a roasting or broiling pan.

2. In a small saucepan, heat the olive oil over medium heat. Add the garlic and shallot and gently sauté until softened but not browned, about 2 minutes.

3. Add the thyme and remove from the heat. Stir in the parsley and enough of the bread crumbs to absorb the oil. Season with the salt and pepper.

4. Spread the bread crumb mixture over the tops of the tomatoes. *(The tomatoes can be prepared up to this point several hours in advance.)*

5. Just before serving, preheat the broiler. Place the tomatoes 3 to 4 inches from the heat until they are heated through and the crumbs are browned, 3 to 4 minutes. If the tomatoes are ripe they will emerge from the broiler hot (but not fully cooked), soft, moist, and flavorful.

Serving Suggestion: Serve the tomatoes with roasted lamb or chicken, or with grilled lamb, chicken, steak, or fish. When available, sprinkle a little freshly chopped basil on top of the tomatoes as they come from the broiler.

Most recipes for these tomatoes instruct you to remove the seeds and excess juice, and to fill the emptied spaces with the flavored bread crumbs. I find the tomatoes more succulent when the seeds are left intact, and have therefore eliminated this time-consuming step here.

Ratatouille Niçoise

*R*atatouille niçoise is a traditional dish from the area of southern France known as Provence, specifically the city of Nice (hence the term *niçoise*), where its few simple ingredients are grown in abundance. There are many recipes for *ratatouille* and although the shapes of the vegetables and the proportions used may vary, the basic ingredients do not. Onion, green pepper, eggplant, zucchini, and tomato are always used.

There are two methods of preparing *ratatouille*. In the first, each vegetable is cooked separately and then mixed together for serving. The liquid left over from the cooking is usually discarded.

I prefer a second method in which all the vegetables are cooked slowly in one pot, often for several hours, until they are soft. Their colors darken and blend, creating a rich earthy hue, while their flavors and liquids blend and thicken to create a savory sauce. This method allows you to do other things as the *ratatouille* cooks, while the first method requires more time and attention.

There are two aspects to my technique that are important to the *ratatouille*'s texture and richness. The first is the size of the cut-up vegetables—I cut the eggplant, tomato, and zucchini into ½- to ¾-inch dice, which makes the *ratatouille* easier to use as a spread or a filling. Second is the way I enrich the *ratatouille* by reducing the excess cooking liquids to a rich, syrupy sauce for the vegetables. This simple procedure makes a world of difference.

Serves 6

Serving Suggestion:
Ratatouille is an extremely versatile dish. It can be served hot as a vegetable accompanying a sautéed, roast, or grilled chicken, or with grilled lamb, beef, or fish. It is served chilled or at room temperature as a first course, and I often serve it on crackers as an hors d'oeuvre. It can be used to fill crêpes and omelets, or mixed with scrambled eggs. Sprinkle grated Swiss or Parmesan cheese on top and reheat under a broiler, to serve it au gratin.

4 tablespoons olive oil, extra-virgin if available
2 onions, halved and sliced
2 green bell peppers, cut into thin strips
4 garlic cloves, finely chopped
1 eggplant (about 1 pound), peeled and diced
2 zucchini (about 1 pound), peeled and diced
2 pounds tomatoes, peeled, seeded, and diced or 4 pounds
 canned tomatoes, drained and diced
Bouquet Garni (page 346) with ¼ teaspoon extra thyme
¼ teaspoon salt
⅛ teaspoon freshly ground pepper
2 teaspoons tomato paste (optional)
4 sprigs parsley, chopped, for garnish

1. In a large saucepan or Dutch oven, heat the olive oil over medium heat. Add the onions and green peppers and cook until softened but not browned, about 4 minutes.

2. Add the garlic and stir several seconds. Add the eggplant and zucchini. Cover and cook gently over medium-low heat for 15 minutes. The vegetables should be partially cooked and there should be some liquid in the bottom of the pan.

3. Add the tomatoes and bouquet garni and season with the salt and pepper. Simmer gently over low heat, uncovered, stirring occasionally, until the vegetables are soft, 35 to 45 minutes.

4. By this time, the liquid in the pan should have reduced to a syrupy sauce. If your liquid is not thick enough, drain the vegetables well in a colander set over a large bowl. Remove the bouquet garni and return the liquid to the pot. Over high heat, reduce the liquid until it attains a saucelike consistency. Taste and add more salt and pepper, if necessary. If the tomatoes used were not red or flavorful enough, add the tomato paste at this time.

5. Place the vegetables in an ovenproof dish and gently stir in the sauce.

6. **To serve:** Reheat in a 350° to 400° oven for 15 to 20 minutes until bubbling. Sprinkle with the chopped parsley just before serving.

PEELING AND SEEDING TOMATOES

It is often necessary to peel and/or seed tomatoes for a recipe. Seeding tomatoes removes excess moisture and thereby also reduces the cooking time of some recipes. For example, if you don't seed the tomatoes for Sauce Tomate (page 372), it will take at least 20 minutes longer than the 5 minutes indicated in the recipe to achieve its desired consistency. In other sauces, tomatoes are added just before serving. If not seeded and well drained, the sauce will be too thin.

Tomatoes are always peeled before going into sauces in France, unless the sauce will be strained at the end. Tomatoes are not usually peeled when being cut for salads, but some varieties have thick or tough skins, and in such cases I would recommend peeling them.

Peeling: A vine-ripened tomato peels easily, but most store-bought tomatoes do not. To make peeling easy, bring a large saucepan of water to a boil. Using a paring knife, remove the stem area of each tomato. With a skimmer or slotted spoon, carefully lower 3 to 4 tomatoes at a time into the boiling water. After 8 to 10 seconds, remove the tomatoes to a plate or bowl. Their skin should now be easy to peel; if it is not, return the tomatoes to the water for an additional 4 to 5 seconds. The riper the tomatoes, the less time they need in the hot water.

If you are working on a gas range, and need to peel only 1 or 2 tomatoes, use a fork to turn them over a flame. The heat from the flame will cause the skin to blister and loosen, and it will then peel easily.

Seeding: To seed a tomato, cut it in half crosswise (through its equator and not its poles). Gently squeeze the tomato over a bowl, and shake out the seeds and excess liquid. Do not worry if a few seeds are left. Whatever you can remove by squeezing and shaking is sufficient.

Zucchini skin is sweet when it is very fresh, but turns bitter several days after picking. While trimming the stem, I cut off and taste a piece of the skin. If it's bitter, I peel the zucchini. If it's sweet, I just wash it. Peeled zucchini is fragile when cooked, and care should be taken in handling it.

Courgettes Farcies
Zucchini Stuffed with Mushrooms and Ham

One of my favorite ways of preparing zucchini is to fill scooped-out halves with a combination of ham, mushrooms, and onions and top with a cheese sauce. The stuffing and sauce can be made in advance and assembled with the zucchini the day of serving.

As a first course, one half zucchini is sufficient, and for a lunch or light supper I serve two together with bread, wine, and dessert.

Serves 4 or 8

4 zucchini, 6 to 8 inches long, peeled if necessary
¼ pound ham (boiled, baked, or smoked), finely chopped
¼ teaspoon thyme
5 sprigs parsley, chopped
Duxelles (page 212)
Sauce Mornay (page 358)
2 tablespoons milk
2 ounces Swiss-style cheese, such as Gruyère or Emmenthaler, grated (about ⅔ cup)
Butter for baking dish

1. Preheat the oven to 475°.
2. Cut the zucchini in half lengthwise and scoop out the seeds with a teaspoon.
3. Place the zucchini halves in 4 quarts of boiling water and blanch until tender, 3 to 5 minutes, depending on freshness. Drain on paper towels.
4. Stir the ham, thyme, and parsley into the *duxelles*. If the *sauce Mornay* was made ahead of time, reheat it. Thin the sauce with the milk and bring to a boil. Whisk well. Stir 5 to 6 tablespoons of the hot sauce into the stuffing.

5. Fill each zucchini half with stuffing and place in a buttered baking dish or on an ovenproof platter. Spoon the sauce over the stuffed zucchini and sprinkle with the grated cheese. *(This dish can be prepared to this point up to 1 day in advance and refrigerated.)*

6. **To serve:** Place the zucchini in the upper third of the oven for 6 to 8 minutes or until the sauce is bubbly and the cheese begins to brown.

There are many possible fillings for a stuffed zucchini. Cooked chicken, lamb, or ground beef can replace the ham in the recipe above. Cooked rice or bread crumbs can be added when unexpected guests appear. Or use a fresh tomato sauce (Sauce Tomate, page 372) with or in place of the cheese sauce.

Pommes de Terre à la Vapeur
Steamed Potatoes

Perhaps the easiest way to prepare potatoes is to steam them. In France, steamed potatoes are served with all poached fish, as well as being added to many stews or ragoûts. I also serve steamed potatoes with grilled, sautéed, and roasted meats, although their traditional partners are sautéed or fried potatoes.

Serves 6

18 small new potatoes
3 tablespoons butter, melted (optional)
Salt, to taste
Chopped parsley

1. Peel the potatoes, if desired; otherwise just wash them. Place them in a steamer basket set over boiling water and cover with a lid.

2. Steam until tender, 20 to 30 minutes. Insert a small knife into a potato; if the potato does not cling to the knife, it is done. *(If the potatoes are cooked in advance, reheat for several minutes in the steamer before serving.)*

3. Transfer the potatoes to a warm bowl. Coat with the melted butter, and sprinkle lightly with the salt and chopped parsley.

Steamed potatoes are usually served lightly coated with melted butter and sprinkled with chopped parsley; if they are going to be served on a plate with a sauce, I generally omit the butter. In formal settings they are traditionally served peeled, but whether you want to leave them unpeeled is a matter of preference.

Pommes de Terre Sautées
Sautéed Potatoes

Classically, sautéed potatoes are parboiled before being cooked in butter and browned. The initial cooking softens the starch, allowing the potatoes to brown easily when sautéed. Most European potatoes are of the firm, waxy variety, and remain firm after boiling, making this procedure easy to handle. Most American potatoes are pulpy and break or fall apart after cooking. To simplify this technique, and to save cleaning an extra pot, I sauté potatoes as follows.

Serves 6

6 large potatoes
4 tablespoons butter, or more as needed
¼ teaspoon salt
Pinch freshly ground pepper
3 sprigs parsley, chopped, for garnish

1. Peel the potatoes and cut them into ½-inch dice. Soak in cold water until ready to use.

2. In a 12-inch nonstick skillet, heat 4 tablespoons of butter. Drain the potatoes and place in the skillet over medium-low heat. Cover the pan and steam the potatoes for 2 to 5 minutes. They should be tender, but not brown.

3. Uncover, turn the heat to medium-high or high, and sauté, shaking the pan frequently, until the potatoes brown, about 10 minutes. If not shaken, the potatoes may stick and not brown evenly. If the pan seems dry, add more butter, 1 tablespoon at a time. *(The potatoes can be prepared up to 1 hour in advance and reheated by sautéing over medium-high heat just before serving.)* Season with the salt and pepper and sprinkle with the chopped parsley to serve.

Les Pommes Frites
French-Fried Potatoes

The French are famous for their fried potatoes. Most Americans probably know only plain *pommes frites*, which are like skinny American French fries. But the French have a whole range of fried potatoes, each with a different shape, size, and name: *chips*, *julienne*, *pailles* (straws), *allumettes* (matchsticks), *Pont-Neuf* (thick-cut), *gaufrettes* (waffled), and *soufflées*.

Most chefs peel their potatoes before trimming them into a basic rectangular shape that then can easily be cut into any other shape desired. I trim the potato with its skin on, thereby peeling it at the same time and saving myself one step (see step 1, below).

The general method for deep-frying potatoes below is followed by specific instructions for preparing and cooking the individual varieties of *pommes frites*.

Serves 4 to 6

8 large potatoes
2 to 3 quarts light vegetable or peanut oil, for deep-frying
Salt

1. Trim one side of the potato so it rests flat on your cutting board. Keep trimming the sides and turning the potato until four sides are square. Trim the ends, stand the potato on one end, and trim the remaining peel at the four edges. You will now have a classically trimmed potato ready for slicing. (If you don't want to waste any potato, just peel it and don't trim it, but realize that some of your finished product will not be perfectly shaped.)
2. Prepare the potatoes according to the style of

When I am asked why potatoes fried in America don't taste like the potatoes fried in France, I reply that both our potatoes and the oil we use to fry them differ from what is used in France. The best flavor is achieved when a combination of animal fats (beef, veal, and pork) is used. Since animal fats are unhealthy, however, we avoid frying with them, sacrificing that true French flavor. The texture of fried potatoes in America also differs from the French because most of ours are made from the brown-skinned Russets, while the French use a yellow potato closer in texture to our red-skinned potatoes (see "Yellow Potatoes," page 225).

French-fried potato you want (see Variations), and soak the potatoes in a bowl of cold water until ready to use.

3. Place the oil in a deep-fryer with a frying basket and heat to the temperature specified for the style of potato you are making (see Variations). Temperatures will range from 320° to 400°, depending on the thickness of the potato.

4. Drain the potatoes and dry between several layers of paper towels. Place about two handfuls of potatoes in the frying basket (any more and the temperature of the oil will drop, increasing the frying time and causing the potatoes to absorb too much oil). Slowly lower the potatoes into the hot oil. If the potatoes are wet, the oil may boil violently. Remove the basket at once. In such cases it may be necessary to lower the basket in steps to avoid excess spattering which can be dangerous. Shake the basket frequently to prevent the potatoes from sticking.

5. When the potatoes are done, drain them in the frying basket, then on paper towels. Sprinkle with salt before serving.

Variations

Pommes Chips *(Potato Chips):* The potatoes should simply be peeled and thinly sliced (a food processor works well), then fried in very hot oil (390° to 400°). The chips should be golden brown in about 2 minutes.

Pommes Julienne *(Julienned Potatoes):* The potatoes are first thinly sliced and then cut into thin julienne and fried as for *pommes chips* (above).

Pommes Pailles et Allumettes *(Potato Straws and Matchsticks):* Both are cut about ⅛ inch thick; *allumettes* (matchsticks) are 2 inches long and *pailles* (straws) are as long as the potato will allow. Both are fried at 375° until golden brown, about 3 minutes.

YELLOW POTATOES

One reason for the superior results the French achieve with fried potatoes is the yellow potato. Used extensively in Europe where they are prized for their flavor, creamy texture, and superb cooking qualities, yellow potatoes are now beginning to make their appearance in American markets. Varieties to look for are Yellow Finnish, Yellow Corolla, Delta Gold, and Golden Delite.

Pommes Pont-Neuf *(Thick-Cut French Fries):* These are 3½-inch-long French fries cut ½-inch square that need to be fried at two temperatures. First fry them at 350° for about 7 minutes. At this point the potatoes should be cooked but not browned. A potato pressed between thumb and forefinger should crush. (If you are unaccustomed to handling very hot food, do not attempt this test. Instead, use the back of a spoon to crush the potato on a plate or counter.) This first frying can be done several hours ahead of time. Just before serving, the potatoes should be fried again at 390° to 400° for 1 to 2 minutes until golden brown.

Pommes Frites *(French Fries):* This term generally refers to potatoes cut into strips ¼-inch square and about 2½-inches long. They can either be fried like the *pommes Pont-Neuf*, requiring only about 5 minutes for the initial frying, and about 1 minute to brown at the higher temperature, or they can be fried all at once at 350° until they color, 7 to 8 minutes.

Pommes Soufflées *(Puffed Sliced Potatoes):* These little air-filled crunchy pillows take care and time to prepare, but are a guaranteed hit. Instead of cutting the potatoes into a rectangle, simply peel them. Slice them lengthwise into ⅛- to ³⁄₁₆-inch-thick ovals and then fry in small batches at two temperatures. Care should be taken when slicing the potatoes to make sure they are evenly cut. Drop the slices by the handful into 325° oil. When the bubbling of the oil ceases, this first frying should be done. Use a frying skimmer to remove the slices and drain on paper towels. At this point, the potatoes should have little or no color. The second frying is done at 400° and the slices should immediately puff and brown. If they have not browned sufficiently, they will collapse on cooling. Should this happen, refry them and some will puff again. Not all slices will puff. These potatoes need to be practiced on your family and friends before attempting to impress guests. Serve the potatoes salted, in a napkin-lined serving dish.

Pommes Gaufrettes
(Waffled French Fries)

To make *gaufrettes*, you will need a vegetable slicer with a ripple blade. The *gaufrettes* are round and are cut ⅛ inch thick. Make the first cut with the ripple slicer, then rotate the potato one-quarter turn to make the next cut. Continue to rotate the potatoes one-quarter turn back and forth as they pass across the rippled blade to give them the traditional open basket-weave design that resembles a waffle. Cook as for the Pommes Chips on page 225, for about 3 minutes.

Gratin Dauphinois
Sliced Potatoes Baked in Cream

A *gratin* is a dish having a crusted or browned surface. Originating in the region of the Alps known as
the Dauphine, this simple and easy potato dish is truly
one of France's great *gratins* and is ideal to serve with
roast beef, lamb, and poultry.

Many different versions of this *gratin* recipe exist.
Some are made with cream and cheese, while others are
made with milk, eggs, and cheese. I feel the best are
made just with a combination of milk and cream, which
I heat before baking to cut the baking time in half. (If
you are not in a rush, you can eliminate this step, but
cook the potatoes 1 hour.)

Serves 6

Butter for baking dish
4 pounds large potatoes (about 8), peeled and cut into
    ⅛-inch-thick slices
1 garlic clove, chopped
1 teaspoon salt
⅛ teaspoon freshly ground pepper
1 cup milk
1 cup heavy cream

1. Preheat the oven to 450°. Butter a large (9 × 14
inches) baking dish.

2. Layer the sliced potatoes in the baking dish and
sprinkle with the garlic, salt, and pepper.

3. In a small saucepan over medium heat, combine
the milk and cream and bring to a boil. Pour over the layered potatoes.

4. Bake in the middle of the oven until the potatoes are
brown and tender and a knife easily penetrates them, 35

Recipes differ in how the
potatoes for a *gratin
dauphinois* are prepared.
Some chefs insist on slicing and soaking the pota-
toes in cold water to rid
them of their surface starch
before baking. Others,
including myself, believe
the starch is necessary for
the creamy consistency of
the potatoes. However, if
you prepare the potatoes
ahead of time, they *do*
need to be soaked to pre-
vent them from discolor-
ing. Therefore, for this
recipe, if you slice the
potatoes in advance, soak
them in the milk and cream
in which they will be cooked
so as not to lose the starch.

to 40 minutes. The potatoes should simmer or gently boil while in the oven. If they begin to boil rapidly, or brown before they are tender, reduce the heat by 25 to 50 degrees.

5. Remove the dish from the oven and serve. The potatoes will stay hot for about 30 minutes. *(The* gratin *can be made ahead of time. Let cool to room temperature, cover, and refrigerate. Reheat by bringing back to room temperature and then placing in a 350° oven for 15 minutes.)*

Variation

Sprinkle 2 ounces (about ⅔ cup) grated Swiss-style cheese, such as Gruyère or Emmenthaler, over the *gratin* in step 3.

Pommes de Terre à la Boulangère
Potatoes and Onions Baked in Stock

It was the practice on Sundays in many towns throughout France to leave a piece of meat at the baker's shop to be roasted. The roast would be dropped off on the way to church, and picked up, fully cooked, on the way home.

The baker would place the meat on racks in his bread ovens and position baking dishes filled with sliced potatoes and onions beneath the roasts to catch their juices while cooking. Sometimes the bakers would roast the meat directly on top of the sliced potatoes and onion. The potatoes were simply moistened with water, but would pick up flavor from the dripping fat and meat juices. Thus, the origin of the name *à la boulangère*, or "in the style of the baker."

I have specified that the onions be sautéed, a step that slightly increases your work but substantially increases the flavor of the finished dish.

Pommes de Terre Savoyarde
(Potatoes with Ham and Cheese Baked in Stock)

You can turn *pommes de terre à la boulangère* into a hearty main dish from the high alpine region of France by adding 3 ounces of diced ham or cooked bacon and 2 ounces (about ⅔ cup) of grated Swiss-style cheese, such as Gruyère or Emmenthaler. When served with a green salad and fruit for dessert, these potatoes become a wholesome meal.

Serves 6

1 tablespoon butter
2 onions, chopped
4 pounds large potatoes (about 8), peeled and cut into
    ⅛-inch-thick slices
1 teaspoon salt
⅛ teaspoon freshly ground pepper
2 cups chicken or beef stock, homemade or canned
    (see chart, pages 348–349)

1. Preheat the oven to 450°.
2. In a skillet, heat the butter over medium-high heat. Add the onions and sauté until lightly browned, about 4 minutes.
3. Layer the potatoes and onions in an ovenproof casserole or baking dish and season with the salt and pepper.
4. In a saucepan, bring the stock to a boil and pour it over the potatoes and onions. Bake the casserole in the oven until the potatoes are tender, about 45 minutes. Adjust the oven temperature if necessary so that the stock boils gently. *(These potatoes are best served hot from the oven, but may be cooked in advance and reheated. When reheating, add 2 tablespoons stock or water.)*

Pommes de Terre Rôties
Roasted Potatoes

*P*ommes de terre rôties, or roast potatoes, are small new potatoes or large potatoes cut to resemble small ones that are served with roast beef, roast lamb, and roast chicken.

Always remember to shake the pan frequently to make sure none of the potatoes stick. Once cooked, remove the potatoes from the hot pan. If you are not ready to serve them, they can be reheated in a hot oven for 5 minutes.

Serves 6

6 tablespoons butter
18 small new potatoes, peeled, or 6 large potatoes, peeled
    and quartered
¼ teaspoon salt
Pinch freshly ground pepper

1. Preheat the oven to 475°.
2. In a roasting pan large enough to hold the potatoes in one layer, heat the butter in the oven or on top of the stove. Add the potatoes, shaking the pan to coat them with butter.
3. Place the pan in the oven. Shake the pan frequently, about every 10 minutes, making sure none of the potatoes stick to the pan. Turn the potatoes if necessary, to brown evenly. Cook until well browned, crisp on the outside, and tender when pierced with a knife, about 45 minutes. Remove the potatoes from the hot butter, sprinkle with the salt and pepper, and serve.

Another method of preparing the potatoes is to place them in a large roasting pan together with your roast, and in 45 minutes to 1 hour the potatoes will be crisp and brown on the outside and soft and tender inside.

Pommes de Terre Dauphine
Potato Puffs

*P*ommes de terre dauphine are potato puffs, made from mashed potatoes and cream-puff pastry, that are fried just before serving. The batter can be prepared up to a day in advance to make their preparation easier. It is important to dry the mashed potatoes to extract any excess cooking moisture. If the potatoes are too wet, the puffs will be heavy instead of light. For the same reason, make sure any ingredients mixed with the batter (see Variations) are also dry.

Serves 4 to 6

1½ pounds potatoes, peeled, boiled, and mashed*
Pâte à Choux Salée (page 269)
½ teaspoon salt
¼ teaspoon freshly ground pepper
2 quarts vegetable oil, for deep-frying

1. Dry the mashed potatoes a little by stirring them in a saucepan over medium heat until they begin to lightly coat the pan.

2. Mix the potato and *pâte à choux* together and season with the salt and pepper.

3. In a deep-fryer, bring the oil to 375°. Drop the mixture by teaspoonfuls into the hot oil and cook until puffed and a rich brown color, 2 to 3 minutes.

4. Drain on paper towels and sprinkle with salt to taste. Serve very hot.

* Do not use a food processor to mash the potatoes or they will be pasty.

Variations

In addition to the specific variations below, you can also mix 2 tablespoons chopped fresh herbs, ¼ pound chopped cooked ham or chicken, or ¼ pound grated cheese or combinations of any of the above into the pastry mixture.

Pommes de Terre Elisabeth *(Potato Puffs with Spinach):* Add ¼ pound spinach that has been cooked, squeezed dry, and chopped to the potato and pastry mixture.

Pommes de Terre Idéales *(Truffled Puff Potatoes):* Add 1 large julienned truffle to the potato and pastry mixture.

Purée de Pommes de Terre à l'Ail
Mashed Potatoes with Garlic

Mashed potatoes are always popular, and this version, with its added delicate flavor of garlic, never fails to bring an expression of surprise to the faces of diners.

A classic French purée of potatoes is first dried by being stirred over heat before it is moistened with milk or cream and enriched with butter. Although delicious, I prefer to save all those calories for dessert. The following recipe uses only the flavorful cooking water to produce a light and healthful purée that can be consumed without guilt. When the flavor of garlic does not complement the rest of your meal, simply omit it.

If preparing the potatoes in advance, cover the surface with plastic wrap or a little milk to prevent them from drying out. Keep warm or reheat in a water bath (*bain-marie*) to prevent the potatoes from scorching on the bottom of the pan.

Serves 6 to 8

8 large potatoes
8 garlic cloves
¾ teaspoon salt
Milk (optional)
⅛ teaspoon freshly ground pepper

1. Peel the potatoes and cut them into large chunks. Place them in cold water until you are ready to cook them.

2. To cook, place the potatoes and garlic in a 4-quart pot and barely cover with water (the tips of several potatoes

will not be covered). Add ½ teaspoon of the salt and bring to a boil over high heat.

3. Boil, uncovered, over medium-high heat until tender, 20 to 30 minutes. The potato is tender when a point of a knife goes in and out without the potato clinging to it. Drain the potatoes, reserving the cooking liquid (about ⅔ cup).

4. Purée the potatoes using a potato masher, food mill, or similar device. <u>Do not use a food processor</u> as it will cause the potatoes to become pasty. Moisten the purée with the reserved cooking liquid until the desired consistency is reached. If more liquid is necessary, use milk. Season with the remaining ¼ teaspoon salt and the pepper.

Riz au Blanc
Boiled White Rice

This is the easiest method I know of preparing fluffy white rice. It is ideal to serve with any sauce, but is especially suited to white sauces. It is also the best way to cook rice that is destined for a stuffing or a salad. Classically, the rice is first cooked in a large quantity of water, then drained, rinsed, and either towel dried or steam dried in an oven. The rice can be cooked in advance and reheated for serving. I simplify the drying and reheating process by steaming the rice quickly just before serving. Some people prefer their rice firmer than others, and I have indicated a cooking time of 15 to 18 minutes. Start tasting the rice after 15 minutes, and stop the cooking when the rice reaches the texture you prefer. The only equipment needed for steaming is a metal strainer.

Serves 4

1½ quarts water
½ teaspoon salt
1 cup long-grain white rice

1. In a medium saucepan, bring 1½ quarts of water and the salt to a boil over high heat. Add the rice and stir, making sure none sticks to the bottom of the pan. Boil for 15 to 18 minutes. The water needs to boil constantly to keep the rice moving so it does not stick to the pan. Taste the rice to determine when you want to stop the cooking.

2. Drain the rice into a metal strainer and rinse well under warm or cold water to remove the excess starch. Place the strainer over the pan used for cooking the rice and allow to drain.

3. **To reheat and serve:** Fill the pan with at least 1 inch of water. Place the strainer in the pan and cover with a lid. (The strainer should not touch the water.) Steam the rice for about 5 minutes, or until hot. Blot the bottom of the strainer with several layers of paper towel or a folded kitchen towel to absorb any excess moisture, and then empty the strainer of rice into a hot bowl and serve.

Riz Pilaf
Rice Pilaf

Rice pilaf is a basic recipe with great versatility. The basic ratio of liquid to rice is two to one. If you prefer your rice softer and moister, add another ½ cup of liquid. If you prefer the rice to be firmer, use ¼ cup

QUICK STOCKS FOR RICE PILAF

When making a rice pilaf, you can make a quick, light stock to use in place of the water. For example, you may have some poultry parts (omitting the liver) or shrimp shells left over from another recipe that together with some onion and mushroom trimmings and a few sprigs of parsley can be simmered in 2½ cups of water to produce a light, flavorful stock in less than 20 minutes.

LADLES

Most people probably don't realize that ladles come in sizes and can be used to measure ingredients. A 1-cup ladle is the size most often used, although I also use ½-cup and ¼-cup ladles. The size is often marked (in ounces) on the ladle's handle.

A ladle is particularly useful for transferring a measured amount of hot liquid out of a pot. Instead of pouring the hot liquid into a measuring cup and then into your pan or work bowl, simply ladle out what you need.

I often use a ladle for making rice pilaf, which is made with two parts water or stock to one part rice. Just measure the rice in the ladle, then scoop up twice as much liquid to pour over the rice.

less. Once you know the basic technique, you can create your own variations to complement whatever you are serving. Here are a few suggestions: You can use chicken, beef, fish, or vegetable stock; and you can flavor the stocks with herbs, or spices such as curry or saffron. A few sliced mushrooms or some diced ham may be cooked with the rice. Dried fruit and nuts also can be chopped and added before serving. Don't use all of these suggestions in one recipe, but try several combinations.

Serves 4

2 tablespoons butter
½ onion, chopped
1 cup long-grain white rice
2 cups water or stock
¼ teaspoon salt
⅛ teaspoon freshly ground pepper

1. In a medium saucepan, heat the butter over medium heat. Add the onion and cook several minutes until softened but not browned. Add the rice and stir with a wooden spoon until the rice takes on a milky opaque appearance, 1 to 2 minutes.

2. Add the water or stock, salt, and pepper and bring to a boil. Stir, making sure the rice does not stick to the pan. Reduce the heat, cover tightly, and cook for 18 minutes over very low heat*.

3. Remove the pan from the heat. (The rice will remain hot for 20 minutes and can be kept warm in a water bath [*bain-marie*] or 200° oven.)

4. **To serve:** Fluff the rice with a fork, adjust the seasoning, if necessary, and transfer to a warm serving bowl.

* You can also bake the pilaf. In step 1, sauté the onion and rice in a flameproof casserole or ovenproof saucepan. Add the stock, bring to a boil, cover tightly, and bake in a 300° oven for 18 minutes.

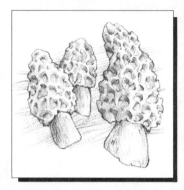

Riz Sauvage Forestière
Wild Rice with Mushrooms

Wild rice, a purely American product still harvested to a large degree by American Indians, is becoming a present-day classic in France. Some of their finest restaurants now import it to offer on their menus. I find that its earthy color and flavor, combined with its slightly crunchy texture, make it an ideal companion for duck, squab, and game birds in general.

Serves 8

8 ounces wild rice, rinsed in cold water
4 tablespoons butter
1 small onion or 3 shallots, chopped
¾ pound cultivated or wild mushrooms, washed, dried,
*   and chopped*
4 chicken livers, chopped (optional*)
¼ teaspoon salt
⅛ teaspoon freshly ground pepper
10 sprigs parsley, chopped

1. Place the wild rice in a saucepan with 5 quarts of water. Bring to a boil and cook until the rice grains open and are tender, 45 to 60 minutes. Drain and rinse the rice under cold water. Set aside.

2. In a 12-inch skillet, heat the butter over medium-low heat. Add the onion and cook until softened but not browned, about 3 minutes. Add the mushrooms, turn the heat to high, and cook until lightly browned, about 3 minutes. Add the livers and cook quickly, about 30 seconds. Season with the salt and pepper and add the mixture to the rice.

3. Stir in the parsley; taste and adjust the seasoning, if necessary.

4. Reheat the rice mixture, covered, in a water bath (*bain-marie*) or in a 200° oven until hot, about 15 minutes, stirring occasionally. Serve.

✳ The liver can be left out, but if you like liver and you are serving squabs, ducks, or game birds, use their livers in the recipe. If you are serving this dish with game birds, in addition to using the liver from the bird in place of the chicken livers, also add ¼ teaspoon thyme to the mushrooms while they are cooking. You can also sprinkle the rice with a tablespoon or two of Madeira when reheating it.

USING A MICROWAVE OVEN FOR REHEATING

Although many recipes can be reheated in a microwave oven, I was surprised and disappointed to find that when reheating wild rice this way, it had lost its good flavor. For this reason, I do not recommend using the microwave oven to reheat any wild rice recipes. It is, however, especially good for reheating vegetable purées, sauces, ragoûts, and dishes with a dense consistency which take longer to reheat, such as the Cassoulet Maigre (page 181).

In my view, a meal is never complete without a dessert, be it cake, fruit, ice cream, or pastry. When serving a meal, try to pace the courses so your guests will be satisfied after finishing the entrée, yet will still be looking forward to dessert. Children seem to do this naturally, and in our home, no matter what the main course has been, my girls always ask, "What's for dessert?".

In the following two chapters, I have included most of my favorites, omitting only those that take an excessive amount of time to make. Most of these desserts and pastries can be made either completely or partially in advance, while others need only a quick, final assembly before serving. Since the final course often determines the success of a meal, knowing that you already have a marvelous dessert ready allows you to relax and prepare the rest of the meal with confidence.

Desserts

Pastries

Before the early '70s French restaurants offered chocolate mousse, fruit tarts, crème caramel, poached fruit, and the like, but rarely offered pastry. The average restaurant chef in France prepared only those desserts known as *entremets*. Pastry chefs did their work in pastry shops and large hotels.

Today no top restaurant in France can reach or maintain its standing without a superb pastry chef. As well, many American restaurants now proudly present superb homemade pastries.

The recipes and techniques I have developed can make home cooks comfortable in an area once the sole domain of the pastry chef.

Successful pastry making requires accuracy in measuring ingredients. Hence, the use of gram measurements in this chapter (see also "The Metric System in Cooking and Pastry Making," page 404).

FRAISAGE

Pâte Brisée
Unsweetened Tart or Quiche Pastry

French tart pastry is designed to be self-supporting when baked, and is firmer and crunchier than American pie dough—qualities that come in part from a more thorough incorporation of fat and flour in a blending/kneading process called *fraisage* (see illustration, left).

Although *pâte brisée* is traditionally made by hand, the food processor method included below makes an excellent tart pastry and takes much of the risk out of the procedure for the novice (inexperienced bakers tend to overwork the pastry, causing it to be tough and to shrink when baked).

Both *pâte brisée* and *pâte sucrée* (variation follows) call for a whole egg (although many recipes for tart pastry call for no egg or the yolk only). The egg white acts as a sealant, preventing liquids baked in the tart from being absorbed or from seeping through the crust. The yolk enriches the pastry and adds color.

Makes enough for a 10- to 11-inch tart

Food Processor Method	Hand Method
1 ⅓ cups (190 g) all-purpose flour	*Same*
1 stick (115 g) unsalted butter, cut into 8 pieces	*Same, but cut into ½-inch cubes*
1 egg	*Same*
⅛ teaspoon salt	*Same*
1 ½ tablespoons cold water	*2 to 3 tablespoons cold water*

1. **Food processor method:** Place all of the ingredients in the bowl of a food processor fitted with a metal blade and process until the mixture blends together to form a mass, about 20 seconds. If it doesn't form a mass after 25 seconds, add another teaspoon of water.

Hand method: Place the flour on a work surface, or in a large bowl, and form a well in the center. Add the butter, egg, salt, and 1 tablespoon of water to the well and mix with a pastry blender. The pastry should have a coarse, granular texture and be moist enough to begin to stick together. If it is too dry, add up to 2 tablespoons more water.

2. Turn the pastry out onto a lightly floured work surface, dust the pastry lightly with flour, and begin the blending or kneading process known as *fraisage:* With the heel of your hand, push the pastry away from you a little at a time and repeat this process three or four times or until the pastry is smooth and does not stick to the work surface*.

3. Lightly dust the pastry with flour and shape it into a flat round much like a thick hamburger. The pastry can be used immediately unless it is too warm and soft, in which case wrap it in plastic wrap and refrigerate for 10 to 20 minutes.

* The processor does such a good job of blending, that most cooks do not see the purpose of kneading at this point. However, if not kneaded the pastry will be too fragile and will either break while you are lining the pan, or later after baking.

Variation

Pâte Sucrée *(Sweet Tart Pastry):* The techniques for making and handling *pâte sucrée* are identical to those for *pâte brisée*. The only changes are in the ingredients: ¼ cup (50 g) sugar is added and the salt is omitted. If you have never made *pâte sucrée*, start by using only 1 tablespoon (15 g) of sugar. The more sugar you add (you can use up to 5 tablespoons or 75 g), the more fragile the pastry will be.

MAKING A DECORATIVE RIM

A decorative rim typically found in pastry shops can be created as follows:

1. After placing the pastry in the tart pan, place your bent index finger at the upper inside edge of the mold. Push about ½ inch of the overlapping pastry in over your finger and press gently with your thumb. Continue around the mold to form a rim.

2. Cut off the excess pastry by rolling the pin across the top of the pan; remove it from the edge.

3. Lift the rim up at a 45-degree angle and press between the thumb and forefinger. Supporting the inner wall of the rim with the forefinger of one hand, use a fork or pastry pinch (a tweezerlike instrument used to give a decorative edge to both tarts and quiches) to decorate the top edge.

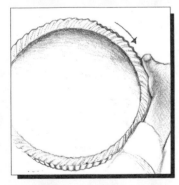

4. Gently run your thumb along the outer top edge of the pan to ensure that the pastry remains on the inside of the pan when baked. This will prevent problems when unmolding.

Tarte aux Myrtilles
Blueberry Tart

In France, where blueberries are usually uncooked in a fresh fruit tart, I have always missed the wonderful, juicy cooked-berry taste of an American blueberry pie. For the best of both worlds, my *tarte aux myrtilles* cooks blueberries in a traditional French tart pastry, and unlike American blueberry pie, is not too sweet. The natural flavors and sweetness of the fruit are complemented by a currant jelly glaze (*glaçage à la gellée de groseille*).

Serves 6 to 8

Butter for tart pan
Pâte Sucrée (tart pastry, page 242)
2 tablespoons (20 g) cornstarch
2 pints fresh blueberries
2 to 3 tablespoons (30 to 45 g) sugar (optional*)
Glaçage à la Gellée de Groseille (page 396), hot

1. Preheat the oven to 475°. Lightly butter a 9½- to 10-inch tart pan with removable bottom. Line the pan with the tart pastry (see "How to Line a Tart Pan," page 75). Prick the bottom of the pastry several times with the point of a sharp knife to prevent it from puffing during baking. Refrigerate or freeze the shell until you are ready to fill and bake it.

2. Sprinkle the cornstarch over the bottom of the tart shell and fill with the blueberries. At this point the blueberries will mound slightly above the rim of the tart. Sprinkle with the sugar, if using.

3. Place the tart on the bottom rack of the oven and bake for 10 minutes. Reduce the temperature to 425° and continue baking for an additional 30 to 35 minutes, until

the berries are gently boiling and the rim of the tart is dark brown.

4. Unmold the tart as soon as possible and allow to cool on a pastry rack (see "Unmolding a Tart or Quiche, page 246).

5. **To serve:** When the tart has cooled, dab the hot *glaçage à la gellée groseille* over the surface of the tart with a pastry brush. Slide the tart off the pastry rack and onto a serving platter. (When you cut into the tart, the berry juice should run very slowly. If the juice does not run at all, use a little less cornstarch when next making the tart. Similarly, should the juice be too liquid, add more starch.)

* If your berries are sour, you may find it desirable to sprinkle them with 2 to 3 tablespoons of sugar before baking, although I have always enjoyed the tartness on such occasions.

Variations

Tarte aux Pêches et aux Framboises *(Peach and Raspberry Tart):* In place of the blueberries, use about 2½ pounds of peaches, peeled, in large, 1-inch-thick slices and ½ pint raspberries. Starting at the outer edge of the tart, overlap the peach slices in concentric circles and place the raspberries in the center. Sprinkle the fruit with 1 to 2 tablespoons of sugar, depending on the sweetness of the fruit. After it's baked, glaze the peaches with hot Glaçage à l'Abricot (page 396) and the raspberries with Glaçage à la Gellée de Groseille (page 396).

Tarte aux Quetsches *(Italian Prune Tart):* Replace the blueberries with 2½ pounds of washed, pitted, and halved Italian prune plums. Use only 1½ tablespoons of cornstarch. Starting at the outer edge of the tart, overlap the plums, flesh side up, in a clockwise or counterclockwise direction, covering the entire surface of the tart. Sprinkle the plums with 1 to 2 tablespoons of sugar, depending on the sweetness of the fruit, and bake for a total of 40 minutes. Glaze with Glaçage à la Gellée de Groseille (page 396).

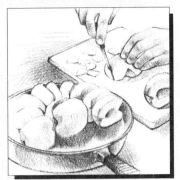

**Peel, halve, and core the
apples. With the cut side
down, trim off a small slice
from each apple half so they
will stand on their sides.**

There is a special pan sold
in France, and imported
by a few companies in the
United States, called a *tarte
Tatin* mold. Made of cop-
per with relatively high,
gently sloping sides and no
handle, it is very expensive.
I use a heavy aluminum
skillet with a handle that
can withstand high temperatures without breaking.
Many of my students use
their black cast-iron fry
pans with equally good
results. While cooking the
apples on the stove, the
sugary juice tends to bubble over the side of the pan,
so if you have a choice of
pans, choose the one with
the highest sides.

Tarte Tatin
Upside-Down Caramelized Apple Tart

The *tarte Tatin*, an upside-down caramelized apple
tart, was made famous by the Tatin sisters, who
served this tart in their hotel restaurant in the early
1900s. It has been a very popular dessert ever since,
and is my favorite apple dessert.

Every chef has his own way of making the tart. Some
bake it totally in the oven, while others cook the apples
on top of the stove and finish baking it with its pastry in
the oven. I use the second method.

The pastry used in this recipe is normal tart pastry,
but if you have puff pastry in your freezer, by all means
use it, as do most restaurants in France. A half recipe
of *pâte brisée* is exactly the amount of dough needed,
and the remainder can be frozen for another use. If,
however, you are not sure of your pastry-rolling skills,
use the whole recipe and roll out until ⅛ inch thick
before using.

I use less butter and sugar than most *tarte Tatin*
recipes call for, and because of this I occasionally
indulge by serving *crème fraîche* along with the tart.

Serves 8

10 Golden Delicious apples (about 4½ pounds*)
7 tablespoons (100 g) butter
½ cup plus 3 tablespoons (150 g) sugar
1 tablespoon lemon juice or water
½ recipe Pâte Brisée (tart pastry, page 241) or ½ pound
    Pâte Demi-Feuilletée (page 277)
Whipped cream or crème fraîche (optional)

1. Preheat the oven to 425°.

2. Peel, halve, and core the apples. With the cut side down, trim off a small slice from one side of each apple half so it can stand on its side.

3. In a 10-inch ovenproof skillet, heat the butter over medium heat. Add the sugar and lemon juice (if the apples are sour, use the water) and mix well. (The sugar will not be completely dissolved at this point.)

4. Starting at the outside of the pan, stand the apple halves on their sides, one next to the other, filling the skillet tightly. Once the outer circle is complete, place two halves together in the center and then continue placing the apples around until all are tightly packed. There may be one or two large holes that should be filled by cutting a piece of apple to fit. At this point, the apples should stand a little above the rim of the skillet (after a few minutes of cooking, the apples will begin to soften and you may be able to wedge additional pieces into the pan).

5. Continue cooking over medium to medium-high heat for 25 to 30 minutes. The juice from the apples will first dissolve the sugar, then evaporate, and the sugar will slowly cook to the caramel stage. When the sugar bubbling around the apples is pale brown in color, place the skillet in the upper third of the oven for 5 minutes. The apples will settle in the skillet.

6. Remove the skillet from the oven and increase the heat to 475°.

7. Roll out the pastry as you would for a tart, keeping it round. When it is large enough to fully cover the top of the skillet, about 12 inches in diameter, roll it up onto your rolling pin and unroll it over the top of the apples. The pastry will drape down the sides of the skillet. Run a paring knife around the edge, trimming off the excess pastry.

8. Place the skillet in the upper third of the oven and bake until the pastry is lightly browned, 15 to 20 minutes.

9. Remove the tart from the oven and run your knife around the inside edge of the skillet to make sure that the apples and pastry are not stuck to it. Holding a round heat-resistant platter inverted on the pastry with one hand, and

UNMOLDING A TART OR QUICHE

1. When the tart has finished baking, place it on your countertop. Fold a kitchen towel to cover your hand and forearm. Slide the tart pan off the countertop and onto your hand.

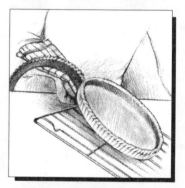

2. The rim will drop away and hang on your wrist. Transfer the tart on its metal bottom to a pastry rack. The removal of the metal bottom is a little more difficult but also essential.

3. Slide a long, narrow metal spatula between the metal bottom and the tart. It should slide freely across the bottom. (If the spatula sticks in the middle, the pastry has not been sufficiently cooked, and you should return the tart, rack and all, to the oven for a few minutes additional baking.) Holding on to the edge of the metal bottom with one hand, raise it, tilting it 10 to 15 degrees. Again, slide the spatula underneath the pastry and pull the metal bottom away, while supporting the tart with the spatula, as you lower the tart to the rack.

the handle of the skillet (wrapped in a pot holder) with the other, turn the skillet upside down and place the platter on the counter. Slowly lift off the skillet, unmolding the tart. The apples will have some spaces between them. Run a long metal spatula around the outside of the apples several times, drawing them toward the center. A border of pastry will be revealed as the apples are compressed. Use the spatula to smooth the top of the tart.

10. A *tarte Tatin* is best when served warm, and may be reheated if necessary. It may be served with whipped cream or *crème fraîche*, if desired.

* Depending on the size of the skillet and the apples, you may need as many as two more or less than the apples called for in this recipe.

Variation

Tarte Tatin aux Poires *(Upside-Down Caramelized Pear Tart):* Use an equal weight of Bosc pears, peeled and halved, in place of the apples.

UNMOLDING A TART OR QUICHE

A tart should be unmolded while it is hot so that the pastry dries as it cools. A tart pan with a removable bottom makes unmolding possible. Because of the false bottom, it is important to lift and move the tart pan by holding the outer rim only.

The procedure at left may sound difficult, and many people prefer not to try it. The results are a soggy bottom. It may take you two or three tarts to master the technique, but the results are well worth it. Once the tart has cooled, it can slide easily from its rack to a flat tart plate or platter for presentation and serving.

Tarte Alsacienne aux Fruits
Alsatian Fruit Tart

Alsace is an area of France that produces a great variety of fruit. Fruit tarts from this area use a custard made with flour, eggs, and heavy cream—sort of a fruit quiche. The custard holds the fruit in place when cut, which makes serving this tart very easy. I have generally found these tarts to be a bit too heavy and rich for my taste, and rather rustic looking. In the recipe that follows, I have lightened the custard by using powdered almonds in place of some of the flour, egg yolks instead of whole eggs, and milk rather than heavy cream. I also glaze this tart, something usually not done, because I feel it both improves the flavor of the tart and enhances its appearance.

The fruits usually used in this tart are those native to Alsace—apples, apricots, cherries, pears, peaches, and plums—the only thing that changes will be the glaze: currant jelly glaze (*glaçage à la gellée de groseille*) for dark fruits (such as plums and cherries) and apricot glaze (*glaçage à l'abricot*) for light fruits. I sometimes make this tart with raspberries, and when doing so, I omit the glaze, finding the flavor better. My favorite Alsatian tart is made with fresh sour cherries. If you are fortunate enough to find them in the market, or if you or a neighbor has a tree in the backyard, I encourage you to make one. The frozen unsweetened variety is almost as good, but the canned is not.

Serves 6 to 8

Butter for tart pan
Pâte Sucrée (tart pastry, page 242)
¼ cup (50 g) blanched almonds, whole or slivered

ARRANGING FRUIT IN AN ALSATIAN FRUIT TART

1. "Quarter" and core the apples as shown.

2. Cut the round pieces into thin slices.

3. Spread out the apple slices with your hand.

4. Transfer the flattened slices to the tart shell.

5. Dice the remaining apple pieces and place in between the apple slices.

6. The finished tart.

¼ cup (50 g) sugar
1 tablespoon (10 g) all-purpose flour
2 egg yolks
½ cup milk
½ teaspoon vanilla extract
1 tablespoon fruit eau-de-vie or brandy (optional*)
2 pounds fruit (apples, apricots, cherries, pears, peaches, plums)
Glaçage à l'Abricot or Glaçage à la Gellée de Groseille (page 396), hot

1. Preheat the oven to 500° and lightly butter a 9½- to 10-inch tart pan with removable bottom. Line the pan with the tart pastry (see "How to Line a Tart Pan," page 75). Prick the bottom of the pastry several times with the point of a sharp knife to prevent it from puffing during baking. Refrigerate or freeze the shell until you are ready to fill and bake it.

2. Using a food processor, grind the almonds and sugar into a fine powder. Add the flour and egg yolks, creating a paste. Add the milk slowly and process until smooth. Flavor this custard mixture with the vanilla and eau-de-vie.

3. Peel, core, and slice the apples or pears. Pit cherries, and halve and pit all other fruits used; slice the peaches. Fill the tart shell with the fruit (see "Arranging Fruit in an Alsatian Fruit Tart," opposite) and pour the custard over the fruit.

4. Bake the tart on the bottom rack of the oven for 10 minutes. Reduce the heat to 425° and bake an additional 20 minutes, until the crust is golden brown.

5. Unmold the tart as soon as possible and allow to cool on a pastry rack (see "Unmolding a Tart or Quiche," page 246).

6. **To serve:** Coat the cool tart with the hot *glaçage à l'abricot* or *glaçage à la gellée de groseille*. Slide the tart from the rack to a serving platter.

* If you are making an apricot or peach tart, use Cognac. For an apple tart, use Calvados. For a cherry tart, use kirsch. For a pear tart, use Poire Williams. For a plum tart, use quetsch.

Génoise
Basic French Cake

*G*énoise is the all-purpose cake used most often in France. Basically a sponge cake made with butter, it is used to make round cakes, square cakes, and jelly rolls. Its firm texture allows it to be cut into thin layers that, when layered with a variety of buttercreams, whipped creams, liqueur- or coffee-flavored syrups, sugar icings, toasted nuts, praline, and *ganache*, transform it into elaborate and delicious creations (see "Les Gâteaux," right). Once you master the techniques for making this cake, the possibilities are endless. For two good examples, try Gâteau Chocolat au Grand Marnier (page 254) and Gâteau Moka (page 256).

In the technique for making a classic *génoise*, there are two areas that can cause problems for cooks, inexperienced and experienced alike. The first is in the initial beating of eggs over heat—the warmth helps the eggs to increase their volume but can also be awkward and time consuming. And the second problem area arises when melted butter must be folded into this lightened egg mixture without deflating it.

To make the whole procedure easier, and to reduce the risk of failure, I do two things. Instead of beating the eggs over heat, I simply warm them in a bowl of hot tap water while I assemble the other ingredients. The water is poured out of the bowl and the eggs are then cracked into it while it is still warm and beaten with the sugar to produce a thick, firm batter in a relatively short time (5 to 8 minutes).

When it comes time to incorporate the butter, I use creamy, soft butter in place of the traditional melted

Les Gâteaux
(Layer Cakes)

Though the combinations of flavors and fillings and icings in French layer cakes are infinite, there are a great number of cakes whose fillings and decorations are well defined. In fact, the name is often written on top of the cake, or the icing decoration will be so particular to that cake that when you see it in the pastry shop you know exactly what the inside will be like.

Mascotte Pralinée: *Génoise* **layers filled with praline buttercream, coated with toasted almonds, and dusted with confectioners' sugar.**

Lutetia: *Génoise* **layers filled with walnut buttercream and coated with apricot glaze. Walnut halves are embedded in the top and sides of the cake and the cake is iced with chocolate fondant. It is finally decorated with a vanilla-flavored chestnut purée.**

Financier: *Génoise* **layers made from almonds and flour and baked with a layer of candied fruits in the batter. Topped with confectioners' sugar.**

Régent: Three *génoise* layers filled with buttercream or a thick chestnut purée, coated with apricot jam, and decorated with candied fruits, then frosted with rum fondant. The outline of the fruits shows through the fondant.

Cluny: *Génoise* layers filled with pistachio and Benedictine buttercream, coated with apricot jam, and topped with Benedictine fondant and roasted hazelnuts. Decorated with chocolate.

SIFTING FLOUR

The only time I sift flour in my recipes is when I want to prevent lumping when adding it to a liquid or to keep it light while folding it into a cake batter, such as *génoise*. In these instances, or anytime you need to sift flour, there is no need for a special flour sifter. Just use an everyday kitchen strainer, tapping the outer rim against the palm of your hand. Any lumps or foreign matter will be left in the strainer.

butter. Instead of adding it directly to the batter, I blend a small amount of batter into the butter first to make its consistency similar to the batter, and thereby easier to fold back in.

If you are familiar with French cake recipes, you will notice that I have reduced the amount of sugar in the classic sugar syrup by at least 75 percent, since I find most classically made French cakes too sweet.

Makes 1 layer

Butter and all-purpose flour for cake pan

For a 9-inch Round Cake	For an 8-inch Round Cake
4 eggs	*3 eggs*
3 tablespoons (45 g) unsalted butter, cut into 4 pieces	*2½ tablespoons (35 g) unsalted butter, cut into 3 pieces*
½ cup (110 g) sugar	*⅓ cup plus 1 tablespoon (85 g) sugar*
1 teaspoon vanilla extract or 1 teaspoon orange or lemon juice and the grated zest of 1 small orange or lemon	*¾ teaspoon vanilla extract or ¾ teaspoon orange or lemon juice and the grated zest of 1 small orange or lemon*
⅔ cup (100 g) all-purpose flour	*½ cup (70 g) all-purpose flour*

1. Preheat the oven to 350°. Butter and flour an 8- or 9-inch round cake pan.

2. Place the unbroken eggs in a large mixing bowl filled with hot tap water.

3. In a small saucepan, warm the butter over low heat. When the pieces are about half melted, remove the pan from the heat and stir until completely melted; the butter should be the consistency of light cream. Set the saucepan aside. When you are ready to use the butter, it will have cooled further, and should be the consistency of heavy cream or light mayonnaise.

4. Remove the eggs from the bowl and pour out the

water. In the same bowl, beat the eggs with the sugar and vanilla until they triple in volume, 5 to 8 minutes. The batter should be very thick. It will fall slowly from the beaters and stand on the surface.

5. Sift the flour one-third at a time onto the surface of the batter. Using a rubber spatula, fold the flour in gently. Fold no more than 10 to 12 times after each addition. After the last addition you may still see a small amount of flour; this will disappear when the butter is added.

6. Fold approximately 1 cup of the batter into the creamy butter until well blended. Pour this mixture into the remaining batter, and fold gently no more than 10 to 12 times. The batter will begin to fall and you may see streaks of butter. A completely smooth batter is not necessary.

7. Pour the batter into the prepared pan, filling three-quarters full. Tap the filled pan firmly on a counter several times to make sure no large air bubbles have been trapped in the batter.

8. Place the pan in the middle of the oven and bake for 25 to 35 minutes, until the cake begins to come away from the sides of the pan and is golden brown and springy to the touch.

9. Unmold the cake onto a rack and allow it to cool, covered with the cake pan. *(If not used immediately, the cake should be wrapped in plastic. It can be refrigerated for several days or frozen for up to 2 months.)*

Variation

Génoise au Chocolat *(Basic French Chocolate Cake):* For an all-purpose chocolate cake that can be used in the same way as the plain *génoise*, simply replace one-third of the flour in the above recipes with cocoa powder. Mix the flour and cocoa together before sifting into the batter. The measurements are as follows: *For an 8-inch cake*: ⅓ cup (50 g) all-purpose flour and ¼ cup (20 g) unsweetened cocoa powder. *For a 9-inch cake*: ½ cup (70 g) all-purpose flour and ⅓ cup (loosely spooned and packed) (30 g) unsweetened cocoa powder.

HERRINGBONE DECORATION

1. Coat the assembled cake with an even layer of ganache.

2. Apply horizontal lines of royal icing about ½ inch apart.

3. Draw the point of a knife through the center of

DECORATING A CAKE WITH GANACHE AND ROYAL ICING

Before attempting to use Ganache (page 391) and Glace Royale (page 395) together, I recommend that you simply coat a cake with *ganache* first to make sure you can successfully frost the cake.

To use *glace royale* (royal icing) and *ganache* together to make a herringbone or spider-web design, it is important to have both a similar consistency before starting. As soon as the cake has been coated with the *ganache* icing, use the royal icing in a decorating cone (see "Making and Using a Decorating Cone," page 394) to make the following designs:

Herringbone: Squeeze horizontal lines the size of spaghetti on the top of the cake, leaving a ½- to ¾-inch space between bands. The royal icing should sink into the *ganache* at this point. Immediately draw the point of a small knife, like a paring knife, down through the center of the lines. As the knife passes through the two icings, it should draw the band of white down into a V-shaped design. Working quickly, repeat this at equal distances from both sides of the first line.

Turn the cake 180 degrees and make four equally distanced cuts through the icings.

If the consistencies of the two icings are just right, and you work quickly, you will have a beautiful herringbone design. If the icings are not of the same consistency, the following can happen:

• If the white bands run down the side of the cake, the chocolate icing was too thin.

• If the white bands crack instead of flowing smoothly, the royal icing was too stiff.

• If the cut marks made by the knife are visible, you probably did not work fast enough and the chocolate stiffened. It should be soft enough to flow back to cover up the marks made by the knife.

Spider-Web Design: Make a spiral design with the royal icing on top of the soft *ganache*. Start at the center and spiral the icing out to the outer edge of the cake, leaving a ½- to ¾-inch space between the lines of the spiral. Immediately draw the point of your paring knife from one side of the cake to the other through the center of the spiral. Turn the cake 90 degrees and repeat the cut from edge to edge. Now divide each quarter by making similar cuts. The cake should now exhibit a spider-web design.

The same problems as mentioned above can occur. In time, if not at first, you will be making perfect designs.

the lines. Repeat this at an equal distance from both sides of the first line.

4. Turn the cake 180 degrees and make four equally distanced cuts through the icing.

Gâteau Chocolat au Grand Marnier
Orange–Chocolate Génoise with Grand Marnier–Chocolate Icing

The layers in this delicious chocolate cake are moistened with orange juice and Grand Marnier in place of the traditional heavy sugar syrup. You can serve it just as is, or decorate it with royal icing (Glace Royale, page 395) or candied orange peel.

Serves 8 to 10

½ cup orange juice
2 tablespoons Grand Marnier
8- or 9-inch Génoise au Chocolat (page 252), batter
*   flavored with the grated zest of 1 orange*
Canache (page 391), flavored with Grand Marnier

1. Combine the orange juice and Grand Marnier.
2. Using a serrated knife, cut the chocolate *génoise* into two layers. Turn the top layer cut side up on the cake rack. Using a pastry brush, moisten both layers with the flavored

SPIDER-WEB DESIGN

1. Starting at the center, spiral a line of icing out to the edge of the cake.

2. Draw the point of a knife through the icing from one side of the cake to the other through the center. Turn the cake 90 degrees and divide each quarter with the knife point as before.

orange juice. (Several tablespoons of juice will remain when making an 8-inch cake.)

3. Place the cake rack over a baking sheet. Spread an even layer of *ganache* over the bottom layer.

4. Replace the top layer. Pour the remaining *ganache* over the top of the cake so it runs down the sides. Tap the rack on the pastry sheet to help the *ganache* fall evenly. If there are spots that were missed, coat them with the excess *ganache* from the pastry sheet, using your spatula.

5. Refrigerate or freeze the cake on the rack. When the icing is firm, transfer the cake to a doilied serving plate. *(The cake will keep refrigerated for several days, or can be frozen for several weeks. Bring to room temperature before serving.)*

Variations

Sachertorte *(Chocolate Génoise with Apricot Glaze and Chocolate Icing)*: Sachertorte, which I find dry, becomes moist and delicious in this variation. Using raspberry jam provides yet another dimension. After moistening the layers with the orange juice, coat with some apricot glaze (Glaçage à l'Abricot, page 396) or strained raspberry jam. Spread some of the *ganache* on the bottom layer. Replace the top layer. Coat the top and sides with more apricot or raspberry glaze and refrigerate to set. Finally, coat with the remaining *ganache*.

Before moving your cake, chill it to ensure that the frosting has set. When it has, move the cake from the pastry rack to a serving plate with a long metal spatula. Use one hand to support the bottom of the cake while moving it.

Gâteau Chocolat au Café *(Chocolate-Mocha Cake)*: Omit the orange zest from the chocolate *génoise*. Make a light coffee syrup (see Gâteau Moka, step 1, page 256) flavored with 1 tablespoon Cognac, rum, or Kahlúa to use in place of the Grand Marnier–flavored orange juice. Flavor the *ganache* with Essence de Café (page 401) or Essence de Café Rapide (page 402)—2 tablespoons for an 8-inch cake, 3 tablespoons for a 9-inch. Moisten the cake layers with the coffee syrup and frost with the *ganache*. Instead of the *ganache*, you might want to try a coffee buttercream (Crème au Beurre au Café, page 393).

Gâteau Moka

Vanilla Génoise with Coffee Buttercream

1. Score the cake around the outside edge with a serrated spatula or knife.

This is a light cake with an irresistible coffee buttercream. As with most cakes made with *génoise* and buttercream, it can be made several days or even weeks ahead (it freezes well).

Serves 8 to 10

½ cup boiling water
2 tablespoons (30 g) sugar
2 tablespoons (10 g) instant coffee
8- or 9-inch Génoise (page 250)
Crème au Beurre au Café (page 393)
⅔ cup (100 g) chopped toasted almonds (see Pâte de Pralin, page 399)

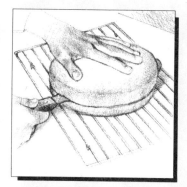

2. Holding the cake gently, cut through along the scored line.

1. **Make a light coffee syrup:** In a small bowl, combine the boiling water, sugar, and instant coffee. Stir to dissolve.

2. Using a serrated knife, cut the cake into two layers. Turn the top layer cut side up on the cake rack. Using a pastry brush, moisten both layers with the syrup. (Several tablespoons will remain when making an 8-inch cake.)

3. Spread a thin, even layer of *crème au beurre au café* over the bottom layer. Replace the top layer.

4. Ice the top and sides of the cake with a thin layer of the remaining buttercream. If you have a pastry bag and starred decoration tube, you can use them to make a decorative border on top of the cake.

5. Scoop up the toasted almonds in your hand and press them gently onto the sides of the cake. Refrigerate or freeze the cake on the rack. When the icing is firm, transfer the cake to a doilied serving plate. *(The cake will keep*

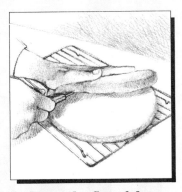

3. Using the flat of the spatula, turn the top layer over, cut side up, onto the cake rack.

refrigerated for several days, or can be frozen for several weeks. Bring to room temperature before serving.)

Variations

Gâteau Moka à la Ganache *(Chocolate-Mocha Cake):* This cake combines two of my favorite flavors. Follow the recipe above through step 4 without making a decorative border. Chill in the refrigerator until firm and then pour a coating of Ganache (page 391) over the buttercream. If desired, decorate the top of the cake with any leftover coffee buttercream. Omit the almonds, or sprinkle them on the buttercream layer in step 4. Try this same treatment with a chocolate *génoise.*

Gâteau au Grand Marnier *(Orange Génoise with Grand Marnier Buttercream):* Flavor the cake batter with the grated zest of an orange and moisten the layers with Grand Marnier-flavored orange juice (see Gâteau Chocolat au Grand Marnier, page 254, step 1). Make a buttercream (Crème au Beurre, page 392) flavored with the grated zest of 1 orange and ¼ cup Grand Marnier, which gets added, 1 tablespoon at a time, in step 3 of the buttercream recipe.

Biscuit Roulé à l'Abricot
Apricot Jam Roll

The classic jelly roll is made with a *biscuit* or French sponge cake batter, similar to a *génoise* but made without butter and with egg yolks and egg whites beaten separately. The resulting batter is quite stiff. I have found that for jelly rolls the batter does not have to be as thick as tradition has dictated. So, I simplify the recipe by using a butterless *génoise*, modifying the *génoise* recipe slightly by adding 2 tablespoons of liquid, which both lightens and moistens the resulting sponge cake.

Serves 6

4 eggs
Butter and all-purpose flour for jelly-roll pan
½ cup (110 g) granulated sugar
2 tablespoons orange juice
Grated zest of 1 small orange
⅔ cup (100 g) all-purpose flour
8-ounce jar apricot jam (see Note)
¼ cup (25 g) sliced almonds, toasted
Confectioners' sugar for dusting (optional)

1. Place the unbroken eggs in a large mixing bowl filled with hot tap water.

2. Preheat the oven to 350°. Lightly butter the bottom of a 17 × 11 × 1-inch jelly-roll pan and line with wax paper. Butter and lightly flour the pan.

3. Remove the eggs from the bowl and pour out the water. In the same bowl, beat the eggs with the granulated sugar, orange juice, and orange zest until tripled in volume, 5 to 8 minutes. The batter should be very thick. It will fall slowly from the beaters and stand on the surface.

4. Sift the flour, one third at a time, onto the surface of the batter. Using a rubber spatula, fold the flour in gently until smooth.

5. Pour the batter into the prepared pan, spreading to fill the pan evenly. Tap the filled pan firmly on a counter several times to make sure no large air bubbles are trapped in the batter.

6. Place the pan in the middle of the oven and bake for 10 to 12 minutes, or until the cake begins to come away from the sides of the pan and is golden brown and springy to the touch.

7. Run a knife around the sides of the pan, making sure that the cake is not sticking. Unmold the cake onto a

Note: Buy lightly sweetened preserves, or use your own homemade jams (see Confiture, page 397) for jelly rolls so that the end results will be full of the fruit flavor, and not overly sweet. This is an easy dessert to make, and is popular with children and adults alike.

clean kitchen towel lined with wax paper. The wax paper that had lined the pan will be attached to the surface of the cake. Remove this paper, then replace it loosely on the surface of the cake. Roll the cake up in the towel between the layers of wax paper and cool. You may roll the cake in whichever direction you prefer to produce either a long, thin cake or a short, thick one. *(The cake can be made up to this point 1 day in advance and refrigerated as is.)*

8. A few hours before serving, warm the jam in a saucepan on the stove (or in a bowl in the microwave) until it is thin enough to spread easily.

9. Unroll the cake and spread a thin layer of jam evenly over the surface of the cake. Reroll, trim the ends, and transfer to a serving platter. Coat the outside of the cake with a thin layer of jam. Sprinkle the almonds over the sides and top of the cake and dust with confectioners' sugar.

Variation

The apricot jam can be replaced by 2 cups of flavored whipped cream or buttercream.

Pain de Gênes sur Coulis de Framboise
Almond Cake with a Raspberry Purée

A *pain de Gênes* is an almond cake that is, traditionally, served with tea in France. When I first tasted it I found the cake dry, but enjoyed its rich almond flavor. Classically made with three eggs, I found myself short an egg one day, but made the cake anyway. The result was a moist and delicious cake that became an instant hit. Although good by itself, this simple cake turns into an elegant dessert when served surrounded with raspberry purée.

Serves 6 to 8

1 tablespoon kirsch, framboise, or Cointreau (optional)
Coulis de Framboise (page 386)
1 tablespoon melted butter and all-purpose flour for
    cake pan
⅔ cup (100 g) whole blanched almonds or ¾ cup
    slivered almonds
¼ cup (40 g) all-purpose flour
½ cup plus 1 tablespoon (125 g) granulated sugar
1 stick (115 g) unsalted butter
2 eggs
1 teaspoon vanilla extract
2 tablespoons dark rum
Confectioners' sugar for dusting

1. Add the kirsch, framboise, or Cointreau to the *coulis de framboise. (The* coulis *can be made a day in advance and refrigerated until used.)*

2. Preheat the oven to 350°. Cut a round of wax paper to fit the bottom of an 8- or 9-inch cake pan. Brush the bottom of the pan with the melted butter and attach the paper to it. Butter and lightly flour the wax paper-lined bottom and sides of the pan.

3. Combine the almonds with half the granulated sugar in a food processor and grind to a fine powder. Add the flour to this mixture and set aside.

4. In a food processor, cream the 1 stick of butter and the remaining granulated sugar. When smooth, add the eggs, one at a time, mixing well after each addition. Blend in the vanilla and rum. Add the almond-flour mixture and process quickly just until smooth.

5. Pour the batter into the cake pan. (It will only fill about one fourth of the pan.) Bake in the middle of the oven for 30 to 35 minutes, or until the cake is golden in color

Pain de Gênes au Sorbet et aux Fruits
(Almond Cake with Sorbet and Fruit)

In summertime, with *sorbet* (page 327) in the freezer and fresh fruit readily available, I make an extra-special presentation of this dessert. For example, I simply add a scoop of pineapple *sorbet* (Sorbet à l'Ananas, page 328) on one side of the cake and several tablespoons of blueberries on the other. The raspberry purée complements all, and you'll have a dessert that any fine French restaurant would be proud to serve. This cake goes nicely with other fruit purées. Try strawberry, blueberry, or peach.

and comes slightly away from the edge of the pan. Unmold onto a pastry rack and allow to cool.

6. **To serve:** Dust with confectioners' sugar to coat the surface of the cake. Cut into 8 wedges. Pour about 3 tablespoons of *coulis de framboise* onto each serving plate. Tilt the plates so the sauce coats them evenly and place a slice of cake in the center of each plate.

Gâteau Mousse au Chocolat
Chocolate Mousse Cake

This light and luscious mousse cake combines both baked and unbaked chocolate mousse for a unique taste experience. All flavor variations that work for the mousse recipe can be used for this cake. This cake can be made a day or two in advance, and can be frozen for later use, if desired.

Serves 8

Butter for cake pan
Double recipe Mousse au Chocolat (page 315)
Unsweetened cocoa powder and whipped cream for
    decoration (optional; see Note)

Note: If desired, decorate the cake before serving by dusting the mousse center with cocoa powder and piping whipped cream around the outer edge.

1. Preheat the oven to 350°. Butter a 9-inch cake pan.

2. Pour three-fourths of the chocolate mousse mixture into the pan. (Refrigerate the remainder until ready to use.) Bake on the middle rack for 30 to 35 minutes. The cake will rise at first; when it falls back, it is done.

3. Unmold onto a cake rack to cool. When cooled, the cake will have a concave center. Transfer the cake, with the aid of a long metal spatula, to a serving platter and fill the center with the remaining mousse mixture. Refrigerate until the mousse sets, about 1 hour.

Savarin au Rhum
Rum Cake

The yeast dough that is used to make this delicious rum-soaked cake is the same that is used for *baba au rhum*. *Babas* are baked in small metal cups or *baba* molds, while a *savarin* is baked in a ring-shaped *savarin* mold. Once risen, baked, and unmolded, these cakes are soaked with rum and a hot sugar syrup. Finally, they are glazed with hot apricot jam and decorated with sliced almonds and candied fruits.

Those who have had a *savarin* will find my recipe far less sweet. The light sugar syrup (*sirop de sucre*) is one-quarter as sugary as the usual French syrup.

In France there are special cake pans designed for making *savarins*. They are heavy, tinned-steel ring molds with a center rim that rises higher than the outer rim, helping the cake to rise straight. However, you can use an American ring mold for baking *savarin*.

Serves 16

2 tablespoons butter, melted, for mold
2 packages active dry yeast or 1 ounce fresh yeast
¼ cup (50 g) sugar
6 tablespoons warm (90° to 115°) water
2 cups plus 2 tablespoons (300 g) all-purpose flour
4 eggs
7 tablespoons (100 g) unsalted butter, melted
1 teaspoon vanilla extract
Light Sirop de Sucre (page 403), brought to a boil
¾ cup dark rum
Glaçage à l'Abricot (page 396)
¼ cup sliced almonds and/or candied fruit and violets,
    for decoration

1. With 2 tablespoons melted butter, completely coat the inside of a 9½-inch *savarin* mold.

2. Dissolve the yeast and 1 tablespoon of the sugar in the warm water. Let sit for 2 to 5 minutes, or until foamy and showing signs of life. If the yeast is nonactive, discard and start again with new yeast.

3. In the workbowl of a food processor combine the flour, sugar, eggs, 7 tablespoons melted butter, vanilla, and yeast mixture and process until a smooth sticky batter forms, about 1 minute.

4. Preheat the oven to 400°.

5. Drop the batter, 1 tablespoon at a time, into the mold, taking care not to drip batter on the sides of the mold. The mold should be filled halfway. Place a towel on the counter and bang the filled mold several times firmly on the towel to level the batter and to bring any air bubbles to the surface. Cover the mold with a large inverted bowl or pot and let rise until the batter reaches to within ⅛ inch of the top, approximately 30 minutes.

6. Place the mold onto the lowest rack of the oven and immediately lower the temperature to 350°. Bake 40 to 45 minutes. The cake will have risen and be dark brown on top and golden brown on the bottom and sides. Unmold the *savarin* onto a cooling rack and let cool, 20 to 30 minutes.

7. Place the *savarin*, on its pastry rack, over a large bowl or deep pan. (A roasting pan or sauté pan works well.) Spoon or slowly pour the boiling light *sirop de sucre* over the *savarin* and repeat until most of the syrup has been absorbed, 8 to 10 applications. As the syrup cools, it should be reheated.

8. When there is only about ½ cup of syrup remaining, stop and slowly spoon the rum over the *savarin*. Follow the rum with the remaining syrup.

9. In a small saucepan bring the *glaçage à l'abricot* to a boil over medium heat. Using a pastry brush, coat the entire *savarin* with a layer of the glaze. Decorate as desired.

10. Using two long metal spatulas, transfer the *savarin* to a large rimmed serving platter. Pour any remaining syrup around the *savarin*.

The *savarin* is a sticky yeast dough (and must have rising time), that is made in seconds using a food processor. To make the preparation of this dessert even easier, I often bake the cake itself the night before I plan to serve.

Variation

Savarin Chantilly aux Fruits *(Kirsch Cake with Fruit and Whipped Cream):* This elegant dessert will serve 18 to 20 because of the additional ingredients. Prepare the *savarin* as above, replacing the rum with an equal amount of kirsch. Fill the center of the *savarin* with 1 cup whipped cream. Place 1 pint of strawberries, raspberries, or blueberries around the outside and in the center of the ring, on top of the cream.

Gâteau aux Fonds à Succès
Almond Meringue and Buttercream Layer Cake

There are a number of cakes in France made with layers of baked meringue, or meringue and ground nuts, that are filled and frosted with buttercream. If the meringue is made with almonds the layers are called *fonds à succès*. Layers made with almond-hazelnut meringue are *fonds de progrès*. (Another variation can be made with pecans.) The layers are light, sometimes chewy, and have a wonderful roasted-nut flavor.

One of the nicest features of this cake—apart from its luscious taste and wonderful combination of creamy and chewy textures—is that it can be done well ahead of time and in stages. The layers can be kept wrapped airtight in plastic for a week or more. The completed cake keeps refrigerated for several days and also freezes well.

Serves 12 to 14

Butter and all-purpose flour for baking sheets
1 ¼ cups (150 g) slivered almonds plus ½ cup (60 g) slivered almonds, chopped and toasted
½ cup plus 3 tablespoons (150 g) sugar

Nut meringue and buttercream are delicious together, but are very rich. For a number of years, I would serve a small wedge of the cake, just enough to enjoy without too many added calories, but many students complained that the slices looked too small when served. My solution to this problem was to make the layers rectangular instead of round, constructing a loaf-shaped cake that, when sliced, appears satisfyingly large.

PASTRY BAGS

Pastry bags and tubes make the forming and filling of cream puff pastry quick and easy. Once you learn to use them well, you will use them to make lady-fingers and meringue nut layers and to decorate cakes with buttercream and whipped cream. They are often confused with decorating bags and tubes, which are much smaller.

The most popular pastry bags are 14 to 16 inches long and are made of light canvas that has been plastic coated for easy cleaning. More expensive nylon bags are also available. The simplest pastry tubes have plain or starred tips and come in various sizes. For the recipes in this book, I have used #1, #4, #6, and #9 plain tubes, and #2 and #3 starred tubes.

2 tablespoons (20 g) cornstarch or all-purpose flour
6 egg whites
*Crème au Beurre au Café (page 393), for an
    8-inch cake**
*Crème au Beurre au Chocolat (page 393), for an
    8-inch cake**

1. Preheat the oven to 350°. Use two or more baking sheets and prepare them by lining with nonstick parchment paper or by lightly coating with butter and flour.

2. Cut a piece of cardboard into a 10 × 3½-inch rectangle to serve as the pattern for the layers. Mark the outline of the pattern 6 times on the baking sheets with a pencil or toothpick. Leave at least ½ to ¾ inch of space between each.

3. In a food processor, grind the sliced or slivered almonds, the 3 tablespoons sugar, and the cornstarch to a powder.

4. In a large bowl, beat the egg whites until soft peaks form, about 1 minute. Add the ½ cup sugar and beat until very stiff, about 2 minutes. Fold in the almond powder until smooth.

5. Using a pastry bag fitted with a ⅜-inch (#4) plain tube, squeeze the nut-meringue mixture out to fill the outlined rectangles.

6. Bake one sheet at a time in the middle of the oven until evenly browned, 20 to 25 minutes. (Although two sheets can be baked at one time, changing their positions after 8 to 10 minutes, you will get better results if you bake only one at a time.)

7. Slide a long metal spatula under the layers to remove them while hot and place them on a flat surface. The layers, which will initially be soft, stiffen quickly. While layers are soft, place the cardboard pattern on top of each layer, and trim the edges square with a serrated knife. Let the layers cool.

8. Assemble the cake by coating all but one layer with a thin (about ⅛ inch) layer of *crème au beurre au café*. Top with the last layer. Holding the cake in one hand or resting it on a pastry rack, coat it all over with the *crème au beurre au chocolat*.

9. Scoop the chopped toasted almonds in the palm of your hand and gently press them onto the sides of the cake. Hold the cake over a bowl to catch the excess nuts as they fall. Refrigerate the cake until 15 minutes before serving.

10. Serve ½-inch slices on individual dessert plates.

* You may have buttercream left over. Freeze the rest for another use; it will keep for months.

Variations

Succès à la Glace *(Almond Meringue and Ice Cream Layer Cake):* Use homemade or softened ice cream in place of the buttercream to make an ice cream cake.

Succès aux Pacanes *(Pecan Meringue and Buttercream Layer Cake):* You can make the meringue layers with an equal amount of pecans in place of the almonds, but process for only 15 to 20 seconds in step 3 or they will become pasty instead of powdery.

Succès *(Almond Meringue and Praline Buttercream Layer Cake):* Try a popular French combination of chocolate and praline-flavored buttercream (Pâte de Pralin, page 399).

Gâteau Roulé au Chocolat
Chocolate Roll with Whipped Cream

A chocolate roll is usually made with a chocolate sponge, but I make a light, flourless chocolate roll with my basic chocolate mousse. When baked, chocolate reacts a little like flour, resulting in a cakelike consistency.

The recipe as written yields a long, relatively thin chocolate roll, and I generally serve 2 to 3 slices per person. If you like thick chocolate rolls, simply roll the cake in the opposite direction.

Serves 8

Butter for jelly-roll pan
1½ recipes Mousse au Chocolat (page 315)
2 cups heavy cream
3 tablespoons orange liqueur, such as Cointreau or
  Grand Marnier (see Note)
Confectioners' sugar
Unsweetened cocoa powder for dusting

Note: You can flavor the whipped cream with vanilla, unsweetened cocoa powder, instant coffee, or coffee liqueur in place of the orange liqueur.

1. Preheat the oven to 400°. Butter a 17 × 11 × 1-inch jelly-roll pan well and line it with wax paper.

2. Pour the mousse into the prepared jelly-roll pan, spreading it evenly with a spatula. Bake for 10 minutes, or until the cake has begun to come away from the sides of the pan.

3. Run a knife around the sides of the pan, making sure that the cake is not sticking. Unmold the cake onto a clean kitchen towel lined with wax paper. The wax paper that had lined the pan will be attached to the surface of the cake. Remove this paper, then replace it loosely on the surface of the cake. Roll the cake up in the towel between the layers of wax paper and cool. You may roll the cake in whichever direction you prefer to produce either a long, thin cake or a short, thick one.

4. In a bowl set into a larger bowl of ice and water, whip the cream and orange liqueur until stiff. Add confectioners' sugar to taste.

5. Unroll the chocolate roll and remove the top layer of wax paper (don't worry if it cracks a little). Coat the roll with half of the whipped cream. Reroll, trim the ends, and lift it onto a serving platter. Coat with the remaining whipped cream and dust the top with cocoa powder. Or, for a more decorative effect, use a pastry bag and a starred tip to coat the outside of the roll in long strips or bands. Refrigerate until ready to serve. *(The cake can be made 1 day in advance.)*

Pâte à Choux Sucrée
Dessert Cream-Puff Pastry

Cream-puff pastry is the most versatile of French pastry doughs. It can be baked in a multitude of forms, from miniature cream puffs or éclairs to elaborate dessert creations, such as Paris-Brest (page 275).

I have used the terms *sucrée* (sweet) and *salée* (salted) to differentiate between the dessert version and the first-course version (see Variation) of this dough. Although the French would certainly add sugar to a dessert cream-puff dough and salt to a first-course dough, they would call both doughs simply *pâte à choux*.

Makes 20 to 25 profiteroles or a Paris-Brest

½ cup water
4 tablespoons (55 g) unsalted butter
2 tablespoons (25 g) sugar
¼ teaspoon vanilla extract
½ cup (70 g) all-purpose flour
2 "large" (60 to 65 g each) eggs

1. In a medium saucepan, bring the water, butter, sugar, and vanilla to a boil over medium-high heat, stirring occasionally. Remove from the heat.

2. Sift the flour into the liquid and stir with a wooden spoon. The pastry should resemble mashed potatoes at this point. Return to the heat and continue stirring for about 20 seconds. The pastry will dry slightly, forming a smooth mass when shaken in the pan. Remove it from the heat.

3. Add the eggs, one at a time, stirring well after each addition. The pastry should cling to the sides of the pan and to the wooden spatula once all the eggs have been added. Lift your spatula and check the pastry. It should

USING A PASTRY BAG

1. Place the tube inside the bag and push or shake it down so its tip pokes out of the small opening at the bottom of the bag. (If the opening is too small for your tube, you can easily enlarge the opening by cutting off a piece of it.) To keep your batter or icing from leaking through the tube while you fill the bag, simply twist the bag right above the tube and push the twisted portion inside the tube.

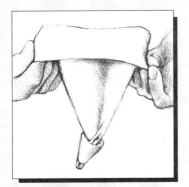

2. Fold the top of the bag down to form a 3- to 4-inch cuff.

3. Slip one hand underneath the cuff while you fill the bag.

4. After the bag is filled, unfold the cuff and make an accordion pleat.

hang down 2 to 3 inches from the spatula. If the pastry clings to the spatula but does not hang, it is still a little stiff and requires a bit more egg. If the pastry runs down from the spatula, you have added too much egg, and although you could add more flour to stiffen the pastry at this point, the texture of your finished pastry would not be as good as it will be if you start again.

4. At this point the pastry is ready to be formed. Once the pastry is formed it can be refrigerated or frozen on the baking sheet until ready to bake. However, as most home cooks do not have enough freezer space for this, you might opt for baking and then freezing them for future use.

Variation

Pâte à Choux Salée *(First-Course Cream-Puff Pastry):* Substituting ¼ teaspoon salt and ⅛ teaspoon freshly ground pepper for the sugar and vanilla, proceed as for Pâte à Choux Sucrée (above).

Beignets Soufflés aux Bananes
Deep-Fried Rum-Flavored Banana Puffs

Ordinarily, a *beignet de banane* would be a piece of banana dipped in a batter and fried. For a lighter version, I make *beignets soufflés* (luscious fritters made from cream-puff pastry and diced banana and served with a hot apricot sauce). Rum adds a Caribbean touch and complements the banana flavor.

Serves 6

1 cup apricot jam
3 tablespoons dark rum
2 tablespoons water
1 banana, diced
1 teaspoon (5 g) granulated sugar
½ recipe Pâte à Choux Sucrée (page 268)
2 to 2½ quarts vegetable oil, for deep-frying
Confectioners' sugar for dusting

1. In a small saucepan, bring the apricot jam, 2 tablespoons of the rum, and the water to a boil. Strain and keep warm.

2. Place the banana in a bowl, sprinkle with the granulated sugar and the remaining 1 tablespoon rum, and set aside while you make the *pâte à choux*.

3. In a deep-fryer, heat the oil to 365°.

4. Gently stir the banana and rum into the cream-puff pastry. Drop the batter by tablespoonfuls into the hot oil. The fritter will take approximately 5 minutes to fry and will puff and turn themselves over several times. They are done when they have puffed, turned a deep brown color, and stopped turning over.

5. **To serve:** Drain the fritters on paper towels. Place them on a plate or in individual serving bowls. Sprinkle with confectioners' sugar and serve with the hot apricot sauce.

5. Twist the pleated area, forcing the filling down in the bag. Tightly grasp the twisted portion of the bag directly above the filling with your thumb and forefinger.

6. Use your other fingers of that hand to squeeze the mixture out. Use your second hand to guide the tip of the tube. When you no longer can comfortably squeeze the bag, stop and twist the bag again, grasping it lower. Continue squeezing with the same hand.

Profiteroles au Chocolat
Chocolate-Dipped Cream Puffs

*P*rofiteroles are small dessert cream puffs. They are classically filled with vanilla pastry cream and stacked in a pyramid-shaped mound. A chocolate sauce is poured over the pyramid, making an attractive display.

The presentation I use is simpler and easier to serve. Instead of making a pyramid and then covering it with sauce, I dip each *profiterole* into a thick chocolate sauce and arrange them on a round platter so that each can be picked up easily.

The *profiteroles* can be filled 4 to 6 hours in advance and allowed to stand at room temperature. (If you have any left over at the end of the meal, be sure to refrigerate them.)

Serves 8

Butter and all-purpose flour for baking sheet (optional)
Pâte à Choux Sucrée (page 268)
1 egg, lightly beaten with a pinch of salt
Crème Pâtissière (page 388)*
Sauce au Chocolat (page 385), made with ¼ cup water,
    cooled to room temperature

1. Preheat the oven to 475°. Use a nonstick baking sheet or prepare a regular baking sheet by lining it with nonstick parchment paper or coating it with butter and flour.

2. Fill a pastry bag fitted with a ½-inch (#6) plain tube with the *pâte à choux*. Form small cream puffs the size of a quarter, about 1 inch in diameter. (You can also form them with a spoon, although they will be rougher looking.) Lightly brush the cream puffs with the beaten egg.

3. Place the baking sheet in the middle of the oven for 5 minutes. Lower the heat to 400° and bake for 25 minutes, or until the cream puffs are evenly colored and firm to the touch. No moisture should be heard escaping from the pastry when the oven door is opened.

4. Remove the cream puffs from the oven and place on a pastry rack. While they are still warm, make a small hole in their bottoms or sides with either the point of the pastry tube or a knife.

5. Place the pastry cream (which should be brought to

Profiteroles à la Glace: Restaurants often serve *profiteroles* filled with ice cream and topped with a hot chocolate sauce. I am not a fan of ice-cold cream-puff pastry, but it is certainly an easy presentation. Let the ice cream get semisoft (or use still-soft homemade ice cream straight from the ice cream machine) and use a pastry bag to fill the cream puffs. Place the filled puffs in the freezer until ready to serve.

room temperature if you've made it ahead and refrigerated it) into a pastry bag fitted with a ³⁄₁₆-inch (#1) plain tube and fill the cream puffs.

6. **To serve:** Dip the filled cream puffs into the cooled chocolate sauce to coat the tops and place on a doilied platter.

∗ For an easier version, substitute whipped cream for the pastry cream.

Variation

Profiteroles au Chocolat Grand Marnier *(Chocolate-Dipped Cream Puffs with Grand Marnier):* Add 2 tablespoons (or more to taste) Grand Marnier to the chocolate sauce and/or pastry cream.

Choux Soufflés au Chocolat
Chocolate Soufflé-Filled Cream Puffs

You can use a cream puff as a container in which to bake any soufflé. In this recipe, I use my basic chocolate mousse recipe and treat it like a soufflé (which is also how I make my Soufflé au Chocolat et au Grand Marnier on page 305). Once the cream puffs are filled with the mousse mixture, they can be frozen and baked several days later. Since the puffs are small, they do not need to be thawed first. The filled *choux soufflés* can be eaten hot or cold—unbaked with a mousse filling or baked with a hot soufflé filling.

USDA Grade A Large eggs weigh 60 to 65 grams, or about 2 ounces each. Although egg size is supposed to be the same throughout the country, I have bought boxes of "Large" eggs containing eggs weighing as little as 50 grams and as much as 75 grams. I recall this happening to me while teaching in Charlotte, North Carolina. I was making cream-puff pastry on two consecutive days, and noticed that on the second day my raw pastry was considerably softer than on the first. I asked my assistant to show me the cartons from the eggs, thinking that she might have accidentally purchased Extra Large, but on examining the cartons, I found that the eggs used on the first day had come from a farm in North Carolina, while on the second day we had used eggs from South Carolina. This is not to say that all South Carolina eggs are larger than those produced in North Carolina, but it is possible for you to buy larger or smaller eggs than you intended.

Serves 8

Butter and all-purpose flour for baking sheet
Pâte à Choux Sucrée (page 268)
1 egg, lightly beaten with a pinch of salt
½ cup (50 g) sliced almonds
Mousse au Chocolat (page 315)
Confectioners' sugar
Crème Anglaise (page 387)

Any problems that people have with *pâte à choux* are due to inaccurate measurement, so a scale is very helpful. Also, if there is not enough egg, the pastry will not puff; if too much is added, it may be too runny to bake or may puff with a concave rather than a flat bottom. It is important to measure carefully and to have the correct-size eggs.

1. Preheat the oven to 475°. Use a nonstick baking sheet or prepare a regular baking sheet by lining it with nonstick parchment paper or coating it with butter and flour.

2. Fill a pastry bag fitted with a ½-inch (#6) plain tube with the *pâte à choux*. Form cream puffs 1½ inches in diameter on the baking sheet. (You can use a spoon, but the cream puffs will be rougher looking.) Brush lightly with the beaten egg and sprinkle with the sliced almonds.

3. Place the baking sheet in the middle of the oven for 5 minutes. Lower the temperature to 400° and bake for 25 minutes, or until the cream puffs have colored evenly and are firm to the touch. No moisture should be heard escaping from the pastry when the oven door is open.

4. Cool the cream puffs on a pastry rack. When cool, use a serrated knife to cut off the tops one-third of the way down. Set the tops aside.

5. Increase the oven temperature to 475°.

6. Use a spoon or a pastry bag fitted with a ½-inch (#6) plain tip to fill the puffs with the *mousse au chocolat*. Replace the tops of the cream puffs. *(The cream puffs can be made ahead to this point and frozen. Bake without defrosting.)*

7. Bake the cream puffs for 3 to 4 minutes or until the soufflé begins to rise, lifting the cream puff tops by about ¼ inch. Sprinkle with confectioners' sugar and serve each cream puff on a plate surrounded by *crème anglaise*, or pass the vanilla custard sauce separately.

CREAM PUFF VARIATIONS

The various desserts that use cream-puff pastry are many, and as with much of French cooking, each variation has its own prescribed size and shape and name.

Profiteroles: The smallest member of the cream-puff family is the *profiterole*. They are small and round and usually about 1 or 1½ inches in diameter and filled with a vanilla pastry cream, ice cream, or whipped cream. They are most often served with a chocolate sauce.

Choux Grillés: These are the same size as *profiteroles*, or larger, and are coated with chopped almonds before baking. They are filled with coffee pastry cream and dusted with confectioners' sugar before serving.

Croquembouche: This spectacular dessert is made from *profiteroles* that have been stuck together with hot caramel to form a hollow pyramid (constructed around a special cone-shaped mold). The pyramid is self-supporting and will not collapse if a puff is plucked from the center.

Salambôs: *Salambôs* are oval cream puffs, traditionally filled with a kirsch-flavored pastry cream. The filled cream puffs are dipped into hot caramel and then into chopped pistachio nuts.

Eclairs: An éclair is a 4½- to 5-inch-long cream puff filled with either vanilla, coffee, or chocolate pastry cream and coated with a chocolate or coffee sugar icing. I coat them with the same sauce I use on *profiteroles*.

Carolines: *Carolines* are shaped like small éclairs and are about 2 inches long. They are traditionally filled with either vanilla- or coffee-flavored pastry cream and then coated with chocolate or coffee sugar icing.

FRENCH WOODEN SPATULA

A French wooden spatula is basically a flat wooden spoon. It has a rounded but flat blade and a flat handle. (Not to be confused with American wooden spatulas, which are square-bladed.) It is ideal for mixing and stirring batters, as well as for general kitchen use. Anytime I call for a wooden spoon in my recipes, I would use my French wooden spatula instead.

Paris-Brest
Cream-Puff Pastry Ring Filled with Praline Cream

MAKING A *PARIS-BREST*

1. Squeeze a ring of pastry onto the baking sheet. Make five or six small cream puffs.

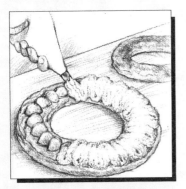

2. Pipe the remaining cream over the cream-puff pieces in the partially assembled Paris-Brest to form ribbons that overlap the edge of the pastry.

This beautiful and delicious cream-puff pastry dessert is one of my favorites. It is a marvelous example of a masterpiece that is created from ordinary ingredients (though it is not a dessert for beginners).

The Paris-Brest is made by baking cream-puff pastry in the form of a crown or wheel. The top of the crown is removed and the pastry is filled and decorated with a praline-flavored *crème St.-Honoré* (also called *crème Chiboust*).

To make the cream filling rise above the edges of the ring, without having to mound the ring with an excessive quantity of filling, Here's a little trick I learned as a student in Paris. Bake a few extra cream puffs at the same time as the ring. Cut the puffs into pieces and place them in the ring after filling halfway with the cream filling. The filling is then piped over the supporting pieces to create a lovely dessert.

Serves 6 to 8

Butter and all-purpose flour for baking sheet
Pâte à Choux Sucrée (page 268)
1 egg, beaten with a pinch of salt
¼ cup (25 g) sliced almonds
4 egg whites
⅛ teaspoon cream of tartar
Praline-flavored Crème Pâtissière (page 388)*
Confectioners' sugar for dusting

1. Preheat the oven to 475°. Use a nonstick baking sheet or prepare a regular baking sheet by lining it with nonstick parchment paper or coating it with butter and flour.

2. Fill a pastry bag fitted with an ¹¹⁄₁₆-inch (#9) plain tube with the *pâte à choux*. Use a pot lid 6 inches in diameter to draw the outline of a circle on the baking sheet. Squeeze a ring of pastry about 6 inches in diameter and 1 inch wide out onto the baking sheet. Make 5 or 6 small cream puffs with the remaining pastry. Brush the ring lightly with the beaten egg and cover with sliced almonds.

3. Dust the assembled pastry with confectioners' sugar.

3. Place the pastry in the oven for 5 minutes. Reduce the heat to 400° and bake another 25 to 30 minutes, or until medium brown all over. Allow the pastry to cool on a pastry rack. Using a serrated knife, cut off the top portion of the pastry and reserve. Cut the cream puffs into quarters.

4. **Make the *crème St.-Honoré*:** In a bowl, beat the egg whites with the cream of tartar until stiff peaks form. Pour the hot *crème pâtissière* into the egg whites and fold rapidly until smooth to produce a firm yet light, soufflé-like mixture. The filling should be firm enough to support a spatula in an upright position.

5. **To assemble:** Spoon half of the *crème St.-Honoré* into the bottom of the pastry ring and top with the cream-puff pieces so their rounded ends stand up to give added height. Fill a pastry bag fitted with a ¼-inch (#2) or ⁵⁄₁₆-inch (#3) star tube with the remaining cream and decorate by squeezing ribbons of cream back and forth over the top, forming loops that hang over the sides of the pastry.

6. **To serve:** Replace the top of the pastry ring gently and sprinkle with confectioners' sugar. Using two long metal spatulas, gently lift the dessert onto a serving platter lined with doilies.

* When you make the pastry cream, add 3 tablespoons of Pâte de Pralin (page 399) in step 4. Once made, cover the surface with plastic wrap and keep warm. Reheat before adding to the beaten egg whites (step 5, above).

If you are eager to try this dessert, but are unsure of your ability, I suggest that you make the pastry in the form of cream puffs or éclairs. With their tops cut off and filled with the praline-flavored *crème St.-Honoré*, they will taste the same as the Paris-Brest but will be easier to make, and can even be made without pastry bags and tubes.

French pastry shops have refrigerated surfaces designed specifically for working with puff pastry— a marble work surface placed on top of a large horizontal refrigerator. Thus, the contents of the refrigerator are kept cold at the same time as the marble top is chilled.

Pâte Demi-Feuilletée
Rough Puff or Half-Puff Pastry

Puff pastry is often thought of as the most difficult of French pastry doughs. And, in fact, it *is* a long, drawn-out procedure that involves rolling and rerolling a flour and water dough with a block of butter to produce the over one thousand individual layers of dough and butter that, when baked, rise to produce flaky layers of pastry.

In between all the rolling, the dough must rest to relax the elasticity built up while rolling. It is these resting times that make classic puff pastry so time consuming.

A second method, which makes what is called rapid, rough, or half puff pastry, shortens the resting time considerably. The butter, instead of being kept completely separated between layers of dough, is interspaced in chunks throughout the dough. This creates much less elasticity. The dough, which looks very rough at first, can be rolled without resting and used shortly thereafter. The end results are so good that I rarely teach the classic version anymore.

The recipe is very simple, and with a scale can be made in any quantity desired. Use equal weights of flour and butter, and the amount of water is half the weight of the flour. I use only a small amount of salt so that the pastry can be used for first-course as well as dessert recipes.

Because of the quantity of butter involved, working on a cold surface is important for success. If you don't have a large plastic pastry board (about 16×20 inches) to chill, fill one or two large roasting pans with ice and place them on your countertop to chill it.

Using plastic wrap, as I do to initially form the pastry, alleviates the need to handle it with warm hands, and makes the beginning stages of making the pastry less sticky than they otherwise would be.

Makes 2½ pounds

3 cups (450 g) all-purpose flour*
1 teaspoon (5 g) salt
1 cup cold water
1 pound (450 g) cold unsalted butter, cut into ½-inch cubes

1. Place the flour in a large bowl and make a well in the center. Place the salt, water, and butter in the well. Quickly and gently blend all of the ingredients together using your fingertips.

2. As soon as all of the ingredients begin to stick together, transfer the contents of the bowl to a sheet of plastic wrap and, with your hands, form the mass into a rectangle approximately 7 × 10 inches. Wrap tightly in the plastic and run your rolling pin over the surface of the wrapped dough to make it tighter and more compact. Refrigerate for 15 minutes or freeze for 5 minutes. At this point, the dough will be very rough looking.

3. Working on a cold, lightly floured surface, give the dough four turns as follows: Roll it out into a 20 × 8-inch rectangle with one short side facing you; fold in thirds as you would a letter and give it one quarter turn to the right or left. You have now given the dough one turn. Repeat this rolling and turning process three more times. Keep the work surface, dough, and rolling pin lightly floured, but brush off any excess flour from the dough before folding.

4. Refrigerate the pastry dough for 15 minutes (or longer). It can be used after these four turns, or it can be given two additional turns before use. The pastry will rise just as much with 4 turns as with 6, but the layers after 6 turns will be thinner, making the finished pastry more tender.

5. The pastry will keep for 3 to 4 days in the refrigerator, or for several months in the freezer. It should be kept

SHAPING *PATE DEMI-FEUILLETEE*

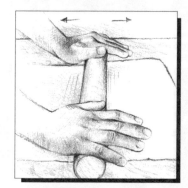

1. Roll out the dough into a 20 × 8-inch rectangle.

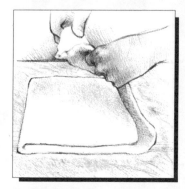

2. Fold the dough into thirds as you would a letter.

3. Mark the finished dough into five pieces.

tightly wrapped in plastic wrap. To use less than a whole recipe, mark the finished dough into five equal portions (½ pound each) and cut off what you need. Wrap and store the remainder.

* To make even finer pastry, replace 100 g of all-purpose flour (⅔ cup) with 100 g cake flour (½ + ⅓ cup).

Feuilleté aux Fraises
Puff Pastry with Strawberries

S ome of the finest fruit tarts are those made with puff pastry, fresh strawberries, or raspberries, and a currant jelly glaze. But they are always made ahead of time and served at room temperature. Unfortunately, this does not take advantage of puff pastry's best feature: the flaky buttery taste it has when it's still warm. By changing the presentation of a traditional puff-pastry tart slightly, this magnificent dessert results. Small individual squares of puff pastry are baked ahead of time, then reheated just before serving and topped with fresh berries and warm currant jelly.

The optional addition of toasted sliced almonds adds a delicate crunch and harmonizing flavor.

Serves 8

Butter for baking sheet
1½ pounds Pâte Demi-Feuilletée (page 277) or 1 pound
    store-bought puff pastry
1 egg, beaten
8-ounce jar red currant jelly
1 to 2 tablespoons kirsch, to taste
3 pints strawberries, quartered if large
½ cup (25 g) sliced almonds, toasted (optional)*

1. Preheat the oven to 400°. Lightly butter a baking sheet.

2. Roll the pastry out into a square approximately 12 × 12 inches and cut it into nine 4-inch squares.

3. Trim off ½-inch strips all around each square. Brush the surface lightly with the beaten egg and place two of the trimmed-off strips on opposite edges of the square, pressing gently to attach the strip to the square. Brush lightly with the egg wash and attach the remaining two strips to the other edges, again pressing gently. Brush again with the egg wash. Trim off any excess pastry at the corners of the square. If desired, decorate the surface of the border by making diagonal slashes with a knife just through the top surface of the pastry.

MAKING *FEUILLETES*, A SECOND METHOD

4. Place the pastry squares on the baking sheet and prick the centers several times with the point of your knife. Bake in the middle of the oven for 20 to 25 minutes, until the pastry has risen and is evenly colored.

5. Cool on a pastry rack and cut out the center of each square to make a well. *(This can be done several hours in advance. Before assembling the dessert, reheat the pastry in a 350° oven, about 3 minutes.)*

6. In a small saucepan, heat the currant jelly over medium heat until it melts and comes to a boil. Add the kirsch.

7. Place the warm pastry on individual serving plates and fill to overflowing with strawberries. Spoon or brush on the hot currant jelly glaze and sprinkle with the toasted sliced almonds.

* Don't use slivered almonds in place of sliced ones, for the thicker-cut almonds are too firm for the combination of textures in this delicate dessert.

Variation

Feuilleté aux Framboises *(Puff Pastry with Raspberries):* Use 2 pints of raspberries in place of the strawberries.

Mille-Feuilles
Napoleons

The most delicious *mille-feuilles* I ever ate was served to me by Jean and Pierre Troisgros when I had lunch with them many years ago in their three-star restaurant in Roanne. The pastry had just emerged from the oven, and was served with a room-temperature pastry cream.

To serve a Napoleon warm requires the hands of a veteran chef. Pastry cream at room temperature is very soft and makes the cutting and serving of this layered pastry difficult. For this reason, most Napoleons are refrigerated before they are cut. When refrigerated, the pastry becomes less flaky and loses some of its allure. Even though the dessert is now easier to handle and cut, it is less than perfect.

In order to get as close as possible to the wonderful warm *mille-feuilles* of my memory, I do not refrigerate them, and for this reason I assemble them only 3 to 4 hours before serving. Make your pastry cream and prepare the puff pastry up to the point of baking it the day before and the process will be easy.

Serves 6

Variation: For an extra-rich version, make a single recipe of pastry cream and fold 1 cup of whipped cream into it.

Butter for baking sheet
1½ pounds Pâte Demi-Feuilletée (page 277) or 1 pound
   store-bought puff pastry
Double recipe Crème Pâtissière (page 388), flavored with
   2 tablespoons Grand Marnier, rum, or kirsch
   *(optional), chilled**
Confectioners' sugar for dusting

1. Preheat the oven to 400°. Lightly butter a 17 × 14-inch baking sheet.

2. Roll the pastry out to fit the baking sheet. The pastry should be less than ⅛ inch thick.

3. Sprinkle the pastry sheet with water. Roll the flattened pastry onto a rolling pin and unroll it onto the pastry sheet. Trim off any excess pastry.

4. Prick the pastry all over with the tines of a fork. Refrigerate it for 15 minutes or more.

5. Place the pastry in the middle of the oven and bake for 20 to 25 minutes, or until the pastry is golden brown and dry. Allow it to cool on a pastry rack.

6. Use a serrated knife to trim the edges of the pastry and to cut it lengthwise into three equal strips.

7. Whisk the chilled *crème pâtissière* to make it smooth and easy to spread. Spread two of the puff-pastry strips with pastry cream and place one on top of the other. Place the last strip of pastry, bottom side up, on top. Sprinkle confectioners' sugar on top to cover well.

8. Use two long metal spatulas to lift the pastry to a doily-covered serving platter. When you are ready to serve, hold the top layer as you cut through it with a serrated knife to form individual Napoleons. *(This can be done in advance, but no more than 3 to 4 hours ahead. Do not refrigerate the pastries before serving. However, do refrigerate any leftovers, which will keep for 1 or 2 days.)*

* If you are using the rum or liqueurs, add it in step 4 of the pastry cream recipe.

SHAPING *TUILES*

You can make these cookies by cooling them on a pastry rack and serving them flat, but part of their glory is their shape. Special *tuile* molds do exist, made up of four or five U-shaped sections, but I have found that French bread pans, especially the *baguette* size, do the job equally well. You can also form the *tuiles* on top of a rolling pin, or over the side of a wine bottle, but it is not as easy as turning them into the bread pans. If you like these cookies, it is worthwhile buying the bread pans solely for the purpose of forming them.

1. Spread the cookie batter thinly to about 3 inches in diameter, leaving 2 inches between each cookie.

Tuiles aux Amandes
Thin Crispy Almond Tile Cookies

*T*uiles are without question France's best cookie. The reputations of many French pastry chefs have been made or broken by the quality of their *tuiles*. These extremely thin, crisp almond cookies, which are

2. Quickly remove the cookies with a long metal spatula.

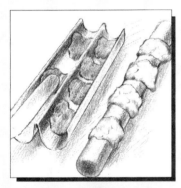

3. Invert the cookies into the baguette mold or lay over a rolling pin.

formed to resemble the roof tiles (*tuiles*) found in Mediterranean countries, are often served with dessert in the finest restaurants. The memory of an otherwise superb meal can be flawed by poor-quality *tuiles*, and imperfections in a meal can be forgiven if it ends with outstanding ones.

From the small number of ingredients in these cookies, it might seem unlikely that there could be so much variation in taste, texture, and quality. But there is. One teaspoon of butter or one tablespoon of sugar one way or the other and you've appreciably altered the *tuiles'* consistency.

After years of tasting and testing, I've finally arrived at what I consider to be the perfect proportions for this cookie. If you follow this recipe exactly—I hope using a scale to measure the ingredients—you will have a *tuile* that you could proudly offer to a three-star pastry chef.

One thing to keep in mind, though, is baking time. You must find the baking time that works best for your baking sheet, oven, and thickness of cookies. Use my baking times first, but if they don't work, try a slightly different time (it may be a matter of only 15 to 30 seconds) and when you find the time that works, make a note of it and use that.

You may not bake perfect *tuiles* at first—although chances are pretty good that you will—but even the mistakes make good eating.

Makes 20 to 24

Butter for baking sheets
3 tablespoons (45 g) unsalted butter
½ cup less 2 teaspoons (100 g) sugar
2 egg whites
¼ teaspoon vanilla extract
3 tablespoons plus 1 teaspoon (30 g) all-purpose flour
1 cup (100 g) sliced blanched almonds

1. Preheat the oven to 400°. Heavily butter two baking sheets.

2. In a small saucepan, heat the butter and remove from the heat.

3. In a small bowl, combine the sugar, egg whites, and vanilla and, without beating, mix together with a whisk. Stir in the flour with a whisk until smooth. Add the melted butter and stir with a whisk until smooth. Using a rubber spatula, fold in the sliced almonds.

4. Drop a teaspoonful of the batter onto a baking sheet. With the back of the spoon, spread thinly to about 3 inches in diameter (you will see the baking sheet through the thin layer of batter), leaving 2 inches between each cookie.

5. Bake 4 to 7 minutes, or until the edges are browned.

6. Using a long metal spatula and working quickly, remove the cookies from the sheet and invert them into a French bread (*baguette*) pan. (If you don't have a French bread pan, you can lay them over a rolling pin.) If the cookies harden before you have a chance to remove them from the baking sheet, place the sheet back in the oven for 20 or 30 seconds to soften them.

7. When cooled, remove the *tuiles* from the mold. As soon as one batch is finished, bake the next.

8. *Tuiles* are served on a doilied platter in overlapping rows. If you are not serving the cookies for several hours, keep them dry in an airtight tin or jar, since humidity can render this thin, crunchy cookie limp, sticky, and chewy.

Madeleines
Small Shell-Shaped Tea Cakes

*M*adeleines are little tea cakes that are good served with fruit or ice cream for dessert. They are classically made from a pound cake batter that is baked in

MADELEINE MOLDS

small shell-like molds appropriately named *madeleine* molds. But the technique I use for making *madeleines* is the same one I use for *génoise* rather than that for pound cake. As with *génoise*, folding the melted butter into the batter can be difficult, even for professionals, for the butter is heavy and rapidly collapses the batter. Softening the butter to the consistency of creamy mayonnaise as I have instructed, makes this procedure easier, and the results lighter and more delicate than the denser pound-cake variety.

Makes 2 dozen

3 eggs
1 stick (115 g) unsalted butter, cut into 8 pieces
½ cup plus 1 tablespoon (120 g) sugar
Grated zest of 1 small lemon or orange or ¾ teaspoon
    vanilla extract
½ teaspoon baking powder
¾ cup plus 1 tablespoon (120 g) all-purpose flour

1. Preheat the oven to 375°.
2. Place the unbroken eggs in a large bowl filled with hot tap water.
3. In a small saucepan, warm the butter over low heat. When the pieces are about half melted, remove the pan from the heat and stir until completely melted; the butter should be the consistency of light cream. Set the saucepan aside. When you are ready to use the butter, it will have cooled further and should be the consistency of heavy cream or light mayonnaise.
4. Brush two *madeleine* molds well with about 1½ tablespoons of the melted butter.
5. Remove the eggs from the bowl and pour out the water. In the same bowl, beat the eggs with the sugar and zest (or vanilla) until they triple in volume, 5 to 8 minutes. The batter should be very thick. It will fall slowly from the beaters and stand on the surface.
6. Mix the baking powder with the flour and sift it, one third at a time, onto the batter, folding gently after each

addition. Stop folding while a little of the flour is still visible.

7. Gently fold one-third of the batter into the creamy butter. Pour this butter mixture back into the remaining batter and fold gently no more than 8 to 10 times. The batter will begin to fall and you may see streaks of butter. A completely smooth batter is not necessary.

8. Spoon the batter (a heaping tablespoonful) into the buttered molds, filling each three-quarters full. (If you have beaten and folded well, you may have a tablespoon of excess batter.)

9. Bake the *madeleines* in the middle of the oven 13 to 14 minutes, or until golden brown. Unmold immediately and cool them on a pastry rack. If the cakes do not fall out when inverting the mold, give one end a firm tap on the counter top. *Madeleines* can be stored in a cookie tin or frozen.

Biarritz
Chocolate-Coated Hazelnut and Almond Cookies

After the Tuiles aux Amandes (page 282), these are my favorite French cookies. Originally made only with almonds, I use half almonds and half hazelnuts for a more unusual cookie. I also bake my cookies on a baking sheet that is only buttered, instead of buttered *and* floured, producing a slightly thinner cookie than the original. If your cookies are too fragile and break often while you are coating them with the chocolate, bake your next batch on a floured cookie sheet. The cookies can be frozen for several months.

Makes 5 to 6 dozen

BAKING OR COOKIE SHEETS

There are many different types of cookie or baking sheets available. There are coated and uncoated sheets, light metal and dark metal sheets, thick and thin metal sheets; and each will affect your baking differently to some degree.

Nonstick coatings are excellent in that they usually eliminate the steps you must normally take to prevent sticking. These coatings can damage easily, however, and care must be taken not to cut on their surfaces. For recipes where cutting is necessary, an uncoated sheet is needed.

Light metal (mostly aluminum) sheets bake cooler than the dark ones, and in most cases are the ones I have used. If you are using a dark sheet, it will probably be necessary to reduce your oven temperature from between 50 and 75 degrees to prevent burning.

Most thin sheets buckle when they go into a hot oven, and although this normally doesn't cause any major damage, it is always disconcerting when it happens. When buying a baking sheet, try to find one that is sturdy and not too flexible.

Just remember, if the bottom of your pastry is burning, reduce your oven temperature or move the baking sheet higher in the oven.

⅓ cup (50 g) hazelnuts
⅓ cup (50 g) whole blanched almonds*
Butter for baking sheets
½ cup less 2 teaspoons (100 g) sugar
7 tablespoons (100 g) unsalted butter
¼ teaspoon vanilla extract
2 egg whites
¼ cup (40 g) all-purpose flour
8 ounces (230 g) semisweet chocolate

1. Preheat the oven to 400°.

2. Place the hazelnuts and almonds in two separate cake pans and roast until the hazelnuts' skins begin to crack and the almonds are lightly browned, 5 to 6 minutes. Place the hazelnuts in a kitchen towel and rub them together to remove the skins. Allow the nuts to cool, about 15 minutes.

3. Increase the oven temperature to 450°. Lightly butter two baking sheets.

4. In a food processor, grind the hazelnuts and almonds with the sugar until a powder forms, about 45 seconds. Add the butter and blend until smooth, about 30 seconds. Add the vanilla, and blend in the egg whites until the batter is smooth, about 15 seconds. Turn the processor off and add the flour. Process quickly, on and off, to mix in the flour, about 5 seconds.

5. Using a pastry bag fitted with a ¼-inch (#1) plain pastry tube, pipe out mounds approximately the size of a quarter, or drop a scant teaspoonful onto the baking sheets, leaving 1 inch between the cookies.

6. Bake in the middle of the oven for 6 to 8 minutes, or until the edges are lightly browned. Remove the cookies with a long metal spatula to a pastry rack to cool.

7. Melt the semisweet chocolate (see "Melting Chocolate," page 337). When the chocolate is smooth and cool to the touch, use a knife or small metal spatula to coat the flat side of each cookie with a thin layer of the chocolate. Place the cookies on a plate or pastry rack. Chill until the chocolate hardens. Serve cool or at room temperature.

* If you can't get blanched almonds, after roasting them in step 2, rub the skins off.

Macarons au Chocolat
Chocolate-Almond Macaroons

I have always found macaroons too sweet. Most recipes contain at least twice as much sugar as almonds, and I have reduced the sugar to a point where many would no longer call them macaroons (although I feel that much of the cookies' original character still remains). The cocoa adds to the subtle, semisweet nature of this cookie.

Similar nut cookies can be made using pecans, macadamia nuts, or hazelnuts. Also try making them with both toasted and unblanched almonds, which changes the flavor and character of the cookie.

Makes 5 dozen

1¼ cups (200 g) whole blanched almonds or 1⅔ cups
    (200 g) slivered almonds
½ cup plus 3 tablespoons (150 g) sugar
⅓ cup (30 g) unsweetened cocoa powder
2 to 3 egg whites

1. Preheat the oven to 350°. Use a nonstick baking sheet or line a regular baking sheet with nonstick parchment paper.

2. In a food processor, grind the almonds and sugar to a powder. Mix in the cocoa.

3. Add 2 egg whites and mix by turning the processor on and off several times to avoid overmixing. Add enough of the third egg white, if necessary, to form a sticky paste.

4. Fill a pastry bag fitted with a ½-inch (#6) plain tube and form the cookies the size of a quarter on the prepared pastry sheet, or drop by teaspoonfuls.

5. Bake the cookies 12 to 14 minutes, until they have puffed slightly. Cool, remove from the paper, and store in an airtight container.

Variation

Macarons *(Plain Macaroons):* Omit the cocoa powder.

Palmiers
Palm Leaf Cookies

Although these delicious, lightly caramelized pastries are called cookies, they really belong in a class by themselves. Sometimes called "elephant ears" in English, *palmiers* (which means "palm trees") are a perfect way to use up any scraps of puff pastry you may have. Although once you've tasted a *palmier*, you're likely to make fresh puff pastry so you can bake a larger batch.

Makes 25 to 30

Butter for baking sheets
About ⅓ cup sugar
½ pound puff pastry, store-bought* or use ¾ pound
   Pâte Demi-Feuilletée (page 277)

MAKING PALMIERS

1. Fold the dough to meet at the center and flatten the edges slightly with a rolling pin.

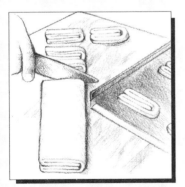

2. Cut the chilled dough, across the folds, into ¼-inch strips. Place the slices cut sides down on baking sheets 1½ to 2 inches apart.

1. Sprinkle the work surface with a light layer of sugar. Then sprinkle the block of puff pastry with a light layer of sugar.

2. Roll the pastry out into a rectangle about 10 inches long and ⅛ inch thick. Continue sprinkling sugar on the dough to make sure the dough is well coated on both sides. Trim the ends square.

3. With a pastry brush or your fingers, lightly sprinkle the surface of the dough with water (this will ensure that the folds stick together when baked). Fold two ends to meet at the center so that the 10-inch side now measures 5 inches. With a rolling pin, roll the pastry slightly to flatten the folded edges.

4. Sprinkle the surface again lightly with water and fold in half so that the 5-inch side now measures 2½ inches. Roll lightly again to flatten the folded edge. Cover with plastic wrap and refrigerate for at least 30 minutes.

5. Preheat the oven to 475°. Butter two baking sheets.

6. Cut the chilled dough, across the folds, into ¼-inch strips. Lay the slices cut sides down on baking sheets, leaving 1½ to 2 inches between them.

7. Bake in the middle of the oven for 5 minutes. Turn the cookies over and bake another 2 to 3 minutes or until glazed and golden brown. Cool on a rack and keep them dry in an airtight container until served. Serve on a doilied plate.

❋ I find, and you may too, that using store-bought puff pastry produces cookies saltier than those made with my recipe.

Biscuits à la Cuillère
Ladyfingers

Ladyfingers are made from a light sponge cake batter that's firm enough to hold its shape when formed with a pastry bag and large plain pastry tube. They are best eaten within several hours of baking, and are ideal for serving with fresh fruit or sorbet. Ladyfingers are used to line molds for desserts like the Marquise au Chocolat (page 333), and are often moistened with liqueurs to become a part of a dessert, as they do in the Marquise Alice (page 311).

A problem often encountered is a runny batter that does not hold its shape when formed on the pastry sheet. This is often caused by the use of vanilla extract in the recipe. For this reason I call for a very small amount. Other ways of avoiding the use of liquid vanilla are to use vanilla sugar (sugar in which a vanilla bean has been stored to give the sugar flavor) or to flavor the batter with grated orange or lemon zest. In France a powdered vanilla is used, eliminating the problem.

Makes 20

3 eggs, separated
⅓ cup (75 g) granulated sugar
¼ teaspoon vanilla extract or grated zest of 1 orange or lemon
⅛ teaspoon cream of tartar
½ cup plus 2 teaspoons (75 g) all-purpose flour
Confectioners' sugar for dusting

1. Preheat the oven to 375°. Line two baking sheets with wax paper.

2. In a small bowl, beat the egg yolks and granulated sugar until very thick. Beat in the vanilla.

3. In a medium bowl, beat the whites with the cream of tartar until stiff peaks form.

4. Sift the flour into the yolk mixture. Add half the beaten egg whites and fold until partially mixed. Add the remaining egg whites and fold until smooth.

5. Fill a pastry bag fitted with an ¹¹⁄₁₆-inch (#9) plain pastry tube with the batter. Form the ladyfingers 4 inches long by squeezing the batter from the bag while holding the tube about ½ inch above the surface of the baking sheet. As the batter falls to the sheet, draw your hand in a steady line until the prescribed length has been reached. Stop squeezing, and with a quick down and up motion of the pastry tube, cut the batter off.

6. Sprinkle the ladyfingers twice with the confectioners' sugar and bake 10 to 15 minutes, or until lightly colored.

7. Cool the ladyfingers on the paper, and then gently pry them off. If not using immediately, store in an airtight container.

In addition to making ladyfingers, the batter can be used to make sponge layers by spiraling the batter into rounds as it is squeezed from the pastry bag. These sponge layers can then be used like *génoise* layers.

Pain Français
French Bread

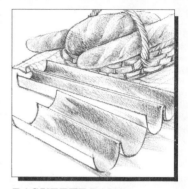

BAGUETTE PANS

The first thing you are served in a French restaurant is bread and butter. And it continues to be an important feature of the meal all the way through to the cheese course.

Only a very few restaurants make their own bread or rolls, for there is usually a bakery within a few blocks that makes good bread, but the top restaurants all have their special bakeries. And with such good bakeries around, it is the rare home cook who makes bread.

In some areas of this country, finding a well-made, freshly baked loaf of French bread may be a rarity and is sufficient reason to make your own. Bread making is easy with the aid of a food processor. And except for the time required for rising it is also quick.

Although I do not consider myself a bread maker, never having formally studied the subject nor worked in a bakery, I do pride myself on the recipe and techniques I've put together for teaching French bread-making to American home cooks. By following the suggestions in the recipe, your first loaf of bread will be a certain success.

The first step in bread making is combining the flour, water, and yeast to form a dough. Mixing these basic ingredients by hand can be a difficult and messy task, but with a food processor it becomes a snap.

Many bread recipes produce a sticky dough that needs to be formed on a floured surface and kneaded with floured hands to keep from sticking. Working with dough in this way can be difficult and messy for the novice. In my recipe the dough is rarely sticky, eliminating the need for additional flour and making

COATING BAKING SHEETS

If you are baking your loaves on a baking sheet, do not oil it as you would a bread pan, or they will spread out rather than up. Instead, coat the sheet with enough layer of flour to keep the bread from touching the sheet. The flour will not change the bread's flavor, but if you feel so inspired, try coating your baking sheet with cornmeal, sesame seed, caraway, or poppy-seed to add another dimension to your bread.

BREAD BASICS

Flour: This is the most important ingredient in bread. I have made bread with many brands of all-purpose flour, and they definitely have different flavors. I prefer unbleached flour to bleached, but I hesitate to mention my favorite brands, knowing that they may not be available in your market, and knowing that there are probably others equally good that I have not tried. Try the different all-purpose flours available to you, and decide which you prefer.

If the flavor or texture of your bread is not up to your expectations, try making your next loaf with 50 percent bread flour. Bread flour contains more gluten (the protein in flour) than all-purpose, so a dough made from it is more elastic, and the bread chewier. I find that bread made with 100 percent bread flour is too difficult to work with, so I mix it 50-50 with all-purpose flour.

When forming loaves made with bread flour, you may find them springy and hard to form. When this happens, stop working, cover the dough with plastic wrap, and let it rest for 2 to

the forming process much easier and neater.

Once the dough is mixed, it must rest to give the yeast time to grow. While the yeast grows, it emits carbon dioxide, which causes tiny air pockets to appear in the dough. This rising or leavening of the dough takes several hours and should not be rushed, because it is during this rising period that the bread also develops some of its flavor. Once the dough has risen to two or three times its original volume, it needs to be deflated, or punched down, and kneaded to release the gas. If the dough is left inflated too long, the bread will have a strong taste similar to baking soda from overexposure to carbon dioxide.

Many bakers allow their dough to rise three or four times, the flavor changing slightly with each rise. I have found that most people are unable to tell the difference in taste between two and three rises, so I suggest that you form your bread after the first rise to considerably shorten the time needed for making it. When you have the time, give it the additional rises, and determine for yourself if they are beneficial.

Traditionally, once formed and risen, and just before going into the oven, its surface is slashed with a sharp knife or razor blade to enhance its beauty and fullness when baked, and to prevent the crust from bursting as the moist interior expands more rapidly than the drier exterior. Slashing a fully risen, fragile loaf can cause it to deflate, producing both a low loaf and a low spirit. I recommend that you slash about halfway through the rise, when the loaf is more resilient, until you become more confident in your slashing. Should you forget to slash, there is no need to panic. Even if your loaf is not picture perfect, it will still taste great.

Many French bakeries use bread ovens that inject steam to moisten the surface of the bread as it bakes, creating a thicker and crunchier crust. Home bakers have tried to simulate the professional steam oven in a variety of ways. Some have put pans of boiling water in their ovens to create steam; some open their oven door to spray their baking loaves with a plant mister; others put ice cubes on the bottom of their hot ovens, while others merely brush their loaves with water to produce the thicker crust. However, if the surface of your dough has been kept moist by being well covered throughout the rising process (in my method, I use plastic wrap instead of the usual kitchen towel, which lets air dry out the dough's surface), no additional moisture is needed to produce a crisp and crunchy crust.

To bake *baguettes*, the typical 16- to 18-inch-long loaf of French bread, you can use baking sheets or, if you have them, you can make them in the special long loaf pans designed for baking French bread.

Makes 2 to 3 baguettes

1 package active dry yeast or ½ ounce fresh yeast
1 teaspoon sugar
¼ cup warm (90° to 115°) water
3¼ cups (1 pound) unbleached all-purpose flour, or half
  bread flour and half all-purpose (see "Bread Basics,"
  page 293)
1 teaspoon salt
¾ cup plus 2 tablespoons cold water
Oil for bread pans or all-purpose flour for baking sheet

1. In a small bowl, dissolve the yeast and sugar in the warm water. Let sit for 2 to 5 minutes, or until foamy and showing signs of life. If the yeast is nonactive, discard and start again with new yeast.

2. Place the flour and salt in a food processor and add the dissolved yeast.

3. With the processor turning, add the cold water in a steady stream and process until the mixture forms a smooth dough, 40 to 60 seconds.

5 minutes to allow the tension in the dough to relax.

Yeast: The other vital component in bread making. It needs to be dissolved in a warm liquid, usually water, and most recipes provide a temperature range. However, if you do not have a thermometer, just put your finger into the warm water. If the water feels warm or even very warm, it is in a good range; but if, after a few moments, it feels hot, it is too warm.

I have used both fresh and active dry yeast with equally good results, so try both to see if you have a preference. Fresh yeast can be stored in the freezer for 2 to 3 months. I do not recommend the "quick rising" yeast now on the market; the difference in rising time is not appreciable and the flavor is not as good as in breads made with traditional yeasts.

Water: If your local water contains chemicals, you may find the flavor of your bread improved by using bottled water.

Causes and Effects: Yeast dough can be temperamental and inconsistent in its behavior. Being aware of the factors that may affect the dough will help you handle its moods.

Occasionally, you may find that your dough is stiffer or softer than usual, and that the amount of rising time it needs increases or decreases substantially. (A stiff dough takes longer to rise than a softer one.) Both the type of flour and the amount of humidity in the air play a role in determining the amount of water your dough may need, so don't hesitate to add up to ¼ cup more if you feel the dough is too stiff. And if the dough is too soft and sticky, add more flour.

Other things that may influence rising time are altitude and room temperature. High altitudes can reduce both the rising and baking times, so keep an eye on your dough. Similarly, a dough left to rise in a warm place will rise more quickly than one left in a cold or drafty room.

A final, perhaps more obvious, factor that will affect your bread is oven temperature. As you can see from the temperatures given for the three sizes in

4. Turn the dough out of the processor onto your work surface. It should be soft, smooth, and easy to knead. To test it, squeeze the dough in one hand, lift it into the air and let it fall back onto your work surface. If the dough leaves your hands clean, it is perfect. If it sticks to your hands, sprinkle it with a little flour and knead until it is smooth and no longer sticky. If the dough is too firm or dry, dip your fingers into water and then plunge them into the dough. Knead the dough and repeat the process until the dough has softened.

5. Tuck the edges of the dough underneath itself, and press to form into a flat round or disc. Place the dough in a large bowl or saucepan (4- to 5-quart), and cover tightly with plastic wrap or a lid (the plastic should not touch the dough). Allow the dough to rest in a cool room until doubled in size, 1½ to 2 hours. The dough is ready when a clear impression remains when a finger is inserted into its center.

6. While the dough rises, oil your French bread pans. If using a baking sheet, sprinkle enough flour on it to prevent the dough from touching it.

7. Punch down the dough and turn it onto the work surface. Knead about 30 seconds, to force out air bubbles that formed during the rising. (If desired, the dough can now be given one to two additional risings in the bowl.)

8. Cut the dough into two or three equal portions, each weighing ½ to ¾ pound, depending on the size of your pans, and cover the pieces you are not working on with plastic wrap to keep them from drying out.

9. Flatten one of the portions of dough with your fingers into a rectangular shape, pressing out the air bubbles as they move to the edge of the dough. Depending on the width of your rectangle, fold the dough in half or in thirds lengthwise to form a long, narrow piece of dough about 2 inches wide. Press down on the edges as you fold the dough to seal them and to break any air bubbles that may still appear. Elongate the dough by rolling it back and forth with the flat palms and extended fingers of your hands, and at the same time moving your hands from the center down

to the ends. The dough should resemble a piece of rope, measuring approximately 1 inch in diameter, and be the same length as your bread pan.

10. If using bread pans, place the loaves into the prepared pans and cover completely with plastic wrap. If using a baking sheet, cover the loaves with a deep roasting pan. Neither the plastic wrap nor the roasting pan should touch the rising dough. If they do, the dough will stick. In such cases, you should remove the plastic wrap (carefully to prevent the loaves from falling) and then carefully re-cover the dough. Let the loaves rise about 30 minutes, or until risen by half.

11. Uncover the loaves and make three or four diagonal slashes in each loaf with a sharp knife—a serrated knife works well. Each slash should be 3 to 4 inches long and about ½ inch deep, and, if possible, the blade should be held at a 45-degree angle to the loaf. Re-cover the loaves and allow them to continue rising until doubled or tripled in size, about 45 minutes.

12. Preheat the oven to 450°.

13. Remove the plastic or roasting pan and bake the loaves on the lowest rack in the oven 20 to 25 minutes, or until evenly browned. If they begin to brown more on top than on the bottom, turn them over in the pans or baking sheet for the last 5 minutes.

14. Transfer the loaves to a pastry rack to cool. Do not be concerned if you hear the crust cracking. When the bread is completely cool, freeze any that is not to be eaten within 24 hours. *(Frozen bread will keep for several weeks, well wrapped in plastic or aluminum foil. To serve, reheat at 350° if frozen, for 10 minutes; and 400° if thawed, for 5 minutes, or until the crust crackles when squeezed.)*

the bread Variations (below), the larger the loaf, the lower the temperature. In any event, French bread is baked at relatively high temperatures to give color, flavor, and crunch to the crust. If you find the temperature too high, lower it 25 to 50 degrees. If you are using black pans or sheets, this is a good rule of thumb anyway.

Variations

Boule *(Round Loaf):* Follow the recipe through step 7 and form one round loaf as illustrated. Preheat the oven to 425°. Place the *boule* on a pastry sheet (sprinkled with flour), cover with a bowl or pot, and let rise until doubled or tripled in size, about 1 hour. Just before placing in the oven, make a slash about 1 inch deep through the center. Bake on the lowest rack of the oven for 25 to 30 minutes. Cool on a rack.

Pain Libanais *(Pita Bread):* Pita is definitely not French, but is being seen more often in France because of the influx of North African and Middle Eastern workers. It doesn't need a final rising before baking, and bakes in just a few minutes.

Follow the recipe through step 5. Preheat the oven to 500° and place an uncoated baking sheet or baking stone on the lowest rack of the oven. After following step 7, form the dough into a long sausagelike shape and cut off 2- to 4-ounce pieces. Keep the pieces covered with plastic wrap when not being worked with. Flatten each piece with your fingers until it is as thin as possible. Place (or toss) these flat, pancakelike pieces of dough onto the hot sheet or stone. The pita will puff and bake in about 4 minutes. If they are beginning to get too brown, turn them after 3 minutes. Cool on a rack.

Pain Complet *(Whole-Wheat Bread):* Substitute ½ pound whole-wheat flour and ½ pound bread flour for the pound of unbleached all-purpose flour. The rest of the recipe is the same; or shape it into a *boule* (see illustration, left).

FORMING A *BOULE*

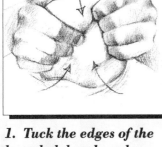

1. Tuck the edges of the kneaded dough underneath itself.

2. Shape the dough into a smooth round ball.

Desserts

Desserts, coming as they do at the end of a meal, have the ability to turn an otherwise ordinary dinner into a memorable one; yet if mischosen, they can ruin the memory of a splendid one. Follow an elegant meal with an elegant dessert such as the frozen chocolate dessert (Marquise au Chocolat, page 333), but a rich meal with a light dessert: sorbet (Sorbet au Poires, page 329).

Although I have in many cases reduced the amount of sugar, butter, and cream used in updating the classic desserts, I also make a point of serving my guests small portions.

Many of the desserts in this chapter can be made partially or totally in advance. By following the advance preparation suggestions, you can make entertaining easy.

Omelette au Cointreau
Cointreau Omelet

Without question, my most successful omelet is an *omelette au Cointreau.* By adding alcohol and sugar to the eggs, they become lighter and have a creamy custard consistency when cooked to perfection. The sugar in my version of this traditional dessert is one-third of that used in the original.

Depending on the size pan you use, and the number of people you serve, you can easily increase or decrease this recipe. For each egg, use 1 teaspoon sugar and 1 tablespoon Cointreau.

Serves 2

3 eggs
1 tablespoon granulated sugar
2 to 3 tablespoons Cointreau, to taste
½ tablespoon butter
Confectioners' sugar for dusting

1. In a bowl, beat the eggs, granulated sugar, and Cointreau together until smooth.

2. In a 7- or 8-inch nonstick omelet pan, heat the butter over medium-high heat.

3. Add the egg mixture to the pan and rapidly and constantly stir with a wooden spoon. If you can, gently shake the pan at the same time. When the eggs are nearly set, yet a little liquid still remains, stop stirring and shake the pan for a couple of seconds, making sure that the bottom of the pan is completely covered by the egg. At this point, the eggs should be set, yet still moist. Stop shaking the pan and allow the bottom of the omelet to firm slightly, 4 to 5 seconds. (After making several omelets, you will be able to stir and shake the pan simultaneously.)

4. Fold the omelet into thirds by lifting the handle and tilting the pan at a 30-degree angle (see "How to Fold an Omelet," page 42). With the back of the spoon, fold the portion of the omelet nearest you toward the center of the pan. Gently push the omelet forward in the pan so the unfolded portion rises up the side of the pan. Using the spoon, fold this portion back into the pan, overlapping the first fold. Turn the omelet out onto a serving plate so that it ends up folded side down. Dust with confectioners' sugar and serve immediately.

Variations

Omelette au Rhum *(Rum Omelet):* Substitute rum for Cointreau.

Omelette aux Fraises et au Cointreau *(Strawberry Omelet with Cointreau):* Place 3 tablespoons diced strawberries across the center of the omelet before folding in step 4. Decorate with 2 strawberry halves.

Omelette aux Fraises *(Strawberry Omelet):* By omitting the Cointreau from the above variation, the omelet becomes a breakfast treat for the whole family.

Omelette Vallée d'Auge *(Omelet with Apples and Calvados):* Substitute 2 tablespoons Calvados for the Cointreau. Place a few tablespoons of sautéed apples down the center of the omelet before folding in step 4. Decorate with additional slices of sautéed apple.

Omelette Soufflée à l'Orange
Orange Omelet Soufflé

This is a quick, elegant—and often overlooked—dessert that will impress and satisfy your guests whenever you have not had time to prepare one in advance.

By beating the egg yolks and whites separately, and then folding them together, an *omelette soufflée*, which is usually cooked in an omelet pan, puffs and browns like a soufflé.

The Orange Omelet Soufflé I serve for dessert is baked in the oven and looks very much like a Baked Alaska. The fluffy egg mixture is first mounded on an *unbuttered* ovenproof platter, and then, using a pastry bag, it is decorated with swirls of the omelet soufflé batter. Browned quickly in a hot oven, the omelet soufflé is served warm, moist, and frothy, a light, delicate ending suitable for a full or rich meal.

Serves 6 to 8

6 eggs, separated
½ cup plus 3 tablespoons (150 g) granulated sugar
Grated zest of 2 oranges
Confectioners' sugar for dusting

There are also first-course or savory souffléed omelets. For example, a cheese omelet soufflé can be prepared by mixing grated cheese with beaten egg yolks and folding stiffly beaten egg whites into this mixture. Poured into a buttered omelet pan, the soufflé is cooked for a few minutes over medium heat and then finished or browned in a hot oven with a little cheese sprinkled on top. The omelet is then slid from the pan to a warm serving plate or platter.

1. Preheat the oven to 475°.
2. In a bowl, beat the egg yolks with half of the granulated sugar until thickened. Stir in the orange zest.
3. Beat the egg whites until soft peaks form. Add the remaining sugar and beat until the egg whites are very stiff. Fold the egg whites into the yolk–sugar mixture.
4. With a spatula, mound the soufflé mixture on an ovenproof platter. The surface of the omelet soufflé may be decorated by using a pastry bag filled with one-sixth of the omelet batter and fitted with a 5/16-inch (#3) star tube.
5. Bake for 4 to 5 minutes, until the omelet soufflé colors but does not rise.
6. Dust with the confectioners' sugar and serve immediately.

Soufflé à l'Abricot
Apricot Soufflé

This is an example of a fruit soufflé made without the traditional pastry cream base. Fruits with a lot of pulp and not much liquid, such as apricots, produce a thick base when puréed. The base can then be simply sweetened and mixed with beaten egg whites to produce a very light and luscious dessert. Fruit soufflés prepared this way are lighter and will rise faster than traditional pastry cream soufflés and require less baking time. Generally they will rise in 8 minutes or less.

For this recipe I use the principle of puréed fruit as a soufflé base, but substitute dried California apricots (I find their flavor more intense than the Turkish variety) for fresh ones because they are available year round. The apricots are puréed in a blender with hot water to replace the fruit's natural moisture and to soften them.

Other fruits you can try are mango, pear, and papaya. With fresh fruit it is not necessary to add water. If the fruit needs sweetening, the sugar should be beaten with the stiff egg whites to dissolve it, or use a heavy sugar syrup (Sirop de Sucre, page 403) instead.

Serves 4

Butter and granulated sugar for soufflé mold
About ¾ cup (100 g) dried California apricots
¼ cup plus 1 tablespoon (75 g) granulated sugar
¾ cup hot water
2 tablespoons orange liqueur, such as Triple Sec
5 egg whites
⅛ teaspoon cream of tartar
Confectioners' sugar for dusting

PREPARING SOUFFLÉS FOR THE OVEN AHEAD OF TIME

To find out just how far in advance you can make your soufflés, I suggest that you try the following: Make any of the soufflés in the book up to the point of baking, and instead of pouring the batter into a 4-cup mold, pour it into individual (¾- to 1-cup) buttered molds. (Only individual size molds should be frozen. The surface of the larger ones tend to dry out and crack in the freezer, preventing them from rising when baked.) Place one of the molds in your freezer, one in your refrigerator, one on your kitchen counter, and one in your oven. You should have no problems with the first one baked. Baking time is only about 5 minutes. Bake the one that is sitting on your counter two hours later, the one in the refrigerator the next day for lunch, and the one from the freezer the following week. If all bake as well as the first, your advance preparation can be done at any time.

Note: **If you have only a food processor, soften the apricots in the hot water first before puréeing them (with the water).**

1. Preheat the oven to 475°. Butter and sugar a 4-cup soufflé mold.

2. Place the apricots in a blender (see Note). Dissolve the granulated sugar in the hot water and add to the blender. Add the orange liqueur. Blend until smooth. Transfer to a large bowl.

3. In second large bowl, beat the egg whites with the cream of tartar until stiff peaks form. With a whisk, fold one-third of the stiffly beaten egg whites into the apricot mixture to lighten it. With a rubber spatula, fold the remaining whites into the mixture until it is smooth. Pour the soufflé batter into the prepared mold and level the surface with a spatula. Run your thumb around the top of the mold to clean off any excess batter.

4. Bake the soufflé on the lowest rack of the oven for 5 minutes. Lower the temperature to 425° and bake for another 3 to 4 minutes, until the soufflé has risen halfway above the top of the mold and is springy to the touch.

5. Dust the soufflé with confectioners' sugar and serve immediately.

Soufflé au Grand Marnier
Grand Marnier Soufflé

One of the most popular dessert soufflés is the *soufflé au Grand Marnier*, yet it is but one of many soufflés that can be made with liqueurs. Use any of your favorite liqueurs in place of the Grand Marnier and produce a soufflé with the name of the liqueur. (Don't be tempted to add any more liqueur than called for in the recipe, for if too much is added, it will fall out of suspension and end up on the bottom of the soufflé dish in a liquid or pasty mass.)

Serves 4

Butter and granulated sugar for soufflé mold
1 cup milk
3 egg yolks
¼ cup less 2 teaspoons (50 g) granulated sugar
3 tablespoons (25 g) all-purpose flour
4 egg whites
⅛ teaspoon cream of tartar
¼ teaspoon vanilla extract
Grated zest of 1 orange
¼ cup Grand Marnier
Confectioners' sugar for dusting

1. Preheat the oven to 475°. Butter and sugar a 4-cup soufflé mold.

2. In a small saucepan, bring the milk to a boil over medium heat.

3. While the milk is heating, whisk the egg yolks and granulated sugar together in a small bowl. Add the flour and mix well, until smooth and free of lumps.

4. Thin the egg yolk mixture with approximately ¼ cup of the warm milk. When the remaining milk begins to boil, add it to the egg yolk mixture and stir well. Return the mixture to the saucepan and whisk rapidly over medium-high heat, making sure to whisk the bottom and the sides of the pan until the cream thickens and boils, about 1 minute.

5. Cook the pastry cream an additional 2 minutes over medium heat, whisking while it boils gently, until it becomes shiny and is easier to stir. Remove the pan from the heat and cover to keep warm.

6. In a large bowl, beat the egg whites with the cream of tartar until stiff peaks form.

7. Pour the pastry cream into a large bowl and stir in the vanilla, grated orange zest, and Grand Marnier.

8. Fold one-third of the stiffly beaten egg whites into the pastry cream with a whisk to lighten it. Fold the remaining whites into the mixture with a rubber spatula until it is smooth. Pour the soufflé batter into the prepared mold and level the surface with the spatula. Run your thumb around

As with most soufflés, the center of this Grand Marnier soufflé will be soft and creamy when cooked to perfection. Although a sauce is never necessary with a creamy-centered soufflé, I realize that many people feel that a soufflé is incomplete without one. For those of you who are so inclined, Grand Marnier-flavored Crème Anglaise (page 387) or fresh raspberry sauce (Coulis de Framboise, page 386) should suit the purpose admirably.

the top of the mold to clean off any excess batter. *(The soufflé can be made ahead to this point; see "Preparing Soufflés for the Oven Ahead of Time," page 302.)*

9. Bake the soufflé on the lowest rack of the oven for 5 minutes. Lower the temperature to 425° and bake another 4 to 5 minutes, until the soufflé has risen at least halfway above the top of the mold, and it is golden-brown in color, and springy to the touch.

10. Dust the soufflé with confectioners' sugar and serve immediately.

Variations

Soufflé Moka *(Mocha Soufflé):* Omit the vanilla, orange zest, and Grand Marnier from above. Add Essence de Café (page 401) or instant coffee to taste to the warming milk in step 3. Taste the pastry cream in step 4, and if the coffee has made it too bitter, add up to 2 tablespoons sugar to the beaten egg white in step 6 and beat again until stiff. Serve the soufflé with chocolate sauce made from 4 ounces (115 g) semisweet or bittersweet chocolate, ⅓ cup water, and 2 tablespoons Cognac (optional).

Soufflé aux Fraises *(Strawberry Soufflé):* Replace the orange zest and Grand Marnier with 2 tablespoons kirsch and add to the pastry cream in step 7. Fold 1 cup diced strawberries into the pastry cream with the second half of the beaten egg whites in step 8.

I usually make the soufflé in advance and refrigerate it. When it is time for dessert, I ask my guests if they would like a chocolate mousse or soufflé. If the majority want a soufflé, I bake it. If they want mousse, it is served cold.

Soufflé au Chocolat et au Grand Marnier
Chocolate Soufflé with Grand Marnier

This is an extremely light chocolate soufflé made from my basic chocolate mousse recipe with the addition of orange zest and Grand Marnier, and a plain chocolate soufflé can be made with their omission.

The soufflé mixture can also be baked in a water bath (*bain-marie*) for a little bit longer, to give you a wonderful, dense fallen soufflé dessert called Pudding au Chocolat (see Variation, opposite).

Serves 4

Butter and granulated sugar for soufflé mold
4 ounces (115 g) semisweet or bittersweet chocolate
4 tablespoons (60 g) unsalted butter
4 eggs, separated
Grated zest of 1 orange
2 tablespoons Grand Marnier
⅛ teaspoon cream of tartar
Confectioners' sugar for dusting

1. Preheat the oven to 475°. Butter and sugar a 4-cup soufflé mold.

2. In a saucepan, combine the chocolate and butter and melt over low heat. Remove from the heat, whisk in the egg yolks, and pour into a large bowl. Stir in the grated orange zest and Grand Marnier.

3. In a large bowl, beat the egg whites with the cream of tartar until stiff peaks form.

4. With a whisk, fold one-third of the beaten egg whites into the chocolate. Fold the remaining egg whites in with a rubber spatula. Pour into the prepared soufflé mold and level the surface with a spatula. Run your thumb around the top of the mold to clean off any excess batter. (*The soufflé can be prepared ahead to this point; see "Preparing Soufflés for the Oven Ahead of Time," page 302.*)

5. Bake the soufflé on the lowest rack of the oven for 5 minutes. Lower the temperature to 425° and bake another 4 to 5 minutes, until the soufflé has risen halfway above the top of the mold and is springy to the touch.

6. Dust with confectioners' sugar and serve the soufflé immediately.

Variation

Pudding au Chocolat *(French Chocolate Pudding):* A French *pudding* is basically a fallen soufflé. As with the Mousse au Chocolat (page 315) on which this is based, the flavor of the *pudding* can be changed easily by replacing the Grand Marnier with coffee, rum, or Cognac and omitting the orange zest. Preheat the oven to 475°. Butter and sugar a 4-cup charlotte or soufflé mold. Pour the mousse mixture into the prepared mold. Place the mold in a deep roasting pan and fill with enough boiling water to come halfway up the side of the mold. Place on the lowest rack in the oven. Reduce the temperature to 400° and bake 15 to 20 minutes. Remove from the oven and allow to cool. (The inflated puffed portion will drop back into the mold.) To serve, unmold onto a platter. The pudding can be served warm or cold, and can be accompanied by Crème Anglaise (page 387).

Any of the soufflés in this book can be baked and unmolded using this method, if desired.

THE COLOR OF CARAMEL

The color of the cooked caramel for *crème caramel* is very important. If it is too pale, it will have little or no flavor. If it is too dark, it will taste bitter or burnt. I cook the sugar until it is a deep amber color and is just about to smoke, and often tell students to wait until they begin seeing smoke before pouring the hot sugar into their mold. After making the dessert several times, you can determine for yourself the color required for the flavor desired.

Crème Renversée au Caramel
Caramel Custard

Crème renversée au caramel, commonly called *crème caramel* and known as *flan* in Spanish, is one of the world's most popular desserts. It is a vanilla custard cooked in a caramel-lined mold, so that when it is unmolded it is covered with a liquid caramel sauce.

I make a classic custard with 2 eggs per cup of milk. In the following recipe, I have removed two egg whites, creating a fragile yet rich tasting custard. Although you can bake the custard in almost any size mold, I have chosen a cake pan so that the finished dessert will be no higher than 1½ inches. If you want the custard to be higher, use a deeper mold, and give it added strength by including the 2 egg whites otherwise removed. The custard can be made with milk, heavy cream, or a mixture of the two, and many people serve it with whipped cream, although I find that unnecessary.

Always unmold the *crème caramel* just before serving, because if it's unmolded too early, it will look dull and dry instead of shiny and bright.

Serves 8 to 10

Caramel

¼ cup water
½ cup (110 g) sugar
2 to 3 drops lemon juice (optional*)
Butter for mold (optional)

Custard

3 cups milk
⅔ cup (140 g) sugar
4 whole eggs
2 egg yolks
2 teaspoons vanilla extract

1. **Make the caramel:** Place the water in a small saucepan and add the sugar. Cook over medium-high heat until the sugar turns amber in color, about 5 minutes.

2. Immediately pour the caramel into an 8-inch cake pan and, using pot holders, turn it until the bottom and sides of the pan are coated. (If for any reason you are unable to fully coat the sides of your mold, wait for the caramel to cool and then lightly butter the sides not coated.) Set aside. (As the caramel cools, it will harden. When the pan cools, the caramel may crack. This is normal and will not affect the dessert.)

3. Preheat the oven to 350°.

4. **Make the custard:** In a small saucepan, bring the milk and sugar to a boil over medium heat.

THE EVER-CHANGING CUSTARD

Custard is one of the foundations of French dessert making. In varying proportions, it is a combination of milk or cream, eggs, and sugar. At its thinnest and most refined it is used as a sauce, called *crème anglaise. Crème anglaise*, or vanilla custard sauce (see page 387), can be served with cake, poached fruit, or as part of a meringue dessert such as Ile Flottante Cardinale (page 314). When you freeze a custard sauce, it becomes ice cream (see Les Glaces, page 330). When you add whipped cream and gelatin to it, a rich dessert called a Bavarian cream is created (see Marquise Alice, page 311, or Riz à l'Impératrice, page 312).

Then there are the baked custards, ranging from the simple and always satisfying Crème Renversée au Caramel (page 307) to the silky and smooth Pots de Crème (page 309). For most custards, but particularly for the very rich recipes such as *pots de crème*, I have reduced egg yolks, cream, and sugar where possible without destroying the satisfying nature of these desserts.

5. In a bowl, whisk the 4 whole eggs and 2 egg yolks until smooth. Stirring constantly, pour the hot milk and sugar slowly into the eggs. Stir in the vanilla.

6. Place the caramel-coated cake pan into a small roasting pan, which will serve as a water bath (*bain-marie*). Strain the custard into the cake pan. Fill the roasting pan with enough boiling water to come halfway up the sides of the cake pan. Place the roasting pan on the bottom rack of the oven.

7. Bake 25 to 30 minutes, or until a cake tester or toothpick placed in the center of the custard comes out clean, not milky. Allow the custard to cool. Refrigerate for 2 hours or more.

8. **To serve:** Unmold the custard onto a large round plate or platter just before serving. To do so, run the point of a knife around the edge of the custard to make sure that it is not stuck to the pan. Place a serving platter upside down on top of the cake pan, and while holding the two firmly together, invert quickly. Remove the cake pan and allow the caramel sauce to flow on top of the custard. Use a cake server to cut and serve the custard.

* The lemon juice will slow the hardening of the sugar and give you more time to coat the pan in step 2. If you have experience working with caramel, you can leave the lemon juice out.

Pots de Crème: Vanille et Café
Rich Vanilla and Coffee Custards

The classic recipe for *pots de crème* calls for 1 quart of heavy cream, 12 egg yolks, and about 1½ cups sugar. This is basically the same formula that is used for *crème brûlée*, a rich vanilla custard served with a crust of melted brown sugar. This dessert was in fashion 35 to 40 years ago, and again in the last four to five years. Although I enjoy these rich custards, I cannot, in good conscience, make and serve anything so high in cholesterol and calories.

The following recipe is made lighter by the reduction of yolks, the addition of egg whites, and the use of milk instead of cream. I have also reduced the sugar considerably, yet it still tastes rich and delicious.

Serves 6

3 cups milk or light cream
½ cup plus 3 tablespoons (150 g) sugar
2 eggs
5 egg yolks
2 teaspoons vanilla extract
1½ teaspoons instant coffee

1. Preheat the oven to 350°.
2. In a small saucepan, bring the milk and sugar to a boil over medium heat.
3. In a bowl, whisk the eggs and yolks together lightly. Stirring constantly, pour the hot milk and sugar mixture slowly into the eggs. Stir in the vanilla.
4. Divide the custard into 2 equal portions. Add the coffee to one portion and stir until dissolved.
5. Strain the custard into small *pots de crème* "pots" or ½-cup ramekins. Be sure that all of the foam is spooned from the top of each.
6. Place the "pots" into a roasting pan. Add water to the roasting pan to come halfway up the sides of the "pots." Place on the lowest rack of the oven. Bake for 20 to 30 minutes, or until a cake tester or toothpick inserted in the custard comes out dry or clean. Do not let the custard boil. If the custard begins to puff, an indication that it is beginning to boil, remove it from the oven immediately.
7. Allow the "pots" to cool and then refrigerate for 2 hours or more. *(The custard can be made a day ahead. Keep refrigerated.)*
8. Serve one vanilla and one coffee to each person.

POTS DE CRÈME

The recipe for *pots de crème* gets its name from the small pots it is traditionally baked and served in. These little ceramic cups with lids have a ⅓-cup capacity, and were often served three per person, one each of chocolate, vanilla, and coffee. Even with my lightened custard, I find three too much to eat, and serve only two: vanilla and coffee (I omit the chocolate because it is grainy and tends to produce a dull rather than shiny finish).

Marquise Alice
Praline-Flavored Bavarian Cream

A Bavarian cream (*bavarois*) is a molded dessert made from a *crème anglaise* base to which gelatin and whipped cream are added. A *marquise Alice* is a praline-flavored Bavarian cream with kirsch-moistened ladyfingers (*biscuits à la cuillère*) buried in the center. The unmolded cream is traditionally covered with whipped cream and decorated with currant jelly.

Although the white-covered Bavarian cream with its deep red decoration is most attractive, I have saved calories by simply serving the unmolded, undecorated dessert surrounded by a band of currant jelly. You can also use small metal molds to make individual servings.

Serves 6 to 8

Kirsch
4 to 6 Biscuits à la Cuillère (page 290) or store-bought ladyfingers
Crème Anglaise (page 387), hot
1 envelope unflavored gelatin softened in ¼ cup cold water
½ teaspoon vanilla extract
2 rounded tablespoons (50 g) Pâte de Pralin (page 399)
¾ cup heavy cream
½ cup red currant jelly
2 teaspoons water

1. Sprinkle enough kirsch over the ladyfingers to moisten them.

2. Place the hot *crème anglaise* in a medium metal bowl and add the softened gelatin, vanilla, and *pâte de pralin*.

3. Set the bowl in a larger bowl of ice and water (see "Over Ice," page 312) and stir until cool to the touch, being sure to scrape the sides and bottom of the bowl. Remove the custard from the ice.

4. In another bowl set in the ice and water, beat the cream until stiff. Fold the whipped cream into the cooled custard. (This is now a Bavarian cream.) Place the bowl containing the Bavarian cream over the ice and continue folding until the mixture is thick and smooth.

5. Pour half of this mixture into an 8-inch round cake pan. Make a layer of ladyfingers, placing them no closer than ¼ inch from the edge. Cover the ladyfingers with the remaining Bavarian cream. Refrigerate for at least 2 hours before unmolding.

6. In a small saucepan, melt the currant jelly and water over low heat. Bring to a boil, remove from the heat, and add 2 teaspoons kirsch. Allow to cool at room temperature, yet remain liquid.

7. **To unmold:** Run the point of a knife around the custard and dip the mold into hot water for 5 to 10 seconds. Place a chilled cake platter upside down on the cake pan. Holding the pan and platter together, invert. Remove the cake pan. If the dessert does not unmold easily after one or two immersions in hot water, give both the plate and the mold a firm downward shake. *(This can be done several hours before serving. Keep refrigerated.)*

8. Just before serving, spoon the currant jelly onto the platter around the dessert.

Riz à l'Impératrice
Rich Molded Rice Dessert
with Raspberry Sauce

The classic *Riz à l'Impératrice* is a vanilla-flavored rice pudding mixed with Bavarian cream (*crème anglaise*, gelatin, and whipped cream) and preserved fruits and molded in a ring mold. It is served unmolded with kirsch-flavored currant jelly around it.

"OVER ICE"

Stirring mixtures over ice is an extremely useful technique. It is used when working with gelatin in order to speed up the jelling process and at the same time give you control over it so it doesn't jell too much (which might happen if you leave the gelatin mixture in the refrigerator). It is also used any time you want to cool down a hot mixture quickly.

To cool things "over ice," place the saucepan or metal or Pyrex bowl containing the mixture in question into a larger bowl filled with ice and a little water. The water is needed in order to completely surround the saucepan or bowl with cold. If you are cooling a hot mixture or thickening a gelatin mixture, you must stir it, which both speeds up the cooling process and, in the case of gelatin, prevents uneven jelling.

The same idea is used by the French when they whip cream, because the cold temperature prevents the cream from turning to butter.

I have reduced the amount of egg yolks and heavy cream originally used by half, and by adding the yolks to the hot rice in step 3, have in effect eliminated the need to make a separate *crème anglaise.* I have also eliminated the preserved fruits, which I find too sweet, and use a raspberry sauce sweetened with currant jelly in place of the jelly on its own. My choice of a cake pan instead of a ring mold is mainly for presentation. I find a wedge of the dessert looks better than a section of a ring. An alternate, and very attractive, solution would be to use individual ring molds.

Serves 8

½ cup (100 g) rice
3 cups milk
½ cup less 2 teaspoons (100 g) sugar
1 vanilla bean or 1 tablespoon vanilla extract
2 egg yolks
1 envelope unflavored gelatin softened in ¼ cup cold water
½ cup heavy cream
½ recipe Coulis de Framboise (page 386), sweetened with
*   red currant jelly*

1. In a small saucepan, cook the rice in 2 or more cups of boiling water for 15 minutes and drain.

2. In a 2-quart saucepan, bring the milk, sugar, and vanilla bean (if using vanilla extract, it is not added until step 3) to a boil. Add the rice, cover, and cook over low heat for 30 minutes. About 1 cup of milk should remain. Remove the vanilla bean, if used.

3. Remove the rice from the heat and whisk in the egg yolks, softened gelatin, and vanilla extract, if using. Pour into a metal bowl and place in a larger bowl of ice and water (see "Over Ice," page 312). Stir until cool to the touch, being sure to scrape the sides and bottom of the bowl. Remove the rice from the ice.

4. In another bowl set into the ice and water, whip the cream until stiff. Fold the whipped cream into the rice mixture. Return the rice to the ice and continue folding until

the mixture begins to set or thicken. Pour into an 8-inch round cake pan or other metal mold. Refrigerate for at least 2 hours before unmolding.

5. **To unmold:** Run the point of a knife around the rice and dip the mold into hot water for 5 to 10 seconds. Place a chilled cake platter upside down on the cake pan. Holding the pan and platter together, invert. Remove the cake pan. If the rice does not unmold easily after one or two immersions in hot water, give both the plate and the mold a firm downward shake. *(This can be done several hours before serving. Keep refrigerated.)*

6. **To serve:** Pour a little of the *coulis de framboise* around the unmolded rice and serve the remaining sauce in a pitcher or bowl. You can also serve the dessert sliced and surrounded with the sauce on individual plates.

Ile Flottante Cardinale
Floating Island with Raspberry Sauce

*I*le *flottante* and *oeufs à la neige* are both desserts made from poached meringue and served with *crème anglaise*. In the case of *oeufs à la neige*, large egg-shaped spoonfuls of meringue are poached in simmering milk or water, while for *île flottante* the meringue is molded and poached in the oven. When unmolded, the meringue becomes an island floating on the *crème anglaise*.

Ile flottante often has crushed praline mixed into or layered with the meringue. I find the praline too sweet in this dessert, so I add chopped toasted almonds instead. I also use raspberry sauce to coat the surface of the floating island, and have added the name *cardinale*, which is classically used to describe a dish robed in red.

A number of years ago I was asked to bring a light dessert to a dinner party at which Paul Bocuse was to be the honored guest. When it was announced that the *île flottante* that was about to be served was mine, I was told by my dinner partner, a close friend of the great chef, that I shouldn't be upset if Monsieur Bocuse merely tasted it, for he rarely ate desserts. I was pleased when he ate not only the portion served, but asked for more.

The complete dessert can be made up to one day in advance and assembled before serving.

Serves 6

Butter for soufflé mold
3 egg whites
¼ cup plus 2 tablespoons (90 g) sugar
¼ teaspoon vanilla extract
⅓ cup (40 g) chopped toasted almonds
Crème Anglaise (page 387)
Coulis de Framboise (page 386)

1. Preheat the oven to 350°. Lightly butter a 4-cup soufflé mold.

2. In a bowl, beat the egg whites until soft peaks form, about 30 seconds. Add the sugar and vanilla extract and beat until very stiff, about 1 minute. Fold in the chopped toasted almonds.

3. Pour the meringue mixture into the prepared mold and bake on the bottom rack in a water bath (*bain-marie*) for 20 minutes, or until springy to the touch and lightly colored on top.

4. Allow the meringue to cool in the mold. Refrigerate for at least 1 hour before unmolding and serving.

5. Present the unmolded meringue on a deep platter surrounded by *crème anglaise* and covered with *coulis de framboise*. Serve each guest a slice accompanied by a little of each sauce.

Mousse au Chocolat
Chocolate Mousse

This simple classic is one of the most versatile recipes that I have ever taught. Not only is it a fabulous chocolate mousse, but it can also be baked to make a soufflé, a cake, a chocolate roll, and a French pudding.

A mousse is light and airy, and can be made with beaten egg whites or whipped cream, but I make mine with egg whites alone. I find that the chocolate, butter, and egg yolks in the recipe supply all the richness needed.

A refreshing variation can be made by adding the finely grated zest of 1 orange. If you want to flavor the mousse with coffee, rum, Grand Marnier, or another liqueur, add only 1 to 2 tablespoons (to taste) just before incorporating the egg whites. If you add more you may lose the light consistency that makes this recipe so good.

Serves 6

4 ounces (115 g) semisweet or bittersweet chocolate
4 tablespoons (60 g) unsalted butter
4 eggs, separated
⅛ teaspoon cream of tartar

1. In a heavy-bottomed saucepan, melt the chocolate and butter over low heat. Stir occasionally until smooth.
2. Remove the chocolate mixture from the heat and whisk in the egg yolks until blended. Immediately pour the mixture into a large bowl. (The melted chocolate and butter will be hot enough to poach the egg yolks, which will lightly thicken the mixture.)
3. In a large bowl, beat the egg whites with the cream of tartar until stiff peaks form.
4. With a whisk, fold one-third of the stiffly beaten egg whites into the chocolate mixture to lighten it. Using a rubber spatula, fold the remaining whites into the chocolate mixture until smooth.
5. Pour the mousse into a crystal serving bowl or individual glasses and refrigerate until set, 2 hours or longer. Serve chilled.

THE MARVELOUS, MULTI-FACETED MOUSSE

Since chocolate behaves much like flour when baked, it is possible to use the basic chocolate mousse recipe to make several desserts that normally contain flour. For example, baked in a cake pan it makes Gâteau Mousse au Chocolat (page 261), or chocolate mousse cake. If you bake it in a jelly-roll pan, you have Gâteau Roulé au Chocolat (page 266), or chocolate roll with whipped cream. Baked in a soufflé mold, it is Soufflé au Chocolat et au Grand Marnier (page 305). For a delicious fallen soufflé dessert called a *pudding*, the mousse is baked in a soufflé mold in a water bath (*bain-marie*) (see Pudding au Chocolat, page 307). You can also make a wonderfully simple variation of the chocolate mousse by freezing it and serving it in slices (see Marquise au Chocolat, page 333).

HOW TO TIE THE LIME ZEST KNOT

Using a vegetable peeler, peel the zest of the lime with a sawing motion from top to bottom. Cut this zest into strips ¹⁄₁₆ inch wide. Gently tie a knot in the center of each strip.

Mousse au Citron Vert
Lime Mousse

Classic fruit mousses are made with fruit purées sweetened with sugar syrup and then folded with whipped cream, molded, and refrigerated. This version uses half whipped cream and half stiffly beaten egg whites. For lime mousse, fruit juice is used instead of a purée and gelatin is used to thicken it.

The tartness of limes varies, and I prefer this mousse on the tart side. If, when you combine the sugar syrup and the lime juice in step 4, you find it too tart, sweeten it to taste by adding confectioners' sugar.

This wonderfully refreshing dessert can be made a day in advance, and remains refrigerated until served.

Serves 8 to 10

8 to 10 limes
1 cup (220 g) granulated sugar
½ cup water
1½ envelopes unflavored gelatin softened in ½ cup
  cold water
1 cup heavy cream
4 egg whites
Confectioners' sugar, to taste

1. With a vegetable peeler, peel the zest from one of the limes from top to bottom using a slight sawing motion. Cut the zest into 10 to 12 thin strips about ¹⁄₁₆ inch wide; discard any remaining zest. Gently tie a knot in the center of each strip and cover them with plastic wrap. They will be used later for decoration.

2. Squeeze the limes to obtain 1 cup of juice.

3. In a small saucepan, bring ½ cup of the granulated sugar and the water to a boil, making sure the sugar is dissolved. Remove from the heat and stir in the softened gelatin to dissolve it.

4. Add the gelatin-sugar mixture to the lime juice and place in a metal bowl set into a larger bowl filled halfway with ice and a little water (see "Over Ice," page 312). Stir the juice until it is cool (see "Cool to Touch," page 392), about 1 minute. Remove from the ice and set aside.

5. In a medium bowl set into the ice and water, beat the cream until stiff, about 1 minute. Set aside.

6. In a large bowl, beat the egg whites until soft peaks form, about 30 seconds. Add the remaining ½ cup granulated sugar and beat until stiff peaks form, about 1 minute.

7. Return the ice and water mixture to its original proportions by pouring off excess water and adding more ice. Stir the juice mixture with a metal spoon over the ice and water, being sure to scrape the sides and bottom of the bowl, until it is very cold and the consistency of heavy cream, 4 to 5 minutes.

8. Fold in half of the beaten egg whites, then three-quarters of the whipped cream. Follow this with the remaining egg whites. The mixture should be smooth and have the consistency of sour cream. Pour into a serving bowl and refrigerate until set, about 30 minutes. *(This can be done up to 1 day before serving.)*

9. **To decorate the mousse:** Whisk in a little confectioners' sugar in the remaining whipped cream to sweeten to taste. Fill a pastry bag fitted with a ³⁄₁₆-inch (#1) starred tube with the whipped cream and pipe rosettes around the edges of the mousse. Place one lime zest knot in the center of each rosette.

Variation

Mousse au Citron *(Lemon Mousse):* Replace lime zest and juice with lemon zest and juice.

Crêpes Sucrées
Dessert Crêpes

Dessert crêpes are made with sweetened batter. In addition to the sugar and vanilla in the recipe, other flavorings can be added to the batter to match the crêpes to the filling. A touch of freshly grated nutmeg or powdered cinnamon for an apple filling, or a little grated lemon zest when filling with a lemon-flavored pastry cream, are just two examples. I use this recipe to make breakfast crêpes for my children. They enjoy spreading a thin layer of jam or jelly on the crêpes and then folding or rolling them to eat.

Crêpes are traditionally made in small iron pans that must be seasoned (see "How to Season a Crêpe Pan," page 69) and lubricated with butter or oil after every few crêpes. I find using nonstick pans much easier and less messy, and therefore recommend their use.

Makes 16 to 24 six-inch crêpes

1 cup plus 1 tablespoon (150 g) all-purpose flour
3 eggs
2 tablespoons (25 g) sugar
½ teaspoon vanilla extract
1½ cups milk
3 tablespoons (45 g) melted butter or vegetable oil

1. Put the flour into a bowl* and add the eggs, sugar, vanilla, and ½ cup of the milk. Whisk slowly until a smooth batter is formed. Add the remaining 1 cup milk and whisk well. If time permits, allow the batter to rest 30 minutes. (As the batter rests, the granules of flour absorb the milk and swell, creating a smoother batter and a slightly stronger crêpe than if used right away.)

2. Whisk in the butter just before using the batter.

MAKING CREPES

1. Tilt the crêpe pan slightly and ladle approximately 2 tablespoons of batter into the pan where the sides and bottom meet.

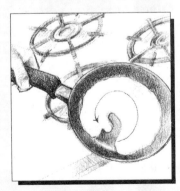

2. Turn the pan in a circular motion to spread the batter evenly.

3. Heat a 6-inch crêpe pan, either well-seasoned or with a nonstick surface, over medium-high heat. The pan is ready when a drop of water dances on the hot surface. Hold the pan in one hand, tilting it slightly. Using a small ladle or coffee measurer, pour about 2 tablespoons of batter into the pan where the sides and bottom meet. Now turn the pan in a circular motion to spread the batter evenly. The amount of batter used should just coat the bottom of the pan. Any excess should be poured back.

4. Cook the crêpe until the edge begins to brown. Turn the crêpe with a spatula or flip it (see Crêpes Salées, page 70). Cook the second side for only 10 to 15 seconds and slide the crêpe onto a plate. (The surface of the crêpe should be medium brown in color. If after making two crêpes you find the color either too dark or too light, adjust your heat accordingly. At the same point, if you find the crêpe is too thick, thin the batter with a little more milk.) Repeat until all the crêpes are made, stacking them one on top of the other, and allow them to cool.

* This can also be done in a blender without worry of lumps forming. Place all ingredients in the container of the blender. Then turn the blender on and off again. Scrape down the flour that has stuck to the sides of the blender and blend until smooth.

3. When the edges of the crêpe begin to brown, flip it.

NEUTRAL CRÊPE BATTER

If you prefer, you can make crêpes to be used in either first courses or desserts by making a crêpe batter flavored only with ¼ teaspoon salt (leaving out the sugar and vanilla).

Crêpes Suzette
Crêpes with Orange Butter

Crêpes Suzette is one of those desserts whose flavor lingers in your memory long after you have finished eating. The unique combination of orange, butter, sugar, and Cognac provides a sauce for the thin, delicately flavored French pancakes.

Those who are familiar with making crêpes will

Crêpes Suzette **was originally designed to be a restaurant spectacle, with the maître d' flaming them for you at the table. I prefer to sip Cognac or Grand Marnier with coffee following dessert instead. However, if you wish to flame the crêpes, simply warm an additional ¼ cup of Grand Marnier and pour it over the crêpes hot from the oven. Carefully ignite and** spoon the flaming sauce over the crêpes until the flames die. If all the alcohol has not evaporated, the delicate balance of flavors can be upset.

DESSERT CRÊPE VARIATIONS

Most classic dessert crêpes are filled—unlike Crêpes Suzette (opposite), which are simply folded and served with a flavored butter sauce. The basic fillings for dessert crêpes are Crème Pâtissière (page 388), whipped cream, and ice cream (see pages 330–33). Diced fruit and chopped nuts are often mixed with the various cream fillings, and raspberry, vanilla, and chocolate sauces are served over the crêpes.

A crêpe filled with a soufflé batter is baked to become a *crêpe soufflée*. You can fill the crêpes with Soufflé au Grand Marnier (page 303) or Soufflé au Chocolat et au Grand Marnier (page 305). To make

notice that for this dessert I have removed 2 egg whites from the traditional dessert crêpe batter, which creates a softer and richer tasting crêpe. It is wonderful to eat, but more fragile (having lost the strength provided by the egg whites). If you have problems with the crêpe tearing, use 3 whole eggs the next time.

Choose an attractive ovenproof platter for serving, and make sure that it has a rim high enough to contain the sauce created by the melting butter. Although not flamed, as is customary for this dessert, the following presentation makes advance preparation and serving easy. When making crêpes for a large party, I use two crêpe pans to speed the process.

Serves 6 to 8

Crêpes Sucrées (page 319), made with 1 egg, 2 egg yolks
1 stick (115 g) unsalted butter, softened to room temperature
¼ cup (50 g) sugar
Grated zest and juice of 1 orange, at room temperature
¼ cup Grand Marnier

1. **Prepare the Crêpes Sucrées** (page 319) using 1 egg and 2 egg yolks in place of 3 eggs. In step 2 of the crêpe recipe, whisk in the 1 tablespoon of Grand Marnier along with the melted butter.

2. **Make the Suzette butter:** (It is best to make the Suzette butter while the crêpe batter is resting, for although the butter can be made ahead and refrigerated, it must be brought back to room temperature before using.) In a food processor, cream the butter. Add the sugar and process until the mixture is smooth and white. Add the orange zest and gradually add the juice. (If the orange juice is cold it will stiffen the butter, making this procedure more difficult.)

3. Add the Grand Marnier a little at a time. Do not worry if the butter does not hold all the liquid.

4. **Assemble the dessert:** Turn the stack of crêpes over so that the lighter side is on top. Spread each crêpe with 1 teaspoon of the Suzette butter and fold in half and

then in half again forming a quarter-circle wedge. Arrange attractively on an ovenproof platter and spread any remaining butter and liquid over them. *(At this point, the crêpes can be covered and refrigerated or frozen. Bake unthawed.)*

5. **To serve:** Preheat the oven to 425°. Place the platter of crêpes in the oven for 10 to 15 minutes, or until the butter is bubbling. Serve 2 to 3 crêpes per person.

the *crêpes soufflées*, spoon about 3 tablespoons soufflé batter down the middle of the crêpe. Fold the two sides of the crêpe over the filling and place the filled crêpes, seam side down, on a well-buttered ovenproof platter. Bake at 475° for 4 to 5 minutes, until they double in size. Serve the *crêpes soufflées* with Crème Anglaise (page 387), flavored to enhance the soufflé filling.

Bananes Flambées au Rhum
Bananas Flamed in Rum

For people who like bananas, *bananes flambées* is a certain winner. Although your guests may enjoy the drama of this dessert, the flaming of the bananas is not just for show, and in fact is most easily done in the kitchen. In addition to cooking off the alcohol, flaming browns the bananas and caramelizes the sugar.

A simple variation can be made by serving half a banana cut lengthwise together with a scoop of vanilla ice cream. Also try plain or toasted grated coconut together with or in place of the almonds.

Serves 4

⅓ cup (70 g) sugar
4 tablespoons (60 g) butter
Juice of 1 lime or lemon
½ cup dark rum
4 small bananas*
¼ cup (25 g) toasted sliced almonds

1. In a large skillet, stir the sugar over medium-high heat until it melts and lightly caramelizes. Remove the pan from the heat.

2. Stir in the butter, lime juice, and ¼ cup of the rum. Return the pan to low heat.

There are many rums with varying flavors. Most of the rum used in France comes from the island of Martinique, and its flavor differs from that of most other rum-producing islands. As hard as I tried to develop an appreciation for it while living in France, I never did. My preference is for one of the dark, full-flavored blended rums from Puerto Rico or Jamaica, and my favorite rum is a Demara rum from Guyana. If you use an ultra-high-proof rum, be careful of the added fire power when flaming.

Anyone who has had diffi-
culty flaming a dessert at
the table will find flaming
in the kitchen much easier.
Before you take your pan
off the heat, be sure to
have the rum you're add-
ing at hand, and the match
ready to strike so the alcohol won't all evaporate
before you're ready to
ignite it.

3. Place the bananas in the pan and baste with the sauce. Cover and cook over low heat until tender, 5 to 10 minutes.

4. **To flame:** Pour the remaining ¼ cup rum into the pan; remove from the heat. Keeping your face well away from the pan, carefully ignite the rum by touching a match to the pan's edge. Baste the bananas until the flames die. Transfer to a serving platter or plates, sprinkle with toasted almonds and serve immediately.

* Use bananas that still have a little green at the stem.

Fraises au Sabayon
Strawberries with Zabaglione

The French *sauce sabayon* is fashioned after the Italian *zabaglione*. In Italy it is made with Marsala, a sweet Italian wine, while in France it is made with a dry white wine and often flavored with a liqueur. *Sabayon* can be served warm, cold, or frozen, and is excellent with both fresh and poached fruit.

Serves 6

2 pints strawberries
3 egg yolks
¼ cup plus 2 tablespoons (90 g) sugar
⅓ cup dry white wine
1 to 2 tablespoons kirsch, Grand Marnier or other liqueur,
  to taste
½ cup (50 g) sliced almonds, toasted

1. Place the berries in individual glass or crystal compote dishes or goblets.

2. Place the egg yolks, sugar, and wine in a metal or heatproof glass mixing bowl and set the bowl over a

saucepan of gently simmering water. (Or use a 2-quart double boiler.)

3. Using an electric hand mixer or whisk, beat the egg and sugar mixture until it is thick and foamy, about 5 minutes. At this point the sauce will be warm to the touch. Beat in the kirsch.

4. The *sabayon* can be served either warm or cold. If it is to be served cold, place the bowl into a larger bowl of ice and water and continue beating until it is chilled. *(A* sabayon *to be served cold can be made 24 hours in advance and frozen. Pour the cold sauce into a cold bowl or container and freeze. When frozen, the sauce will be thick and can be spooned over the berries.)*

5. **To serve:** Pour the *sabayon* over the berries, sprinkle with the almonds and serve.

Poires au Porto
Pears Poached in Port Wine

Several years ago, when it seemed as though everyone was poaching pears in red wine, I was reminded of Fernand Point's recipe for prunes poached in red wine and port (see Variation) and was inspired to try pears instead. By poaching in port, which has a certain sweetness, you can eliminate a large quantity of the sugar normally used in poaching fruit.

Serve the pears with Madeleines (page 284) or Tuiles aux Amandes (page 282). Any excess poaching liquid remaining after the pears have been served can be refrigerated or frozen for future use in poaching pears.

Serves 6

6 pears, preferably Comice or Bosc, peeled
3 cups dry red wine
1½ cups port
½ cup less 2 teaspoons (100 g) sugar
Juice and peeled zest of 1 orange
Juice and peeled zest of 1 small lemon

1. Place the pears upright in a deep pan just large enough to hold them. Add all of the other ingredients and bring to a boil over medium-high heat. Reduce the heat and simmer gently, uncovered, until they are tender, 15 to 20 minutes for unripened pears and 5 to 10 minutes for ripened, ready-to-eat pears.

2. Allow the pears to cool in the poaching liquid.

3. Place the pears in a serving bowl and strain the liquid over them. Refrigerate 2 hours or more. *(This can be done a day or two in advance.)*

4. Serve one pear per person in a bowl or on a plate with some of the poaching liquid.

HOW TO SECTION AN ORANGE

The best oranges to use for sectioning are seedless ones.

Start by cutting off one end so you can see the exposed flesh. You can either slice off strips of skin as shown above, or use the method I prefer which follows on the next page.

Variation

Pruneaux au Porto *(Prunes Poached in Port Wine):* Substitute 2 pounds of pitted prunes for the pears. In step 1, cook the prunes until tender, about 10 minutes.

Oranges au Champagne
Oranges in Champagne

While a Frenchman would never dream of making this simple, elegant classic dessert with anything but French Champagne, I find the selection of

Champagne-style sparkling wines being produced in this and other countries very suitable.

The orange sections are served in a cut crystal or glass bowl or in individual goblets and brought to the table with a chilled bottle of Champagne. The bottle is uncorked at the table and the Champagne poured over the oranges. Accompany the oranges with ladyfingers (Biscuits à la Cuillère, page 290) or Tuiles aux Amandes (page 282).

The best oranges to use are seedless so the sections will be solid and not left with holes made by the seeds. The navel orange is our best-known seedless and is known in France as the Thompson, after the man who developed it. Use oranges in the winter months, at the height of their season, when they are deep orange in color and full of flavor. In addition to the navel, a number of other oranges work well for this dessert, even though they have some seeds. Some of these are the Valencia, Mineola, and Tangelo.

Serves 8 to 10

8 oranges
1 bottle demi-sec Champagne or similar sparkling wine

1. Peel and section all of the oranges, making sure they are completely free of all membranes (see "How to Section an Orange," page 325). Place the oranges in a colander (they will hold their shape better than if allowed to sit in their own juice) and refrigerate until ready to serve.

2. Place the sectioned oranges in a crystal serving bowl or individual goblets and bring to the table with a chilled bottle of Champagne.

3. Pour the Champagne over the oranges and serve.

1. *Hold the paring knife as you would to peel an apple, but instead of just drawing your knife along the flesh, move it up and down with a sawing motion at the same time, enabling it to cut through the thick skin more easily. Keep the knife under the membrane but as close to it as possible so as not to cut away too much flesh. Continue cutting around the orange until all the skin and membrane are removed.*

2. *Section the oranges by cutting them toward the center as close to each sec-*

tional membrane as possible. This will yield shiny, smooth individual orange sections. Once all the sections have been removed, squeeze the membrane that is left to extract any juices that remain.

Sorbet
Sorbet or Fruit Ice

A fresh fruit sorbet provides an ideal ending for a meal, especially during the summer months when the variety and quality of fresh fruit is at its best. A sorbet captures the essence of fruit in a smooth, frozen state.

Easy to make, sorbets are simply sweetened fruit purées frozen in an ice cream machine. They will keep in your freezer for several weeks.

In most cases I use a very heavy sugar syrup to ensure a smooth sorbet (see Note), but I add it to taste, according to the fruit being used. A few fruit juices are thin and sweet, and produce a sorbet that is a bit icy. Adding an egg white in these few cases will produce a smoother texture.

This recipe, which is constructed loosely in order to give you freedom, will make as much or as little sorbet as you want or as the size of the fruit dictates. The fruit quantities given in the flavor variations that follow will produce about 1 quart of sorbet.

Fruit (see suggestions)
Heavy Sirop de Sucre (page 403), to taste
Lemon juice (optional)

1. Purée the fruit using a food processor or blender.
2. Strain only when necessary to remove large seeds or fibrous content, for example, raspberries, pineapple, or citrus juices.
3. Sweeten to taste with the heavy *sirop de sucre*. If you add too much sugar, adjust the sweetness with lemon juice. Keep in mind that the purée will taste a little less sweet when frozen.

Note: The amount of sugar added to the purée plays a large role in the consistency of the finished sorbet. If too little sugar is added, the sorbet will be hard and icy; if too much is added, it will not freeze. In French cooking, sugar is added to achieve the proper consistency without regard for the natural sweetness of the fruit, often resulting in an overly sweet purée. When this happens, lemon juice is added to adjust the sweetness.

4. Freeze following the directions for your ice cream machine. If you do not have a machine, you can use a food processor (see "Making Ice Cream the New Old-Fashioned Way," page 331).

5. Store sorbets in covered plastic containers in the freezer for up to a month. If the sorbet becomes too hard or icy, it can be melted and refrozen in your ice cream machine.

Variations

Sorbet aux Framboises *(Raspberry Sorbet):* This is my most often used flavor. It is excellent when served with other sorbets, with vanilla or coffee ice cream, and with fresh fruit. For about 1 quart, use 2 pints fresh raspberries or 2 packages (10 ounces each) unsweetened frozen raspberries.

Sorbet aux Fraises *(Strawberry Sorbet):* Use dark red, full-flavored berries. For about 1 quart, use 2 pints of fresh strawberries or 2 packages (10 ounces each) unsweetened frozen.

Sorbet aux Myrtilles *(Blueberry Sorbet):* I like the taste of both fresh and cooked blueberries (the flavor of blueberry pie). For cooked blueberry sorbet, after puréeing and sweetening the fruit, bring it to a boil, then chill before freezing. I often add a tablespoon or two of *crème de cassis* (black currant liqueur), which creates an unusual flavor. For about 1 quart, use 2 pints of fresh blueberries or 2 packages (10 to 12 ounces each) unsweetened frozen.

Sorbet à l'Ananas *(Pineapple Sorbet):* Pineapple makes an excellent sorbet when the fruit is ripe and full of flavor. Choose a pineapple that has a sweet, ripe smell to it. It is excellent when served with fresh raspberries, strawberries, blueberries, or mango, or sorbets made from these fruits. To surprise your guests, hollow out a pineapple and fill it with sorbet. For about 1 quart, use a medium pineapple, peeled, cored, and cubed.

SERVING SORBETS

I find sorbets so easy to make, especially as quantities don't really matter and sugar is added to taste, that I make sorbets whenever fruit looks particularly good or is in season. I often have a whole range of flavors in my freezer to choose from and will serve several together.

If you have a variety of flavors, use a small scoop (1½ inches in diameter) and fill a wine glass with the different flavors. If you're planning this in advance, take the colors of the sorbets into consideration to make an attractive arrangement.

To serve a single flavor of sorbet, use a large (1¾- to 2-inch) scoop and, if desired, surround the sorbet with fresh fruit. Even better for sorbets is an egg-shaped scoop; the oval scoops of sorbet can be arranged on a cold dessert plate, with or without added fresh fruit. When using this scoop, I generally serve three scoops per person.

Sorbet aux Poires *(Pear Sorbet):* Use ripe, juicy Comice pears when in season. Purée with a little lemon juice and sugar syrup to retard discoloration. Use one pear per person, or four for about 1 quart.

Sorbet au Citron ou au Citron Vert *(Lemon or Lime Sorbet):* Both juices create extremely refreshing sorbets. Strain the pulp and dilute the juice with an equal amount of water before sweetening. You can increase the flavor of all citrus sorbets by adding the grated zest of the fruit; you can leave the zest in or strain just before freezing. Serving lemon and raspberry sorbet together makes a wonderful combination. For about 1 quart, use 4 cups of diluted and sweetened juice.

Sorbet au Pamplemousse *(Grapefruit Sorbet):* This sorbet is extremely easy to make with fresh squeezed grapefruit juice that is available at most supermarkets. Try it flavored with a little white vermouth or Campari. If you squeeze your own grapefruits for this, you can add the grated zest for a more pronounced flavor; leave the zest in or strain just before freezing. Although I do not serve sorbets between courses as a palate refresher, grapefruit sorbet would work well for this purpose. For about 1 quart, use 4 cups of sweetened juice.

Sorbet à la Mangue *(Mango Sorbet):* When ripe and full of flavor, mangos make a marvelous sorbet. This purée requires very little sugar, and its flavor is improved with a touch of lime juice. I often serve mango sorbet surrounded by fresh blueberries in the summer. For about 1 quart, use 4 ripe mangoes.

Sorbet Tropical *(Banana, Orange, and Rum Sorbet):* For 1 quart, use 3 bananas, 3 cups of orange juice, and 6 tablespoons of dark rum. Add sugar syrup if needed, or adjust sweetness with either lemon or lime juice.

Sorbet au Melon *(Melon Sorbet):* Melon sorbet is only good when melons are truly at their perfection. Otherwise it is

Sorbet au Chocolat et à l'Orange
Chocolate–Orange Sorbet

This recipe is for all those who want their chocolate without cream. I often flavor the sorbet with a little Essence de Café (page 401) or Grand Marnier before freezing. I also make another wonderful variation by adding a cup of raspberry purée.

Makes about 1 quart

6 ounces (170 g) unsweetened or semisweet chocolate
½ cup water
2 cups fresh orange juice
Heavy Sirop de Sucre (page 403), to taste

1. In a small saucepan, melt the chocolate in the water over medium heat. Bring to a boil and whisk into a smooth sauce. Remove from the heat and cool.

2. Blend the chocolate sauce with the orange juice and sweeten as necessary with heavy *sirop de sucre*.

3. Freeze following the directions for your ice cream machine. If you do not have a machine, you can use a food processor (see "Making Ice Cream the New Old-Fashioned Way," page 331).

Les Glaces
Ice Cream

French ice cream is simply frozen *crème anglaise*. This produces a rich ice cream, which many chefs make richer by using cream in place of the milk.

MAKING ICE CREAM THE NEW OLD-FASHIONED WAY

For those without top-of-the-line automatic ice cream machines (or those with no machine at all), try this easy method for ice cream made with a food processor. It stands up surprisingly well to the machine-made.

Place the ice cream base in a bowl or other container and place in the freezer until frozen. (If you taste it, you will notice that large ice crystals have formed, making it crunchy.) Place the frozen base in a processor and process until smooth, 1 to 2 minutes. Pour the smooth mixture back into the cold container from which it came and place in the freezer for another 2 to 3 hours, until frozen. The ice cream may still have a few tiny ice crystals, but not enough to keep you from enjoying it and proudly serving it to guests.

When making ice cream, I use one part heavy cream to three parts milk, and reduce both the number of egg yolks and the amount of sugar normally found in a *crème anglaise*.

Here is my basic ice cream recipe, followed by the various flavors I make. Because the canisters of ice cream makers can make anything from 1 cup to 2 quarts, the flavoring instructions are given per cup of ice cream base. This way you can make as little or as much as you like of each flavor.

Makes 5 cups base / about 1½ quarts ice cream

3 cups milk
1 cup heavy cream
½ cup less 2 teaspoons (100 g) sugar
6 egg yolks

1. In a large saucepan, bring the milk, cream, and sugar to a boil over medium-high heat, about 3 minutes.

2. Place the egg yolks in a mixing bowl. Slowly beat in about 1 cup of the hot milk. Return the mixture to the saucepan and whisk rapidly over medium-high heat for several seconds. Do not boil. Remove the pan from the heat. The sauce should thicken sufficiently to coat a spoon. If the sauce is too thin, return the pan to the heat and whisk several more seconds. This procedure should take no more than 15 seconds.

3. Strain into a large bowl and allow to cool.

4. Freeze following the directions for your ice cream machine. If you do not have a machine, you can use a food processor instead (see "Making Ice Cream the New Old-Fashioned Way," above).

Glace à la Vanille *(Vanilla Ice Cream):* I often serve vanilla ice cream together with a variety of fruit sorbets, and it is a perfect match for ripe cantaloupe. A few well known French desserts use vanilla ice cream as a base: *Coupe Jacques* or *royale* is simply diced fresh fruit with vanilla ice cream. *Poires* or *Pêches Belle Hélène* is poached pears (*poires*) or peaches (*pêches*) with vanilla ice cream and topped with chocolate sauce. Peaches, pears, or strawberries with vanilla ice cream and a raspberry sauce are called *Cardinal* or *Melba.*

To make vanilla ice cream, add 1½ teaspoons vanilla extract to each cup of base. (Or, you can flavor the base with a vanilla bean when you cook it. Add a vanilla bean to the milk when you bring it to a boil in step 1. Then remove the vanilla bean, split the pod, and scrape the seeds into the milk.)

Glace au Chocolat *(Chocolate Ice Cream):* Use 1½ ounces of your favorite semisweet chocolate for every cup of base. Although you can simply melt the chocolate in the base, the ice cream will be smoother if you make a chocolate sauce first. Use 1½ tablespoons water for every 1½ ounces of chocolate to make the sauce. Bring the chocolate and water to a boil. Stir until smooth and add to the ice cream base.

Glace Moka aux Pacanes Grillées *(Mocha Toasted Pecan Ice Cream):* This is one of my favorites. I flavor Chocolate Ice Cream (above) with 1 teaspoon Essence de Café (page 401) or instant coffee per cup of base. When the mixture is nearly frozen, I add ¼ cup (25 g) chopped, toasted, unsalted pecans per cup of base used. The combination is ideal.

Glace au Chocolat et aux Amandes Grillées *(Chocolate Toasted Almond Ice Cream):* The lightly toasted and thinly sliced almonds give a wonderful flavor and delicate crunch to the Chocolate Ice Cream (above). For each cup of base used, add ¼ cup (25 g) lightly toasted sliced almonds to the ice cream while it is still soft but nearly frozen.

Glace au Café *(Coffee Ice Cream):* Use about 1 tablespoon Sirop de Café (page 402) or 1 tablespoon sugar and 1 tablespoon instant coffee for each cup of base. By using decaffeinated espresso coffee beans to make the coffee syrup, I can make a strongly flavored ice cream that won't keep my children awake. Coffee ice cream is outstanding with Sorbet

I generally reserve ice cream making for special flavors, since for the more ordinary flavors—such as vanilla, chocolate, and coffee—I find many commercial brands quite acceptable.

aux Framboises (page 328) and with Sauce au Chocolat (page 385).

Glace Pralinée *(Praline Ice Cream):* Add 1 tablespoon Pâte de Pralin (page 399) to each cup of base. Use praline ice cream instead of vanilla for a marvelous *Poire Belle Hélène* (see Vanilla Ice Cream).

Glace au Rhum et aux Raisins Secs *(Rum Raisin Ice Cream):* No commercial rum raisin ice cream can ever match the home-made variety. Soak the raisins for two or more hours in your favorite rum. Add ¼ cup rum-soaked raisins to each cup of base used. It is tempting to add some of the liquid, but the alcohol acts as an antifreeze and makes the ice cream more difficult to freeze. It will be delicious but soft.

Glace aux Pruneaux à l'Armagnac *(Armagnac Prune Ice Cream):* Use Armagnac- or Cognac-soaked prunes (page 340) for this delicious ice cream. For each cup of base, use 2 to 3 prunes either finely chopped or puréed. As with the Rum Raisin (above), do not add much of the liquid.

Marquise au Chocolat
Frozen Chocolate Dessert

My version of this classic dessert is simply a chocolate mousse that is frozen in a ladyfinger-lined mold. When unmolded, it is sliced and served with a vanilla custard sauce. The classic version, which I first tasted many years ago at Lasserre, then the top restaurant in Paris, is made with a chocolate buttercream and is refrigerated, not frozen. My *marquise* is a lot lighter and easier to digest after a complete meal.

This make-ahead dessert may look complicated,

but it is actually quite easy to make. Bake your lady-fingers one day (or use store-bought) and complete the dessert the next. It can be made several days in advance.

I designed this dessert for a 5-cup French loaf pan, which is longer and more narrow than ours, but you can use any 5-cup loaf pan.

Serves 6 to 8

1½ recipes Biscuits à la Cuillère (page 290) or about
*   30 store-bought ladyfingers*
Mousse au Chocolat (page 315)
Whipped cream and/or candied violets for decoration
Crème Anglaise (page 387), chilled

1. Line the bottom of a 5-cup loaf pan with wax paper. Trim the ladyfingers at one end and on each side to fit tightly together and flush against the bottom of the pan. With cut ends down, line the sides of the loaf pan with the ladyfingers.

2. Pour the chocolate mousse into the lined loaf pan. Refrigerate for 2 hours to set, and then freeze. (If frozen immediately, the mousse will contract.)

3. Before serving, trim the ladyfingers off at the level of the chocolate and unmold the *marquise* onto a rectangular platter, peel off the wax paper, and decorate the top with whipped cream and/or candied violets. Freeze until ready to use.

4. **To serve:** Cut ½-inch slices, place in the center of a dessert plate, and surround with the chilled *crème anglaise*.

Variation

Fill the ladyfinger-lined mold halfway with the mousse mixture, then add a layer of raspberries or whole small strawberries and cover them with the remaining mousse. In addition to the *crème anglaise*, serve a raspberry sauce (Coulis de Framboise, page 386).

COOKING WITH CHOCOLATE

The process of making chocolate is in some ways similar to the process of making coffee. Both cocoa and coffee beans are roasted and then blended to produce a desired flavor, and with each, manufacturers develop a variety of flavors. The quality of the chocolate varies, depending on its percentage of cocoa butter and the amount of time spent refining it.

When choosing a cooking chocolate, I look for one that tastes good, is smooth on my tongue as it melts, leaves a good aftertaste, and is neither too sweet nor too bitter. (A further consideration when the chocolate is to be used for candy making is to find one that is both dark and shiny.)

In general, Americans prefer eating milk chocolate to the dark, semisweet, or bittersweet variety. Cooks, on the other hand, prefer dark chocolate. The terms "semisweet" and "bittersweet" are often synonymous, and the actual sweetness varies among manufacturers. If a company produces both, its bittersweet will be less sweet than its semisweet chocolate. On the other hand, you may find a bittersweet chocolate made by one company that is sweeter than a semisweet made by another. The only true test is in the tasting.

Besides the semisweet chocolate available in supermarkets, there are numerous qualities of imported and domestically manufactured chocolates that can be purchased in bulk at candy stores and specialty food shops. This can often save you money, and offers you a variety of flavors to choose from.

Truffes au Chocolat à la Crème
Chocolate and Fresh Cream Truffles

Chocolate formed to resemble truffles, covered with "dirt" as they emerged from the earth, have been a Christmas specialty sold in French candy shops for many years. Their popularity, especially in America during the last 10 years, has spawned truffle shops and candy companies specializing only in truffles — although many of the confections carrying this name hardly resemble their namesake. It now seems that anything round and chocolate can be called a truffle.

Originally, chocolate truffles were made of a sturdy, fudgelike mixture, concocted of chocolate, butter, and egg yolks, that could be formed by hand and stand at room temperature without melting. But the contemporary version of the truffle is made with a combination of chocolate and fresh cream (called *ganache*), and must be handled carefully and refrigerated, for it melts at room temperature.

Because they melt easily when handled, the soft creamy chocolates, once formed into balls, are dipped into chocolate to lightly coat and protect them. They are then rolled in cocoa powder, which tastes much better than the soil it represents. Biting into a finished truffle provides a wonderful combination of chocolate sensations. Bitter cocoa covers a thin layer of crunchy bittersweet chocolate, which surrounds a creamy, meltingly soft chocolate center. Only those with incredible will power can refuse a second one.

Trying to make the truffles in one day can be difficult and frustrating, but doing a little work over a two- to three-day period makes truffle making easy and enjoyable.

In addition to the Grand Marnier flavoring used in the following recipe, truffles can be flavored with coffee (Essence de Café, page 401), rum, Cognac, or mint extract. If you enjoy the flavor of praline, try mixing ¼ to ½ cup (50g to 100 g) of Pâte de Pralin (page 399) with the *ganache* for a delicious combination.

Makes 80 to 90 pieces (2 pounds)

Truffle Mixture

12 ounces (340 g) semisweet or bittersweet chocolate
1 cup heavy cream
3 tablespoons Grand Marnier or other liqueur

Chocolate Covering

1 pound (450 g) semisweet or bittersweet chocolate
2 ounces (60 g) unsweetened cocoa powder

1. **Make the truffle mixture:** In a saucepan, heat the chocolate and heavy cream over low heat, stirring occasionally until the chocolate is melted.

2. Remove from the heat and pour into a bowl. Stir in the Grand Marnier.

3. Place the mixture in the refrigerator for a minimum of 2 hours until it is firm.

4. Cover a baking sheet with a piece of wax paper. Using two spoons, scoop out and drop onto the paper mounds of ½ to 1 teaspoonful, depending on the size you wish to make. Refrigerate overnight.

5. When cold, loosen the mounds from the paper and use your fingers to make them relatively round, if not already so. Refrigerate until ready to coat.

6. **Make the chocolate covering:** In a saucepan, melt the chocolate in a very low oven (see "Melting Chocolate," page 337).

7. When the chocolate has melted, stir it well from time to time as it cools to body temperature. (This is determined when no difference in temperature is noticed when you touch the chocolate with the knuckle of the smallest finger.)

8. Spread the cocoa powder evenly in a chilled jelly-roll pan or on a chilled plate.

9. Remove the truffles from the refrigerator and drop two at a time into the coating chocolate. Using two forks, turn the truffles, coating them well with chocolate. Lift a truffle with one fork, tapping that fork with the other to eliminate excess chocolate, then drop the coated truffle onto the pan containing the cocoa powder. Using a spoon, quickly roll and coat with the powder, then push it to the side.

10. When the truffles are firm enough to handle, transfer them to a bowl and refrigerate or freeze until ready to serve. *(They will keep well in the refrigerator for about two weeks and can be stored in the freezer for several months.)*

11. **To serve:** Mound the truffles in a serving dish. They are delicious when served at room temperature or cold from the refrigerator.

MELTING CHOCOLATE

If chocolate is melted alone, at a temperature that is too high, two things can happen. The first and most damaging effect is that the chocolate can scorch, dry out, and stiffen. The second, which is noticeable only when using the chocolate for coating, is that the cocoa butter comes out of suspension or separates, causing the chocolate to be streaky and grayish and to lose its gloss. Theoretically, chocolate should be melted at temperatures below 120° to keep it from drying out, and below 90° to prevent the separation of the cocoa butter from occurring.

In practice, I have melted chocolate at much higher temperatures without damaging effects. Following either of the two methods given below for melting will prevent the chocolate from scorching, and if you stir it well while it is cooling for coating, any cocoa butter that may have separated will be mixed back into suspension. If you make lots of chocolate candy, a stricter control of melting and the maintenance of temperature may be advisable, but for this book it is not necessary.

It is, however, necessary, when melting chocolate by itself, to prevent moisture from mixing with it. Although chocolate can be melted with a sufficient amount of water, milk, or cream (½ ounce per ounce of chocolate) to make sauces and icings, a drop or two added to a bowl of melted chocolate can cause it to stiffen and make it useless for coating. For this reason, extreme care should be taken to prevent moisture from coming in contact with melted chocolate.

Stirring the chocolate as it cools is important. Generally when you melt chocolate the cocoa butter floats to the surface, as butter would in a sauce. When it cools and sets, it leaves a dull white film on the surface. By stirring it well as it cools, you keep the cocoa butter well mixed, and the chocolate remains smooth and even colored.

Melting in a Warm Oven: When using chocolate to coat fruit (Fruits Glacés au Chocolat, opposite) or chocolate truffles (Truffes au Chocolat à la Crème, page 335), I most often melt the chocolate using the warmth generated by the light bulb in my oven. Place the chocolate in a saucepan and place the pan in your oven with the light on. In about 20 minutes the chocolate should be melted and ready to use. I often leave the chocolate in the warm oven for several hours and, on occasion overnight, without ill effect to the chocolate.

In a gas oven with a continual gas pilot, the oven will be warm without the light. In an electric oven without a light, set the temperature at the lowest possible setting for similar results.

Melting in a Water Bath (*Bain-Marie*) or Double Boiler: Heat about 1 inch of water in an 8- to 10-inch skillet until it comes to a simmer. Turn off the heat and place a saucepan, with the chocolate in it, into the hot water. Stir occasionally until melted, about 5 minutes. In a double boiler, the chocolate should also be melted off the heat, over hot, not simmering, water.

Fruits Glacés au Chocolat
Chocolate-Dipped Fruit

Some of the most delicious candies are very simple to make. For example, chocolate-coated dried and fresh fruits, as well as assorted nuts, add an elegant touch to the end of a meal when served with coffee or Cognac. All you need to do is melt chocolate, stir it well as it cools, dip the fruit to coat, and let it cool on wax paper. You can use either semisweet or milk chocolate for these candies.

When dipping, the chocolate should feel cool to the touch. The chocolate will be thick and close to setting. Chill a plate or cookie sheet and cover it with wax paper. The chilled surface helps the chocolate set once dipped. The chocolate-covered fruits should be kept covered in a cool room or in the refrigerator, but should be served at room temperature.

To make chocolate-dipped fruits, melt the chocolate in a low oven (see "Melting Chocolate," page 337) and use the following suggestions.

Apricots: Choose deep orange, dried California apricots. Stretch them gently, if necessary, to straighten them and arrange them flat on a plate. Dip them only halfway into the chocolate and allow the excess to drip off before placing the coated apricot on the wax paper.

Prunes: Take large, soft pitted prunes and cut them into two to four pieces. Drop the pieces into the chocolate, and use two forks to turn and coat each piece. Lift a piece out of the chocolate with one fork and tap with the other fork to shake off any excess chocolate. Drop the coated prune onto the wax paper.

Candied Ginger and Candied Citrus Peel: Coat the same way you coat the prune pieces (above).

Nuts and Raisins: Toasted unsalted nuts and raisins are delicious when coated with chocolate. I enjoy eating clusters made with a combination of both. Stir enough nuts and raisins into your melted chocolate so they become lightly coated. Drop them by teaspoonsful onto the wax paper.

Strawberries: If washed, leave the stems on the strawberries and make sure they are completely dried before dipping. If water gets into your chocolate, it will stiffen and become unusable for this purpose. Use paper towels to pay dry and then air dry the strawberries for several hours before dipping. For best results, dip the berries the day you serve them.

Pruneaux à l'Armagnac
Prunes Marinated in Armagnac

Prunes soaked in Armagnac or Cognac are a delicacy to be shared with guests after dinner, with coffee. The longer the prunes sit in the alcohol, the better they get. If you find you enjoy these "stewed" prunes as much as I do, store them in an attractive jar that can be brought to the table.

Makes 1 pound

1 pound pitted prunes
Armagnac or Cognac

1. Place the prunes in an attractive jar and cover them with Armagnac or Cognac.
2. The prunes will absorb the Armagnac, so add more

as necessary to keep them covered. When the level of Armagnac remains constant, the prunes are ready to serve. This takes about one week.

3. Serve two or three prunes per person in a wine glass with a little of the Armagnac from the jar.

Variation

Pruneaux au Madère *(Prunes Marinated in Madeira):* For a slightly milder version with a different but equally interesting taste, marinate the prunes in Madeira.

Classic sauces provide much of the glory of French food. Although many beginning cooks are often intimidated by even the idea of sauce making, once they realize the relative ease with which a few basic sauces can be prepared, and the wonderful elegance they add to the simplest dishes, they'll soon find themselves making them often.

In this section are the stocks and sauces that are basic to French cooking, including the sweet sauces used in a number of different dessert recipes. Pastry Cream, Crème Anglaise, and icings are also located here since they are important components of many French desserts. The following recipes form a cornerstone of most of French cooking.

Basics

Stocks

Most books on the subject of French cooking stress the importance of making your own stocks to use in soups and sauces. Stocks themselves are not difficult to make, and I encourage you to make them to learn their delicate flavor. Then try reducing them to a richer, more intense glaze (*glace*) to better understand their full potential. Knowing the characteristics of homemade stocks and glazes will enable you to use commercial products successfully when homemade ones are not available (see "Using Canned Stocks," page 348).

Over the years I have found that only about 25 percent of my students regularly make their own stock. They tell me that they have difficulty finding the bones and the time necessary for making it. The time problem can be alleviated by shortening the cooking process, as I have done here, but because of the way meat and fish are currently being processed, unless you live in one of the major cities on

either coast, chicken bones may be the only bones you can easily find.

Meat glaze, or *glace de viande* – as well as *glace de volaille* (chicken), *glace de poisson* (fish), and *glace de gibier* (game) – is an essential part of fine sauce making. It is the essence of stock and the result of a long reduction. Its full flavor and body add character and color to sauces. By reducing stock until it has practically no water, glaze can be stored in your refrigerator or freezer until you are ready to use it. A hot glaze has the consistency of a thick syrup; when cold, it will be firm and gelatinous.

Unlike stocks, glazes are not readily available in the supermarket, and for this reason I have made their use in my recipes optional. Most of the recipes call for only 1 to 2 teaspoons of *glace de viande*. Without it, the sauce will be very good; with its addition, it will be even better.

Fonds Brun Economique
Economical Brown Beef Stock

A classic brown beef stock is made with meat and bones and is simmered for eight hours. Without the meat it becomes less expensive and hence more economical. The bones and vegetables are usually cooked whole or in large pieces, which helps to keep the stock clear, but they require a long cooking time to extract their flavor. In this recipe I cut the bones and vegetables into smaller pieces, thus reducing the cooking time by more than half.

Once the stock has come to its initial boil, it is important to adjust the heat to prevent rapid boiling during the lengthy cooking time. If the stock boils vigorously, it will become cloudy, and it may even appear as though milk has been added. The cloudy stock can be used, but when a clear one is needed, it will have to be clarified (see "Clarifying," page 351).

To make this recipe, you will need a 16- to 20-quart stockpot. If one is not available, the ingredients can easily be halved to fit the size pot you have. Be sure to leave the stock uncovered while it is cooling. Trapped warm air can sour a stock, making it unusable.

Makes 5 to 6 quarts

8 to 10 pounds beef or veal bones, cut into 2-inch pieces *****
4 tablespoons vegetable oil or butter
4 carrots, thickly sliced on the diagonal
4 onions, halved and sliced ¼ inch thick
8 quarts cold water
4 stalks celery
2 leeks, washed and diced (optional)
1 turnip, cut into 4 pieces, each piece stuck with 1 clove
4 garlic cloves
Double Bouquet Garni (page 346)
15 peppercorns

1. Preheat the oven to 500°.
2. Place the bones in a large roasting pan, and brown in the oven, 45 minutes to 1 hour.
3. Meanwhile, in a stockpot, heat the oil over high heat. Add the carrots and onions and cook, occasionally scraping the browned bits from the bottom of the pan, until well browned, 20 to 25 minutes.

BOUQUET GARNI

A bouquet garni consists of 4 to 5 sprigs parsley, 1 bay leaf, and 2 to 3 sprigs fresh thyme (or ¼ teaspoon dried) which I tie up in a celery stalk cut in half. The reason for tying the ingredients together is to enable you to discard them easily once the cooking is finished. If you plan to strain the stock or sauce in which the bouquet garni has been cooking, it is not necessary for you to tie up the ingredients, although it makes skimming easier.

1. Place the fresh or dried thyme in the hollow of the celery stalk half and cover with the bay leaf and parsley sprigs.

2. Cover with the remaining celery stalk half and tie together.

Double Bouquet Garni: If a recipe calls for a double bouquet garni, just double the ingredients and tie with the same celery stalk.

4. Add the browned bones to the stockpot and cover with the water. Add all the remaining ingredients and bring to a boil, 30 to 45 minutes.

5. Reduce the heat and *simmer*, uncovered, for 3½ hours. Skim the surface several times during the simmering to remove any foam that appears.

6. Strain and allow the stock to cool *uncovered* before refrigerating. Remove any fat from the surface when cold, or before using. Freeze the portion not used, or reduce to form meat glaze (Glace de Viande, page 352). Four quarts of stock will reduce to yield about 1½ cups of *glace de viande*.

✻ Beef bones have become increasingly hard to find in supermarkets, since meat is now cut and packaged at a central warehouse and shipped to local stores without bones. When bones are not available, use 2 pounds beef shank and 6 pounds of chicken backs or necks.

Variations

Fonds Brun Rapide *(Quick Beef Stock):* This version of beef stock cuts the preparation time by about 1 hour. Place all the ingredients, without browning, into a pot, cover with water, and bring to a boil. While the stock comes to a boil, blacken an onion as follows: Cut the onion in half and place both halves, cut side down, in a hot, dry (without butter or oil) skillet. The onion will blacken within 3 to 4 minutes. Adding the blackened onion to the stockpot will give the stock the brown color it would otherwise be missing.

Although their flavors are slightly different, either stock works well as a brown beef stock. One word of caution: The time saved by not browning the bones and vegetables may be equaled by the effort needed to clean your skillet after blackening the onion.

Fonds de Gibier *(Game Stock):* Follow the steps in the beef stock recipe to make a game stock, using 6 pounds of game meat and 7 pounds of bones. Add 10 juniper berries and 2 sage leaves.

USING CANNED STOCKS

A properly made stock has a delicate flavor that does not overtake the dishes it's in. Most people using a commercial stock follow the manufacturer's instructions and unfortunately end up using too strong a stock.

If, for example, you use a can of Campbell's beef broth diluted with one can of water, as the manufacturer instructs, you will taste this product in all your finished recipes. If, however, you use additional water (see below), you will have a liquid to use that will be equivalent in strength (although not taste) to your homemade beef stock. Other brands of commercial beef stocks, and some chicken stocks, may be less concentrated and require less additional water. The charts that follow list just some of the commercial stocks that were tested for this book. Instructions are given for diluting both canned beef and chicken stock to create a "normal-strength" stock, which you can use any time stock is called for, and a "double-strength" stock, which is used to make Consommé (pages 19–21). For the beef stock, there is also an extra-fortified dilution that is called for when making Jus Lié Rapide (page 365) (see Note).

When using a brand of commercial stock that is not in the chart, keep in mind that in most cases you're better off with an overdiluted canned stock than one that is too strong.

BEEF STOCK

BRAND (*Can size*)	**AMOUNT OF ADDED WATER (FOR REGULAR STRENGTH)**	**AMOUNT OF ADDED WATER (FOR DOUBLE STRENGTH)**
Campbell's Double Rich Bouillon (10½ ounces)	5 cans (to make about 8 cups stock)	2½ cans (to make about 4½ cups stock)
Campbell's Beef Consommé (10½ ounces)	4 cans (to make about 6½ cups stock)	2 cans (to make about 4 cups stock)
College Inn Beef Broth (13¾ ounces)	3½ cans (to make about 6½ cups stock)	1¾ cans (to make about 4¾ cups stock)

CHICKEN STOCK

BRAND *(Can size)*	AMOUNT OF ADDED WATER (FOR REGULAR STRENGTH)	AMOUNT OF ADDED WATER (FOR DOUBLE STRENGTH)
Swanson's Chicken Broth (14½ ounces)	2 cans (to make 5¼ cups)	1 can (to make about 3½ cups)
Campbell's Chicken Broth (10¾ ounces)	3 cans (to make 5½ cups)	1½ cans (to make about 3¼ cups)
College Inn Chicken Broth (13¼ ounces)	2 cans (to make 5 cups)	1 can (to make about 3¼ cups)

Note: To make Jus Lié Rapide (page 365), which uses canned stock to make a quick substitute for a classic brown sauce, you will need an extra-fortified stock. To dilute the above brands to the proper strength, use the following: Campbell's Double Rich Bouillon (dilute with 2 cans water); Campbell's Beef Consommé (dilute with 1½ cans water); College Inn Beef Broth (dilute with 1¼ cans water).

Fumet de Poisson
Fish Stock

A *fumet de poisson* is a fish stock, which can be made from the bones and heads of any fresh fish you buy. It is used in cooking fish and for making soups and sauces. The fish stock can also be reduced to a syrupy Glace de Poisson (page 353), which can be stored and used for sauces and soups when stock is not available.

Fresh fish may be difficult to find in many areas of the country, making heads and bones nonexistent. In such cases, search for a fish wholesaler in the area. Although most fish is being processed on the two coasts and flown minus heads and bones to many parts of the country, many wholesalers buy large whole fish, because they remain fresher in that condition. They fillet them locally before selling in smaller portions. You may be able to buy bones from these wholesale markets for your stock.

Makes about 3 cups

2 pounds fish bones and heads (avoid oily, strong-flavored
    fish such as mackerel and bluefish)
2 tablespoons butter
1 onion, sliced
¼ pound mushrooms, light parts only, sliced (optional*)
10 sprigs parsley
¾ cup dry white wine
3 cups water

1. Cut away all traces of the liver and the gills from the bones and fish heads. If you have time, soak the bones and fish heads in ice water for at least 20 minutes to extract any remaining blood.

2. In a large saucepan, heat the butter over medium heat. Add the onion, mushrooms, and parsley and gently sauté over medium heat until the onion is softened but not browned, about 3 minutes.

3. Add the fish heads and bones, cover, and cook for 15 minutes.

4. Add the wine, increase the heat to high, and reduce the liquid, uncovered, by half, about 3 minutes.

5. Add the water, bring to a boil, reduce the heat, and simmer, uncovered, for 15 minutes.

6. Strain the stock and allow it to cool *uncovered* before refrigerating.

* If using mushrooms, do not use the dark brown undersides of the cap (the gills); use only the light-colored portions of the cap and stems.

When buying heads and bones to make a fish stock, use a variety of fish. Make sure to remove all traces of liver and to cut away the gills. If time permits, soak the bones and heads in ice water to extract any remaining blood. This will help to produce a light and delicate stock.

Fonds de Volaille
Chicken Stock

CLARIFYING

When a stock needs to be absolutely clear, as when making a chicken consommé (see Consommé de Volaille, page 19) or aspic, it should be clarified. To clarify a stock, add 1 egg white per quart of stock and stir continually while the stock reheats. When the stock begins to boil, stop stirring, reduce the heat, and simmer gently for 20 minutes. As the egg white cooks, it will float to the top of the stock, carrying with it the particles that would otherwise cloud the stock; you can then remove it easily with a spoon or a skimmer.

Chicken stock is easier to make than beef stock because chicken parts are more readily available today than are beef bones. Although I occasionally use a whole chicken or parts to make the stock (and then use the cooked meat for chicken salad), I normally use backs and necks, which are more economical. Hearts and gizzards can also be used, but not the liver, which has too strong a flavor.

The cautions that apply to beef stock (Fonds Brun Economique, page 345) also apply here.

Makes about 3½ quarts

1 chicken (4 pounds) or 4 pounds chicken parts, rinsed
4 quarts cold water
1 leek (white part only), washed
2 onions, each studded with a clove
3 carrots
3 stalks celery, cut in half
Bouquet Garni (page 346)
6 peppercorns

1. Place the chicken in a large stockpot. Cover with the water and bring to a boil over high heat, 25 to 30 minutes. Skim the foam from the surface and reduce the heat.

2. Add the remaining ingredients and *simmer*, uncovered, for 2 hours, occasionally skimming any more foam.

3. Strain the stock and allow it to cool *uncovered* before refrigerating. Remove the fat from the surface when it is cold or before using. Freeze the portion not used, or reduce to form Glace de Volaille (page 353), which can be stored in the refrigerator or freezer. Two quarts of stock will reduce to yield approximately ¾ cup *glace de volaille.*

Glace de Viande
Meat Glaze

I encourage you to make stocks in order to use them to make meat glaze. *Glace de viande* (meat glaze) is homemade beef stock (Fonds Brun Economique, page 345) that has been reduced so that nearly all the water in it is removed. When hot, the glaze has a thick, syrupy consistency; when cold, it is firm yet springy. It can be cut into chunks that can be added to soups and sauces to increase their flavor, or used like a bouillon cube to reconstitute a stock. *Glace de viande* is a convenient way to store large quantities of stock.

Continue using the commercial stocks you use for your soups and sauces, but have *glace de viande* on hand to add to them to improve their flavor.

If you make chicken stock frequently and beef stock rarely, use your chicken stock to reduce to Glace de Volaille (see Variations), and use it whenever *glace de viande* is called for. Although you will be adding a different flavor, you will be contributing a richness and intensity to your sauce that otherwise would be missing.

After making a glaze, allow a small piece to melt in your mouth and notice the wonderful intense flavor it releases. You will find the glaze salty, even though no salt was added when making the stock. The salt you taste is the natural salt extracted from the bones and vegetables used in making the stock.

Makes 1 to 1½ cups

4 quarts Fonds Brun Economique (page 345)

1. After removing all the fat from the surface of the stock, boil it uncovered over medium-high heat until only 3 cups remain, about 1½ hours. Skim the stock as it reduces to remove all foam and impurities.

2. Strain the stock into a small heavy-bottomed saucepan and continue reducing over medium heat until the liquid thickens to coat a spoon, about 30 minutes. The liquid will at this point be dark and shiny and will bubble slowly.

3. Pour the hot glaze into a heatproof custard cup or bowl and refrigerate. When cold it will be firm and can be easily unmolded. Invert the cup or bowl, and with your thumb, push or pull the glaze from the edge of the cup toward the center. This will loosen the glaze and allow it to fall into your hand.

4. Wrap the glaze well in plastic wrap and refrigerate or freeze it. To use, simply cut off teaspoon-size chunks, and rewrap the unused portion. A glaze will keep this way for many months.

Variations

Glace de Volaille *(Chicken Glaze):* Make chicken stock (page 351) and reduce to about 1½ cups of glaze.

Glace de Poisson *(Fish Glaze):* Triple the recipe for fish stock (page 349) and reduce to about ¾ cup.

Glace de Gibier *(Game Glaze):* Make game stock (page 347) and reduce to about 1½ cups.

Sauces

French cooking's fame is in great part due to its many superb sauces. A plain piece of poached fish takes on elegance when served with a *sauce beurre blanc*; an ordinary steak becomes anything but ordinary with a *sauce béarnaise*, and a simple chicken is transformed into a delicate masterpiece when served with a *sauce suprême à l'estragon*.

The repertoire of classic sauces available to a trained chef is so vast that a mere listing of their names baffles a beginner. Learning a few basic sauces, however, will give you the ability and freedom to produce many others.

A sauce is a flavorful liquid that has been thickened. An unthickened liquid is called a *jus* (or juice). A sauce can be created separately from the main dish—as is *sauce hollandaise*—or it can be an integral part of the dish.

A sauce can be thickened by simple reduction (rapid boiling to evaporate excess liquid), or it can be thickened by the addition of a starch, egg yolks, or cream. There are even some sauces, rarely made today, that use animal blood as the thickening agent.

By far the majority of classic sauces are thickened by a starch. Most of these sauces are rarely found in restaurants today because of the *nouvelle cuisine* movement of the early '70s, when a small group of prominent chefs decided to eliminate starch as a thickening agent on the premise of producing purer and simpler sauces.

Although few restaurant goers have minded the move away from classic starch-based sauces, there are good reasons why the home cook should not forget them. What the *nouvelle* legacy has given us are sauces that are thickened or enhanced with butter or cream, and which often rely on meat glazes like *glace de viande*. Not only are these sauces higher in calories, but reproducing them at home, with the required reductions and meat glazes, is time-consuming. The flour- or *roux*-based classic sauces can be successfully made with commercial stocks, making them more convenient and, generally speaking, lower in calories.

Although you can use commercial stocks successfully, it is my hope that while learning the sauces in this book you will progress to homemade ones.

A brief description of the classic basic sauces follows.

Basic Sauces

Sauces fall into two general categories, hot and cold; within the hot sauce category, there are white sauces and brown sauces. Sauces are further divided by the way they are thickened. For a better understanding of the following definitions, it is helpful to know what a *roux* is. A *roux* is flour cooked in butter, and is the base for most classic sauces. A white *roux* is flour cooked in butter until the flour is pale yellow and frothy. A brown *roux* is cooked until the flour turns a reddish brown.

HOT WHITE SAUCES

Velouté: White stock (veal, chicken, or fish) thickened with a white *roux*. Recipe on page 360.

Allemande/Parisienne: A *velouté* enriched by egg yolks. See Filet de Sole Granville (page 110).

Suprême: A *velouté* enriched by heavy cream. See Poule au Pot Sauce Suprême (page 129).

Béchamel: A sauce made with a white *roux* and milk. Recipe on page 357.

Crème: A sauce made with a reduction of a dish's cooking liquids and heavy cream. See Steak au Poivre (page 159) or Poulet au Riesling (page 135).

Hollandaise: Hollandaise (page 373) is the classic butter sauce made from an emulsion of egg yolks and butter. Other sauces in the same family include Sauce Béarnaise (page 374), Sauce Choron (page 376), and Sauce Paloise (page 375).

Beurre Blanc: The contemporary *nouvelle* butter sauce made without egg yolks. Recipe on page 376.

HOT BROWN SAUCES

Demi-Glace: The basic brown sauce made with a brown *roux*, a brown stock, a browned *mirepoix* (diced vegetables), and tomatoes.

Jus Lié: A brown stock lightly thickened with arrowroot, potato starch, or cornstarch. Recipe on page 364.

Tomate: A tomato sauce. Recipe on page 372.

COLD SAUCES

Mayonnaise: Mayonnaise (page 378) is an emulsion of egg yolks and oil. Other sauces in the mayonnaise family include Aïoli (page 379) and Sauce Verte (page 381).

Vinaigrette: A sauce with a base of vinegar and oil. Recipe on page 383.

Sauce Béchamel
White Cream Sauce

When preparing the sauce in advance, cover the surface with plastic wrap to prevent a skin from forming. As with most flour-based sauces, béchamel keeps well for several days in the refrigerator, and can be frozen for longer periods.

A béchamel sauce is the classic white "cream" sauce, made from milk and a white *roux*. Although it has been replaced in most restaurants today by a sauce made completely of heavy cream, it still has a number of important uses. A béchamel is used whenever you want a creamy sauce without using cream. It may be mixed with puréed vegetables for richness without many added calories. Add cheese and transform it into a Sauce Mornay (page 358) for a gratin or to coat vegetables or crêpes. When made correctly, it is smooth and creamy; poorly made, it will be thick and pasty.

Simple variations of the sauce can be made by adding tomato paste, mustard, or curry powder to taste.

Makes 2 cups to serve 8

2½ tablespoons butter
3 tablespoons all-purpose flour
2 cups milk
¼ teaspoon salt
⅛ teaspoon freshly ground pepper

1. In a medium saucepan, heat the butter over medium-high heat. Add the flour and cook, stirring frequently, until the *roux* is pale yellow and frothy, 30 to 45 seconds. Add the milk and stir well with a whisk until the sauce thickens and comes to a boil, 2 to 3 minutes.

2. Reduce the heat to maintain a gentle simmer and season with the salt and pepper. Whisk vigorously for about 10 seconds. Simmer gently, whisking the sauce well from time to time, until the sauce is a little thicker than heavy cream, 2 to 3 minutes. Skim off any butter that rises to the surface. *(The sauce can be made ahead and refrigerated for several days or frozen for later use. Cover the surface with plastic wrap. Before using, bring to a boil and check the consistency and seasoning. If the sauce is too thick, add a little milk or water to thin it.)*

Sauce Mornay
Cheese Sauce

A *sauce Mornay* is a cheese-flavored béchamel sauce that can be used with poached eggs, crêpes, vegetables, and meat. The cheese used for the sauce in France is usually Gruyère, or a combination of Gruyère and Parmesan. Any Swiss-style cheese can be used;

if you use other than a Swiss-style cheese, such as Camembert, the sauce takes on the name of the cheese. Classically, a Mornay is made with an addition of 3 to 4 tablespoons of butter just before serving. I find this added richness unnecessary, and have eliminated it with today's eating habits in mind. When browning the sauce as in a *gratin*, I always sprinkle additional cheese on top.

Makes 2 cups to serve 8

2½ tablespoons butter
3 tablespoons all-purpose flour
2 cups milk
⅛ teaspoon salt
⅛ teaspoon freshly ground pepper
Pinch freshly grated nutmeg
2 ounces Swiss-style cheese, such as Gruyère or
    Emmenthaler, grated (about ⅔ cup) or 1 ounce each
    Gruyère and Parmesan, grated

1. In a medium saucepan, heat the butter over medium-high heat. Add the flour and cook, stirring frequently, until the *roux* is pale yellow and frothy, 30 to 45 seconds. Add the milk and stir well with a whisk until the sauce thickens and comes to a boil, 2 to 3 minutes. (This is a béchamel sauce.)

2. Reduce the heat to maintain a gentle simmer and season with the salt, pepper, and nutmeg. Whisk vigorously for about 10 seconds. Simmer gently, whisking the sauce well from time to time, until the sauce is the consistency of heavy cream, 2 to 3 minutes. Skim off any butter that may rise to the surface.

3. Stir in the cheese and bring to a boil while whisking. At this point the sauce should be slightly thicker than heavy cream and ready to use. *(The sauce can be made in advance and refrigerated for several days or frozen for later use. Cover the surface with plastic wrap. To reheat, bring to a boil and check the consistency and seasoning before using. If the sauce is too thick, add a little milk or water to thin it.)*

Sauce Velouté
White Sauce with Stock

A *sauce velouté* is a velvety smooth sauce that is made with a white *roux* and a white stock (veal, chicken, fish, or vegetable). It is one of the finest sauces to come from the classic French kitchen. In this sauce, perhaps more than any other, the quality of the stock is very important. Although *veloutés* can be made with canned stock, those made with fresh stock are far preferable, and for this reason I have used *veloutés* in this book only at times when a stock is made as a part of the recipe; for example, Blanquette de Veau aux Morilles (page 189).

Classically, *veloutés* are slowly simmered for an hour or more, with additional stock added as needed to achieve a beautifully smooth consistency. During this time the sauce is skimmed frequently to remove the butter and impurities that rise to the surface. While the sauce cooks, the flavor develops and intensifies.

Normally I shorten the process, and simply reduce some of the stock rapidly to make a glaze, and add it to the sauce. With careful skimming, and vigorous whisking, a beautifully smooth and flavorful sauce can be made quite rapidly. Just keep in mind that the more you whisk, the smoother and more shiny your sauce becomes.

Makes 2 cups to serve 8

2½ tablespoons butter
3 tablespoons all-purpose flour
3 cups veal, chicken (page 351), fish (page 349), or
*   vegetable stock*

VARIABLE *VELOUTÉS*

When making a *velouté*, look around your kitchen to find any liquids that you might want to use in conjunction with stock when preparing your sauce. For example, besides the fish stock used in a recipe such as Filet de Sole Granville (page 110), you may have liquid created while steaming oysters and mussels. You may also have flavorful liquid from poaching fresh mushrooms, or from soaking dried ones. There may be some tomato liquid collected while seeding tomatoes. Taste these liquids to determine which will complement your final dish. If they are strong or salty, just add a little. If they are mild, reduce to strengthen, and taste again before adding them to your sauce. Spices like saffron and curry, and herbs like tarragon and chives can be added for color and flavor shortly before serving. Use all these potential flavorings as an artist uses the many colors of his palette.

¼ teaspoon salt
⅛ teaspoon freshly ground pepper

1. In a small saucepan, reduce 1 cup of the stock until reduced to 1 tablespoon of glaze. Remove from the heat and reserve.

2. In a medium saucepan, heat the butter over medium-high heat. Add the flour and cook, stirring frequently, until the *roux* is pale yellow and frothy, 30 to 45 seconds. Add the remaining 2 cups of stock, and stir well with a whisk until the sauce thickens and comes to a boil, 2 to 3 minutes.

3. Reduce the heat to maintain a gentle simmer and season with the salt and pepper. Add the reserved glaze and whisk vigorously for about 10 seconds. Simmer gently, whisking the sauce from time to time, until the sauce is the consistency of heavy cream, 2 to 3 minutes. Skim off any butter that rises to the surface. *(The sauce can be made in advance and refrigerated for several days or frozen for later use. Cover the surface with plastic wrap. To reheat, bring to a boil and check its consistency and seasoning before using. If the sauce is too thick, add a little additional stock or water to thin it.)*

Sauce Aurore
Tomato-Flavored Velouté Sauce

A *sauce aurore* is a tomato-flavored *velouté*. It can be made with either chicken or fish stock, depending on what you intend to serve. A classic *sauce aurore* calls for tomato purée, where this recipe uses a more concentrated tomato paste. This reduces the cooking time necessary to achieve the desired consistency of the sauce. I use it mainly with poached fish and *mousseline de poisson*, but it is also an excellent accompaniment to crab, lobster, or poached chicken.

Makes 2 cups to serve 8

3 tablespoons butter
¼ cup all-purpose flour
3 cups fish stock (page 349) or chicken stock (page 351)
¼ teaspoon salt
⅛ teaspoon freshly ground pepper
1 tablespoon tomato paste
4 tablespoons butter or ⅓ cup heavy cream

1. In a small saucepan, heat the 3 tablespoons butter over medium-high heat. Add the flour and cook, stirring frequently, until the *roux* is pale yellow and frothy, 30 to 45 seconds. Add the stock and stir well with a whisk until it thickens and comes to a boil, 2 to 3 minutes.

2. Reduce the heat to maintain a gentle simmer and simmer gently, whisking the sauce well from time to time, until the sauce is the consistency of heavy cream, 10 to 15 minutes. Skim off any butter that rises to the surface.

3. Season with the salt and pepper. Add the tomato paste and whisk until smooth. Simmer for 5 minutes longer. The sauce will have thickened slightly and should be smooth and creamy. *(The sauce can be made ahead to this point. Cover the surface, let cool, and refrigerate for several days or freeze for later use.)*

4. Just before serving, bring the sauce to a boil and whisk in the 4 tablespoons butter or ⅓ cup cream. If butter is used, do not boil the sauce once it has been added.

SKIMMING SAUCES

Skimming is used to remove foam, fat, and impurities from the surface of liquids. It is one of the most important and often overlooked steps in preparing fine sauces, soups, and jams. In most cases, it should be done during the cooking process. The importance of skimming can easily be understood by merely tasting the foam or fat removed. You can also notice the difference it makes while cooking jam. If not skimmed, the foam will cause a jam to be cloudy and dull instead of clear and shiny. If you make skimming a regular habit, you will find it improves the general quality of your cooking.

Sauce au Safran à la Tomate Fraîche
Saffron Sauce with Fresh Tomatoes

I f you like the flavor of saffron, you will probably find this transformation of a classic *sauce velouté* to be one of your favorites to serve with poached fish or fish mousse (Mousseline de Poisson, page 56). I use two large pinches of saffron for this sauce, but you may want to start with only one and see if you like the flavor. I have made this sauce a little thicker than a normal *velouté*, but it will thin to a perfect consistency, a little lighter than heavy cream, after the tomatoes have been added.

Makes 2 to 2½ cups to serve 8 to 10

5 to 6 tablespoons butter
¼ cup all-purpose flour
3 cups fish stock (page 349)
2 large pinches saffron threads (see Note)
¼ teaspoon salt
Pinch freshly ground pepper
2 tomatoes, peeled, seeded, chopped, and drained
2 to 3 tablespoons chopped fresh chives, basil, tarragon,
*   or parsley, to taste*

1. In a small saucepan, heat 3 tablespoons of the butter over medium-high heat. Add the flour and cook, stirring frequently, until the *roux* is pale yellow and frothy, 30 to 45 seconds. Add the stock and stir well with a whisk until it thickens and comes to a boil, 2 to 3 minutes.

2. Reduce the heat to maintain a gentle simmer and season with the saffron, salt, and pepper. Whisk vigorously for about 10 seconds. Simmer gently, whisking the sauce well from time to time, until the sauce is slightly thicker than heavy cream, 30 to 45 minutes. Skim off any butter that rises to the surface. *(The sauce can be made to this point up to one day ahead. Cover the surface with plastic wrap, let cool, and refrigerate for several days or freeze for later use.)*

3. Just before serving, bring the sauce to a boil. Off the heat, whisk in the remaining 2 to 3 tablespoons of butter, to taste. Gently stir in the tomatoes and all but 1 teaspoon of the herbs. Heat for several seconds, but do not boil.

4. **To serve:** Spoon the sauce over the fish or fish mousse and sprinkle with the remaining herbs.

Note: The saffron slowly dissolves into the sauce, and when the threads are translucent it is completely dissolved. If you wish to add more saffron near the end of the cooking time, crush the threads to speed the dissolving.

Jus Lié
Thickened Brown Stock

Whenever I need a basic brown sauce (called a *demi-glace*), but do not have the time to make one, I use a thickened beef stock called a *jus lié*. Since my beef stock is very mild, I reduce the stock by half and add some *glace de viande* to heighten its flavor. To thicken the stock, I use arrowroot, potato starch, or cornstarch (in order of preference) dissolved in a little cold water.

The tomato traditionally found in a classic *demi-glace* is omitted from this thickened stock, giving the sauce a greater clarity, which is characteristic of contemporary brown sauces.

If you don't have time to make homemade stock, you might want to try the Jus Lié Rapide made with canned stock, which follows on the next page.

Makes 2 cups to serve 12

1 quart beef stock (page 345)
3 tablespoons Glace de Viande (page 352)
2 tablespoons arrowroot, potato starch, or cornstarch
  dissolved in 2 tablespoons cold water
¼ teaspoon salt
⅛ teaspoon freshly ground pepper

1. In a medium saucepan, bring the stock and *glace de viande* to a boil over medium-high to high heat. Boil gently, uncovered, until the stock reduces by half, 15 to 20 minutes, skimming off any fat and impurities as they rise to the surface.

2. Whisk the dissolved arrowroot into the gently boiling stock. Whisk vigorously until the sauce thickens and lightly coats a spoon, 15 to 20 seconds, and remove from

SAUCE *DEMI-GLACE*

Demi-glace, the basic brown sauce that was once the mainstay in the classic French kitchen, has all but vanished from today's top French restaurants. The classic *demi-glace*, or *espagnole* as it was known, took at least two days to make.

The principles used in making *demi-glace* are still used in such dishes as Canard à l'Orange (page 149). But in most instances where a brown sauce is called for, I use Jus Lié (page 364), which makes a thinner and clearer brown sauce that I find more refined (and certainly less time-consuming) than the classic sauces made with *demi-glace*.

the heat. Season with the salt and pepper. *(This thickened stock can be made in advance. Cover the surface with plastic wrap, let cool, and refrigerate for several days or freeze for later use.)*

Variations

Sauce Madère *(Thickened Brown Stock with Madeira):* For a very simple sauce made with *jus lié*, bring 1 cup of *jus lié* to a boil, add ¼ cup Madeira, and serve.

Sauce Porto *(Thickened Brown Stock with Port):* For a quick port sauce, bring 1 cup of *jus lié* to a boil, add ¼ cup port, and serve.

Jus Lié Rapide
Quick Brown Sauce

For an almost instant brown sauce, when you don't have time to make beef stock, use this *jus lié* made with canned stock. It is important to use the dilution of the stock indicated in the chart on page 348. In this recipe, the *glace de viande* is optional; in the preceding one, it is not.

Makes about 2 cups to serve 12

2 cups canned beef stock, jus lié strength (see chart, page 348)
3 tablespoons Glace de Viande (optional; page 352)
¼ teaspoon salt
⅛ teaspoon freshly ground pepper
2½ tablespoons arrowroot, potato starch, or cornstarch dissolved in 2½ tablespoons cold water

1. In a medium saucepan, bring the stock and *glace*

de viande, if using, to a boil over medium-high to high heat. Reduce the heat to medium.

2. Whisk the dissolved arrowroot into the gently boiling stock. Whisk vigorously until the sauce thickens and lightly coats a spoon, 15 to 20 seconds, and remove from the heat. Season with the salt and pepper. *(This thickened stock can be made in advance. Cover the surface with plastic wrap, let cool, and refrigerate for several days or freeze for later use.)*

Sauce Bordelaise
Red Wine Sauce

This rich red wine sauce is a perfect match for beef. It is traditionally served with slices of beef marrow that have been poached in water and a little vinegar. In a classic kitchen, if the sauce were intended to go with a roast, the marrow would be added to the sauce along with fresh parsley just before serving. However, since marrow can be difficult to find, I have omitted it as well as the parsley, but have kept a small amount of butter to round out this full-bodied sauce.

Makes about 1¼ cups to serve 6

2 shallots, finely chopped
1 pinch thyme
¼ bay leaf
1 tablespoon Glace de Viande (optional; page 352)
⅛ teaspoon freshly ground pepper
¾ cup red Bordeaux wine or any dry red wine
1½ cups Jus Lié (page 364)
2 teaspoons Cognac
1 tablespoon butter

REDUCING LIQUIDS

In making sauces a recipe will often instruct you to "reduce by half" or "reduce until only 1 cup remains." The reasons for reducing are to intensify flavors and to thicken or reduce the quantity of a liquid. Most reductions are done uncovered rapidly over high heat. To increase the speed of reduction, transfer the liquid to a larger pan. The greater the surface area, the faster the evaporation. Conversely, when reducing a sauce or soup slowly, you should use as small a pan as possible. The smaller the surface area, and the greater the depth, the slower a liquid will evaporate.

1. In a small saucepan, combine the shallots, thyme, bay leaf, *glace de viande*, pepper, and wine. Over high heat, reduce the liquid by two-thirds, about 5 minutes.

2. Add the *jus lié* and simmer until the liquid lightly coats a spoon, 5 to 7 minutes. Whisk gently occasionally and skim if necessary. Strain the sauce through a double-mesh sieve. *(The sauce can be made in advance up to this point. Cover the surface with plastic wrap, let cool, and refrigerate for up to a week or freeze for later use.)*

3. Just before serving, bring the sauce to a boil over medium-high heat and add the Cognac. Remove the sauce from the heat and whisk in the butter.

Sauce Robert
Mustard-Flavored Brown Sauce

This mustard-flavored brown sauce is ideal to serve with sautéed or roasted pork, and can be used with sautéed rabbit and chicken as well. The amount of mustard you use will depend on your personal taste, but I always use less when serving the sauce with chicken.

A pinch or two of sugar is often added to cut the bite of the vinegar. Although I have never found this necessary, you might.

Makes 1 cup to serve 6

1 small onion, finely chopped
¾ cup dry white wine
¼ cup white (distilled) or white wine vinegar
1 cup Jus Lié (page 364)
1 teaspoon Glace de Viande (optional; page 352)
1 to 2 tablespoons Dijon mustard, to taste
¼ teaspoon sugar (optional)
4 to 5 sprigs parsley, chopped*

1. In a small saucepan, combine the onion, wine, and vinegar. Bring to a boil and cook over high heat until the liquid is reduced by two-thirds, about 5 minutes.

2. Add the *jus lié* and *glace de viande*. Reduce the heat to low and simmer, uncovered, until the sauce thickens enough to lightly coat a spoon, 2 to 3 minutes. If necessary, skim during the simmering.

3. Strain the sauce, and stir in the mustard. Taste and adjust the seasoning, adding the sugar, if necessary. (The sauce can be kept warm in a water bath [*bain-marie*].) Stir in the parsley just before serving.

* When preparing the sauce to be used with Médaillons de Porc Sauce Robert (page 177), omit the parsley.

Marinade Pour Gibier
Wild Game Marinade

This marinade is classically made with white wine, but I prefer making it with red wine, because I find it less acidic and the resulting sauces have a richer color and smoother flavor. Either version can be used to flavor the meat of such game as venison, elk, antelope, hare, and wild boar. I use a marinade whenever I have meat cut from animals that have not been aged.

Since most people do not prepare game at home, I have adapted it for use with a leg of lamb (see Gigot en Chevreuil, page 176). While the lamb is roasting, I use the marinade to prepare one of three sauces, also traditionally served with game.

Depending on the amount of meat to be marinated, you can easily increase the quantities shown below.

Makes about 4 cups / enough for about 5 pounds of meat

If you are fortunate enough to have game, marinate it for several days and then either braise it, using a little of the marinade together with some game stock as the braising liquid, or make a stew or ragoût using the same combination of liquids.

If you are making any of the game sauces below, reserve the marinade and the vegetables.

1 small onion, halved and sliced
1 carrot, sliced
2 shallots, sliced
1 stalk celery, sliced
2 garlic cloves, smashed
3 sprigs parsley
¼ teaspoon thyme
¼ teaspoon rosemary
1 bay leaf, crumbled
8 fresh or dried juniper berries, crushed
5 peppercorns, crushed, or ¼ teaspoon freshly ground pepper
1 whole clove or whole allspice berry
1 bottle dry red wine
½ cup white (distilled) vinegar
½ cup vegetable oil

1. Mix all the ingredients together in a large bowl or deep roasting pan and place the meat you are using in it. The meat should be at least half covered by the marinade. Cover with plastic wrap and marinate in the refrigerator for two to four days. Turn the meat in the marinade twice a day.

2. When you are ready to cook the meat, drain the marinade, and dry the meat before browning.

Sauces Poivrade, Chevreuil, et Grand Veneur
Game Sauce with Pepper, Game Sauce with Cream, and Game Sauce with Currant Jelly and Cream

These three classic game sauces are traditionally served with venison, elk, antelope, hare, and wild boar. The aromatic *sauce poivrade* goes well with all these meats, while the *chevreuil* and *grand veneur*, a little milder and sweeter than the *poivrade*, are especially good with venison.

The base for these sauces uses the game marinade above, which for the purposes of this book I've used to marinate a leg of lamb (see Gigot en Chevreuil, page 176). Although game is becoming more and more available (much of it being raised on ranches and shipped precut and packaged to specialty markets), you can experiment with game marinades and game sauces by serving them with the leg of lamb before venturing on to venison.

What makes these three sauces different from one another is how they are finished, and the differences are only slight: One has a small amount of butter added, one has some cream added, and the third a bit of cream and currant jelly. It is extremely easy to prepare all three at once, and I suggest that the first time you make the recipe you do this to decide which is your favorite.

Makes about 3 cups to serve 18

Game Sauce Base
Marinade Pour Gibier (page 368)
2 tablespoons butter or vegetable oil
½ pound ground game or lamb (optional; see Note)
¼ cup Madeira
3 cups Jus Lié (page 364)
1 tablespoon tomato paste
30 peppercorns, crushed, or ½ teaspoon freshly
*   ground pepper*

Finishing Touches
Sauce Poivrade: 2 tablespoons softened butter per cup of
*   sauce base*
Sauce Chevreuil: ¼ cup heavy cream per cup of sauce base
Sauce Grand Veneur: 1½ teaspoons currant jelly and
*   ¼ cup heavy cream per cup of sauce base*

ADDING BUTTER TO A SAUCE

Butter is often added to sauces just before serving. The purpose is to make strong sauces milder, light sauces richer, or sharp sauces smoother. The sauce should never boil after the butter has been added, although it may be boiling at the moment you add it. Boiling will cause the butter to come out of suspension and float to the surface. I have often been asked, "Why skim butter from the surface of a sauce during cooking if you plan to beat butter in at the end?" Butter used in cooking tastes like oil and detracts from the sauce's flavor, whereas butter added at the end contributes a fresh buttery flavor. Butter that has been at room temperature beats into a sauce more easily than does butter taken directly from the refrigerator. For this reason, take the butter from the refrigerator when beginning your recipes.

Note: If you are making these sauces to go with the Gigot en Chevreuil (page 176), the ground meat can be made from the excess meat trimmed from the H-bone (see "French-Style Leg of Lamb," page 175).

1. If you have not already done so, strain the marinade and set the marinade and vegetables aside.

2. In a heavy-bottomed 4- to 4½-quart saucepan, heat the butter over medium-high to high heat. Add the reserved vegetables and the ground meat. Cook, stirring only occasionally, until the meat and vegetables begin to brown, about 10 minutes.

3. Add 2 cups of the marinade and the Madeira. Cook over high heat and reduce until no liquid remains, 15 to 20 minutes. Pour off any excess fat.

4. Add the *jus lié*, another ½ cup of marinade, and the tomato paste. Stir well and bring to a boil. Reduce the heat and simmer gently for 15 minutes, skimming off butter and impurities as they rise to the surface. Add the crushed peppercorns and continue simmering until the sauce thickens to lightly coat a spoon, 10 to 15 minutes longer.

5. Strain the sauce through a fine-mesh sieve, taste, and adjust the seasoning, if necessary. *(The sauce can be made ahead to this point and refrigerated for several days or frozen for later use.)*

6. **To make the Sauce Poivrade:** Just before serving, bring 1 cup of the sauce base to a boil. Remove from the heat and beat in the butter, 1 tablespoon at a time. Do not allow the sauce to boil again once the butter has been added. Keep hot in a water bath *(bain-marie)*. *(The sauce can be made ahead and refrigerated for several days or frozen. Reheat in a water bath* [bain-marie].*)*

To make the Sauce Chevreuil: Just before serving, bring 1 cup of the sauce base to a boil. Add the cream and simmer 10 to 15 minutes. Skim the sauce and adjust the seasoning, if necessary. *(The sauce can be made ahead and refrigerated for several days or frozen. To reheat, bring to a boil.)*

To make the Sauce Grand Veneur: Just before serving, bring 1 cup of the sauce base to a boil. Add the currant jelly and cream and simmer 10 to 15 minutes. Skim the sauce and adjust the seasoning, if necessary. *(The sauce can be made ahead and refrigerated for several days or frozen for later use. To reheat, simply bring to a boil.)*

Sauce Tomate
Tomato Sauce

This simple, chunky tomato sauce can be used with pasta, veal, chicken, or fish. When your tomatoes are not as ripe or as red as you may wish them to be, add 2 teaspoons of tomato paste or ½ cup tomato purée to improve both the color and flavor of the sauce (or use canned tomatoes). A variation can be made by using a blender or processor to purée the cooked sauce to make it smooth.

Makes 2 cups to serve 6

3 tablespoons olive oil, extra-virgin if available
1 onion, chopped
3 garlic cloves, chopped
3 pounds tomatoes, peeled, seeded, chopped, and drained
    of excess liquid or 6 pounds canned tomatoes, chopped
    and drained
¼ teaspoon salt
⅛ teaspoon freshly ground pepper
10 to 12 fresh basil leaves, chopped, or 1 teaspoon
    dried basil

1. In a saucepan, heat the oil over medium-low heat. Add the onion and sauté until softened but not browned, about 2 minutes.

2. Add the garlic and the tomatoes, increase the heat to high, and cook the sauce until most of the moisture has evaporated, leaving a medium-thick sauce, 4 to 5 minutes. Season with the salt and pepper. *(The recipe can be prepared ahead to this point one to two days in advance. Cover and refrigerate. Bring back to a boil before proceeding.)*

3. Remove the sauce from the heat and stir in the basil. Use at once.

Most classic recipes for this sauce call for the butter to be clarified. To clarify butter, it must be heated sufficiently to separate the milk solids from the fat, yielding clear butter. When this is done, the sweet, fresh taste of butter is destroyed. For this reason, I am careful to just melt the butter, and often remove my pan from the heat before the butter is completely melted.

REPAIRING A CURDLED HOLLANDAISE

Should your sauce curdle, try one of the following:
• Place a fresh egg yolk in a clean bowl and slowly whisk in the curdled sauce a little at a time, making sure the sauce is smooth before adding more curdled sauce.
• Put 1 to 2 teaspoons of cold water in a clean bowl and slowly whisk in the curdled sauce a little at a time, making sure the sauce is smooth before adding more curdled sauce.

In both cases, the sauce should return to its emulsified state provided the egg yolk has not set. If that is the case, strain the sauce and serve the flavored butter.

Sauce Hollandaise
Butter and Egg Yolk Sauce

The classic *sauce hollandaise*, an emulsion of egg yolks and butter flavored with lemon, is a perfect match for fish. The sauce is also used with poached eggs, and with vegetables. For eggs I omit the lemon juice completely, and I use only a touch of lemon when serving with vegetables. I often vary the sauce by adding chopped fresh chives when available.

The sauce is most often made in a double boiler. This technique is tedious and the resulting sauce is quite heavy. When made with the following technique, the sauce is much lighter and quickly made. It will help if you have a small heavy saucepan that conducts heat well, preferably one with a core of either aluminum or copper. Also important is a good 8-inch wire whisk with several layers of wire of varying lengths.

Once made, the sauce can be kept warm in a water bath (*bain-marie*) for 15 to 20 minutes while you put the finishing touches on the meal. The water in the water bath should never be hotter than warm to the touch. If the water gets too hot, the sauce will curdle.

Makes 1¼ cups to serve 8 to 10

2 egg yolks
2 tablespoons water
1½ sticks (6 ounces) butter, melted
¼ teaspoon salt
Lemon juice to taste
1 to 2 tablespoons chopped fresh chives, to taste (optional)

1. In a small saucepan, whisk the egg yolks and water together over medium heat until thick and fluffy, 2 to 3

minutes. As soon as the sauce thickens enough so you can see the bottom of the pan while whisking, remove it from the heat. (Too much heat at this point can cause the yolks to set and look like scrambled eggs. If this happens, start again.) Continue whisking the mixture off the heat for several seconds. The sauce should be thick enough to cling to your whisk.

2. Allow the pan to cool for a minute before slowly adding the melted butter, which should be no hotter than the egg yolks. Whisk continually while adding the butter, a little at a time, as you would for a mayonnaise. Add the salt and lightly flavor with lemon juice. Stir in the chopped chives, if using, and keep <u>warm</u> in a water bath (*bain-marie*) for 15 to 20 minutes.

Sauce Béarnaise
Tarragon-and Shallot-Flavored Hollandaise Sauce

A *sauce béarnaise* is essentially a hollandaise sauce with a reduction of tarragon, chervil, shallots, pepper, wine, and vinegar. Its unique blend of flavors makes it one of France's most popular sauces. Although usually served with grilled steak, it is also ideal with other grilled meats, fish, and poultry.

Classically, the shallots are first sautéed to soften and only vinegar is used in the reduction. I do not sauté the shallots, creating a slightly stronger flavor, which I find most people enjoy. Adding white wine to the vinegar reduction rounds out the flavor.

Leftover *béarnaise* is excellent on sandwiches made with leftover roasts, and I often serve the sauce at room temperature with cold, sliced fillet of beef.

BAIN-MARIE

It is often necessary to keep things warm at temperatures well below the boiling point, and a *bain-marie* (water bath) is ideal for this purpose. The temperature of the pan is kept below boiling by placing it in another pan containing water (this second pan is the *bain-marie*). Even if the water in the *bain-marie* boils, the contents of the pan will not. (A double boiler is in effect a *bain-marie*.)

When making a *bain-marie*, use a pan considerably larger than the one you want to heat or keep warm. For example, I would choose an 8-inch square cake pan as the *bain-marie* for a 1-quart saucepan, or a 10-inch skillet for a 3-quart saucepan. By using large pans, you can easily monitor the temperature of the water in the *bain-marie*.

Makes 1⅓ cups to serve 8 to 12

2 shallots, finely chopped
2 teaspoons tarragon, chopped or crushed
1 teaspoon chervil, chopped or crushed
⅛ teaspoon freshly ground pepper
2 tablespoons tarragon vinegar
2 tablespoons dry white wine
2 tablespoons water
2 egg yolks
1½ sticks (6 ounces) butter, melted
¼ teaspoon salt

1. Place the shallots, tarragon, chervil, pepper, vinegar, and wine in a small saucepan. Over high heat, reduce the liquid until only 1 teaspoon of liquid remains, about 2 minutes. Remove from the heat. *(This can be done several hours in advance.)*

2. Over medium heat, add the water and egg yolks and whisk constantly until thick and fluffy, 2 to 3 minutes. As soon as the sauce thickens enough so you can see the bottom of the pan while whisking, remove it from the heat. (Too much heat at this point can cause the yolks to set and look like scrambled eggs. If this happens, start again.) Continue whisking the mixture off the heat for several seconds. The sauce should be thick enough to cling to your whisk.

3. Allow the pan to cool for a minute before slowly adding the melted butter, which should be no hotter than the egg yolks. Whisk continually while adding the butter, a little at a time, as you would for a mayonnaise. Add the salt. The sauce should taste of tarragon and have a slight bite from the vinegar and a hint of salt. If necessary, add 1 to 3 drops of vinegar, additional tarragon, and a sprinkle of salt. Keep <u>warm</u> in a water bath (*bain-marie*) for up to 15 to 20 minutes.

Variations

Sauce Paloise *(Béarnaise-Style Mint Sauce):* Substitute an equal amount of mint for the tarragon.

Sauce Choron *(Béarnaise Sauce with Tomatoes):* This delight-
ful variation of *béarnaise* is wonderful with roast or grilled
lamb as well as with grilled fish. Use it in the summer when
you are sure to get a full-flavored, ripe tomato. Peel, seed,
and finely chop 1 tomato before placing it in a fine strainer
to drain well. If the pulp is not well drained, it will thin the
béarnaise too much. The sauce should remain thick enough
to lightly coat the meat or fish. Mix in ¼ cup chopped fresh
tomato pulp, well-drained, or 2 heaping teaspoons tomato
paste just before serving.

Sauce Foyot/Valois *(Béarnaise Sauce with Meat Glaze):* A *sauce
béarnaise* with the addition of *glace de viande* is known by
either the name Foyot or Valois and is served primarily with
beef. I have made similar sauces using *glace de volaille* and
glace de poisson to serve with grilled chicken and grilled
fish, but I have never seen names for these sauces. This
sauce can also be made with the reduced deglazed liquid
from a roasting pan. Just before serving add 1 tablespoon
Glace de Viande (page 352) and salt to taste.

Sauce Beurre Blanc
White Butter Sauce

*B*eurre blanc nantais, now known as *beurre blanc*, is
a velvety white butter sauce, traditionally made
from a reduction of vinegar and shallots to which butter is added. It was created in the area of the Loire
Valley between the towns of Angers and Nantes to
serve with the pike, shad, and salmon that populate
the Loire River.

The recipe below, which is based on the original
and uses only vinegar, will surprise those familiar with
a contemporary *beurre blanc* that uses wine or a com-

In the early '70s, Paul
Bocuse and other chefs
abandoned hollandaise
sauce, the butter sauce of
the classic French kitchen,
and started using *beurre
blanc* exclusively. Variations developed, with wine
being used in place of the
vinegar. Even red wine was
used to create a *beurre
rouge* (red butter sauce).
Beurre blanc soon became
the mainstay of *nouvelle
cuisine*, and is used today
with fish, veal, chicken,
and vegetables.

bination of wine and vinegar. It is wonderful with all forms of fish. Although flavored vinegars can be used, I generally use plain white (distilled) vinegar. Freshly chopped herbs, or even puréed herbs, can be added at the end to vary the flavor and appearance of the sauce.

Makes 1 cup to serve 6 to 8

2 shallots, finely chopped
½ cup white (distilled) vinegar
2 sticks (8 ounces) lightly salted butter (see Note), softened
    to room temperature

Note: You will note that I use lightly salted butter for this recipe in place of the unsalted butter I normally use. When made with unsalted butter, the sauce tends to be a little thinner.

1. In a small heavy saucepan, cook the shallots slowly in the vinegar over medium-low heat until only 1 tablespoon of liquid remains, about 10 minutes.

2. Remove the pan from the heat. Whisk in the butter 2 tablespoons at a time, waiting for each addition to melt before adding the next. The sauce will be warm and thick enough to lightly coat a spoon. Keep the sauce <u>warm</u> in a water bath (*bain-marie*) until ready to use.

Variations

Beurre Blanc au Basilic *(White Butter Sauce with Basil):* Stir in 1 to 2 tablespoons chopped fresh basil at the end of step 1.

Beurre Blanc à la Ciboulette *(White Butter Sauce with Chives):* Stir in 2 to 3 tablespoons chopped chives after step 1.

Beurre Blanc à l'Estragon *(White Butter Sauce with Tarragon):* Stir in 2 to 3 tablespoons chopped fresh tarragon at the end of step 1.

Beurre Blanc au Cresson *(White Butter Sauce with Watercress Purée):* Make a dry purée of watercress following step 1 of Pâtes Fraîches Vertes (page 92), using only 1 bunch of watercress. Whisk in enough of the puréed watercress to lightly color the sauce.

Mayonnaise

Store-bought mayonnaise serves me well for normal daily uses, but whenever a special sauce merits it, or a large quantity is called for, I whisk up a homemade one especially for the occasion.

Mayonnaise is an emulsified sauce. Egg yolk is used to hold oil in suspension, and vinegar or lemon juice is used to thin and to add flavor and acidity to the sauce. Besides adding salt and pepper to season the mayonnaise, you can add any number of other seasonings to change or enhance its flavor. The most common addition is Dijon mustard. Others include curry powder, tomato paste, horseradish, saffron, a purée of fresh herbs and greens for Sauce Verte (page 381), and garlic for Aïoli (page 379).

My technique for making mayonnaise differs from most cookbook writers' in one significant way. Most start by combining the egg yolk and vinegar before adding the oil, whereas I add the oil before the vinegar. My reason is simple. I find the egg yolk holds the oil in suspension easier when it is thick, and I can add the oil faster with less danger of separation than when the yolk is first thinned with vinegar. It is difficult to separate a mayonnaise once a good emulsion is formed. I add the vinegar or lemon juice when the sauce becomes too thick to stir. While adding the vinegar, I taste the mayonnaise, making sure not to add too much. If the mayonnaise tastes good yet is still too thick, simply thin it with a little water.

Although the classic mayonnaise is made only with egg yolks, it is just as easy to make it with a whole egg, producing a lighter, slightly less rich, and perhaps healthier version.

FLAVOR VARIATIONS

Oil is the major component of a mayonnaise, and will lend its taste to the sauce. I prefer the combination of mild oils in this recipe, but you should try your own combinations and proportions. Nut oils such as hazelnut and walnut are very strong, but can add an interesting accent when used in small amounts.

Traditionally either lemon juice or plain white (distilled) vinegar is used for making mayonnaise, but with all the various flavored vinegars now available, you may wish to try one if you feel its flavor will add to your presentation.

One egg yolk will hold up to 1 cup of oil in suspension, and I frequently make mayonnaise with only ¾ cup of oil per egg yolk. The more oil you use, the thicker the mayonnaise becomes.

Makes 2½ cups

1 egg
1 egg yolk
½ teaspoon salt
¼ teaspoon freshly ground pepper
½ cup light olive oil
1½ cups vegetable oil, such as soy, sunflower, corn, or peanut
2 to 3 teaspoons vinegar or lemon juice

1. Place the egg, egg yolk, salt, and pepper in a food processor fitted with a metal blade. Process until well blended.

2. With the processor running, slowly pour in the oils, gradually increasing the amount added as the sauce thickens. As soon as the sauce is very thick, thin with 2 teaspoons of the vinegar, followed by the remaining oil.

3. Stop the machine and taste the mayonnaise. Add more vinegar, if necessary, and adjust the seasoning to taste. Cover the surface of the mayonnaise with plastic wrap. It can be stored in the refrigerator up to 2 weeks.

REPAIRING A SEPARATED MAYONNAISE

If a mayonnaise separates, it is usually due to one or more of the following:
• Oil is added too rapidly at first.
• The egg or the oil is too cold.
• Too much oil was added for the amount of egg used.

The easiest way to restore it is to beat the curdled sauce, slowly at first, into a bowl containing either a fresh egg yolk or 1 teaspoon of Dijon mustard. If your problem is due to temperature, you can first try beating the curdled sauce vigorously while adding 1 tablespoon of boiling water.

Aïoli
Garlic Mayonnaise

*A*ïoli, the "butter" of Provence, is found in every restaurant in the south of France. The area, which traditionally is not known for its dairy products, uses this strong garlic mayonnaise instead of butter in many instances. Spread on bread and lightly toasted, it makes wonderful garlic bread. It can be used as a dip for raw vegetables, or be spread on a piece of fish and broiled, and it is a must to serve with Soupe de Poisson (page 24) or Bouillabaisse Américaine (page 114).

The sauce is easily made in a blender, by first puréeing the garlic and then adding the yolk, salt, and oil, thinning it in the end with lemon juice.

Makes 1 cup

1 egg yolk
Salt
5 garlic cloves, crushed through a press or finely chopped
    (see Note)
¾ cup olive oil, extra-virgin if available
Juice of 1 lemon

Note: **If you find the sauce too strong on garlic, simply use less the next time and thin your first batch with a little plain mayonnaise.**

1. In a small bowl, whisk the egg yolk with a pinch of salt. Add the garlic.

2. Whisking, slowly begin adding the oil, drop by drop at first. As the mixture thickens, more oil can be incorporated more rapidly.

3. Thin the sauce with some lemon juice when it becomes very thick and follow with the remaining oil. Whisk in salt and additional lemon juice to taste. The *aïoli* should be the consistency of mayonnaise.

Variations

Rouille *(Garlic Mayonnaise with Red Chili Pepper):* Traditionally served with *bouillabaisse*, *rouille* gets its rusty color (*rouille* means rust) and its fiery hotness from a small, crushed fresh red chili pepper. When not available, I use a crushed small dried red chili pepper or add cayenne powder to taste (¼ teaspoon or more). The traditional recipe also calls for soup-soaked bread or potato, but I leave it out.

Aïoli au Basilic *(Garlic Mayonnaise with Basil):* Add 5 to 10 chopped fresh basil leaves (to taste) to make a delicious basil and garlic mayonnaise. Try it as a dip for shrimp or vegetables.

Sauce Verte

Green Mayonnaise

*S*auce verte is a green mayonnaise sauce used with cold poached fish and seafood. The sauce is made with a variety of greens and herbs that are first briefly blanched and refreshed to heighten their color, then squeezed dry and chopped along with the mayonnaise ingredients in a blender or food processor. It is not always possible to find all the herbs listed (see Note).

If you already have some homemade mayonnaise on hand, simply chop the herbs after squeezing them dry and mix them with the prepared mayonnaise.

Note: Try to use at least four different herbs. The proportions can vary, and the amounts given in the ingredients are to be used as a guide. The greater the variety of greens and herbs, the better the sauce will be. I have not given dried equivalents for the fresh chervil and basil in the recipe, for I do not like them in this sauce.

Makes 2 cups

12 leaves spinach, stemmed
25 chives or 2 scallions
15 sprigs watercress, stemmed
4 sprigs fresh tarragon or 1 teaspoon dried tarragon
6 sprigs parsley
12 sprigs chervil
6 fresh basil leaves
1 egg
1 egg yolk
½ teaspoon salt
⅛ teaspoon freshly ground pepper
½ cup light olive oil
1 cup vegetable oil, such as soy, sunflower, corn, or peanut
2 to 4 teaspoons tarragon vinegar or lemon juice

1. Drop all the greens into a small pot of boiling water for 30 to 45 seconds. Drain and refresh under cold running water. Press or squeeze the greens to extract their moisture. Place in paper towels and squeeze dry.

2. Place the egg, egg yolk, salt, and pepper in a food processor fitted with a metal blade. Process until well blended.

3. With the processor running, slowly pour in the oils, gradually increasing the amount added as the sauce thickens. As soon as the sauce is very thick, thin with the vinegar or lemon juice to taste.

4. Stop the machine and taste the mayonnaise. Add more vinegar or lemon juice, if necessary, and adjust the seasoning to taste. Cover the surface of the mayonnaise with plastic wrap.

Sauce Rémoulade
Mayonnaise with Herbs, Capers, and Chopped Pickle

This classic French sauce, similar to a tartar sauce, is also a member of the mayonnaise family of sauces. It is excellent with both fried and cold poached fish and seafood. Try mixing it with mussels, crab meat, shrimp, or tuna for seafood salads with a new twist. *Cornichons* are small sour French pickles, which can be found in the imported food section of most supermarkets.

Makes 1¼ cups to serve 8 to 10

6 medium cornichons, finely chopped
1 tablespoon capers, finely chopped
2 teaspoons Dijon mustard
1 sprig tarragon, chopped (see Note)
3 sprigs parsley, chopped
1 cup Mayonnaise, homemade (page 378) or store-bought

Mix all ingredients together in a small bowl. Refrigerate until ready to serve.

Note: If fresh tarragon is not available it can be omitted entirely, but if you are making your own mayonnaise, use tarragon vinegar to add more flavor.

Sauce Raifort
Cold Horseradish Sauce

This cold horseradish sauce is ideal to serve with cold roast beef. I also like to use it with sliced cold boiled, braised, or corned beef.

The classic version of this sauce is made with bread crumbs, which are moistened in milk and then squeezed dry; then mustard, fresh horseradish, vinegar, sugar, and heavy cream are added.

The interpretation that follows does away with the bread crumbs, vinegar, and sugar. I whip the cream to replace the body the bread crumbs add to the sauce.

Serves 8

1 cup heavy cream, whipped
1 teaspoon Dijon mustard
2 to 3 tablespoons prepared horseradish, to taste

Mix all the ingredients together and serve chilled.

Sauce Vinaigrette
Vinegar- and Oil-Based Salad Dressing

A vinaigrette, or French salad dressing, in its simplest form is one part vinegar or lemon juice to three or four parts olive or vegetable oil. It is seasoned with a little salt and pepper. Mixed extremely well just before using, the vinaigrette is smooth and delicate tasting; if not well blended, it can be harsh and oily. If the oil and vinegar used have excellent flavor, nothing else is needed to sauce a mixed green salad.

Dijon mustard is often used as a basic ingredient by many chefs. Besides adding flavor to the vinaigrette, it also acts as an emulsifier, holding the oil and vinegar in suspension longer. Other ingredients added to a vinaigrette are fresh-chopped herbs, chopped shallots, chopped hard-boiled egg, and garlic.

Fresh herbs can go over your salad or in the dressing, and I often shred a hard-boiled egg over a salad enhancing both its flavor and appearance.

I generally keep a bottle of vinaigrette in the refrigerator ready to use, shaking it well just before pouring it over a salad.

Using the proportions shown here, it's easy to scale this recipe up or down. I use a blender to help whenever making large quantities of the dressing.

Makes 1¾ cups

3 tablespoons tarragon vinegar
3 tablespoons lemon juice
1 to 2 teaspoons Dijon mustard, to taste
1 garlic clove, halved (see Note)
½ teaspoon salt
⅛ teaspoon freshly ground pepper
¾ cup light vegetable oil, such as soy, sunflower,
*   or peanut*
½ cup plus 1 tablespoon light olive oil

1. In a small bowl or jar, mix the vinegar, lemon juice, mustard, garlic, salt, and pepper together.

2. Add the vegetable and olive oils and mix all ingredients until well blended and smooth. Blend well again just before using.

VINAIGRETTE PROPORTIONS

If you want to use either all vegetable oil or all olive oil in the vinaigrette instead of the blend here, keep in mind the proportions that follow.

Olive Oil Vinaigrette: Three parts oil to one part vinegar or lemon juice.

Vegetable Oil Vinaigrette: Four parts oil to one part vinegar or lemon juice. If the vegetable oil you use has a strong flavor, use the ratio of 3:1 instead.

Note: Because garlic can overpower a salad, add a halved garlic clove instead of chopped garlic to the dressing. In this way you can remove it when the dressing has acquired sufficient garlic flavor.

When entertaining, I make the dressing keeping in mind what I am serving before and after the salad. For example, if garlic is not present in the other dishes, I do not use it in the vinaigrette.

Dessert Sauces

Here are the basic sauces, fillings, icings, and flavorings that you will need to make the desserts in this book. I have included among them my recipe for quick and easy homemade jam, which is only lightly sweetened and intense with fruit, and my sugar syrups (used for moistening cakes and making sorbets). You will notice that for all of my dessert sauces, I use less sugar than most classic recipes call for.

Sauce au Chocolat
Chocolate Sauce

If you start with a good-tasting chocolate, it is a simple matter to make a good sauce. A chocolate sauce can be made with water, milk, or cream. In the following recipe, I use the most convenient and least caloric of these liquids to produce a dark, shiny sauce.

You can create a thin or thick sauce by merely changing the amount of liquid used. The amount shown in the recipe below produces a sauce that is thin when hot and thick when cold, the proper consistency whenever a chocolate sauce is called for. It is also an ideal consistency for flavoring ice creams, custards, and the like. Using half the amount of liquid produces a thick, hot sauce that becomes fudgy when cold. In this form, it is perfect for pouring over ice cream, and at room temperature mixes well with buttercreams and makes a wonderful coating for cream puffs and éclairs.

You can add a teaspoon or two of Cognac, rum, Grand Marnier, or liqueur to change the flavor of your sauce, or make it richer by using milk or cream.

Makes ¾ cup

4 ounces (115 g) semisweet or bittersweet chocolate
½ cup water (see Note)

1. In a small saucepan, melt the chocolate together with the water over medium heat, about 2 minutes. When the water and chocolate come to a boil, stir gently with a whisk until smooth. Continue stirring while the sauce gently boils for 1 minute.

2. If the sauce is too thin, cook it longer. If it is too thick, add more liquid and return to the boil.

3. Remove the sauce from the heat and allow to cool to room temperature for coating cream puffs and the like, or pour into a pitcher to serve with a dessert.

Note: For a thick sauce to use hot as an ice cream topping or at room temperature as a coating for cream puffs and éclairs, use only ¼ cup of water. If you use Baker's Semi-Sweet Chocolate, it will make a thicker sauce than most of the other chocolates on the market. You may need to add as much as another ¼ cup of liquid to reach the desired consistency.

Coulis de Framboise
Raspberry Sauce

A raspberry purée is an extremely versatile sauce. Its flavor and color can dramatically alter a dessert and, in effect, create a new one. Many years ago Auguste Escoffier did so when he created his now famous *pêche Melba* by adding a sweetened raspberry purée to a poached peach perched on top of vanilla ice cream. The addition transformed the simple peach and ice cream into an extraordinary dessert.

Serve the sauce with peaches, pears, strawberries, vanilla and chocolate cakes, custards, and ice cream. When fresh raspberries are unavailable, or too expensive, you can use one of the brands of frozen unsweetened raspberries.

STRAINING THE *COULIS*

Makes 1½ cups

1 pint raspberries or 1 package (10 ounces) unsweetened
frozen raspberries, thawed but undrained
Confectioners' sugar or red currant jelly to taste
1 tablespoon kirsch or framboise (optional)

In a food processor or blender, purée the raspberries. Taste and add confectioners' sugar or currant jelly if too sour. Add the kirsch and strain through a fine sieve to remove the seeds. *(This sauce can be made a day in advance and refrigerated until used.)*

Crème Anglaise
Vanilla Custard Sauce

When using the rapid technique in this recipe, it is helpful to have a good whisk and a heavy-bottomed saucepan that conducts heat well (see "Pots and Pans," page 14). If the sauce boils, it will curdle, so make it first in small quantities before trying large ones.

*C**rème anglaise* is a vanilla custard sauce with many uses. It is usually used as a sauce and served both warm and cold to accompany cakes, French puddings, crêpes, fruit, and soufflés. It is the base from which both French ice cream (Les Glaces, page 330) and Bavarian cream desserts (such as Marquise Alice, page 311) are made, and it can be easily flavored with chocolate, coffee, or any variety of liqueur.

The classic technique for making a *crème anglaise* requires beating the egg yolks and sugar to the "ribbon" stage, adding warm milk, and stirring over a double boiler until the sauce thickens enough to coat a spoon. This procedure takes between 10 and 20 minutes.

For my *crème anglaise*, I skip the beating of the egg yolks and sugar and eliminate the use of the double boiler. Once the milk and sugar come to a boil, it takes no more than 10 seconds to make the sauce. The classic technique leaves the surface of the sauce smooth and shiny, while this one leaves it with many small bubbles. The bubbles are easily removed with a spoon (but if you're using the *crème anglaise* in ice cream or a Bavarian cream, don't worry about the bubbles).

Makes 1½ cups to serve 4 to 6

1 cup milk
3 tablespoons (40 g) sugar
3 egg yolks
¾ teaspoon vanilla extract

1. In a small, heavy-bottomed saucepan, bring the milk and sugar to a boil over medium-high heat.

2. Place the egg yolks in a bowl. While whisking, add the hot milk slowly. Return the mixture to the saucepan and whisk rapidly over the heat for several seconds. *Do not boil.* Remove the pan from the heat. The sauce should have thickened enough to lightly coat a spoon. If the sauce is too thin, return the pan to the heat and whisk several seconds more. This procedure should take less than 10 seconds.

3. Strain the sauce into a bowl and flavor with the vanilla. The sauce can be served hot or cold. If it is to be served cold, cover the surface with plastic wrap and refrigerate. The sauce will be slightly thicker when cold.

"THICK ENOUGH TO COAT A SPOON"

Many recipes instruct the reader to cook a sauce until it is "thick enough to coat a spoon." To use this test, dip a wooden or metal spoon into your sauce; remove it, and draw your finger down the center of the back of the spoon. If a clear, clean path has been left by your finger, the sauce has thickened sufficiently. The thickness, however, can vary. A sauce must be thick enough to coat whatever it is accompanying. Sauces like *beurre blanc* and *crème anglaise* are thin and are meant to coat lightly, while a *sauce Mornay*, for example, provides a heavier coating.

Crème Pâtissière
Pastry Cream

A pastry cream—the cream used in éclairs, Napoleons, as the base for most dessert soufflés, and as the filling for many fruit tarts—is made by boiling milk, flour, sugar, and egg yolks together until a smooth, thick, and creamy sauce is formed.

One of the most common mistakes in making a pastry cream is to undercook it. People generally stop cooking when the pastry cream first comes to a boil. If you follow the method below and cook and whisk the pastry cream an additional minute or two, you will notice a dramatic change in its consistency. The pastry cream will become shiny, smoother, and thinner, instead of thick and pasty, with the disagreeable raw-flour taste of an undercooked pastry cream.

Since many people do not cook this pastry cream sufficiently, I am including another, widely-used version, using cornstarch (recipe follows). I normally use the classic version because I prefer the taste. However, you may find the recipe with cornstarch easier to make because it requires less cooking time. If it is undercooked, it will not have the grainy taste that the flour-based recipe would have.

Pastry cream will keep, well covered with plastic wrap, for several days in the refrigerator, and it can be frozen.

Makes 1¼ cups

1 cup milk
3 egg yolks
3 tablespoons (40 g) sugar
3 tablespoons (25 g) all-purpose flour
1 teaspoon vanilla extract

1. In a small saucepan, bring the milk to a boil over medium heat.

2. Meanwhile, whisk the egg yolks and sugar together in a small bowl. Add the flour to the egg yolks and mix well, until smooth and free of lumps.

3. Thin the egg yolk mixture with approximately ¼ cup of the warm milk. When the remaining milk begins to boil, add it to the egg yolk mixture and stir well. Return the mixture to the saucepan and whisk rapidly over high heat,

whisking the bottom and the sides of the pan until the pastry cream thickens and boils, about 1 minute. Turning the pan as you whisk helps to easily reach all areas of the pan.

4. Reduce the heat to medium and cook an additional 2 minutes, whisking as the pastry cream gently boils. It will become shiny and easier to stir.

5. Pour the pastry cream into a bowl and stir in the vanilla. Place plastic wrap directly on the surface of the pastry cream (this prevents a skin from forming on the surface) and allow it to cool.

Crème Pâtissière à la Maïzena
Pastry Cream with Cornstarch

If you are having trouble making a classic *crème pâtissière*, try this version that many of my students find easier.

Makes 1¼ cups

1 cup milk
3 egg yolks
3 tablespoons (40 g) sugar
2 tablespoons plus 2 teaspoons (20 g) cornstarch
1 teaspoon vanilla extract

1. In a small saucepan, bring the milk to a boil over medium heat. Meanwhile, whisk the egg yolks and sugar together in a small bowl. Add the cornstarch to the egg yolks and mix well, until smooth and free of lumps.

2. When the milk boils, add it to the egg yolk mixture and stir well. Return the mixture to the saucepan and whisk rapidly over high heat, whisking the bottom and the sides of the pan until the pastry cream thickens and boils, about 1 minute. (Turning the pan as you whisk helps to easily reach all areas of the pan.)

A pastry cream can be lightened with beaten egg whites, creating *crème Chiboust* or *crème St.-Honoré*, and it can be mixed with softened butter to produce a rich buttercream filling.

3. Reduce the heat to medium and cook an additional 1 minute, whisking as the pastry cream gently boils. It will become shiny and easier to stir.

4. Pour the pastry cream into a bowl and stir in the vanilla. Place plastic wrap directly on the surface of the pastry cream, and allow it to cool.

Ganache
Chocolate Cream Icing

Ganache is a creamy, smooth chocolate icing that is basic to French pastry making, and for the most part it has taken the place of the more classic chocolate fondant or sugar icing. It can be poured over cakes, yielding a dark, rich finish, or it can be whipped, when cool, to produce a lighter, fluffier icing that can be used like a chocolate buttercream. I also use a *ganache* for the centers of my Truffes au Chocolat à la Crème (page 335).

Ganache can be flavored with strong coffee, rum, Cognac, Cointreau, Grand Marnier, Kahlúa, or another liqueur or brandy of your choice. Adding liqueurs will thin the *ganache*, and you will need to wait until it is cold, instead of cool, to the touch before pouring it.

To Cover an 8-inch Cake
*6 ounces semisweet
   chocolate**
½ cup heavy cream
*2 tablespoons liqueur or
   other flavoring
   (optional *)*

To Cover a 9-inch Cake
*9 ounces semisweet
   chocolate**
¾ cup heavy cream
*3 tablespoons liqueur or
   other flavoring
   (optional *)*

1. Place the chocolate and cream in a small saucepan

over low heat. When the chocolate begins to melt, about 2 minutes, stir gently until it is nearly melted. *Do not allow to boil.* Remove from the heat and stir until the chocolate is completely melted and smooth.

2. Slowly add the liqueur or other flavoring, if using, and stir gently until smooth. Be sure to be gentle when you stir the *ganache*; overzealous stirring will cause air bubbles to form, which will remain on the cake once it is coated.

3. When the chocolate is cool to the touch, it will thicken and be ready to use. To see if the *ganache* is ready to pour, spoon some out of the saucepan and pour it back. If it remains on the surface for a few seconds, it is ready. It should be thin enough to pour, but not so thin that it runs right off your cake. *(The ganache can be made ahead. If it is too stiff by the time you use it, reheat gently over low heat, stirring occasionally.)*

* If you use Baker's chocolate, it will produce a thicker *ganache* than will most chocolates, and it will need additional liquid. If you are not planning on adding the liqueur or other flavoring in step 2, add an equal amount of water.

"COOL TO TOUCH"

The knuckle of your little finger is very sensitive to temperature. Use the knuckle to test the temperature of liquids. When a gelatin mixture feels cool, it will be close to setting.

Crème au Beurre
Buttercream

Buttercream, one of France's most famous culinary creations, is used for frosting cakes and as a filling for chocolates. A well-made buttercream is velvety smooth and melts in your mouth. It also spreads easily and makes beautiful designs when piped through the decorating tube of a pastry bag.

Although there are several methods for making buttercream, the one that follows produces the best results.

To Cover an 8-inch Cake
½ cup less 2 teaspoons
   (100 g) sugar
2 tablespoons water
3 egg yolks
1½ sticks (170 g) butter,
   softened

To Cover a 9-inch Cake
½ cup plus 2 tablespoons
   (135 g) sugar
2½ tablespoons water
4 egg yolks
2 sticks (225 g) butter,
   softened

1. In a small heavy-bottomed saucepan, bring the sugar and water to a boil over medium-high heat, about 2 minutes. Stir the sugar several times to assist dissolving. When the sugar is fully dissolved, the mixture will be clear and boiling rapidly.

2. In a small bowl, with an electric beater, start beating the egg yolks slowly while adding the hot sugar syrup. Continue beating at high speed until the mixture is cool, 5 to 6 minutes. The mixture will be thick and pale yellow.

3. Beat in the softened butter until smooth. This unflavored buttercream can now be flavored to taste (see Variations, below). Buttercreams are best used at room temperature, but are often served chilled. *(They can be made in advance and kept in the refrigerator for several days or frozen for months.)*

Variations

Crème au Beurre à la Vanille *(Vanilla Buttercream):* Add 2 to 3 tablespoons (to taste) of vanilla extract.

Crème au Beurre au Chocolat *(Chocolate Buttercream):* For an 8-inch cake, add the whole Sauce au Chocolat recipe (page 385) made with ¼ cup water. For a 9-inch cake, make the chocolate sauce with 5 ounces of chocolate and 5 tablespoons of water. Cool the sauce before adding to the buttercream.

Crème au Beurre au Café *(Coffee Buttercream):* Use 2 tablespoons Sirop de Café (page 402) or make Sirop de Café Rapide (page 402). Cool before adding to the buttercream.

Made from butter, egg yolks, and sugar, buttercream is undoubtedly one of the richest preparations you can eat. When compared with the imitation buttercream often found on commercial cakes, the "real thing" is so superior that you will forgo all the others. Use it sparingly, and save it for special occasions.

Crème au Beurre à l'Eau-de-Vie *(Liqueur or Eau-de-Vie Butter-cream):* Add 2 to 3 tablespoons (to taste) of Grand Marnier, framboise, or any liqueur or *eau-de-vie* (fruit brandy) of your choice.

Crème au Beurre Pralinée *(Praline Buttercream):* Add 2 to 3 rounded tablespoons (to taste) of Praline Paste (page 399).

MAKING AND USING A DECORATING CONE

To write "Happy Birthday" or to make a simple decoration on a cake, it is necessary to have either a small pastry bag fitted with a small decorating tube, or a decorating cone. It is extremely difficult to explain how to make a cone from a triangular-shaped piece of paper, but it should be easy for you to follow the drawings.

Start with a square piece of parchment or wax paper and fold it in half to form two triangles, cutting to separate them.

The triangle in front of you should resemble a pyramid. Bring one of the corners up to the top of the pyramid, twisting it gently so that the two points meet, forming a cone. Holding the two points together with one hand, wrap the third up and around the cone so that it joins the other two points from behind. If the point of the cone is not tightly closed, adjust the ends to close it. Use a stapler to fasten the three points together or fold over to secure them. Fill the cone half to three-quarters full with royal icing and fold the top of the cone over several times to securely enclose it. Again, use a stapler to fasten the folds shut.

The icing is now secured in an airtight paper cone and can be refrigerated until you are ready to use it. When ready to use the icing, snip off enough of the point with a pair of scissors to allow the icing to be squeezed out. The amount of the tip that is snipped off will determine the thickness of your lettering.

Before decorating your cake, practice your decoration on a plate or a piece of wax paper.

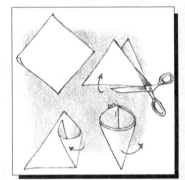

1. Cut a square piece of parchment or wax paper into two triangles. Bring the lower corners to the top of the triangle, twisting them to form a cone, as shown above, and staple together.

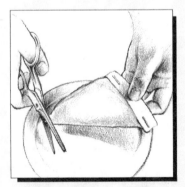

2. Snip off the tip of the filled and sealed cone to form the desired size opening.

Glace Royale
Royal Sugar Icing

You can make an even less complicated icing simply with confectioners' sugar and water called *glace au sucre glace*. A similar coffee icing can be made using Essence de Café (page 401) in place of the water. Another version is *glace à la liqueur*, made with confectioners' sugar and a small amount of any liqueur or alcohol you choose. These icings are not as smooth or strong as *glace royale*, and since it is so easy to make, I seldom use the others.

A royal icing is a quickly made sugar icing that can be used in place of fondant, a cooked sugar icing. It is made by stirring confectioners' sugar and egg white together and brightening it with a little lemon juice.

Glace royale is used in a thin consistency to frost small cakes and cream puffs, and it is a little thicker when used in combination with Ganache (page 391) to decorate cakes (see "Decorating a Cake with Ganache and Royal Icing," page 253). To use for lettering on a cake, it is thickened to a point where it will hold its shape well when squeezed from a decorating cone.

Once made, the icing begins to dry or harden rapidly. If it is not going to be used immediately, it should be covered tightly with plastic wrap. Most often, I use royal icing for decoration and spoon it into a parchment or wax paper decorating cone. I often divide one recipe to make a variety of colors. When doing this, I use vegetable coloring sparingly to create pastel shades and fill individual cones with the different colors.

Makes enough to decorate one 8- or 9-inch cake

About ⅔ cup confectioners' sugar
About 1 tablespoon egg white
About ¼ teaspoon lemon juice
Vegetable food colors (optional)

1. With a wooden spoon, mix the confectioners' sugar, egg white, and lemon juice together to form a thick, smooth paste that falls slowly from your spoon.
2. If the icing is too thick, add a few drops of water or a very small amount of additional egg white. If the icing is

too thin, add a little more sugar.

3. If the icing is to be colored, stir in vegetable coloring, one drop at a time, until the desired color is reached.

4. If not used immediately, cover the surface of the icing with plastic wrap or store in airtight decorating cones (see "Making and Using a Decorating Cone," page 394) and refrigerate.

Glaçage à l'Abricot, Glaçage à la Gellée de Groseille
Apricot and Currant Jelly Glazes

Tarts have traditionally been glazed with either strained apricot jam or red currant jelly. The apricot is used for light fruits, and the currant jelly for darker fruits. However, in the past 15 years, in striving for "purity," many chefs have started glazing tarts with jelly made from the fruit that is in the tart itself. Classically, an apple tart would be glazed with apricot jam; today, chefs might glaze it with apple jelly. I have always found a tart's flavor more interesting and complex when the classic glazes are used.

Most glaze recipes call for the jam or jelly to be melted over heat with a tablespoon or two of water. Since most jams and jellies vary in consistency from one manufacturer to another, the amount of water you might need will vary.

Both apricot and currant glazes can be thinned further with water or liqueur to make colorful and flavorful sauces. For example, an apricot glaze thinned with a little water and rum or Cognac makes a delicious sauce for Beignets Soufflés aux Bananes (page 269), poached fruit, or pound cake.

APPLYING A GLAZE

Glazes are used to both decorate and sweeten fruit tarts and other desserts. <u>Use the glaze while it is still hot</u>, and apply it with a pastry brush. Do not make strokes across the fruit with the end of the brush as you would with a paint brush. Instead, dip the pastry brush into the glaze and then dab it onto the tart with the side of the brush. This is a softer motion than an ordinary brush stroke; it doesn't disturb the delicate fruit, and allows the glaze to be applied gently.

Makes about 1 cup

8- to 10-ounce jar of apricot jam or red currant jelly*
Water

1. In a small saucepan, melt the jam or jelly slowly over low heat.

2. If you are making apricot glaze, it is usually strained at this point. Most of the time I find this an unnecessary step since the pastry brush used to apply the glaze picks up the liquefied jam but leaves the heavier fruit in the pan, in effect, straining the glaze. However, if you need a perfectly smooth jam for glazing a cake, strain it. If necessary, thin the jam with a little water to make it flow more easily through the strainer.

3. For either glaze, once melted, dip a spoon (or a piece of the fruit for the tart to be glazed) into the hot glaze. If the spoon or fruit comes out nicely coated, then it is not necessary to add water. On the other hand, if the glaze runs off the fruit or spoon, increase the heat and boil the jam or jelly until it thickens sufficiently to coat. If the coating seems very thick, add enough water to thin it and make sure to boil it and recheck its consistency before using.

* Most jams and jellies come in one of the two sizes given above. Two ounces one way or the other will make no difference to the recipes in this book. In most cases, you will have a small amount of glaze left over, which can be kept, refrigerated, for future use.

Confiture de Framboises
Raspberry Jam

J am is made by cooking fruit and sugar together to the point where the moisture in the fruit evaporates and the sugar and fruit thicken. Most jams in France are made with either equal weights of fruit and sugar, or four parts fruit to three parts sugar (i.e., 1 pound fruit to ¾ pound sugar). I find that these proportions are too sweet for my taste, and therefore use two parts fruit to no more than one part sugar. Using less sugar results in less jam, but a greater intensity of flavor is achieved. The results are expensive but worthwhile, and a little goes a long way.

Although almost any fruit can be used, my three favorites are raspberry, apricot, and strawberry. Both raspberry and apricot work very well with the 2:1 ratio of fruit to sugar, but I find strawberry jam made with this ratio a little sweet. To adjust the sweetness, I either add a little lemon juice, or start by using a ratio of 3:1, which produces a marvelous jam.

Jam cooks in two distinct stages. During the first stage, the moisture of the fruit evaporates, and during the second the fruit and sugar thicken. In the thickening stage, the fruit and sugar can easily stick to the bottom of your pan and burn if they are not stirred frequently.

The recipe and variations that follow are for relatively small quantities of jam. They cook rapidly and are easily prepared. Larger amounts take considerably more time, and should not be tried until you understand the process with the smaller quantities. I keep the small quantities of jam in my refrigerator or freezer.

Traditionally, in France, a large, unlined copper pan was used for making jam, and is still used by many cooks today. Although pots made of copper and aluminum are most often recommended for cooking jam, and a heavy bottom will help to prevent burning, any pan can be used if care is taken.

Makes 3½ cups

2 pounds fresh raspberries (about six ½-pint baskets)
*   or unsweetened frozen raspberries*
1 pound (2 cups) sugar

1. In a large, heavy-bottomed saucepan, combine the fruit and sugar and bring to a boil over high heat. Stir frequently with a wooden spoon.
2. Allow the jam to boil rapidly for about 10 minutes, but adjust the heat, if necessary, to prevent it from boiling

over. Spoon off the pale pink foam that rises to the surface into a glass or small bowl. Stir the jam each time after spooning. As the foam collects in the bowl, you will notice clear jam settling under the foam. Discard the foam and return the clear jam to the saucepan.

3. After about 15 minutes you will begin to feel and hear the jam sticking to the bottom of your saucepan as you stir. This is an indication that the jam is thickening and will be finished in about 5 minutes. Lower the heat to medium-high and cook, stirring frequently to prevent burning. The jam is done when the liquid thickens to coat a spoon with some of the seeds or small pieces of fruit.

4. Pour the jam into heavy glass or porcelain jam jars. Cover the surface with a layer of plastic wrap. Refrigerate or freeze for up to 6 months.

Variations

Confiture de Fraises *(Strawberry Jam):* Use 3 pounds fresh (about 6 1-pint baskets) or unsweetened frozen strawberries in place of the raspberries.

Confiture d'Abricots *(Apricot Jam):* Use 2½ pounds fresh apricots (halved or, if large, quartered and pitted to yield 2 pounds) in place of the raspberries. In step 1, add ½ cup water along with the fruit and sugar. Apricots are not as juicy as berries, so water is needed to dissolve the sugar and to prevent it from caramelizing or burning.

New Orleans praline is made with pecans and brown sugar, but in France it was originally made with almonds and caramelized sugar. Quite a few years ago hazelnuts were mixed with the almonds because they were less expensive, and it is this combination that is used commercially today.

Pâte de Pralin
Praline Paste

Praline paste is found in the supermarkets in France and can easily be used for making candies or flavoring ice cream, pastry creams, and Bavarian creams.

It is a uniquely French flavor, and many Americans do not appreciate it at first. Given time, however, I have never met anyone who has not learned to like it in one form or another.

Finding blanched hazelnuts in the market is easy in France, but almost impossible in the United States. For this reason you may prefer making the original, all-almond version.

Makes 1 pound

¼ pound (¾ cup) whole blanched almonds
¼ pound (½ plus ⅓ cup) whole blanched hazelnuts*
½ pound (1 cup) sugar
½ cup water

1. Preheat the oven to 400°.
2. Roast the almonds and hazelnuts on ungreased baking sheets until the nuts are beige and shiny, 5 to 7 minutes. Do not let the nuts burn.
3. Lightly oil a marble surface or baking sheet (if you have only nonstick baking sheets, oil the *back* of one as the hot caramel is too hot for the nonstick coating and will damage it).
4. In a small saucepan, bring the sugar and water to a boil over medium-high heat. Boil the mixture without stirring until it turns to a medium caramel color, about 5 minutes. Remove the saucepan from the heat and stir in the nuts so they become coated with the caramel. Immediately pour the mixture onto the lightly oiled baking sheet or marble surface and allow to cool.
5. Break the caramelized nuts into small pieces and place in a food processor or blender. If a blender is used, blend in small quantities. Process for several minutes until a smooth paste is formed. This paste can be stored in the refrigerator or freezer for several months.

   * Blanched hazelnuts are hard to find. To remove their skins, simply rub them together in a kitchen towel while still hot after roasting them in step 2. The skins should fall off easily.

Variations

Pralin Granulé *(Granulated Praline):* In step 5, process for only a few seconds. Praline in this form can be sieved for uniformity and used for decorating pastries and desserts by sprinkling or pressing onto a buttercream pastry.

Pralin en Poudre *(Praline Powder):* In step 5, process for several seconds beyond the granulated praline stage. Praline powder can be used in baking cakes and cookies by using it in place of a portion of the flour, e.g., half flour and half praline powder.

Essence de Café
Coffee Essence

Note: Use your favorite coffee to make the essence. I prefer dark roasted French-, Italian-, or Viennese-style coffees, and often use a decaffeinated variety. Once on hand, you will find many uses for this wonderful flavoring. It is easy to double or triple the recipe, if necessary.

Coffee essence is a concentrated, strongly brewed coffee for flavoring desserts. It should be stored in a small bottle, and used like vanilla to flavor ice cream, pastry cream, soufflés, candies, cookies, cakes, sauces, and milkshakes. It is used in concentrated form, as are other flavoring extracts, to not upset recipes by adding excess liquid. You may need to add more sugar to some of your recipes, since the essence is unsweetened. If you find that you always add sugar when using it, make a coffee syrup (recipe follows).

Makes ½ cup

1 cup water
1 cup ground coffee (see Note)

1. In a small saucepan, bring the water to a boil. Stir half the coffee into it. Allow to infuse for 10 to 15 minutes. Strain the mixture through a coffee filter.

2. Place the remaining ground coffee in another filter. Bring the strained coffee to a boil and pour it over the ground coffee.

3. Store in a small jar or bottle and keep tightly closed.

Variation

Essence de Café Rapide *(Quick Coffee Essence):* I make this quick essence as I need it. Any leftovers can be stored as above. Dissolve two parts instant coffee in one part boiling water.

Sirop de Café
Coffee Syrup

I f you find the Essence de Café (above) too bitter as a flavoring, make this coffee syrup and use it instead.

Makes ½ cup

Essence de Café (page 401)
Sugar or Heavy Sirop de Sucre (page 403), to taste

If you sweeten the coffee essence with granulated sugar, add it while the coffee essence is still hot.

Variation

Sirop de Café Rapide *(Quick Coffee Syrup):* Dissolve one part instant coffee and one part sugar in one part boiling water.

Sirop de Sucre
Sugar Syrup

The classic French sugar syrup (*sirop de sucre*) is what we know as a "simple syrup." It is used to sweeten drinks, poach fruit, moisten cakes, and to make *sorbets*. I find this syrup, which is made with equal parts of sugar and water too sweet for just about everything except lemonade. When making sorbets I find it too thin. For this reason I make an extremely light syrup to use generally, and a very heavy one for a few special uses, such as the making of *sorbets* and flavoring syrups.

The proportions for the three syrups are given in the following recipe enabling you to make whichever one suits your purpose. I usually make double the quantity shown, keeping any leftover covered in the refrigerator. It will keep for months, and you will find many uses for it if you have it on hand.

Makes 1 cup Light Syrup	*Makes 1½ cups* "Simple Syrup"	*Makes 2 cups* Heavy Syrup
1 cup water	*1 cup water*	*1 cup water*
¼ cup sugar	*1 cup sugar*	*2 cups sugar*

1. In a saucepan, bring the water and sugar to a boil over medium-high heat. Boil for 30 to 45 seconds until the syrup is perfectly clear. Stir to make sure all the sugar has dissolved, and remove from the heat.

2. Allow the syrup to cool and pour it into a glass or plastic container. Store in the refrigerator.

Appendix A
The Metric System in Cooking and Pastry Making

Cooking is more an art than a science, and as such gives the individual a considerable amount of freedom. Pastry making, on the other hand, being a science, requires precision and accuracy for consistently successful results.

For years, Europeans have had the advantage of the metric system in the kitchen. When correctly used, this system of weights and measurements not only preserves the freedom inherent in cooking, but also ensures accuracy in pastry making, while the system of measurement we presently use in America creates more work and less freedom for the cook and an awkward and imprecise form of measurement.

The key to the advantage of the metric system lies in the principle of weighing solids and measuring liquids as compared to our system of measuring both. Ideally, recipes should list ingredients as we find them or buy them at the market—e.g., 1 eggplant, 1 pound (500 g), diced. This describes the size and weight of the eggplant to buy and what to do with it once you get it home. Most of our recipes follow the standard form of measuring in cups—e.g., 3 cups diced eggplant; ½ cup chopped onion; 6 cups sliced apple; a slightly rounded cup of grated cheese. This is impractical.

A "slightly rounded" cup of grated cheese always puzzled me until one day when I was writing a recipe for a cheese sauce. In making the sauce, I took a piece of cheese (100 g) out of my refrigerator, cut it into a few pieces, and melted it in the liquid in my saucepan.

METRIC KITCHEN SCALE

BUYING A SCALE

A scale must be easily readable to be useful. Perhaps the best scales, in this respect, are the digital ones that came on the market several years ago. Unfortunately, they are quite expensive and not affordable for every household.

For accurately measuring small quantities, do not get a scale that can weigh more than 16 ounces, or 500 grams. Small-capacity gram/ounce scales can read 5 grams easily and are excellent for weighing flour, eggs, sugar, butter, nuts, cheese, etc. When it comes to weighing larger items like meat, fruit, and vegetables, use the scales at the food markets.

Simple enough. But, in writing the recipe for a non-scale-using audience, I found that I had to describe the amount of cheese in cups. I grated the cheese and then sprinkled it into a cup. Finding it was slightly more than one cup, I described it as a slightly rounded cup of grated cheese. I could have easily pressed it gently and then called it a "lightly packed" cup of grated cheese. In both cases, the grating and measuring are time-consuming procedures. They were not needed when I made my sauce. They were needed only because the average reader doesn't have a small, inexpensive kitchen scale (see "Buying a Scale," opposite).

Although the scale is only helpful in making cooking easier, in the science of pastry making it is indispensable. Most problems in baking come from the inaccurate measurement of flour.

Back in the '30s, when the first Betty Crocker cookbook was written, readers were told to sift flour onto a piece of wax paper and then spoon it into their liquid measuring cups. (Solid measuring cups had not come onto the market yet.) Since the book was so popular, this form of measuring flour became the norm until Julia Child appeared on the scene. In her first book, she measured flour by sifting it directly into a solid measuring cup and leveling it off. In her subsequent books, her flour has been measured by dipping the cups into the flour and leveling them off.

How do you measure flour? How do your friends, who give you recipes, measure their flour? And, most important, how do the authors of your cookbooks measure flour?

My results in weighing the above measurements of all-purpose flour were as follows:

Method A   *1 cup (sifted and spooned) = 130 g*
Method B   *1 cup (sifted and leveled) = 105 g*
Method C   *1 cup (dipped and leveled) = 140 g*

If the author of a book measures with Method B, and you use Method C, you have a failure. If you use Method A and the author Method C, your results are different. But, if you both use a scale, you can have the same results.

Why, then, don't we weigh? Because we don't have scales in our kitchens. And why don't we have scales? Because most writers and publishers don't want to use both weight and volume measurements in their recipes.

If recipes had weights, we would have scales. It is as simple as that!

With a scale in the kitchen, we can use recipes from around the world, as well as endless variations of them. Without a scale, however, we are limited to those recipes that conveniently fit into cups. Once in the kitchen, the scale and the metric system will become so useful that you will wonder how you ever got along without them.

Appendix B
High-Altitude Cooking

For the past 13 years, I have taught classes in Denver, the "mile-high city." A number of my students live in the mountains near Denver at considerably higher altitudes. Although all the recipes in the book have been tested at sea level, they have also been successfully prepared at altitudes of one mile or more.

Certain things happen at high altitudes that necessitate some changes in sea-level recipes. Understanding the effects of high altitudes will help you successfully prepare these recipes at whatever altitude you may happen to be.

Atmospheric pressure decreases at high altitudes; consequently, water boils at a lower temperature, and it evaporates more quickly. As a result, you will find that recipe ingredients that require boiling will take longer to cook. Normally I will tell you how to judge when something is properly cooked, and you will look for those signs rather than using the cooking times.

Since the moisture evaporates more rapidly, you may find that your sauces are too thick at the end of the cooking time. To remedy this, add a little more water to thin the sauce to the desired consistency. When a recipe calls for a tight-fitting lid, its purpose is to retain moisture in the cooking utensil. At high altitudes, this is more important than at sea level.

While boiling usually takes longer at high altitudes, baking and some roasting take less time. If a pastry recipe calls for baking 25 to 30 minutes, you should check for doneness at 20 minutes.

Similarly, because of the dryness generally found at high altitudes, recipes for tart dough (*pâte brisée*), noodle dough (*pâtes fraîches*), and similar recipes will require small amounts additional water or moisture, since the flour is much drier at high altitudes than at sea level.

The rising time for yeast doughs is decreased at high altitudes. Because there is less atmospheric pressure, expansion is more rapid. For a similar reason, the baking time of cakes and bread is usually shortened by 5 to 10 minutes. The proper rising of a *génoise* at high altitudes can be guaranteed by reducing the butter called for in the recipe by one half.

Books on high-altitude cooking often instruct the reader to increase the oven temperature when baking or roasting. Since the French use considerably higher temperatures in their ovens than Americans do, I have not found it necessary to alter the temperature of recipes when cooking at high altitudes.

Index